A Lapidary of Sacred Stones

A Lapidary of Sacred Stones

Their Magical and Medicinal Powers
Based on the Earliest Sources

Claude Lecouteux

Translated by Jon E. Graham

Inner Traditions
Rochester, Vermont • Toronto, Canada

Inner Traditions
One Park Street
Rochester, Vermont 05767
www.InnerTraditions.com

Copyright © 2011 by Éditions Imago
English translation copyright © 2012 by Inner Traditions International

Originally published in French under the title *Dictionnaire des Pierres magiques et médicinales* by Éditions Imago, 7 rue Suger, 75006 Paris
First U.S. edition published in 2012 by Inner Traditions

All rights reserved. No part of this book may be reproduced or utilized in any form or by any means, electronic or mechanical, including photocopying, recording, or by any information storage and retrieval system, without permission in writing from the publisher.

Library of Congress Cataloging-in-Publication Data
Lecouteux, Claude.
 [Dictionnaire des pierres magiques et médicinales. English]
 A lapidary of sacred stones : their magical and medicinal powers based on the earliest sources / Claude Lecouteux ; translated by Jon E. Graham. — 1st U.S. ed.
     p. cm.
 Includes bibliographical references (p.   ).
 ISBN 978-1-59477-463-8 (hardcover) — ISBN 978-1-59477-508-6 (e-book)
 1. Precious stones—Folklore—Dictionaries. 2. Precious stones—Therapeutic use—Dictionaries. I. Title.
 GR805.L4313 2012
 398'.465—dc23

2012013499

Printed and bound in the United States by Courier Companies, Inc.

10 9 8 7 6 5 4 3 2 1

Text design and layout by Virginia Scott Bowman
This book was typeset in Garamond Premier Pro with Packard and Caslon Antique used as display typefaces

Inner Traditions wishes to express its appreciation for assistance given by the government of France through the National Book Office of the Ministère de la Culture in the preparation of this translation.

Nous tenons à exprimer nos plus vifs remerciements au gouvernement de la France et au ministère de la Culture, Centre National du Livre, pour leur concours dans la préparation de la traduction de cet ouvrage.

Contents

Acknowledgments vii

Introduction: The Bones of the Earth 1

◆

Dictionary of Magical and Medicinal Stones 29

An A to Z Guide to the Sacred Power
of Gems from Antiquity to the Middle Ages

◆

Notes 336

Bibliography 344

Acknowledgments

With the end of this long labor now at hand, I would like to acknowledge my debt of gratitude toward all my colleagues who generously allowed me to profit from their work: Leo Carruthers (Sorbonne), Chantal Connochie-Bourgne (University of Provence), Elena di Venosa (Milano), Françoise Féry-Hue (IHRT, Paris), Christoph Gerhardt (Trier), Valérie Gontéro (Aix), Denis Hüe (Rennes II), and Jens Haustein (Jena), who placed at my disposal his copy of the lapidary *Liber defota anima;* and to my friends Baukje Finet van der Schaaf (Metz) and Ronald Grambo (Oslo). Without them, this dictionary would have been woefully short of many entries.

I would also like to express posthumous thanks to the late Father Brunet S.J., for permitting me to photograph the incunabula housed in the Les Fontaines Center in Chantilly.

INTRODUCTION

The Bones of the Earth

Stones have an extraordinarily long history and since antiquity they have deeply stirred the human imagination as quintessential representatives of the domain of the marvelous.[1] During the Middle Ages, lapidaries gathered together traditions with remote origins going back to ancient India, Mesopotamia, and Egypt. These traditions had been adopted by Greek authors such as Theophrastus, Dioscorides, and Meliteniotes,[2] followed by Roman authors such as Pliny the Elder and Solin,[3] and then were given new life thanks to Isidore of Sevilla,[4] Hraban Maur, and Marbode of Rennes.[5] All of these authors form the pedestal for a body of knowledge that extended into the seventeenth century, at which time it became more scientific in nature. Concurrently with the aforementioned authors, other texts—like the collection of the *Kyranides*[6] and the lapidary of Damigeron and Evax—were translated from the Greek, further feeding the flow of information that culminated in the second half of the twelfth century with the translations of Arabic lapidaries (which were themselves adaptations of Greek, Hebrew, and Latin texts). With the rise of literature as entertainment, poets and novelists had a vast body of work—essentially about stones with extraordinary properties—from which to draw material for embellishing their stories. This is why romances in medieval France were among the first literary works to make liberal use of gems.

The study of stones drew scant interest in post-Enlightenment France. In 1871, when Leopold Pammier sought to obtain an edition of the lapidary by Marbode of Rennes (circa 1035–1123), his friends were surprised to see him engaged in what they considered "such an unappealing domain, with such arid soil and such a limited horizon."[7] In short, despite a few books (a list of which can be found in the bibliography), this field of research had become fallow.

The stone is ubiquitous in human history. It has been used as a weapon since prehistoric times. In the Bible, David flattened Goliath with a stone from his sling. During the Middle Ages, it was viewed as the weapon of giants; certain tiny islands were said to be formed from the stones they once cast at their foes. A stone can sometimes resemble an axe, but it is also the weapon of those who have no other means to defend themselves. In *Henry VI*, Shakespeare puts these words in the mouth of one of his characters: "If we be forbidden stones, we'll fall to it with our teeth!"[8]

The Bible has left us a number of sayings that feature stones, such as "cast the first stone" (John 8:7), "stumbling stone" (Isaiah 8:14), "corner stone" (1 Peter 2:6), "if his son ask bread, will he give him a stone" (Matthew 7:9), "there shall not be left here one stone upon another" (Matthew 24:2), and proverbs[9] such as "a rolling stone gathers no moss" and "you cannot get blood out of a stone" confirm the importance of the mineral. Myths also bring in the stone motif, such as the myth of Sisyphus, for example, or the story of Deucalion and Pyrrha, who on Zeus' orders cast stones over their shoulders onto the ground, which then gave birth to men and women.

I. Stones of the Middle Ages

The Genesis of Stones

Following in the footsteps of Aristotle, medieval scholars believed that the dry and moist exhalations occurring inside the earth combined to form minerals. According to another belief—and one that survived in folk traditions until fairly recently—stones grew in the ground and would continue to grow as long as they were not moved. To do so would be tantamount to uprooting them.

Hildegard von Bingen provides the following explanation for the genesis of precious stones: "Gems are born in very hot regions of the East from the meeting of water with fiery mountains: the water foams and adheres to the rocks, then solidifies over a length of a time that can run from one to three days" (*Physica,* preface). Several different opinions are recorded in the Old French dialogue *Placides et Timéo:* "Others say they are formed from air in the earth as solid works of the planets."[10]

In the Scandinavian cosmogony myths, stones are the bones of the primordial giant Ymir, whose dismembered body formed the earth, sky, and sea. Another medieval dialogue, the Middle High German *Lucidarius,* tells us: "The earth is made like man. The ground is the flesh and its skeleton is the stones."[11]

Some stones are ascribed a different origin. Crystals are considered to be solidified snow. According to John Mandeville, Indian diamonds grow on the crystals formed by frozen water.[12] Other stones are giants or dwarves that have been petrified by the rays of the sun.

Lastly there is a category of stones called bezoars, a term used to designate those that form in the bodies of animals, somewhat similar to gallstones.[13] The Byzantine treatise of the *Kyranides* names sixteen stones of animal origin,[14] while other lapidaries offer a smaller number. *Alectoria* are created in the gizzards of roosters; the *borax,* also known as *crapaudine,* is formed in the head of the toad; the *celidonius* in the stomach of a swallow; the *chelonite* in the body of a turtle; and the *draconite* in the head of a dragon. Everyone knew the legend of the *vouivre,** popularized in the 1941 novel of the same name by Marcel Aymé, and the carbuncle it wears on its forehead, an avatar of the one described by Philostratus in his *Life of Apollonius of Tyana,* in which he says of *draconite* (dragon stone): "it must be extracted from the dragon's skull while it is still living, otherwise the stone will have no powers."[15] In his *Parzival* (482, 29–483, 1), Wolfram von Eschenbach says the carbuncle is taken from the unicorn's forehead. In the great Armenian national epic *David of Sasun,* the basic plot of which goes back to the

---

*[Meaning either "wyvern" or "woman-serpent" —*Trans.*]

tenth century, a dragon holds in its mouth a precious stone to which a powerful charm is attached.[16]

Bartholomaeus Anglicus ("Bartholomew the Englishman," thirteenth century) maintains in the same way that the *quandros* can be found in the head of the vulture and, citing Avicenna, says that the *rosten* or *reiben* lies in the head of the crab.[17] If we believe what Hildegard von Bingen says concerning the *magnet*, it would be born from the pus of a venomous reptile (*Physica* V, 18). The *lyncurius* or *ligure* comes from the urine of the lynx[18] and the *hyenia* is a hyena's eye.[19]

The lithic imagination was first stirred by foreign-sounding names—*gagatromeus, cegolites, zimur, ranim,* or *kakabre*—some of which it then reinterpreted. For example the *panchrous*, the "multicolored stone," became the *panther* and the *opalius* (opal) transformed into *ophthalmius*, because it is good for eyesight. An examination of the manuscripts provides evidence of permanent shifts, when it is not a case of substitutions or confused terms (i.e., a single name being applied to several stones, such as *adamas,* meaning both loadstone and diamond). When Arabic names invaded lapidaries at the end of the twelfth century, thanks to the translation of the lapidary by a Pseudo-Aristotle, gems answering to the names of *elbeneg, dehenc, elendhermon,* or *haalkec* appeared. And in the latter third of the thirteenth century, the *Lapidario del Rey Alfonso* (Lapidary of King Alfonso)[20] introduced "Chaldean" stones. Only one of these has been identified: the *bezebekaury,* a name for ruby.

The Stone Is a Person

In La Réponse du Seigneur (The Lord's Answer; II), Alphonse de Châteaubriant declares: "People say that stones do not speak, they do not feel. What an error!"

The stone has been regarded as a living being, a male or female creature capable of reproducing, believing, and having feelings. Albertus Magnus says that the peanite is of the female sex and that it conceives and engenders a stone that is similar to it. It is also said that the balagius (balas ruby) is the female carbuncle.[21] According to John Mandeville, diamonds can be either sex and can engender children:

Men find them more commonly upon the rocks in the sea and upon hills where the mine of gold is ... They grow together, male and female, and are fed with the dew of heaven. And according to their nature they engender and conceive small children, and so they constantly grow and multiply.[22]

Philippe de Thaon mentions *turobolein* (in other words, pyrite)[23] in his *Bestiary*. When the male stone approaches the female, both catch fire. Bartholomaeus Anglicus says that *idachite* perspires and that *silenite* contains a white spot that grows and shrinks with the moon.[24] The Argonauts used a stone for an anchor, but as it had a habit of straying from its spot, they had to fix it in place with lead—a fine example of *lapis fugitives*! In the *Kojiki*, written in seventh-century Japan, we learn that stones can be frightened and flee what they perceive as danger. One day when Emperor Ojin was under the influence and traveling through a mountain pass, he found a stone in the middle of the path and struck it with his cane. The stone fled away from him, giving rise to the saying: "Even a solid stone can avoid a drunkard," meaning one should never try to thwart a drunk.[25] Some stones, such as the *aetites*, are pregnant. Some cry out for vengeance (*Habakkuk* 2:11); some can be swayed, as in the myth of Baldur (*Gylfaginning*, chapter 49), in which the stones promise Frigg they will cause no harm to her son; and they can, conversely, be inflexible, as seen in expressions like "to be hard as stone." This physical hardness has been equated with insensitivity. But in hagiographic legends, especially those concerning persecuted virgins, stones are capable of displaying kindness.[26] They open to conceal the fugitive from her pursuers, as in the case of Saint Dietrine and Saint Odile. Saint Dietrine's stone can be seen in the Morvan region in the Vaupître Valley, in other words the Val Petrae,* and Odile's stone (Odilienstein) stand on the Schlossberg near Freiburg-im-Breisgau. The *Acta Sanctorum* (Acts of the Saints) tells how on October 17, in the legend of Saints Cosmas and Damian, the prefect Lysias ordered them

---

*[Vale of Stones —*Trans.*]

stoned, but the stones refused to strike the targets and instead turned back on the ones who had thrown them.

Stones speak and are used for divinatory purposes, especially the mineral siderite, which can be treated in the following fashion so that its voice may be heard.

> If one fasts and purifies oneself, if one washes the stone in pure waters and wraps it in white linen, then when the lights are lit something like the voice of a newborn will suddenly be heard, and the stone shall answer questions. Then, toward the end, it breathes like a living creature.[27]

Helenos raised a siderite like a child: "He pampered this divine stone, it is said, he held it in his arms like a mother holding her young son against her body."[28]

One thing that becomes apparent to the student of magical stones is the notion of character: they only give up their secret or surrender their power to someone who is worthy, either because the individual has respected a ritual or been chosen by fate. This is the meaning of stones that represent an ordeal or a test. The only individuals that can approach them are fearless knights who are above reproach. A variation is the stone that can only be sat upon by people bearing these same qualities. The motif of the "sword in the stone," which is primarily found in the Arthurian romances, is of this nature: the stone will only release the sword after it has identified the person to whom it should be given.

The Worship of Sacred Stones

Regarded as the bones of the earth or the home of unspecified numinous powers, stones were an object of worship. Nevertheless, from the beginning to the end of the Middle Ages, decretals, penitentials, and the decrees of synods and councils proclaimed anathema those who swore oaths by them or worshipped them.

A very interesting passage from the Bible perfectly illustrates how stones were sanctified. Jacob rests his head on a stone and his contact with it gives him a divine vision while he sleeps. Upon awakening, he recalls the ladder that appeared to him in dream. He stands the stone upright, pours oil over it, and gives it the name of *beit El,* in other words, "dwelling of God."[29] There is evidence for the worship of stones throughout Europe long before the Middle Ages, and the ecclesiastical writs, texts, canons, decrees, and penitentials offer some details. Between 443 and 452, the Council of Arles condemned those who worshipped stones; in 506, the Council of Agde forbade the swearing of oaths to stones; and in 557, the Council of Tours condemned those who performed actions near stones that were incompatible with the rules of the church. The Synod of Toledo mentioned stone worshippers in 681, and Charlemagne's *Admonitio Generalis* (cap. 65) of 789 informs us that fires were lit and certain practices performed around stones. In tenth-century England, the *Law of the Northumbrian Priests* condemned those who gathered around stones.[30]

What is behind all these practices? One council's writ provides a precise description: the stones are used as an altar, "as if some deity resided within it."[31] During the Middle Ages, these deities became dwarves, elves, and genies. Evidence is supplied by the *Kristni Saga* (The Saga of Icelandic Christianization; chapter 2):[32] "In Gilja [in northwest Iceland] stood the stone to which Kodran's folk had made their sacrifices and in which, it was said, dwelt, their tutelary deity." And in *Þorvalds þáttr víðförla* (The Tale of Thorvald the Far-Traveled), which gives us a variation on the same theme, the spirit is called "seer" (*spámaðr*), undoubtedly because it predicts the future.[33]

People therefore came to the ancient megaliths in search of healing or to ask for their wishes to be granted. We should emphasize that the church was unable to eradicate these practices and rites, which were often connected with fertility,[34] but it did Christianize them. This is evident from the Christian symbols covering some Breton menhirs, such as in Trégunc, or the stone "of the Twelve Apostles" cited by Philippe Walter,[35] which was referred to by that name as early as 713.

Two basic points emerge from all of these ecclesiastical texts. First, they almost always involve stones in the plural, which suggests megalithic remnants. Next, these stones were frequently part of a complex that included a tree and a spring or fountain. In this case, the stone involved was often pierced through and/or contained a basin, and the sacred nature of the site was dependent on this complex of elements. Consider the fountain of Barenton in the Broceliande Forest, as described in Chrétien de Troyes' twelfth-century romance *Yvain, le Chevalier au Lion* (Yvain, the Knight of the Lion): when water is drawn and poured over the block of stone, this causes a violent storm to break out.

In the poem *Merlin* by Robert de Boron (twelfth–thirteenth century), there is an interesting reaction from the people leaving mass when they see the stone block supporting the anvil with the sword in it (which only Arthur can pull free). They stand in wonder and cast holy water at it as a kind of exorcism of the supernatural and diabolical (i.e., pagan) powers that may be hiding there.

II. The Use of the Stones

Precious stones abound throughout courtly literature.[36] This can be seen in the romances of Apollonius of Tyre; in Benoît de Sainte-Maure's *Le Roman de Troie* (The Romance of Troy), with the description of Hector's room; or in Gautier d'Arras' romance *Eracle*.[37] In such stories they appear on clothing, weapons, the harnesses of horses, and on various objects such as lamps, furniture, or games. The presence of these stones falls into what is called the "courtly representation"[38]—they are a polysemic symbol that refers to the social rank, power, wealth, and capabilities of their owner. There are even doors made of precious stones![39] In *Diu Crône* (The Crown), an Arthurian romance written by Heinrich von dem Türlîn around 1230, the castle of Dame Fortune is built from twenty-five different kinds of gems.[40]

We need to reexamine the long descriptions involving gems in terms of their magical and symbolic values. Some of the twelve mystical stones mentioned in the Apocalypse primarily turn up again on the knight who is fearless and above reproach, establishing a connection between gem and owner. It can be inferred from numerous statements scattered throughout the various versions of the *Letter of Prester John*,[41] as well as with the allegorical appropriation of gems in which each possesses several meanings. Here are just a few examples: crystal represents the angels or virginity; carbuncle, the Virgin Mary; jasper, faith or the apostles; diamond, the archangels; and so forth.[42] Philippe de Thaon, a twelfth-century Anglo-Norman poet, clearly notes that stones "possess several meanings, but their primary meaning forms a veritable sermon."[43] As mediators between man and the supernatural powers, stones held a very important place in the mental world of our ancestors. In Prester John's palace, the tabletop was an emerald resting on legs of amethyst "so that no one would become intoxicated during a meal."[44] The monarch's bed was made from "sapphirean wood" because the sapphire is so chaste that one who sleeps upon this bed will not be tempted by the workings of Venus.[45] Thanks to other scriptural accounts, light has been shed on the phrase "sapphirean wood": the bed is made from ebony and studded with sapphires.

Magical stones are highly esteemed in literature, such as the stone that makes Yvain invisible in the romance by Chrétien de Troyes. Similarly, there is the "Israel stone" from the romance of *Perceforest,* undoubtedly a *lapis judaicus*, which was used to mark newborns so no demons would abduct them and replace them with their own progeny (the belief in the changeling).

Stones and Magic

For stones, nothing is impossible![46] They protect against harm, accidents, poison, ambushes, lies, envy, demons, and witchcraft; they help in the granting of wishes, flying, becoming rich, ascertaining the future, and improving memory. They heal diseases, stop hemorrhages, and allow one to forget painful memories, especially the pain of lost love. They confer invisibility and the gift of languages. I will stop here, though I am well aware that this list could go on an on.

A statistical analysis of the specific powers of stones reveals that these are unevenly distributed between two poles, one consisting of purely magical properties (5%) or protective properties (30%), and the other of therapeutic properties (65%). It should be noted that these numbers vary depending on the type of text—lapidaries, encyclopedias, or grimoires—and that literature for entertainment has a definite predilection for magical stones (while remaining notably vague in how it describes them). Treatises like the *Kyranides* or the lapidary of Damigeron-Evax offer an almost equal distribution between the two poles, whereas the lapidary by Marbode of Rennes, whose information was regarded as almost canonical throughout the whole of the Middle Ages, favored the medical aspect. Earlier, Saint Augustine noted that his contemporaries used stones and herbs for therapeutic purposes, something that smacked to him of magic.[47]

For example, the *ostolanus* (*ophthalmius*) and *heliotrope* make a person invisible, but for the latter stone to have this power it must be combined with the plant of the same name and a charm must be recited.[48] A fourteenth-century German text, *Der Junker und der treue Heinrich,* features a stone that allows its bearer to transform into a bird. The marvelous stone from the romance of *Eracle* is renowned: it protects its bearer from drowning, fire, and weapons. In *Kormáks saga* (The Saga of Kormak; chap. 12), Bersi owns a "life stone" (*lífsteinn*) that he wears in a pouch around his neck. It allows him to win a swimming contest.

There are numerous stones that secure victory, and I shall only mention *gagatromaeus, alectory, pyrophilius,*[49] and the *memonius*. The Middle High German texts designate them with the name *sigestein* (*seghesten*), "victory stone." We should note in passing that Norse literature is rather lacking in stones, outside of those we encounter, for example, in the *Þiðreks saga af Bern* (Saga of Theodoric of Bern).[50] The medieval treatise *Secretum Secretorum* (Secret of Secrets) tells us that the Philosopher's Stone has the same properties.[51] It is also said that *draconite* grants victory over all foes provided it is attached to the left arm.[52] The genre of the *exemplum* sometimes echoes this marvelous motif too, as in the writings of Caesarius von Heisterbach.[53]

Let us briefly look at phylacteries and other protective devices.

Stones that are commonly used against evil spells of all kinds include: *gagates* or *jayet* (jet), pyrite, *anthropocrinus*, topaz, *melas* (black stone), *galactites* (milk stone), *hephestites* (Vulcan stone), coral, and *aetites* (eagle stone). The *chrysolite* is effective against nightmares, the infamous "night terrors."[54] When set in silver, jasper drives ghosts away. When worn on the left arm, *chrysolite* sends devils fleeing, and *jayet* expels spirits and dispels sorceries and charms.[55]

Stones can also serve as charms, primarily when combined with enchantments and spells. An example can be found in Hildegard von Bingen's *Physica* (IV, 2). Someone who is bewitched should take warm rye bread and cut a cross into its crust, then draw a jacinth down through the cut, saying, "Just as God has taken from the Devil all the preciousness of stones, let these spells be taken from me in the same fashion and deliver me from the pain of madness." Or, when a person has lost the power of speech because of a spell, smear a magnet with his saliva and rub it over the top of his head while saying, "Tu furens malum cede in virtute illa qua Deus virtue de coelo ruentis dyabuli in bonitate hominin mutavit" (IV, 18).*

Lastly there are those stones that can be described as marvels because of the legends attached to them. Such is the case for jacinth, which protects travelers, or *jayet,* which is used to prove a woman's virginity, or the *magnet* that makes it possible to detect if one is a cuckold or not. It was common knowledge that in Scythia, griffins guard emeralds and that the Arimaspians—allegedly a race of one-eyed people—try to steal them.

There is much to say about magnets. Recall that there exist all kinds: magnets for silver, copper, lead, meat, fingernails, cotton, wool, scorpions, animals, and men.[56] These claims of Eastern origin[57] can be found in the work of the thirteenth-century encyclopedists. Dimishqî [the "Damascan," Shams al-Din al-Ansari al-Dimashqi (1256–1327)] also cites hematite, without saying what it attracts: "Its force of attraction increases," he says, "when left to steep overnight in the blood of a

---

*"You, raging evil, cede to that virtue by which God transmuted the strength of the devil who fell from heaven, to human goodness."

recently slain goat; if rubbed with garlic, it loses its properties."[58] If we take the romance of *Eneas* at its word, magnets were used to build the ramparts of cities.

Sigil Stones

Our remote ancestors attributed particular virtues to sigil stones, of which there are two types:[59] those possessing a natural imprint and those that have been engraved. These latter are either cameos or intaglios, depending on whether the image is a raised relief or one that is set into the stone. In the great thirteenth-century debate on the notion of natural magic,[60] the first type (with naturally occuring images) were fully authorized, whereas in the case of the second type (with man-made images), it depended upon the author.

Let us look at two examples of engraving:

Chalcedony: On it was carved an Athena on foot holding a heron in her right hand and a helmet in the left. If worn following its consecration, one will triumph over all enemies and rivals; it makes one kind, understanding, capable of fulfilling all undertakings and overcoming shipwreck (*Kerygma* 29; Damigeron 27).

Panchrus: This is a holy stone on which Lato and Harpocrates have been carved on the front and three greyhounds on the back; it is useful against all the magic arts (Damigeron 37).

But if one wishes to increase the stone's magical powers, it is necessary to gather together the forces that the stars have scattered throughout the whole of nature. In the *Livre des secrez de nature* [Book of the Secrets of Nature], greatly inspired by the *Kyranides*, it is said concerning the stone Rhinoceros:

se tu entaillez en la pierre dessus dicte l'oisel dessus dit (rumphea) et a ses pièz le poisson (rumphis) et desoubz la pierre tu metz un pou de la racine d'iceste herbe et encloz tout ce en un anel come dessus, celui qui le portera nul mauvaiz esperit ne le pourra approuchier; et qui le mettra desous le chief de aucun, il ne pourra dormir (IV, 15).*

The carvings are quite varied and range from *paranatellonta* (figural depictions of the stars, the signs of the Zodiac, and the decans), to magical inscriptions reminiscent of the Gnostic gems from early antiquity. Concisely, we can say that everything is made possible through the use of sigil stones: winning the favor of the great, of love, or in a trial; destroying the house or city of an enemy; finding protection against the perils of travel; and so forth. The vernacular lapidaries do not say it is necessary to follow a precise ritual in order to consecrate these stones. These texts are often content to recommend that one simply be chaste or *"blans dras li convient vestir kil portera, et abstenir soi de char de columb"* (it is necessary to be clad all in white robes and to abstain from eating the flesh of the dove),[61] otherwise the stone in question will remain without effect.

Lithotherapy[62]

A stone never possesses only a single virtue. As the centuries go by and traditions from other lands are discovered, the number of its properties continues to grow. Every ailment, or nearly every one, can be treated with stones, either by themselves or in combination with another substance. This treatment can be implemented in various ways: by the application or rubbing of the stone on the patient; by reduction of the stone to a powder used to make a beverage; and by wearing it as a bracelet or necklace. In the twelfth century, Philippe de Thaon indicates four protocols in his lapidary: "There are four ways to utilize stones in medicine: by touching them, by wearing them, by ingesting them as a drink, and by looking at them."

---

*Translation: If you carve in the aforementioned stone the aforementioned bird (*rumphea*) and at its claws a fish (*rumphis*), and beneath this stone you place a bit of the root of said herb and enclose it all within a ring like above, the person who wears it cannot be approached by any evil spirit; and if placed beneath the head of someone, he will not be able to sleep.

For nosebleeds, one can use a carnelian that has been immersed in heated wine; for stomach ailments, a ligure that had been steeped for an hour in wine, water, or beer; against poisons, a beryl was grated into effervescent water or another liquid. Round, black orite protects from bites if it is reduced in rose oil.

Hildegard von Bingen (1098–1179) offers an excellent account on the lithotherapy of her day in her *Book of Simple Medicines*,[63] better known under the title *Physica*. Jasper and sardonyx are effective against deafness; emerald for heart diseases, epilepsy, and headaches; jacinth for the eyes; magnet for paralysis, jaundice, and apoplexy; and chrysoprase for gout, epilepsy, and possession. According to Albertus Magnus (?—1280), the emerald cures tertian fevers and epilepsy; sapphire heals abscesses; beryl works for hepatic pains; and amandine and daemonius are effective against poisons. He also says that jasper and orite have contraceptive properties and hematite has astringent virtues. Sometimes the etymology of the stone's name becomes a starting point for the beliefs about it. This is why ophthalmius is good for the eyes (Greek ophthalmos means "eye"), chalcophane against hoarseness (in Greek, this term means "voice of bronze"), and the tecolith dissolves gallstones (Greek tyko: "to melt, dissolve").

Stones were used as amulets for this reason. Here are a few examples taken from the Greek medico-magical text the *Kyranides,* originally compiled in the fourth century. Worn around the neck, stones from the head of the sea bream heal consumptives; those found in the head of the porgy cure tooth aches; the stone taken from the head of the hydra is helpful for dropsy sufferers; and the stone taken from the head of the weever, taken in a drink, heals bile stones. Occasionally we come across surprising recipes such as this: "Take the stones from the head of the hake and wear the one from the right side against the right testicle and the one from the left against the left testicle: this will produce an erection."

When a stone's virtues are exhausted, there are prayers for restoring its powers (*Oratio et benedictio ad sanctificandum lapides*). "When you see that your stones have lost their virtues, you should place them in a linen cloth and then set them on the altar until three masses have been said. When the last priest has said the third mass, clad in his sacred vestments, he will speak the blessing that begins with *Dominus vobiscum, Oremus.*" This prayer includes references to the twelve stones of heavenly Jerusalem and the other twelve on Aaron's breastplate.[64]

When scholarly and clerical literature provides this kind of information, it is no surprise to find it in the romances. Just one example from among hundreds would be Lohengrin, which mentions stones expelling fevers, healing ills, bestowing courage, and protecting one from lust (str. 652).[65]

The Stone as Test of Virtue

Medieval German Arthurian literature tells us of marvelous stone platforms that only allow a knight or a man beyond reproach to sit upon them. The motif appears for the first time in Ulrich von Zatzikhoven's Lanzelet (end of the twelfth century) with a stone called an "honor stone" (*eren stein*); the topic is so well known that the author does not bother to elaborate on it.

> The virtuous Walwein [Gawain] was sitting on the stone of honor. You have been told enough times how it cannot tolerate duplicity or hostility (v. 5177ff.).[66]

Wirnt von Grafenberg describes it with more detail in his *Wigalois,* written between 1204 and 1215. The stone is located at the foot of a linden tree; it is square in shape and blue with red and yellow streaks. "None who had performed an evil act could lay his hand upon it" (v. 1477ff.);[67] "He who had committed the slightest dishonorable act could not approach within a footstep of it" (v. 1495ff.). A Danish folk book, *Viegoleis med Guld hjulet,* says about the stone (chap. 6): "Whoever has the slightest taint cannot reach it; to do so one must be as pure and innocent as when he left his mother's womb. Of all the knights gathered at Caridol, none could approach it except King Artus himself, who often sat upon it, and Lord Gabon, who could touch it with his hand." The anonymous author adds that this was so because the knights "conversed with and courted the beautiful ladies and beautiful young girls there too frequently."

The young Wigalois, naturally oblivious to all of this, ties his horse to the tree and sits smack on the middle of the stone to the astonishment of all who are watching. Although Renaut de Beaujeu's *Bel Inconnu* (twelfth–thirteenth century) derives from the same source as *Wigalois,* it does not include this episode, although we can find it again in Middle English in the fourteenth-century *Libeaus Desconus.*

Lanzelet and *Wigalois* are the source texts for two other tales written by Ulrich Füetrer (died circa 1493). In the *Persibein,*[68] the stone lies in the middle of a field and glows so strongly it dispels the gloom of the night, which brings to mind a carbuncle. It is also engraved: on it the seven planets "such as found in the Zodiac" can be seen (str. 15). Despite their efforts, Gabon and his companions cannot get near it and continue on their way toward Nantes (str. 16). This passage is directly inspired by *Wigalois* in which it is said that "Sir Gauvain could at best reach out his hand toward it" (v. 1505f.), but he had committed an indecent act and this prevented him from ever approaching the stone (v. 1507–15).

Füetrer seems to have appreciated this motif, since he employs it in his *Poytislier* as well.[69] While riding toward Cardeuil (Karidol), Poytislier spied near a linden tree a stone that "none could approach unless he was courageous and virtuous" (str. 199). He sat down upon it, and the author notes: "Thus was his valor proved" (str. 200, 3).[70]

It would perhaps be prudent to compare these accounts to what I have said earlier about coronation rites, and in this regard it is well worth mentioning Fortunat's ninth-century *Vie de saint Pair* (Life of St. Pair). There was a red marble seat on Mount Phanus called "Pulpit of Saint Vigor," in which every new bishop had to sit during his coronation.

One fourteenth-century text clearly distinguishes itself from its pre-

decessors by indivisibly coupling a stone to the water of a spring. The story of *Wigamur*[71] describes a hollow stone from which flows water from a spring murmuring near a linden tree. "In this stone," says the text, "no man whose spirit had ever taken a bad turn could bathe, else he would fall ill and lose his color and the strength of his body. But he who plunged in having ever loved pure virtue, he would forget all cares by the force and qualities of the stone and by the nature of the spring; his body would strengthen, his heart would rejoice, his energies would increase, his spirit would soar, and he would become wise" (v. 1202–14). This particular stone, named Aptor (v. 1100), was red in color but would turn murky if a man who had slept with a woman gazed at it or if a woman contemplated it. If the lady was a maiden, however, she could see its true color. Whoever wished to bear this stone should free himself of hatred, wrath, envy, infidelity, and felony; he should give preference to decency and steadfastness instead. The stone prevented misfortune if looked at once a day, but only dispensed this protection to virtuous men; it had been hollowed out to form a tub (v. 1215–49). Here the anonymous author is combining information gleaned from a lapidary together with elements from the tradition represented by Lanzelet and Wigalois.

Lastly, the stone can be used to prove one's strength, as in *Guiron le Courtois,* in which Melyadus carries a block of stone (the front steps) to a church to prove his strength to his son, Tristan.[72]

The Stone and the Law

The stone played a role in ancient law, a fact we often forget. Charters from the year 1225 tell us that the judges sat near a stone (*apud lapidem, apud longum lapidem*) or sat on stones. The accused did likewise.[73] In medieval Sweden, there could be three, seven, or twelve of these stones. The story of *Reynke de Vos* (Reynard the Fox), written in Low German, says that King Noble won a stone platform from which to judge Reynard (v. 2569–71).[74] Oddly enough, the illustrator of the Lübeck incunabula (1498) did not follow the text and chose to depict the seat as a wooden platform (see illustration on the following page).

To summon someone to appear in court, a stone would be turned over in front of his house, and if the individual was not at home, three stones would be placed on the threshold.[75] In Lorraine, judgments and municipality rulings were posted on granite blocks that were the remnants of ancient menhirs. Condemnations were sometimes proclaimed there and this was called "justice on the stone."[76]

The stone was an object that played a role in the preaching of sermons. As early as the Roman era, Livy informs us that when treaties or contracts were finalized, a piglet would be slain with a flint, which was afterward cast aside while speaking the following oath: "In the case of oath-breaking, may the people be slain like this animal and the signatory be cast aside as I throw this stone."[77] Centuries later, in the Eddic poem *Helgakviða Hundingsbana II* (Second Lay of Helgi Hundingsbane [= Hunding's murderer]; str. 31), we have the "stone of Unn," by which Dag swore the oaths he later betrayed. The *Hænsna-Þóris saga* (Saga of Hen-Thorir) includes a scene in which Hersteinn swears an oath in the following way: "He went to the place where there was a certain stone, placed his foot upon the stone and spoke: 'I solemnly swear that before the Althing ends I shall have had the goði [priest-chieftain] Arngrim banished completely.'"[78]

This custom should certainly be likened to the rites of royal coronation. When he is being crowned, the new monarch climbs atop a stone—undoubtedly, one set deeply in the ground, a *jordfast stein*—to receive consecration and be acclaimed. This stone is called Mora in

Sweden and Danaerygh in Denmark. The *Hlöðskviða* (Lay of Hlöd), a heroic poem from the Eddas, alludes to it (str. 7). The ancient Celts had a stone of sovereignty called Lia Fáil (Fál) that had the ability to let out a roar under the feet of the legitimate king during his coronation.[79]

In an ordeal by water (judicium aquae), a stone had to be plucked from a cauldron of boiling water, as the Grágás (chap. 55), a collection of early Icelandic laws, informs us. In the *Poetic Edda,* a prominent figure, Gudrun, exonerates herself of an accusation in this way: "She stretched her bright hands down to the bottom / and there seized the precious stones / 'Look now, warriors—acquitted am I, / by the sacred test—how this cauldron bubbles.'"[80]

In Old Icelandic this was called *taka i ketill,* "to take from the cauldron." We should note in passing that stones were used to be certain God's judgment would be favorable, something we learn from Burchard of Worms[81] and the ninth-century *Arundel Penitential* (cap. 78).[82]

Stones were used for two different methods of execution: stoning and drowning. The first method is fully attested in the Bible (Leviticus 20:27; Joshua 7:25)—whence the expression "cast the first stone"—and in Gregory of Tours' *History of the Franks.* In the latter text, Euric, king of the Goths, is stoned to death as punishment for his debauchery (II, 20), and the populace inflicts the same fate on Parthenius, who is despised for the heavy tributes he imposed during the lifetime of Theodebert (III, 36).

The second method of punishment appears in the Gospel of Saint Matthew (18:6): "But whoso shall offend one of these little ones which believe in me, it were better for him that a millstone were hanged about his neck, and that he were drowned in the depth of the sea."[83] For his part, Gregory of Tours reports in his *History of the Franks* (I, 35) that during the persecutions under Diocletian, Bishop Quirinus, in other words Cerin, was thrown into a river with a millstone around his neck. Gregory later (II, 28) describes how Chilperic's wife is slain in this same manner on orders of Gundobad. The *Acta Sanctorum* tells of the martyrdom of Crepin and Crispinian on the date of October 25: stones were tied to their necks before they were thrown into the Aisne River, but in vain. We might further note that Bayard, the steed of the four sons of Aymon, suffered a similar execution, but one adapted for his size: he was tossed into the water with a stone around his neck and one on each hoof. In the Scandinavian North, Freyfaxi, the horse dedicated to the god Freyr, is cast into a river from the top of a large boulder.[84]

Much less well known, surely, is the punishment for quarrelsome and slanderous women. They were sometimes condemned to pay a fine or, if not, to wear a stone around their neck and walk through the city. A French text confirms this:

> The woman who shall speak villainous things about others, shall like a whore, pay five *sols* [*solidi*] or carry the stone, naked but for her shirt, in a procession and afterward she [the insulted woman] shall poke her with the point of a needle."[85]

A 1497 law from the city of Hamburg says the same thing, as do other testimonies, too, such as the charter of Henry I, Duke of Brabant, dating from 1229, which mentions two stones connected by chains: one hangs over the chest and the other over the back. One of these accounts states explicitly: "If a woman strikes another woman, she shall bear the chained stones."[86] In Germany, these stones had different regional names. In the north they were "shame stones" (*schandsteene*), whereas elsewhere they were the "noisy stone," "quarrel stone," or "insult stone" (*klapperstein, pagstein, lasterstein*).

Olaus Magnus informs us that adulterers also wore stones,[87] and medieval Scandinavian common law included an arrangement that is worth citing for its extremely burlesque nature: "If a married woman surrenders to lust with a married man, they should pay a fine... If he cannot pay, a string shall be tied to his penis and the woman will tie it to the communal stone, then she will lead her lover through the entire town."[88]

One form of capital punishment was to drop a huge stone, typically a millstone, on a person's head. The Swedes executed the Icelander Ref in this way: "they resorted to villainy and got rid of him while he slept by crushing him with a rock; what they did was suspend a millstone high up and later cut the ropes so that it fell on his neck as he lay beneath."[89] In his *Skáldskaparmál*, a treatise on skaldic poetry and its mythological sources (chapter 2), Snorri Sturluson relates that when the wife of the giant Gilling mourned the death of her husband, who they had slain, the dwarves Fialar and Galar slew her: "Then he [Fialar] told his brother Galar that he was to go up above the doorway she was going out of and drop a millstone on her head, and declared he was weary of her howling; and Galar did so."[90] It may be worth comparing this information with Gregory of Tours' account of Senator Euchirius' demise. King Euric had him removed from prison one night and, after ordering him bound to a wall, he had this same wall pushed over onto his victim (II, 20).

The use of millstones may also allude to another very widely attested method of execution, which consists of crushing a person between two of them.[91]

Another form of implicit judgment and execution can be found in the *Vie de Madoc de Ferns* (Life of Madoc of Ferns). Madoc built a church and bequeathed a specific virtue to the stone there: "Whosoever acts unjustly . . . will not live through the end of the year, provided this stone is turned three times contrary the course of the sun, as wished by the sages of this land."[92]

The execution of witches seems to have given rise to a unique method of putting someone to death. If we can give creedence the *Saga of King Olaf Tryggvason*, which Snorri Sturluson wrote down around 1230 as part of his Norwegian royal history *Heimskringla*, witches were transported to a large rock that would be submerged under water at high tide. This is what happened to a certain Eyvind, and from that point on the rock was known as Skrattasker, "witches' skerry."[93] The same author provides us with another interesting tidbit of information at the conclusion of the story of Gilling, which was referred to earlier. Suttung, the son of Gilling, seized the dwarves Fialarr and Galar, took them out into the open sea, and left them on a skerry that would be covered at high tide. He spared their lives in exchange for the wonderful mead made from the blood of Kvasir.[94]

The stone also seems to have served as a chopping block for execution. In the legend of Saint Colombe, the heroine was decapitated at the first milestone north of Sens.

The stone also played a role in suicides. Pliny the Elder tells us that the Scythians would hurl themselves from a rock into the sea,[95] and Pomponius Mela says the same of the Hyperboreans.[96] The *Gautreks Saga* features a rock called *Ætternisstapi,* meaning "Family Rock," found at the top of Gilling Cliff (*Gillingshamarr*). "The drop's so great there's not a living creature could ever survive. It's called Family Rock simply because we use it to cut down the size of our family . . . in this way our elders are allowed to die straight off . . . And then they can go straight to Odin."[97] The saga states explicitly that those who choose this death go to Valhalla. A later redaction of the *Landnámabók* (Book of the Settlement of Iceland), the *Skarðsárbók,* indicates that during a famine, the elderly and indigent would be slain by hurling them from the tops of giant boulders.[98]

III. Lapidary Typologies

A considerable portion of this knowledge about stones was transmitted via the lapidaries, and a few remarks about the texts themselves are in order. Slightly simplifying things, we can divide these books into three groups:

1. Pagan lapidaries containing the information from Greek and Latin works.
2. Christian lapidaries, which add a symbolic interpretation to the physical, medical, and magical virtues of stones.
3. Mixed lapidaries blending traditional data with religious considerations (symbolic, allegorical, moral); this "collage" is immediately apparent, as in the lapidary of manuscript 164 from the Méjanes

Municipal Library of Aix-en-Provence (Res. ms. 12), the first part of which consists of a list of twelve stones and their properties, while the second part explicates the meaning of each gem (v. 657–1300).

The lapidaries of engraved stones, which belong to the first group, can be further divided as follows:

1. Planetary lapidaries: the stone bears the sign of a planetary body or should be carved under its influence, or even at a certain hour.
2. Composite or complex lapidaries: the engraved stone must be set in a certain metal or combined with a bird, a fish, or a plant. For example: "A crowned man seated on a stool lifting his arms toward the sky, with four men who seem to be carrying the stool: take mastic and terebinth, and place it beneath the stone in a silver ring that weighs twelve times the weight of the stone; if placed beneath the head of a sleeper, he will dream of his waking desire."
3. Lapidaries referring to the constellations or decans.
4. Gnostic lapidaries, in which we again find well-known Greco-Egyptian intaglios, such as of Abraxas and others. This was how Thetel expressed it, according to Konrad von Megenberg: "A man holds the head of a winged, horned devil in one hand and a snake in the other, and beneath his feet there is a lion, while the image above him holds the sun and moon—this stone must be set in lead; it will then possess the power to force demons to answer the questions put to them."

All these various types of information have been combined with one another and it is impossible to find a text that is free of any borrowings. Furthermore, information taken from medical treatises, such as those of Dioscorides or Galen, has been used to complete the different categories.

Von dem electuario

Electua rius ist ein stein an der grossen als ein bone glichet einer cristallen an der varben Und ist etwas tunckel Ist der stein weh sset in eines hanes magen wenn man dem da kappet noch drÿ zt joren Und lut in dar noch vij vor leben Wer den stein in dem munde trait dem löschet er den durst Er machet den men schen sighafte Und kom het freÿden Und widermüeget er Und mar het wol gespreche Und machet dem menschen gemeine aller dinge Und allen lüten Und aller meist machet er die frö wen hey ren mynnen Und das Und heysset er zu latin aketuarius Das spricht zu samelt Und das er das alles wircket an dem menschen Do sal man zu beslossen tragen in dem andwort

Von dem absmitten stein

Asmith eub ist ein smaetzer stein du rech mit stet mit sne witzen öbetten Der hat die art wenn er erhitzet wirt von dem fure so haltet er die hitze siben tage

Von dem Alabander

Alabander ist ein tót stein Und ist ger stho Und ist an der stat glich einem granaten Une dz sin rötte veister ist wan des granaten Und ist vil nohe also der rob in Es ist aber einer anderleÿ Der stein gefichet an der varben einem sander ist einer Dunckeln oder einer dotten bleichen rötti Also das rotti ertet ist das afra heysset In dem lande Alabrandra Und da von hat der stein den namen Der stein er wer het das blutes fluss Und me ket das

The engraved stones are effective in every possible circumstance and here again, if we collect the information, we have a reflection of profoundly human desires.[99] These stones can make one kind, eloquent, robust, courageous, or bold; they can secure joy, happiness, favor, victory in battle or in the courtroom; they can provide protection from illness, drowning, fire, and storms; they can give one the upper hand in negotiations, and so on. In this sense, these magical lapidaries are not only a record of ancient knowledge but also ethnological documents of the highest order if we know how to analyze them. These intaglios, cameos, and bezoars (stones extracted from an animal) draw their powers from gods, demons, or planetary bodies, and they often have to be consecrated in a precise manner, which corresponds more or less to what the ancients say about the gathering of herbal simples.

This rich and fascinating world of stones plays an interesting part in the history of mentalities; in the history of science, religion, magic; and in the incorporation of scholarly literature by romances, epics, poetry, mysticism, and legends. Philology is also important here, because the successive distortions of the names of the gems raise many problems (see, for example, the entries for *tarnif* and *turcois*). While we have good editions of the translations and adaptations of the lapidaries of Marbode, Damigeron-Evax, King Alfonso the Wise, the Pseudo-Aristotle, and the *Kyranides,* a number of manuscripts have never been published or studied, and the lapidaries of Solomon, Thetel, Chael, Raizel, and so forth, are still waiting to be brought out of the shadows. Despite the work of Max Wellmann and Moritz Steinschneider, the routes of distribution remain poorly known.[100] Researchers are still hampered by a lack of the necessary tools for their work; only the very incomplete dictionary of Hans Lüschen is available.[101] How can one study Mandeville's lapidary[102] without knowing what preceded it and without knowing the orgin for the extraordinary names of certain stones such as *vermidor, reflambine, gasticoq, hanon, decapitis, otriche,* and *sorige*?[103] The task is immense and can only be accomplished by a team, since the requisite linguistic knowledge is rarely found in a single individual.[104]

IV. How the Dictionary Is Organized

I have left the names of the stones in classical or medieval Latin as entries, when they exist, because they do not always correspond to the names of modern mineralogy and many stones remain unidentified, and I am going by the medieval nomenclatures. For stones without specific names, I have created entries of the type "stone + virtue" or "stone + location."

> ✦ *introduces the most significant variations of a stone's names. These are often so distorted they are unrecognizable.*
>
> 📖 refers to the sources: given the number of lapidaries, I have chosen a representative selection.
>
> 📖📖 refers to the existing studies on the stone in question, if there are any.

I have taken into account representatives of the Greek and Latin scholarly traditions and those written in the vernacular languages, as well as several texts from the literature of epics, romances, and travelers' tales, but I have left out the category of marbles entirely. It should come as no surprise that the vernacular name of each stone is not included. The works that refer to the stones most often do so in medieval Latin.

The illustrations come from various ancient Latin and German editions of Johannes von Caub's *Hortus sanitatis,* the *De proprietatibus rerum* by Bartholomaeus Anglicus, Anselm Boëtius de Boodt's treatise, the manuscripts of Konrad von Megenberg's *Buch der Natur* (Book of Nature), and various other manuscripts.

fueillet C.lvii

De pꝫrigio et pꝫingetes.

Ꝑꝫigius ꞇ pꝫingetes. Yſidoꝛe. Pꝫꝛigius eſt ainſi dicte du lieu/ pour ce quelle naiſt en frigie. Elle eſt de couleur paſſe moyēnemēt peſāte ꞇ graue/ ꞇ eſt une tochē dure pōgieuſe. Elle bruſle quāt y auoit elle eſt moiſſee en vin ꞇ puis ſoufflee de ſoufflet; tant que elle deuiēgne rouge. Et de rechief eſt eſtaincte troiz foiz en vin douly. Et eſt tāt ſeulement utile a taindꝛe ſes robes et veſtemens.

Les operatiōs de pꝫingites.

Yſidoꝛe. Pꝫingites autremēt pꝫengites eſt une pierre de capadocie dure cōme marbꝛe/ reſplēdiſſante ꞇ treſreluyſante. De laquelle anciennement fut edifſie et conſtruict dung top ung teple ou il miſt poꝛtes doꝛ/ leſquelles quant elles eſtoient cloſes il y auoit dedans icel luy temple clarte diuturne ꞇ lōgue. Sim?
En copadocie fut trouuee la pierre pꝫigites ſoubz neron prince/par raiſon et argumēt ainſi appellee. Car ſes voines cheurēt en couleur ou rouſſeur reſplendiſſantes et treſreluyſantes. Et dōna fortune a ceſte pierre ceſte choſe/laquelle ilz appellent ſciam.

Chapitre. C.v.

Poderos et pontica. Yſidoꝛe. Poderos eſt une gēme la ſeconde apres la Marguerite laquelle eſt la plus reſplendiſſant des gēmes reſplendiſſantes/ de laquelle eſt enquis de quelle couleur elle doit eſtre nōmee/tant de foiz gectee par les eſtranges beaultes du nom: tellemēt que elle eſt faicte du nom prerogatiue de beaulte.

Les operatiōs de potica.

Luy meſmes yſidoꝛe. Les gēmes pontices ſont reſplēdiſſantes de gouttes aurees:les unes ayans eſtoilles: et les autres ſont lignees de longe menemēs ꞇ traicts de couleurs. Elles veulent eſtre poꝛtees ſobꝛemēt ꞇ chaſtemēt
Chapitre. C.iiii.

Abbreviations

OE = Old English (names attested in the glosses)

Ar. = Arabic (names found essentially in the Latin translations of the Pseudo-Aristotle's lapidary)

Heb. = Hebrew (as found in the translations of the Pseudo-Aristotle's lapidary)

MDu. = Middle Dutch (as found in Jakob van Maerlant's *Der naturen bloeme* and *Van den proprieteyten der dinghen,* the translation of the encyclopedia by Bartholomaeus Anglicus)

ME = Middle English

MFr. = Middle French

MHG = Middle High German

MItal. = Medieval Italian (as found in *Il Libro di Sidrach*)

OIc. = Old Icelandic

ON = Old Norse

MSp. = Medieval Spanish (names found in the Lapidary of King Alfonso and the *Poridat de las poridades*)

Dictionary of Magical and Medicinal Stones

AN A TO Z GUIDE TO
THE SACRED POWER OF GEMS
FROM ANTIQUITY TO THE MIDDLE AGES

A

Abel: A stone by this name appears in Twinger and Closener's *Vocabulary* (fifteenth–sixteenth century). It should, in fact, refer to the name of a Baltic island off the shores of Frisches Haff (Eastern Prussia) where amber is found. See *succinum*.

📖 Closener ab 31.

Abeston: Iron in color, asbestos comes from the mountains of Arcadia and Arabia. Once ignited, it cannot be extinguished because—or so it is said—it has a wooly texture called "salamander feather." See *asbeston*.

✦ *abesios, absectos, abston, besteon, bestion, asbestus, asbostus, aspectus, aspecus, albestus, albeston, arbestos, abestos;* MFr. *abestos, ebesto, asbeste, ageste, egeste;* MHG *abestô, bestîôn;* MSp. *asençio, abestus.*

📖 Albertus Magnus 2, 1, 1; *Summarium Heinrici* VI, 2, 3; *De lapidibus preciosis* 4; Wolfram von Eschenbach 791, 4 and 16; Arnoldus Saxo 1; Konrad von Megenberg VI, 4; Saint Florian v. 555–64; Thomas de Cantimpré 14, 5; *Secrez* 3, 26; *Liber secretorum* II, 1, 10.

Absinctus: Having been warmed by fire, this heavy black stone streaked with red veins will remain hot for seven days; this is an interpretation of its name, which in Greek means "that which cannot get cold again." It is thought to possibly be some kind of lignite. It was believed to be effective against chills and paralysis.

Under the name of *asiste,* the Lapidary of King Philip describes this as a Spanish stone resembling a top, or sometimes alum. If one rubs it lightly, it will glow again like fire. If one touches or rubs one's clothing with it, then places them in the fire, they will not burn but will be cleaned and bleached. It resists poisons and necromancy.

✦ *absynthus, absectos, absictus, abistos, asyctos, asycto, apsyctos, absuctos, absictos, absyctos, adsyctos, absictus, absintus, abaccintus, absiccos;* MFr. *absictos, absite, as(s)iste;* MHG *absist;* MSp. *asençio;* MDu. *abscicus.*

📖 Pliny 37, 137–42; 148; Isidore of Sevilla 16, 11, 2; Marbode 52; Lambert de Saint-Omer 55, 55; Lapidary of Marbode, 1st Romanesque translation LII; Meliteniotes v. 1136; *De lapidibus preciosis* 7; Cambridge Lapidary v. 1245–52; Wolfram von Eschenbach 791, 19; Arnoldus Saxo 2; Bartholomaeus Anglicus XVI, 13; *Albertus Magnus* 2, 1, 3; Vincent de Beauvais VIII, 36; Saint Florian v. 710–25; Thomas de Cantimpré 14, 8; Lapidary of King Philip 65; Konrad von Megenberg VI, 7; Jacob van Maerlant XII, 10; Leonardi II, 7, 13 and 20; *Poridat* 23; *Phisice* 44; *Hortus sanitatis* V, 4.

Absturt: A deformation of the name of the *apsyctos / absinctus.*

📖 Lapidary of King Philip 52.

Abtalune: A deformation of the name of the opal (ophthalmius).

📖 Lapidary of King Philip 50.

Achates: A black stone with white stripes that exceeds other stones of this type in size. It comes in many varieties, hence the many nicknames. Distinctions are made between iaspachates; cerachates; smaragdachates;

haemachates; leucachates; dendrachates, which appears to be decorated with small bushes; autachates, which when burned has an odor similar to that of myrrh; and coralloachates, which like sapphire is spotted all over with specks of gold. It is quite common in Crete where it is considered sacred. It is good against the stings of spiders and scorpions. The mere sight of it is good for the eyes, and when placed in the mouth, the agate eases thirst. Magicians distinguish those that resemble lion hide and are effective against scorpions. In Persia, the fumigation of these stones is used to divert tempests and hurricanes and for stopping the course of rivers. They are recognized as possessing this virtue if, when tossed into a boiling pot, they turn the water cold, although the same is said of rubies. For them to be truly useful, however, they must be attached with hairs from a lion's mane. Magicians detest those that resemble hyena skin and spread discord in homes. The stone that is a single color renders athletes invincible and makes men desirable to women; it incites desire. The one that has the color of lion hide is good against scorpion stings if it is tied on to the body or is crushed and mixed with water to make a balm, as it removes the victim's pain. When crushed into powder it can be sprinkled on viper bites or drunk with wine. When worn on a ring, it renders one eloquent, sociable, persuasive, powerful, vigorous, and makes one look good and amiable in all matters pertaining to God and men. It is made sacred by carving *Iachó* on it with a bronze pin, after which it should be set in a ring and worn.

The agate provides rich harvests when placed on the horns of draft animals; it earns men women's favor and grants the gift of bewitching mortals with the power of words; if held in the hand, it helps against all diseases, notably those of the bladder, and it relieves the ills of aging. The agate strengthens he who wears it. It will make one invisible if held in one's closed hand with the plant called heliotrope (*Solsequium*, a distorted form of which can be seen in the Old French *sorsique*). To learn if the stone you are holding is a good one, you should rub it while warming it next to a fire: the true agate will release a very pleasant aroma.

In the *Physiologus* and certain bestiaries, the agate works as a pearl magnet, and fishermen use it at the end of a line.

Camillo Leonardi notes: "There are several kinds of agates, to wit:

the agate of Sicily, India, Crete, and Cypress. Each of these species possesses a specific different property that emanates from it. This is why we find different sculptures in each type that designate the specific property of each kind. For example, since the specific virtue of the Sicilian agate is protection against the poison of vipers, so that the effect of this property is visible, one finds on it a human figure holding a viper in his hand, in order for the engraving to demonstrate the stone's property. But if the Serpent present in the celestial constellations is carved on this Sicilian agate, the presence of the constellation multiplies the stone's power."

If a winged horse (the constellation of Pegasus) is depicted in its entirety (as opposed to the constellation of the Small Horse [*Equulus*]) on a stone, particularly an agate, it brings to its bearer victory and prudence in all his actions.

An agate adorned with a rooster or three young girls gives its owner the favor of other men; it enables one to dominate the spirits of the air and it is useful in the magical arts.

According to Damigeron, the agate is the gem of Saturn, but other authors maintain it is the stone of Hermes. When decorated with a seated Ops, it was carried by free men, while the freed men had Fides Publica on it, and slaves had an image of a sleeping lion.

Today agate designates a variety of chalcedony quartz, which is given different names depending on the color: cherry-red color is called carnelian, brown is sardonyx, and apple-green is chrysoprase.

✦ *achaten, acate, accates, agat(h)es, agattes, agapis, chates;* MFr. *acates, achate, agate, acaste, aacate, scace;* MHG *achâtes, achat, achalat, aghetstein, acatstein, achaten, achades, agathan, agates, ekates, aitstein, aytstein, augstein, ioachat, aghaed;* MItal. *agate;* MDu. *agathes;* Ar. *alaquech.*

Varieties: *iaspachates, cerachates, zmaragdachates, haemachates, leucachates, dendrachates, aethachates, corallachates, agates, chates.*

📖 Theophrastus 31; Pliny 37, 139ff.; Solin 5, 26; Orpheus v. 232–43; 610ff.; Kerygma 21; Epiphanes 8; Damigeron 17; Pseudo-Hippocrates 2; Isidore of Sevilla 16, 11, 1; Marbode 2; Hildegard von Bingen IV, 16; 11, 1; Old English Lapidary 22; Lambert de Saint-Omer 55, 54; Alphabetical Lapidary 2–3;

Lapidary in prose 2; 2nd Lapidary in prose 10; *Sidrac* 8; Meliteniotes v. 112; *Physiologus* Y 22; Alexander Neckham v. 171ff.; Bodl. Digby 13 53; Cambridge lapidary v. 53–104; *De lapidibus preciosis* 2; Wolfram von Eschenbach 791, 11 and 22; *Liber lapidarii* 7; Gossouin de Metz v. 320–65; Arnoldus Saxo 4; Bartholomaeus Anglicus XVI, 11; Thomas de Cantimpré 14, 3; Albertus Magnus 2, 1, 4; Vincent de Beauvais VIII, 37–38; Lapidary of King Philip 8 and 20; Konrad von Megenberg VI, 2; Jacob van Maerlant XII, 3; Christian lapidary, v. 471–530 and 1069–98; Saint Florian v. 99–130; Volmar v. 197–220; *Secrez* 3, 22; Psellos 6; *Liber defota anima* v. 3102–318; *Vocabularius ex quo* a 83; a 133.2; a 261; *Liber ordinis rerum* 129, 13; Mandeville I 3; *Hortus sanitatis* V, 2; Pseudo-Mandeville 5 and 39; Closener ac 29; *Libro di Sidrach* chap. 46; Leonardi II, 7, 2; *Liber secretorum* II, 1, 12; *De virtutis lapidum* II, 29; *Poridat* 22 (under the name *smeradgus*); *Phisice* 4.

📖📖 Thomas Rogers Forbes, *The Midwife and the Witch* (New Haven and London: AMS, 1966), 64–79, in the chapter "Chalcedony and Childbirth."

Acopos: A gem that resembles niter; it is porous and spattered with specks of gold. Boiled with oil, it relieves lassitude.

📖 Pliny 37, 143.

Adamas (I): Six species of diamonds exist (*indicus, arabicus, cenchros, macedonius, cyprius, siderites*); it is also called *ananchitis*. Sometimes *adamas* is used to designate the loadstone (magnetite) and many lapidaries confuse the two stones. The Indian diamond is transparent and possesses six joined sides terminating in a point. It is the size of a hazel nut. The diamond of Arabia resembles that of India, only smaller. The other diamonds are pale like silver and are only born amidst the most perfect gold. They resist blows so well they cause iron to rebound and even split apart the anvil. Their hardness diminishes if plunged in goat's blood and then hit sharply. Around 1180, Alexander Neckham added vinegar to the blood (*De naturis rerum*, II, 92). This legend provided by Pliny the Elder can also be found in the works of Saint Augustine (*City of God*, XXI, 4) and numerous other authors. Diamonds triumph over fire and never get hot; it is this strength that earned them their name in Greek, "the indomitable one" (*adamas*). One tradition claims that the diamond grows on rock crystal and loadstone and another that it is the foam of water. Furthermore, they are male and female and engender more stones together, creating small ones that multiply every year. One can therefore place a male and a female in a box with a little of the rock on which they grew, moisten them often with heaven's dew, especially from the month of May, and they will engender and grow in accordance with their nature.

The diamond has a very strong antipathy to the magnet. If a magnet is in the diamond's proximity, it will not allow it to catch fire, or else, if the magnet has already attracted metal to it, the diamond will grab the iron and steal it away. It is also said to be a magnet for gold: when it is brought near gold, the gold becomes attached to it. Notker maintains that the diamond is the stone of Capricorn and the month of January.

Circa 1350, Konrad von Hamburg made the diamond the symbol of the Virgin's strength to endure suffering. In a poem entitled *Anulus*, he offers Mary a ring adorned with twenty gems. A pious legend maintained that Aaron's ring changed color and would grow dark when the Hebrews deserved capital punishment for their sins; when they needed to be executed by the sword, it appeared bloody, and when no crimes had been committed, it glowed in an extraordinary fashion.

Enchanters used the diamond. It provided protection against enemies, disease, wild animals, the largest blades, and typhoons. It rendered those who carried one in a silver walnut invincible and, when consecrated, it would drive away apparitions (*fantosmes*), specters of the dead, incubi, and false visions and dreams. It would also repel poisons, vain dreams, resolve brawls and trials peacefully, dispel delirium and vain terrors, relieve the insane, repulse bitter enemies, destroy enchantments and spells, maintain the happiness between married couples, and in the event of a dispute, encouraged their reconciliation. It prevented demons from entering the home. This required making a bracelet of gold, silver, iron, and copper twisted together and wearing it on the left wrist. One tradition maintained that looking at it was good for the eyes and a diamond that cured cataracts was once kept at Virville Castle in Isère.

In his *Voyages,* John Mandeville spoke at length about the diamond. He discussed where it was found, recycling the legend maintaining that they grew in male and female pairs on rocks, "nourished with the Dew of Heaven. And they engender commonly and bring forth small Children, that multiply and grow all the year." He specifies that they should be worn on the left side, "for it is of greater Virtue than on the right Side; for the strength of their Growing is toward the North, that is the Left side of the World." The diamond provides boldness and physical health, victory over enemies if the cause is just, protects from sedition, disputes, nightmares, wild animals, magic, and evil spirits, and heals the possessed. If a witch or enchanter tries to bewitch the wearer of a diamond, the spell will rebound. The diamond starts to perspire when in the presence of poison. The gem will lose its virtues due to its owner's sins; it is then necessary to restore the virtues—an allusion to the blessing of stones. A diamond should be given without compensation or haggling; its strength will be all the better for it.

The diamond's powers are increased if set in gold or steel, and sometimes in silver, and worn on the left, "as it is born in the North." To obtain an amulet, Venus is carved on the stone with rays around her feet. A man's head carved with a long beard and a little blood around the throat brings victory and audacity; it preserves the body from wounds and makes it possible to obtain the favor of kings and princes.

Around the year 1000, Ibrahim Ibn Wasif Shah recorded the following legend about the diamond in his *Summary of Wonders:* "In the mountains of Serendib (Sri Lanka) is the Vale of the Diamond. It is a very deep valley that is home to large venomous serpents. In order to take diamonds out, freshly scorched hot meat is cast into the valley. Eagles, which are numerous in the region, pounce on it and then carry it away to eat it elsewhere because of their fear of the serpents. The diamond hunter climbs up to the place where they feed to collect the diamonds that adhered to the meat. These stones are the size of a lentil, a bean, or a pea; the largest reach the size of a broad bean. The kings there carve their seals on them." Aristotle, the author of *Logic*, reports that there are large diamonds there that cannot be removed because of the snakes in the valley. Saint Epiphanius (fourth century) says the same thing about jacinth. This legend can also be found in the *Second Voyage of Sinbad the Sailor* (*The Thousand and One Nights*, 73rd night). One of Grimms' fairytales, *The Little Shepherd Boy*, mentions a mountain of diamonds in Pomerania.

The diamond has long been a symbol of fidelity, both in love and vassalage. In the *Aeneid*, for example, Lavinia gives Aeneas a diamond ring "that has the virtue of guarding from all peril the lovers who faithfully keep it."

The hardness of the diamond has given rise to the expression that someone is "like a diamond under the hammers," which Furetière explains this way: "A steadfast and constant man, who resists persecution. An old mistaken folk belief gave the impression a diamond could not be broken by hammers; this is wrong, since a goldsmith can break as many as one could want."

We should finally note that the French spelling *aymaut* for "diamond" brought about the confusion of this stone for the magnet [*aimant* in French —*Trans.*].

✦ *adamans, adams, adamast, dyamans, diamas, adamantinus*; MFr. *diamant, dieu amant, haneset*; MHG *adamant, adamast, ademaster, demant, diamant, diemant*; OE *dyamounde*; MItal. *diamantes, diamante, adamant*; Ar. *almâs, hager sumbedhig*.

📖 Theophrastus 18; Pliny 37, 55f.; 58; Solin 52, 23 and 56; Philostratus II, 14; Pseudo-Dioscorides II, 161; Lapidaire nautique 2; Isidore of Sevilla 16, 13, 2; Marbode 1; Notker I, 42; *Summarium Heinrici* VI, 5, 9; Hildegard von Bingen IV, 17; Meliteniotes v. 1121; Luka ben Serapion 9; *De lapidibus preciosis* 9; Lapidaire in old English 12; Lambert de Saint-Omer 55, 90; Jacques de Vitry cap. 91; Lapidary of Marbode, 1st Romanesque translation I; Alphabetical Lapidary 1; Damigeron 3; Dimishqî II, 6, 2; Lapidary in prose 1; 2nd lapidary in prose 1; Cambridge lapidary v. 1–18; *Sidrac* 17; Alexander of Neckam v. 325ff.; *De lapidibus preciosis* 3; Bodl. Digby 13 22 and 49; Wolfram von Eschenbach 53, 4; 75, 26; 589, 18; 791, 27; Serapion c. 391 (sumbedig id est lapis adamas);

Physiologus Y 47; *Liber lapidarii* 16 (dyamans); Arnoldus Saxo; Gossouin de Metz v. 509–522 (dyamant); Bartholomaeus Anglicus XVI, 9; Thomas de Cantimpré 14, 4; Konrad von Megenberg VI, 3; Jacob van Maerlant XII, 5; Vincent de Beauvais VIII, 39 and 41; Albertus Magnus 2, 1, 2; Guillaume Le Clerc v. 3333–426; *Lapidario* 31; *Picatrix* II, 10, 5; 42; 53; IV, 4, 65; Lapidary of King Philip 17; Saint Florian v. 408–50; Volmar v. 294–345; Jordan Catalani §43; *Secrez* 3, 21; *Liber defota anima* v. 6248–99; *Liber ordinis rerum* 129, 5; *Hortus sanitatis* V, 1; Pseudo-Mandeville 4; Mandeville I 2; *Vocabularius ex quo* a 154; Closener ad 3; *Libro di Sidrach* chap. 468; Leonardi II, 7, 1; *Liber secretorum* II, 1, 11; *De virtutis lapidum* II, 28; *Poridat* 7 and 26; *Phisice* 3.

📖📖 Friedrich Ohly, "Diamant und Bocksblut," *Wolfram-Studien* III (1975), 73–188; J. Ruska, "Der Diamant in der Medizin," in *Festschrift für Hermann Baas* (Hamburg, 1908).

Adamas (II):
Name given by some authors to the magnet. The *Physiologus* is responsible for this as it combined the properties of the diamond and the loadstone in the same entry. See *magnes*.

✦ *yamas;* MFr. *aymaunt;* MDu. *seil steen.*

📖 Alphabetical Lapidary 1; Cambridge lapidary v. 19–52; Vincent de Beauvais VIII, 34; Konrad von Megenberg VI, 50; Jacob van Maerlant XII, 6.

Adamicos:
A soft, moist, translucent stone whose color is close to that of the jacinth. It makes its wearer good, persuasive, pleasant, and procures a good life. It is useful for eye afflictions.

📖 Damigeron 62.

Ægopthalamos:
This is an agate with orbicular layers that resembles a goat's eye, hence its name. Carried in the left hand, it wards off vile insults.

✦ *egloptalmos, egostalinos, hyophtalmos, apocheamos.*

📖 Pliny 37, 187; Damigeron 62; Isidore of Sevilla 16, 15, 19.

Ægyptilla: This is a white stone cut by a red line and a black line; the more common form of egyptilla is a stone whose lower part is black and whose upper part blue. It gets its name from the region that produces it, Egypt. It is undoubtedly a banded agate.

According to Damigeron, it is the stone of Venus. Free men wore it with an engraving of Venus victorious; slaves with one of a dove.

✦ *egippula, egypcilla.*

📖 Pliny 37, 148; Isidore of Sevilla 16, 11, 3; *Summarium Heinrici* VI, 4; Lambert de Saint-Omer 55, 56; *Hortus sanitatis* V, 53; Leonardi II, 7, 105.

Aerizusa: Persian jasper or sapphirine chalcedony. The stone takes its name from the participle of a verb meaning "to be similar to air."

📖 Pliny 37, 115; Dioscorides V, 142.

Aeroids: A variety of beryl whose name means "sky blue."

📖 Pliny 37, 77.

Æthachates: A variety of agate that gives off an odor of myrhh. See *achates*.

📖 Pliny 37, 139.

Aetites: The "eagle stone"—which is still known as "pregnant stone" (*lapis praegnans*) and "stone of salvation," in other words one that helps someone conceive—is a variety of hydrated iron oxide or yellow ochre. It is round and generally red or purple, although sometimes gray or white, and "pregnant" with another stone. It is found in eagles' nests. Herodotus said that the eagle places aetites in its nest to ward off snakes and to help with laying eggs (Histories II, 14). It is claimed the stones always come in pairs (one male, the other female), and that without them eagles will not conceive. Some also maintain that this is the reason there are never more than two eaglets in the nest at one time. There are four distinguishable species: the

African aetites is small and soft and contains a smooth white clay in its belly. It is crumbly and regarded as female. The male aetites is found in Arabia; it is hard and similar to oak gall, or russet, and contains a hard stone; it is therefore a geode. The third comes from the island of Cypress and in color resembles the African aetites but it is larger and flatter, while the others are spherical. Inside it contains a pleasant sand and tiny stones. It is so soft it can be crushed in the fingers. The fourth is known as Taphiusian and is found near Leucas. The lapidaries give *aquileu* and *erodialis* as synonyms for aetites. It is the stone of twins, the stone symbolizing Castor and Pollux.

When attached to pregnant women or females in their fullness, and wrapped in the skins of sacrificed animals, all the *aetites* will prevent abortions. They should be left in place during the entire pregnancy until the time of parturition, but if they are not removed at this time, the childbirth will not take place. Midwives place it on the belly of those giving birth as it helps them do so without pain. In the tenth century, it gave protection to pregnant women when attached to their left wrist. It brings sobriety (worn around the neck, it enables one to drink a carafe of wine with no noticeable effects), increases wealth, brings victory, procures the favor of other people, prevents epileptics from falling, and ensures the health of young children. Hanging from the left shoulder, it keeps intact the love between married couples; it reduces the danger of becoming scared and fights epilepsy. According to a widespread legend, if it is placed beneath a dish that has been poisoned, the diner responsible for placing the poison will be unable to eat and will start choking immediately and will be incapable of ingesting food until the stone is removed. The innocent person will eat normally, even if the stone remains in his dish.

Whoever carries the aetites wrapped in a wolf hide will dread no evil thing, neither spirit nor demon. No woman shall be able to obstruct him. The stone gives honor and property in all cases.

To make an amulet or talisman from aetites, it is necessary to carve an eagle or fish on the stone. This will protect you from sea creatures and let others find you to be pleasant company. If a fish is carved, the stone procures a good catch. This is what the *Kyranides* and the *Secrez* say: "Take an aetites, carve an eagle on it, then, place a grape seed beneath the stone with the tip of an eagle's wing, and if you do not have one, then that of a sparrow hawk, next, once this is inserted, wear it. It will ward off any illnesses that may threaten you." One author suggests, "If a standing eagle is depicted on an aetites, and this stone is fixed in a lead ring, the person wearing it on his person shall have the power to catch many fish, no wild beast shall harm him, and he will be esteemed by men." Aetites must be set in lead.

Around the year 1000, Ibrahim Ibn Wasif Shah noted in his *Summary of Wonders* that the guard of one of the Egyptian pyramids was entrusted to "a small idol made of aetites, standing on a pedestal. It drew to it any man that looked upon it, and let him die at its feet." See also *okitokius*.

✦ *aethitae, aetitis, ethites, etites, etthites, etytes, ethitus, ethices, echites, echidnes, ecithnes, echinides, actites, anchites, endes, lapis aquilinus/aquile, lapis qui cito facit parere*; MFr. *ethite, echite, achite*; MHG *echites, atyote, atite, antytzy*; Ar. *clitemeth, achtamach, athamach*; Heb. *even takumah*.

📖 Pliny 36, 11; 149ff.; 37, 187; Solin 37, 5; Isidore of Sevilla 16, 4, 22; Aetios II, 32; 20 (another name for *ceraunia*); Damigeron 1; *Summarium Heinrici* VI,

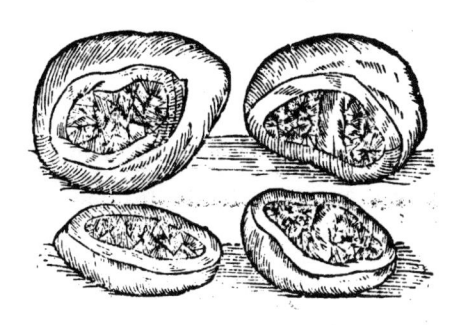

2, 21; Luka ben Serapion 31; *De lapidibus preciosis* 28; *Aristoteles de lapidibus* 374, 28ff.; Dioscorides V, 160; Pseudo-Dioscorides 2, 161; *Kyranides* 1, 1; 3, 1; Lambert de Saint-Omer 55, 43; Bodl. Digby 13 45; 51; *De l'entaille des gemmes* 49; *De la vertu des tailles* 48; *De figura* 15; Meliteniotes v. 1121; *Physiologus* Y 47; Pseudo-Plutarch §19; Lapidary of Marbode, 1st Romanesque translation XXV; Alphabetical Lapidary 36; Lapidaire in prose 20; 2nd lapidary in prose 23; Serapion c. 402 *(hager achtamach)*; Cambridge lapidary v. 621–66; Arnoldus Saxo 29; Bartholomaeus Anglicus XVI, 39; Thomas de Cantimpré 14, 18; Albertus Magnus 2, 5, 1; Vincent de Beauvais VIII, 23; *Picatrix* IV, 8, 7; Jacob van Maerlant XII, 32; *Secrez* 3, 27; 4, 1; Volmar v. 378–411; Leonardi II, 7, 96; Summary of Wonders 186; Hermes 17; Chael Solomon 37; *Phisice* 31; *Hortus sanitatis* V, 10.

📖 C. N. Bromhead, "Aetites or the Eagle-Stone," *Antiquity* 81 (1946): 16–22.

Agapis: On lapidary states: "Agapis, agathes: two names, / one stone is called by." See *achates*.

📖 Alphabetical Lapidary III, 2; Vincent de Beauvais VIII, 42; Leonardi II, 7, 8.

Agnes: See *magnes*.

📖 *Vocabularius ex quo* a 282.

Agnus Castus: Name given to a stone in the Middle French adaptation of the *Kyranides*. This is an Indian gem that gives its bearer the capacity of understanding and protects him from illness and drunkenness. It is also a common name for a plant called "chaste tree" in English, and its French name, *agneau chaste,* means "chaste lamb." Reputedly it soothes sexual tensions. A spice is made from it called "monks' pepper."

📖 *Secrez* 3, 24.

Agstein: This German word originally designated amber, then magnet and jet (gagate). Obsidian was called "black agstein" circa 1800.

✦ *augstein, ackstein, aitstain, aidstein.*

Alabanda: See *alabandina*.

Alabandica, Alabandicus: See *alabandina*.

✦ *alabandra, aabandicus*.

📖 Pliny 37, 123; *Summarium Heinrici* VI, 3, 8; Vincent de Beauvais, VIII, 15; Leonardi II, 7, 18.

Alabandina: Almandine, a kind of dark-red garnet carbuncle that is found in Orthosia and worked in Alabanda (Arabhissar), on the Marsyas River in Caria. In the fifteenth century, it was compared to sardonyx and is now considered to be a natural manganese sulphate. See *amandinus*.

✦ *alabandynia, alabandica, alabantina, alemandina, alamandina*; MFr. *alabandine, baudine, blande*; MHG *alabander, alabandâ*; MDu. *alabandina*.

📖 Pliny 36, 62; Isidore of Sevilla, 16, 14, 6; Aetios II, 33; Marbode 21; Lambert de Saint-Omer 55, 75; Lapidary of Marbode, 1st Romanesque translation XXI; Alphabetical Lapidary 11; Lapidary in prose 49; *De lapidibus preciosis* 8; Bodl. Digby 13 14; Cambridge lapidary v. 565–72; Wolfram von Eschenbach 791, 19; Arnoldus Saxo 5; Bartholomaeus Anglicus XVI, 14; Thomas de Cantimpré 14, 9; Vincent de Beauvais VIII, 16 and 42; Albertus Magnus 2, 1, 5; Konrad von Megenberg VI, 8; Jacob van Maerlant XII, 11; Leonardi II, 7, 7; *Hortus sanitatis* V, 3; Closener al 2; *Phisice* 26 and 65.

Alabastrite: Marbled onyx, native to the Thebaid and Alabastrum in Egypt, and Damascus in Syria. Its color is a shade of white broken up by various other hues. It soothes ills of the mouth, toothache, stomachache, and also serves as a laxative. See *alabastrum* and *onyx*.

📖 Pliny 36, 60; Isidore of Sevilla, 16, 5, 7; Lombard Dioscorides 162; *Summarium Heinrici* VI, 3, 5; Vincent de Beauvais, VIII, 16; *Hortus sanitatis* V, 4; Closener al 3; Leonardi II, 7, 17.

Alabastrum: This name designates two kinds of stone: chalcedony, a variety of lime carbonate, still called alabastrite, and a gypsum variety. See *nicomar*.

✦ *alabaster, alabastron, alabausta, alabaustrum, alabastrites, nycomar, nicomar;* MHG *alabaster, wiß mermelstein.*

📖 Theophrastus 6; Pliny 36, 59–61; Dioscorides V, 135; Isidore of Sevilla 16, 5, 7; 20, 7, 2; Hildegard von Bingen IV, 24; Alphabetical Lapidary 6; Bodl. Digby 13 21; *Vocabularius ex quo* a 299; Bartholomaeus Anglicus XVI, 3; Vincent de Beauvais VIII, 16; Konrad von Megenberg VI, 54; Jacob van Maerlant XII, 4; *Liber defota anima* v. 2654–823; *Liber ordinis rerum* 129, 28; Closener al 4.

Alacharist, Alataruch: Two stones bear this name, one that is red and as big as a cherry, and another rock that is purple in color. Both are effective against toothache.

📖 Pseudo-Mandeville 50; *Phisice* 81.

Alamandina: See *alabandina*.

Alcinio: A stone resembling copper that shines in the sunlight. It is, we are told, a kind of jacinth. When worn, it is useful for vigor and power, and it has Neptune carved on a chariot.

📖 Damigeron 60.

Alectorias: The al(l)ectory or "cock stone" or "capon stone" earns its name from the fact it is created in the belly of a rooster that is nine years old or more. It looks like crystal and is about the size of a broad bean.

Another tradition maintains that the *alectory* is found in the bird's knees. It renders its bearer strong and bold, and invisible, especially when worn on a helmet. It is claimed that Milo of Croton carried one on his person when he went into bouts, and it made him invincible. It makes one eloquent, gracious, and generous; earns one friends; excites sexual desire; makes one friendly and just; and enables one to be cherished by one's lord. One must remain chaste, however, otherwise the *alectory* will lose its virtues. Placed under the tongue, it will banish or ease thirst. It must be set in gold and worn on the right side.

When an *alectory* bearing a carved image of a rooster—that is to say, the star Alhabor holding a crown or belt in its beak—is carried, it will bring victory in a duel. See *clastecolz,* a stone that offers distinctive qualities similar to the *alectory.*

> ✦ *a(l)lectorius;* MFr. *allectorie, alectoire, aletoyre, electoire, dlectorie, ad lectories, clasterole, clastecollz;* MItal. *electria, preta de lo gallo (Pentamerone 4, 1);* MDu. *capoensteen;* Ar. *alector.*
>
> 📖 Pliny 36, 62; Solin I, 77; Damigeron 19; Isidore of Sevilla, 16, 13, 8; Marbode 3; Lambert de Saint-Omer 55, 44; *De lapidibus preciosis* 6; Arnoldus Saxo 6; Lapidary of Marbode, 1st Romanesque translation XXI; Alphabetical Lapidary 11; Lapidary in prose 12; 2nd Lapidary in prose 16; Cambridge Lapidary v. 105–28; Bartholomaeus Anglicus XVI, 17; Thomas de Cantimpré 14, 7; Albertus Magnus 2, 1, 6; Vincent de Beauvais VIII, 43; *Lapidario* 114; Lapidary of King Philip 24; Konrad von Megenberg VI, 6; Jacob van Maerlant XII, 9; Saint Florian v. 824–49; Volmar v. 346–59; Mandeville I, 14; Pseudo-Mandeville 16 and 43; *Secrez* 3, 23; *Vocabularius ex quo* a 318; Closener al 29; Leonardi II, 7, 4; *Liber secretorum* II, 1, 13; *De virtutis lapidum* II, 30; Hermes 19; Poridat 27; *Phisice* 16 and 89 (clasterole); *Hortus sanitatis* V, 6.

Alexandrius:

To the best of my knowledge, this name is only found in the Old English lapidary (17) in the Tiberius Manuscript A III in the

British Museum, which contents itself with the observation that this stone looks like crystal.

Alla Lapsurus: See *lapis lazuli*.

 📖 *Vocabularius ex quo* a 382. 1.

Amandinus: *Almandine* or *alabandine* is a gem of varied colors that takes its name from Alabandina, another name for Ephesus. It is primarily scarlet red in color. It expels all poisons, gives the gift of prophecy, makes one invisible, and facilitates the understanding of obscure matters. See *alabandina*.

✦ *almandina, alimendin, almechin, amandin, asmadus, esmundus;* MHG *amanten, almandreü, almenden, almantin.*

📖 Arnoldus Saxo 7; Albertus Magnus 2, 1, 7; Konrad von Megenberg VI, 9 and VI, 5; Volmar v. 79–86; Leonardi II, 7, 12; *Liber secretorum* II, 1, 14; *De virtutis lapidum* II, 31; *Hortus sanitatis* V, 4.

Ambra: Callistratus states that this stone, which may be amber, is good for all ages in treating madness and dysuria, either in a drink or worn as an amulet. It is under the jurisdiction of the 18° of Taurus and prevents intoxication if touched. See *succinum*.

Ambra also sometimes designates ambergris. See *cymbra*.

📖 Avicenna II, 2, 63; *De lapidibus preciosis* 14 (*clambari*); *Lapidario* 48 (Ar. *alambari*).

Amethystizonite: These stones, whose name means "that which the flame, at the end, draws from the violet of the amethyst," are a variety of carbuncle, balas ruby, or garnet, comparable to the *syrtites*. They were used during the Middle Ages to light fires with the help of oakum.

✦ *amethystizon, ametistizontas, amistunte.*

📖 Pliny 37, 93; Isidore of Sevilla 16, 9, 5; Alphabetical Lapidary 7; *Summarium Henrici* VI, 4, 24.

Amethystus: This is the violet quartz found in Spain in the vicinity of Cartagena, in France near Brioude, and in Hungary, Arabia, and India. According to the etymological interpretation of its name, amethyst is supposed to prevent intoxication. It is sometimes specified that it should be placed with a sardonyx on a drunken individual's navel to dispel his inebriation. A legend tells how the nymph Ametis was pursued by Bacchus and asked Diana for her aid. The goddess changed her into crystal, which Bacchus, in a drunken rage, turned violet by pouring wine over it. Once he sobered up, the god granted amethyst the power to dissipate drunkenness.

Reddish-violet in color, it resembles a drop of wine. There are countless varieties, but distinctions are made only between five species. Amethysts are transparent violet and are easily etched. Those from India have the richest shade of purple. One variety is close to the color of jacinth: the Indians call this color *socon* and this amethyst *socondion*. Another variety has a lighter color and is called *sapenos*. It is also called *pharanitis,* the name of the region where it is found, which borders Arabia. The fourth variety is wine-colored. The fifth is practically white and could almost be mistaken for crystal. According to the Arabic tradition presented by Belenis, its planet is Venus. However one wears it, it facilitates one's access to kings. It wards off hail and grasshoppers when used with a prayer learned from the magi. It heals consumption, banishes headaches, and paralyzes magic charms. Triturated and drunk, it makes women fertile and destroys poison. It is good to wear an amethyst when going hunting as it attracts wild animals, and it should be set in silver.

In the thirteenth century, it was said the amethyst prevented the devil from causing harm and prevented a person from seeing "ghosts" (*fantasme*). It also provided protection from the entity known as a nightmare and from fevers, it granted riches, and made one humble, courteous, and gracious. The Middle French spelling *mastice* has caused it to be confused with hematite.

Etched with the moon and sun and hung around the neck with hairs from a cynocephalus and feathers from a swallow, it protects one from evil spells. Its magical properties are increased if set in gold or silver and if a man on horseback holding a scepter is carved on it.

Whoever finds an amethyst with a foaming horse mounted by a man holding a scepter in his right hand should know that this engraving will be helpful in all matters for its owner and that all the princes and the powerful will obey him. This stone must be attached to a piece of silver or gold that weighs twice as much as the stone itself.

A man armed with a sword in his hand carved on a sardonyx or amethyst will grant its owner a good and trustworthy memory and give him wisdom.

If one finds an image on an amethyst of a man with a sword in hand seated on a dragon, and this stone is then set in a ring of lead or iron, the wearer will obtain the obedience of all the spirits, and they will reveal where treasures are hidden and answer whatever questions he may ask.

A figure of a bear etched on an amethyst has the power to put demons to flight and to protect an individual from inebriation.

In the Bible, the amethyst figures among the gems of the high priest Aaron's *rationale* [the breastplate of the Ephod —*Trans.*]. In the Christian lapidary, it symbolizes the meek who die with Christ and pray for their persecutors, those from whom charity springs forth. In the poem entitled *Anulus*, written circa 1350 by Konrad of Hamburg, he offers Mary a ring adorned with twenty gems. Here, the amethyst symbolizes the love men and God devote to the Virgin. See *socoudios, sapenos, pharanites, pederotes, anterotes*.

✦ *amathystus, amatistes, amaristes, amatiste, amesticus, amiscus;* MFr. *ametiste, amatiste, amistote, amestice, omistite, mastice, qatique;* MHG *amatisten, ametisten, amantiste;* MItal. *amatista;* MDu. *ametist.*

📖 Theophrastus 31; Pliny 27, 121f.; Epiphanes 9; Isidore of Sevilla 16, 9, 1; Marbode 16; Hildegard von Bingen IV, 15; Lambert de Saint-Omer 54, 12 and 55, 20; Meliteniotes v. 1125; Lapidary of Marbode, 1st Romanesque translation XVI; Lapidary in prose 11; 2nd Lapidary in prose 14 v°; *Sidrac* 9; Alexander

Neckham v. 217ff.; *De lapidibus preciosis* 1; Bodl. Digby 13 16 and 53; *De l'entaille des gemmes* 30; Wolfram von Eschenbach 589, 18; *De figura* 14; *Liber lapidarii* 8; Gossouin de Metz v. 360–89; Cambridge Lapidary v. 401–14; Arnoldus Saxo 8; Bartholomaeus Anglicus XVI, 10 and 19; Thomas de Cantimpré 14, 2; Vincent de Beauvais VIII, 44; Albertus Magnus 2, 1, 8; Lapidary of King Philip 9; Konrad von Megenberg VI, 1; Jacob van Maerlant XII, 2; Christian lapidary v. 531–44 and 1099–1158; Volmar v. 221–34; Saint Florian v. 131–64; *Secrez* 3, 19; *Liber de fota anima* v. 3242–3323 and 6030–87; Mandeville I 7; Pseudo-Mandeville 9; Closener am 36; *Liber ordinis rerum* 129, 17; *Libro di Sidrach* chap. 462; Leonardi II, 7, 3; *Vocabularius ex quo* a 435; 448.2; *Liber secretorum* II, 1, 15; *De virtutis lapidum* II, 32; Ragiel 18; Hermes 16; Solomon 5; 15; 44; *Phisice* 8 and 36; *Hortus sanitatis* V, 7.

Amiantos: The "immaculate one" is a cold, dry white stone that wards off all the poisons of witches. It is found in the Nile and the Mountains of the Moon, the name given to the mountains from which flows the Nile River. The amiantos stone is governed by the 21° of Taurus and, when crushed into a powder, is effective in clearing the eyes of rheum. It destroys poisons and offers resistance to enchantments and "the arts of nigromancy."

See *asbeston,* for which this is a white variety, an aluminum and potassium silicate.

✦ *amianton, amianthus, amiathon, amanthos, amiatus, amiliarius, amatides;* MHG *amantes, amaritan;* MFr. *amarite, amanthesar;* Ar. *algodon.*

📖 Pliny 36, 139; Isidore of Sevilla 16, 4, 19; Dioscorides V, 138 and 156; Lombard Dioscorides 165; *Summarium Heinrici* VI, 2, 16; Meliteniotes v. 1126; *De lapidibus preciosis* 5; Thomas de Cantimpré 14, 6; Vincent de Beauvais VIII, 27; *Lapidario* 50; Lapidary of King Philip 62; Konrad von Megenberg VI, 6, 4; Jacob van Maerlant XII, 8; Closener am 37; am 45; Leonardi II, 7, 15 and 23.

Amistes: See *amethystus*.

📖 Closener a 48.

Amites: See *ostracite*.

📖 Leonardi II, 7, 25 and 78.

Ammochrysos: A gem native to Persia, described as resembling a blend of sand and gold, which corresponds with the Greek words *ammos* and *chrysos*.

📖 Pliny 37, 188; Solin 37, 13; Isidore of Sevilla 16, 15, 5.

Amphicomos: Its name means "surrounded by hair." It is another name for the *erotylos* and the *hieromnemon*. This stone is used as a means of divination.

◆ *amphiconios*.

📖 Pliny 37, 160.

Amphidanes: Another name for chrysocolla. This square stone is native to "India, where the ants mine gold," an allusion to a well-known legend passed down in the romances of Alexander and in the scholarly literature. It is the magnet for this metal.

◆ *amphidanas, amphitanes, aphidanes*.

📖 Pliny 37, 147; Isidore of Sevilla 16, 15, 7; Meliteniote v. 1134.

Anactites: This is the "stone without anger"; another name for galactite.

✦ *anachites, mancites.*

📖 Orpheus 2; Kerygma 2; Damigeron 34 (*anancites* as a result of a reading error).

Ana(n)citis: Another name for *adamas* (diamond) according to Pliny, or galactite according to the Pseudo-Orpheus. Some call it leucographite, emerald, or galbanite, but for magicians, this stone was synecite, "because it contained all the stones one could possibly desire," and lethargos, "forgetting of all ills." We find a stone called *camiruca*, which is glossed as *olvidadiza*, "oblivious," and which has the property of making its bearer forget all his reasons for acting the way he does.

Anancite is used in hydromancy and inspires divine apparitions. It was said that "devils" often showed themselves to their possessors but without being able to harm them, so this stone represents the temptation of Jesus by the devil.

✦ *ananchitide, anancithidus, anatida, amantides, amathitis;* MFr. *anatida.*

📖 Pliny 37, 61 and 192; Isidore of Sevilla 16, 15, 22; Orpheus v. 194; Damigeron 7; Meliteniotes v. 1132; Alphabetical Lapidary 1; Vincent de Beauvais VIII, 32; *Lapidario* 60; Leonardi II, 7, 28.

Androdamas: The "man tamer" is a black, square stone, noteworthy for its weight and hardness, which earned it the name it bears.

It is formed in the Red Sea from the shattering of silver, is quadrangular, and extremely similar to pieces of marquetry. It subdues men's fits of rage and their wrath, which is based on an etymological interpretation of the stone's name. It is an excellent remedy for liver disorders. It combats delirium, bad moods, and sorrow; it preserves visual acuity but covers the sight of those around the bearer with a thick fog—so thick it allows thieves to enter houses. It is also called *argyrodamas*.

✦ *androdamans, androdamanta, andromanda, andromantes, androdamma, androdamantus, andromant, andordramanta, antrodiamanta, andravnias, auhetion, andro, amaradama, aramanda;* MFr. *anthrodragme, androdragme, andromame, adroma(n)de, androniade, androdania, idrodamas;* MHG *antrodrâgmâ, andromant;* Ar. *elendhermon.*

📖 Pliny 37, 144; Solin 33, 21; Isidore of Sevilla 16, 15, 8; Marbode 48; *Summarium Heinrici* VI, 2, 14; Lambert de Saint-Omer 55, 83; Lapidary of Marbode, 1st Romanesque translation XLVIII; Alphabetical Lapidary 12; Lapidary in prose 47; *De lapidibus preciosis* 9; Arnoldus Saxo 9; Bodl. Digby 13 19; Cambridge Lapidary v. 1161–70; Wolfram von Eschenbach 791, 8; Thomas de Cantimpré 14, 10; Albertus Magnus 2, 1, 9; Vincent de Beauvais VIII, 28; VIII, 45; Lapidary of King Philip 61; Konrad von Megenberg VI, 10; Jacob van Maerlant XII, 12; Leonardi II, 7, 5; 7; 9 and 32; Closener an 37; *Phisice* 55; *Hortus sanitatis* V, 5.

Anguinum: See *dre concides.*

Animate Stone of the Mountain: See *siderites.*

Annauris: A stone that remains unidentifiable because its name has been distorted by the scribes.

✦ *annauiris, anna virus, annauir, ananaturis.*

📖 Closener an 71.

Antachates: This is the "anti-agate." When used to fumigate, it heals tertian and quartan fevers. If placed beneath a burning horn, it will dissolve without difficulty. See also *achates.*

✦ *antiachates, anthachates, aethachates, autachates, antes.*

📖 Pliny 37, 139; Orpheus v. 633–41; *Kerygma* 40; Closener an 93.

Anterotes: The name of a variety of white amethyst, also called "eyelid of Venus" and *pederotes*. It allegedly prevents drunkenness.

📖 Pliny 37, 123.

Anthracite: This is a hard fossil stone similar to the coal found in Threspotia; sparks sometimes appear and fly about inside which causes people to say that it "glows like a blazing fire or like a shining carbuncle." Cast into a fire, it goes out and seems lifeless; sprinkled with water, it blazes up. If carried from the time one is a child, the *anthrax* prevents drowning in the event of shipwreck.

✦ *anthracitis, antrachites, antrachas, andrachithen, arachites.*

📖 Pliny 36, 148; Isidore of Sevilla 16, 14, 2; Lambert de Saint-Omer 55, 64; Meliteniotes v. 1133; Alphabetical Lapidary 10; Vincent de Beauvais VIII, 45; *Hortus sanitatis* V, 5; Leonardi II, 7, 11.

Anthracitis: A black and saffron colored stone found in Thesprotia, Arcadia, and Africa. It is an excellent ingredient for ophthalmic concoctions. It may be the ruby spinel, an aluminate of magnesia. No distinction was made between this stone and anthracite during the Middle Ages.

✦ *anthracias.*

📖 Pliny 37, 99; 189; Solin 37, 23; Melitenotes v. 1133; Isidore of Sevilla 16, 14, 2; Vincent de Beauvais VIII, 45.

Anthrax: Another name for anthracite. When carried from childhood, *anthrax* and chalcedony prevent drowning during shipwreck.

📖 Theophrastus 18–19; Pliny 37 92f.; *Lapidaire nautique* 1; Meliteniotes v. 1119; Wolfram von Eschenbach 741, 13; Vincent de Beauvais VIII, 45; Psellus 5.

Anthropocrinus: This stone contains stars tousled like a man's hair (*anthropo* + *crinus*). It is helpful in controlling blood flow. Hung from the neck on a multicolored string, it frees one from the magical and malefic arts.

 📖 Damigeron 53.

Antipathes, Antiphates: This gem, an opaque black coral, is found in Mysia [in the northwest of what is now Anatolia, Turkey —*Trans.*]. It is tested by boiling it in milk: if genuine, it turns the color of myrrh. "A person might well expect to find some extraordinary virtues in this stone, seeing that, among so many other substances possessed of antipathetic properties, it is the only one that bears this name," says Pliny the Elder. Magicians claim it offers assistance in counteracting fascinations, enchantments, and nervous pains. Macerated in wine, it makes a remedy against scurf and leprosy.

 ✦ *antipathites.*

 📖 Pliny 37, 145; Dioscorides V, 122; Pseudo-Dioscorides 2, 140; Lombard Dioscorides 149, Pseudo-Plutarch §23; Melitenotes v. 1132; Leonardi II, 7, 24.

Antitaneus: See *chrysocolla.*

 📖 Leonardi II, 7, 30.

Aphrodisiaca: The aphrodisiac is a red stone mixed with white.

 📖 Pliny 37, 148; Melitenotes v. 1136.

Aphroselinus, Afroseline: Still called "moon foam," the *aphroselenite* is engraved with an Isis bearing cow horns, in other words either Hathor-Hecate or a head topped by a crescent. Its zodiac sign is Cancer. When a man who is seated on an Eagle (Mars) and holding a baton in his hand is carved on it, and the stone has then been set in archon (brass), it allows a man to subjugate his foes, provided that he is dressed in white linen and abstains from eating the meat of pigeons.

✦ *affrosolinum, afestrosalinus.*

📖 Damigeron, De sculpturis; *De la vertu des tailles* 38; *De figura* 5; *Hortus sanitatis* V, 76.

Apolokos: See *polophos*.

Apsyctos: See *absinctus*.

Aptor: *Wigamur,* an anonymous thirteenth-century Arthurian romance, calls aptor an extraordinary stone. If an ill individual looks at it, it will appear red; the longer he or see contemplates it, the redder it becomes. It appears murky to someone who has just slept with a woman. The stone becomes cloudy if a woman looks at it, but if she is a virgin, she will see all its colors. The person wearing aptor should avoid ugly thoughts, anger, and envy. Any who look at it shall experience no misfortune on that day. An unfaithful man cannot linger near it but one who is pure shall earn honor and renown. A tub topped by a golden arch is made from this stone. Those who bathe in it forget all their cares and their heart is uplifted, their energies and wisdom alike are revived and this lasts for a month's time— nothing can disrupt their happiness at this time. Evil men will feel wan and weakened.

It is possible that the anonymous author was partly inspired by Geoffrey of Monmouth (*Historia Regum Britanniae* VIII, 10f.), who tells how the giants of Ireland brought many stones with healing powers from Africa; they bathed in them to heal their sicknesses or washed the stones and used that water for bathing.

📖 *Wigamur,* Wolfenbüttel ms. 51.2. Aug. 4°, fol. 30 r°–v°.

Aquileus, Aquilinus: Another name for *aetites*. The lapidaries also talk of a stone that is extracted from the eagle or an ocean fish; it cures quartan fever if carried on one's person. It is called *aquileus lymphaticus*.

📖 Leonardi II, 7, 27 and 31.

Arabica: A kind of onyx that is extremely similar to ivory. It is thought that those wearing it will heal themselves of nervous pains. When charred, it is used as toothpaste. It cures hemorrhoids in particular. To achieve this, it is placed in torn cloths and applied with compresses. Its zodiac sign is Virgo, and it is carved with a cynocephalic creature.

✦ *arabicus, arabus; MSp. arábiga.*

📖 Pliny 37, 145; Solin 33, 22; Isidore of Sevilla 16, 4, 11; Dioscorides V, 131 and 149; Pseudo-Dioscorides 2, 149; Lombard Dioscorides 158; Meliteniotes v. 1130; *Summarium Heinrici* VI, 2, 9; Meliteniotes v. 1127; *Lapidario* 221; Leonardi II, 7, 22.

Argirites: Another name for the argyrophylax, a gem that looks like silver and is collected from the Pactolus River. It had the property of guarding treasures against thieves.

✦ *argyrites, agirites.*

📖 Isidore of Sevilla 16, 15, 7; Lambert de Saint-Omer 55, 82; Bartholomaeus Anglicus XVI, 15; Leonardi II, 7, 29.

Argyrodamas: Some lapidaries maintain that this is talc; for others, it is *androdamas*. See *androdamas*.

 📖 Pliny 37, 144; Meliteniotes v. 1126.

Argyrophilax: A stone found in the Pactolus River and resembling silver. It is placed on the threshold of the place where one's wealth is stored because it will emit the sound of a trumpet at the approach of any thief. Sent fleeing, the scoundrel will find his death by falling into a precipice. According to the *Kerygma* of Orpheus, this stone may correspond to the opal.

 📖 Pseudo-Plutarch §3.

Armenius: The "Armenian" stone is blue and somewhat dull and thick. It is effective against heart failure and prevents conception if a man or woman is wearing one. Some call it the "loadstone." See *vernix*.

 ✦ *armenas, armenus;* MFr. *pierre de armenac;* MSp. *piedra armeniana.*

 📖 Pseudo-Dioscorides 2, 105; Lombard Dioscorides 116; Avicenna fol. 550 r°; Pseudo-Mandeville 61; *Lapidario* 180; *Hortus sanitatis* V, 14; Leonardi II, 7, 26; *Phisice* 99.

Arnostetites: This stone resembles lamb's fat. It is used to calm the wrath of kings and the fury of judges. It must be held clenched in the left hand.

 📖 Damigeron 51.

Aromaticus: The "aromatic stone" is produced, or so it is said, in Arabia, although it is found in Egypt, in Philae. It is stony all over and has the color and odor of myrrh, which is why queens long for it.

 📖 Pliny 37, 145; Meliteniotes v. 1131.

Arsenicus: Arsenic, still called realgar, was highly prized by the sixteenth-century alchemists. In around the year 1525, Paracelsus extolled its virtues. See *auripigmentum*.

> ✦ MHG *rusgel, regalger, ruesgel;* Ar. *zirnih, zarnich, azernec(h).*

> 📖 Dioscorides V, 104; Pliny 34, 178; Pseudo-Dioscorides 2, 121; Avicenna II, 2, 49; Luka ben Serapion 27; *De lapidibus preciosis* 24; *Aristoteles de lapidibus* 373, 12ff.; *Liber ordinis rerum* 130, 29; *Hortus sanitatis* V, 22.

Asbeston: The color of iron, asbestos, whose Greek name means "inextinguishable," comes from the mountains of Arcadia. Once it has been set on fire, nothing can put it out again, the ancients say. In the Middle Ages, it was native to Arabia and had a wooly texture called "salamander feather." Thanks to Marco Polo, we know more about this. There are veins in a mountain located within the borders of the province of Ghinghin Talas, from which the salamander, which is neither beast nor snake, is taken. The ore is heaped in a copper mortar, then washed with water; only the wool-like filaments float to the top. These are woven into salamander cloth. These cloths are brown and bleached in fire.

Writers did not allow any of these properties to escape their notice and have made use of them since the second half of the twelfth century. The *Romance of Aeneas,* for example, describes the tomb of Pallas in which an eternal lamp burns: "*asbestos* was its wick and it was lit by a stone; by its nature and custom it never went out" (v. 6514ff.). This motif can be found in all the adaptations and translations of this romance, as well as in Benoît de Sainte-Maure (*Roman de Thebes* v.

14904ff.; 16800ff.). In the beginning of the twelfth century, the chanson de geste of *Quatre Fils Aymon* [Aymon's Four Sons] (v. 9617–20) mentions "The candles burn night and day, / and neither wind nor rain can ever extinguish them, / for their light can never weaken be it only the size of a bud."

✦ asbestos, asbestus, asbostus, aspectus, aspecus, albestus, arbestos, abestos, abesios, absectos, besteon, bestion; MFr. abestos, ebesto, asbeste, albeston, bestatis, bestunes, cestont; MHG abestô, bestîon; MSp. asençio; MDu. albesten.

📖 Pliny 37, 146; Solin 7, 13; Saint Augustine, *De civitate Dei* XXI, 5; Isidore of Sevilla 16, 4, 4; Dioscorides V, 115; Lombard Dioscorides 142; Marbode 33; Old English lapidary 14; Lapidary of Marbode, 1st Romanesque translation XXXIII; Lapidary in prose 52; 2nd Lapidary in prose 27; Alexander Neckham v. 271ff.; Cambridge Lapidary v. 875–84; Bartholomaeus Anglicus XVI, 12; Vincent de Beauvais VIII, 27; Albertus Magnus II, 1, 1; Marco Polo chap. LX; Lapidary of King Philip 39; Jacob van Maerlant XII, 7; Closener al 20; *Liber secretorum* II, 1, 10; *De virtutis lapidum* II, 9; *Phisice* 37; *Hortus sanitatis* V, 9.

📖📖 Berthold Laufer, "Asbestos and Salamander," *T'oung Pao* 6 (1915): 299–373.

Asinius, Asininus:

The name given to two round or oblong stones that are white verging on yellow and can be found in the wild ass (onager). The one in its head is called *cephalicus*, the other, located in its jaw, is called *maxillaris*. The first variety, if placed on the head, heals headaches as well as epilepsy.

📖 Leonardi II, 7, 21.

Asius, Assius:

This is another name for the *sarcophagus* stone. Assius is light in weight and is white with black spots and scales like fish. Placed in the mouth it tastes like salt. It heals fistulas and scrofula and protects one from gout and other ills. It must be pulverized and drunk, mixed with wine, and then one's health is restored. For wounds, it is used with honey. It is said it will shrink the body, except for the teeth, in less than forty days.

📖 Pliny 37, 1131ff. (*sarcophagus*); Dioscorides V, 124; Pseudo-Dioscorides 2, 142; Lombard Dioscorides 152; Meliteniotes v. 1127; Bodl. Digby 13 15; Avicenna II, 2, 30; Vincent de Beauvais VIII, 46; Alphabetical Lapidary 5; *Hortus sanitatis* V, 8; Leonardi II, 7, 14.

Aspalachites: The "mole stone" is helpful for finding treasures. "Etch on this stone a naked man holding a mattock, and bent over as if digging; and the following names all around him . . . and behind him Aram. It must be set in a gold scarab and then one will be invincible and unshakable wherever riches are to be found."

📖 Kerygma 50; Meliteniotes v. 1155.

Aspisatis: This stone is the color of fire. Individuals with spleen disorders should wear it attached to their persons with camel hair. It is found in the nests of certain birds in Arabia. Another aspilate, which is shiny silver in color, can be found in the same region, in Leucopetra. Those suffering from spleen illnesses should wear it in an amulet with camel dung; it works against mental alienation. It is sometimes compared to *sirites/siderites*.

✦ *aspisates, aspisatim, aspillatis, aspisalis, aspilaten.*

📖 Pliny 37, 146; Meliteniotes v. 1134; Leonardi II, 7, 19.

Asseus: This stone is used against gout in a foot bath or as a poultice with broad beans; it is said to dry the festering sores.

📖 Vincent de Beauvais VIII, 5.

Assiffe: A white stone found in Khorasan (terra de Horazen); it cannot be filed down. Placed on the belly, it soothes stomach disorders.

📖 *Picatrix* IV, 8, 5.

Astamatis: An artificial stone allegedly manufactured by Aristotle for Alexander the Great. It consists of melted iron, sulfur, magnesium, borax, pig brain and suet, the blood of a black crow, orpiment, gold, silver, and bronze. It gives one shelter from prejudices, enemies, and their weapons. One wears astamatis when going to war.

📖 *Picatrix* III, 10.

Asteria: This name designates the star sapphire native to India and Carmania. During the Middle Ages, it was confused with asterite.

📖 Pliny 37, 131.

Asterite: The *asterite* is an agatized madreporite, a star-shaped or radiant stone that contains a bit of light, like the light in the pupil of an eye. It transmits this light, which means it moves about inside, depending on the degree of angle, sometimes through one tip and sometimes through another. In contrast to the sun, it casts white rays, like a star, hence the name

E   F

that has been bestowed upon it. The Pseudo-Plutarch says that it burns at night like a star at the beginning of autumn. According to Notker, who repeats Martianus Capella on this point, the *asterite* is governed by Cancer and the month of July. See *astrios*.

✦ *astrites, alerites, asterytes, asteritus, asteria;* MSp. *gasten.*

📖 Pliny 37, 131; Pseudo-Plutarch §11; Isidore of Sevilla 16, 10, 3; Notker I, 39; *Summarium Heinrici* VI, 4, 27; Lambert de Saint-Omer 55, 47; Alphabetical Lapidary 8; Bartholomaeus Anglicus XVI, 18; Vincent de Beauvais VIII, 46; *Hortus sanitatis* V, 11; Leonardi II, 7, 6; *Poridat* 16.

Astolos: A white stone resembling a fish eye that shines like the sun. See *astrios, asterite*.

✦ *astalon, astrolon, astrobolos.*

📖 Pliny 37, 133; Meliteniotes v. 1130.

Astrapaea: All we know of this stone is what Pliny the Elder tells us: it has flashes of radiance running across a white or blue background.

📖 Pliny 37, 189.

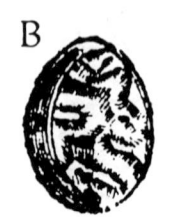

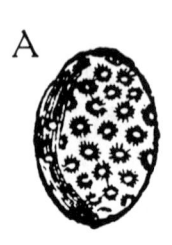

Astrios: The stone named *astrios* is white and resembles a crystal. It is found in India, on the sides of the Pallene headland, in Carmania, and on Mount Ballenus, hence the name ballen that is sometimes given to it. Its center glows like a star whose light resembles that of the full moon. Some attribute its name to the fact that, when set opposite the stars, it steals their light and reflects it. These authors name the most beautiful sort, which is flawless, as being from Germania, and describe a lesser variety that is called *ceraunia*. The least valued resemble the light cast by a lantern. Those involved with the magic arts swear that Zoroaster celebrated its marvelous virtues in magic.

Judging from the names, *astrios* (also called *ceraunia*, "thunder bolt"), the *astroites* extolled by Zoroaster and the magi, and the *astrobolion* all appear to be varieties of the same gem. The *astrion* may correspond to the *asteria*, a kind of opal.

✦ *astriotes, astrion, astrotes, astolos, asirites;* MDu. *astryon*.

📖 Pliny 37, 132–33; Isidore of Sevilla 16, 13, 7; Lambert de Saint-Omer 55, 95; Pseudo-Plutarch §11; Meliteniotes v. 1130 and 1133; Alphabetical Lapidary 9; Bodl. Digby 13 20 and 48; Bartholomaeus Anglicus XVI, 16; Vincent de Beauvais VIII, 46; *Hortus sanitatis* V, 11; *Liber defota anima* v. 3885–996.

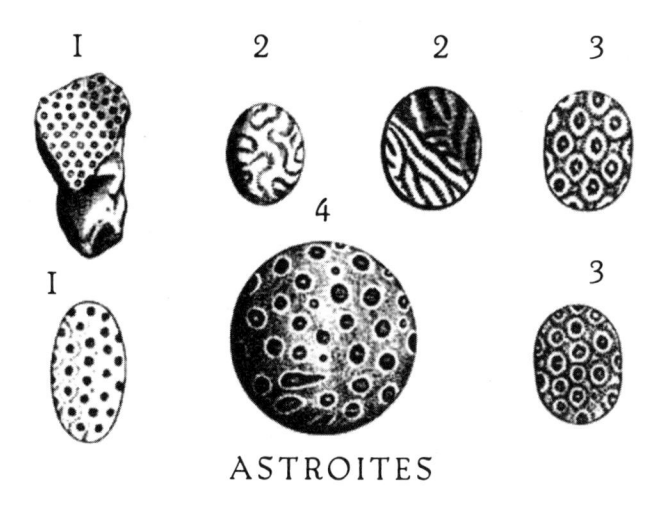

ASTROITES

Atarac: The name of a stone that never breaks.

📖 *Picatrix* IV, 8, 14.

Athomates: A yellowish stone resembling chalcedony with something like a white flower at its center. It is "full of vices" and the lapidary mentions it "in order that people refrain from wearing this stone as it multiplies rage, quarreling, and tension." It renders its wearer hateful. If a man wants to kill his enemy, he gives him this stone set in a ring.

📖 *Phisice* 88.

Atizoe: India, Persia, Mount Acidane, and Mount Ida produce the silvery gleaming *atizoe,* which is about three fingers long and shaped like a lentil. It has a pleasant odor and is necessary to magicians when consecrating a king.

- ✦ *atizon, azitoen, acizoen.*
- 📖 Pliny 37, 147; Meliteniotes v. 1134.

Atyote: see *aetites.*

- 📖 Volmar v. 378–411.

Augetis, Augites: For many authors, this stone, which according to the etymology of its name diffuses "a glowing light," is no different from callaïne (callaina).

- ✦ *angites, quingites.*
- 📖 Pliny 37, 147; Meliteniotes v. 1134.

Auripigmentum: Orpiment is a natural arsenic sulfate. See *arsenicus.*

- ✦ MFr. *orpin, arcenic;* MSp. *oropimente;* Ar. *azarnech, azamec(h), zarnech.*
- 📖 Pliny 33, 79; 35, 30; Bartholomaeus Anglicus XVI, 6; *Lapidario* 223f.

Autoglyphos: This stone can be found in the Sagaris River, and on it is depicted the "Mother of the Gods." If a priest of Cybele finds one of these stones, which is rare, he is no longer shocked by castration and will boldly undertake this operation contrary to nature. It is undoubtedly a frothy agate.

- 📖 Pseudo-Plutarch §10.

B

Babylonios: The Babylonian stone is a variety of sardonyx growing near Babylon, hence its name. Its color verges on white, with sparkling veins. It is dedicated to Ares. An image of Artemis on foot next to a doe, or one of Ares, is etched on it. The Babylonian stone renders its bearer vigorous, noble, and bold, and it weakens one's adversaries. Placed on a wound, this stone prevents swelling and anesthetizes the pain.

📖 Pliny 37, 106; Kerygma 30.

Bacca: Another name for the pearl, and also a name in the fourteenth and fifteenth centuries for a gem that was shaped like an olive.

📖 *Vocabularius ex quo* b 10.

Bahit: Aristotle's Lapidary and many Arab authors tell the story of a laughing stone attracting men and slaying them. Dimishqî (1256–1327), for example, says this:

> According to Aristotle, there is the *Bâhit* stone—a name that, like the *aetites,* designates the stone that is a human magnet—which is found at the mouth of the Al-Hou River behind the source of the

Nile in Egypt, beyond the Mountains of the Moon. It is white in color and shines like silver, but with a more intense whiteness. It is a small rock consisting of a single stone. Any who approaches it feels drawn by a force of love and enchantment; as he is drawn closer, he becomes attached to the stone, remaining in a state of joyful gaiety until he dies. This is what Ptolemy tells us. Travelers and traditions inform us that an association joined together for the purpose of exploring the sources of the Nile followed this river's course to a valley in the Mountains of the Moon, which they were unable to cross because of its dense forests. Then one person climbed back out of the valley to the top of the mountain to look at the course of the river flowing across it. He stood motionless, then let out a cry and vanished from the sight of his companions. The same thing happened to another one of them. They finally attached a rope firmly to another member of their company who, once he reached the same heights as his earlier companions, fainted away while letting out a scream. Pulled back with the help of the rope, once he returned to his senses the man recounted what he had seen there and felt by way of bewitchment and anguish. They retreated after that, daring not to cross through that valley.

✦ *bahtah, beh, elbehtat, behet;* MSp. *alhent.*

📖 Dimishqî II, 6, 18; Albert the Grand II, 11, 1; II, 3, 6; *Picatrix* IV, 8, 9; *Lapidario* 64 and 159; *Poridat* 4; *Liber defota anima* v. 6322–24.

📖📖 Claude Lecouteux, "Der Menschenmagnet: eine orientalische Sage in Apollonius von Tyrland," *Fabula* 24 (1983): 195–214; Edgard Weber, "La ville de cuivre, une ville d'al-Andalus," *Sharq Al-Andalus* 6 (1989): 43–81.

Balagius: This is a balas ruby that takes its name from the Arabic *balschah,* used to designate the spinel ruby, a brilliant, transparent red gem that was believed to be a female carbuncle (*carbunculus*). It was also said to come from Badakchan, the khanate of Turkestan on the Oxus River (Amoo Daria). The lapidaries tell us it could be found in India,

Ethiopia, and Libya, and even on "an island that is between two seas and is called Corinth," which some lapidaries have distorted into "Corable" or "Courable." The balas ruby cools down the man who is prey to lust, removes idle thoughts, lessens sorrow, and makes its wearer gracious, valiant in battle, and joyful. It provides peace and harmony, shields against enemies, and provides protection in perilous places. If one touches it to the four corners of a room or orchard, no venomous reptile will be able to enter, lightning will not strike there, and it will be spared by the storm. It must be set in gold. Its color allows one to predict the weather: if it is clear, this will be pleasant; if it is brown or dark, there will be bad weather. See also *jargonce*.

✦ *balasius, balascus, balandrus, palatius, halasius, halastus;* MFr. *balaiz, jargonce, jacinte;* MHG *balax, paleis, palas;* MItal. *balascio.*

📖 2nd Lapidary in prose 13; Arnoldus Saxo 10; Wolfram von Eschenbach 791, 2; *Liber lapidarii* 12; Gossouin de Metz v. 476–508; Albertus Magnus 2, 2, 1; Lapidary of King Philip 13; Jacob van Maerlant XII, 17; Saint Florian v. 389–96 ; Volmar v. 658–61; Pseudo-Mandeville 3 and 41; *Phisice* 2; *Hortus sanitatis* V, 23 (*balagius*) and 96 (*palagius*); *Libro di Sidrach* chap. 469; Leonardi II, 7, 33.

Balanites: As indicated by its name, this stone resembles an acorn. There are two kinds of *balanite*: one is greenish in color, the other is similar to Corinthian bronze. The first comes from Coptos, Egypt, and the other from Troglodytica. Both have a fiery vein cutting through their centers. See *basanites.*

✦ *balanytes, balanita.*

📖 Pliny 37, 119; Isidore of Sevilla 16, 15, 10; Lambert de Saint-Omer 55, 72; Meliteniotes v. 1138; Vincent de Beauvais VIII, 47; Leonardi II, 7, 41.

Baptes: A soft gem with an excellent aroma.

📖 Pliny 37, 149; Meliteniotes v. 1138.

Baroptis, Baroptenus: *Baroptenus* or *barippe* is black with white and blood-colored markings. Its use as an amulet is rejected as being likely to produce monstrosities.

✦ *aaripta, bariptes.*

📖 Pliny 37, 150; Isidore of Sevilla 16, 11, 5; Lambert de Saint-Omer 55, 61; Closener ba 83.

Basaltes: see *basanites.*

📖 Isidore of Sevilla 16, 5, 6.

Basanites: This stone takes its name from Basan, a city of Palestine. It has the color and hardness of iron.

✦ *basanitis, basaltem.*

📖 Pliny 36, 57ff.; Isidore of Sevilla 16, 4, 36; *Summarium Heinrici* VI, 3, 4; Closener ba 9, 5; Leonardi II, 7, 39.

Batrachites, Batrachius: This is *"crapaudine";* etymologically, it is the "toad stone" still called "bufonite" and composed of silica, aluminum, lime, and iron oxide.

Three different kinds of this stone have been distinguished: one is frog-colored, one is ebony, and the third is black shading to red. An amulet is made by engraving it with the image of a fish in the claws of a kite. See *borax* and *nose*.

✦ *batracites, batrachitas, bathrachites, vatrachitis.*

📖 Pliny 37, 149; *Summarium Heinrici* VI, 2, 17; Meliteniotes v. 1138; Bartholomaeus Anglicus XVI, 71.

📖📖 Christian Fischer, *Dissertatio de bufonite* (Königsberg, 1714); Antoine de Jussieu, "De l'origine des pierres appelées yeux de serpents et crapaudine," *Mémoires de l'Académie royale des Sciences* (Paris, 1723).

BVFONITES

Belioculus: The eye of Belus is a cat's eye, a whitish agate that contains a black pupil in its center that shines amid a "luster akin to that of gold." Because of its beauty, it was sacred to Bel, the most beloved god of the Assyrians. In the Middle Ages, it was described as a white gem with a black ring at its center. Nothing could harm its bearer.

Authors have also compared the *eye of Belus* to the *astrite,* an opaque, milky-white, false opal, which the Italians called *bel occhio* and *ochio del gatto.*

✦ *beli oculus, beloculus, belliculi, belleoculus;* MFr. *bellucolo;* Ar. *astor.*

📖 Pliny 37, 149; Isidore of Sevilla 16, 9, 9; Lambert de Saint-Omer 55, 52; Meliteniotes v. 1137; Alphabetical Lapidary 17; Bodl. Digby 13 12; Lapidary of King Philip 71; Closener be 13; *Hortus sanitatis* V, 25; Leonardi II, 7, 38; *Phisice* 82.

Benediction of the Stones: During the Middle Ages, it was believed that stones could lose their virtues because of our sins and that they could be regenerated through prayer. Several authors have passed the following example down to us:

> May the Lord be with you and your spirit. Let us pray. God, all powerful Father, who, through some insensitive creatures, has revealed to Elijah Your power in all things; You who have commanded Moses, Your servant, to honor among the priestly vestments the rationale of judgment and to adorn it with twelve precious stones; You who have also shown the evangelist John the holy city, Jerusalem, built for eternity with stones signifying the same virtues, and who has the power to resuscitate with stones the son of Abraham, we humbly implore Your majesty, You who have chosen as eternal vehicle of Your power one of these stones, so that you may deign to bless and sanctify these stones by the sanctification and incarnation of Your name, so they may be sanctified, blessed, and consecrated and received from You the effect of the virtues that You have granted their kind in this same consecration, and that the experience of the wise has proven they come from Your gifts; that whosoever shall bear one in his person shall thereby feel the presence of Your power in him with the gifts of Your grace and that we are deserving of receiving these virtues. By Jesus Christ, Your son in whom all sanctification, benediction, and consecration exist, and who lives and reigns with You, as God, in the centuries upon centuries. Amen. Thanks to God.

This benediction takes place within the following ritual. The stone must be wrapped in a clean linen cloth and placed on the altar so that three masses can be spoken over it. Clad in his priestly dress, the priest that speaks the third mass will recite the benediction.

Gervase of Tilbury mentions the consecration of stones at the beginning of the thirteenth century: "There is no precious stone which may not be consecrated to receive its extrinsic virtue with the herb of the same name or with the blood of a bird or animal, in combination with spells (charms), whose knowledge has been handed down to us from Solomon. I said extrinsic; but many stones have, in fact, an intrinsic virtue granted them by their very nature, independent of those that come to them from without when they are conjured or consecrated." Gervase then offers examples of the emerald, sapphire, heliotrope, and agates, before continuing: "Words, herbs, and precious stones provide all the remedies that are beneficial and necessary for human beings, but it is not the stones or their carvings . . . which are at work: all this is the work of God . . . The carving is the sign of its effectiveness but it does not help produce the effect; the nature given the stone with the words of consecration increase and confirm its innate virtue." This clarification, which is intended to Christianize pagan beliefs, is then developed further: "It is necessary, however, that whoever is seeking to feel the stone's virtue by wearing it must be honest in his body and pure in his mind: the dignity of the stone flees the touch of an unworthy man, and the effectiveness of its consecration flees an ignoble consecrator . . . When the donor is not worthy, the authority of the gifts is lessened . . . This is why, just as stones are consecrated by the blessings of bishops, with the addition of herbs and solemn exorcisms, when they have likewise been permeated by the turpitude of their bearer, they are anointed, by the hand of the bishop, with the blood of the dove, and through repeated prayers are restored with the virtue they had lost either partially or completely." Some stones are blessed in one time, Gervase adds, and the consecration of others is made several times, and he mentions a dozen lunar cycles.

📖 Gervase of Tilbury, *Otia Imperialia* III, 28; Thomas de Catimpré XIV, 71; Saint Florian 310; Pseudo-Mandeville, 127f.

Berla: see *margarita*.

✦ *berle, berlin, berullus.*

📖 Volmar v. 512–19; *Liber ordinis rerum* 129, 10; Closener be 35.

Bernic: An Indian gem of a hot, dry nature. Magicians used it in their incantations. One of its properties was to excite the sexual desires of women.

✦ *lampus*; Ar. *barkijj, elbarchi.*

📖 Luka ben Serapion 28; *De lapidibus preciosis* 25; *Aristoteles de lapidibus* 373, 22ff.

Bernin: see *margarita*.

📖 Hildegard von Bingen IV, 22.

> **perlin ccrliii Ca**
> **lapis margarithe latine·ara**
> **bice bageralulo vel brlao·**

Berullus: see *margarita*.

✦ *berle, berlin.*

📖 Closener be 35.

Beryllos: The word designates both beryl and aquamarine. Today, it is said to be a variety of emerald that can be colorless, red, blue, or stony; a more-or-less pure glucinium silicate and aluminum. It is one of the twelve stones of the high priest Aaron's breastplate in the Bible. There are nine kinds of beryl, a pale, clear, transparent stone. India produces it and it is rarely found elsewhere. Jewelers cut all beryls into hexagonal shapes because its subtleties, rather dull in its uniformity, are given life by the reflections produced by the different angles. If it is cut in any other shape, there is no sparkle. The ones that are valued most highly are those that resemble the green of a calm sea. The beryl is placed under the patronage of Jupiter. To be protected during sea voyages, it is necessary to etch an image of Neptune standing in a chariot pulled by two horses. Beryl lightens the mood and makes one communicative, especially when combined with gold. It enhances its bearer, burns the hand of any who hides it there, repels all enemies and weakens them, gives good manners and encourages tender behavior. The beryl is good for liver complaints, shortness of breath, vomiting, and watering eye. It cures fevers and headaches. Whoever drinks water in which it has been steeped will be healed of throat afflictions. It encourages the birth of affection between those who marry and perfect accord in personal relations. It is also said that it strengthens marital bonds and is effective against dangers and disputes. People wore beryl necklaces to ward off toothache. The romance of Reynard the Fox in Low German (Reynke de Vos v. 5041ff.) claims that beryl permits one to see all that occurs within a thousand-foot radius, both night and day.

In the Christian lapidary, it represents the wishes of sage minds. It is "the mysterious doorway to supreme rest." It symbolizes those who are fragile but who, struck by grace, shine through their good works and warm those around them with their charity. The beryl symbolizes innocence and purity, the church and the Holy Virgin, because the sun represents God:

> *Iceste pere senefie*
> *Saint Iglise u sainte Marie.*
> *Par le soleil Deu entendons . . .*

In the thirteenth century, it was sometimes maintained that beryl was formed from water that had been congealed for seven years. It makes one chaste and humble; it procures honors and the love of others.

Mandeville's lapidary provides a strange recipe. If a virgin child holds a beryl with three fingers inside a besieged castle and says, "Like this stone has no door or entrance, may our enemies find no entrance for taking the castle," while turning his face toward the enemy three times, the fortress cannot be captured.

Engraved with a spiny lobster with a crow at its feet, or else a crow on a crab, with a small branch of savin herb and a small piece of the heart of the bird called "Jupiter's Head" beneath, the stone protects love and grants riches, the gift of pleasing, and success in one's undertakings. It is effective against renal colic and dyspnea.

Carved with an image of Venus, the stone becomes an amulet that protects against snakebite, and when plunged in drinking water, it heals wounds. With another form of Venus, it provides travelers freedom from harm.

If a frog is carved on a beryl, the contact of this stone has the power to reconcile enemies and inspire friendship between men.

If it is a hoopoe with the herb *dracontea* in front of it, the beryl will have the power to summon water spirits and prevent them from speaking; it can bring back dead family members and compel them to answer questions.

A greyhound carved on a beryl helps one attain the highest honors, renown, and benevolence.

The German word for eyeglasses is *Brille*, a deformation of beryl, because the early lenses were made from thin layers of this stone.

✦ *berillus, beryllus, berullus, berullios, barillus*; MFr. *beril, bericle, berib, belxil, berith, geril, peril, seril, barine*; MHG *beril, berillen, bril, brylle, parill, barellin, perlin, perel*; MItal. *beriella*; Ar. *zébardjad, almehe*.

📖 Pliny 37, 76f.; 79; Solin 52, 61; Epiphanes 11; Isidore of Sevilla 16, 7, 5; Damigeron 35 and 61; *Lapidaire nautique* 3; Marbode 12; *Kyranides* 1, 2; *Summarium Heinrici* VI, 4, 3; Hildegard von Bingen IV, 4; Old English lapidary 8; Lambert de Saint-Omer 54, 8; 55, 8; 55, 15; Meliteniotes v. 1124; Dimishqî II, 5, 3; Alphabetical Lapidary 14–15; 1st Lapidary in prose 8; 2nd Lapidary in prose 21; Christian lapidary I, XII and 2, XII; *Sidrac* 1; Alexander Neckham v. 185ff.; *De la vertu des tailles* 29; *De l'entaille des gemmes* 50; Bodl. Digby 13 13; *De lapidibus preciosis* 10; Cambridge lapidary v. 305-28; Wolfram von Eschenbach 791, 30; *Liber lapidarii* 11; Gossouin de Metz v. 414-31; Arnoldus Saxo 11; Bartholomaeus Anglicus XVI, 21; Albertus Magnus 2, 2, 3; Vincent de Beauvais VIII, 47–48; Thomas de Cantimpré 14, 11; *Picatrix* II, 10, 3; 58 and 60; Lapidary of King Philip 12 and 89; Konrad von Megenberg VI, 11; Jacob van Maerlant XII, 13; Christian lapidary v. 615-58 and 1239-1300; Saint Florian v. 275-98; *Secrez* 3, 7; 4, 2; Psellos 7; *Liber defota anima* v. 4972-5081; *Liber ordinis rerum* 129, 7; *Vocabularius ex quo* b 97; Closener ba 81; *Libro di Sidrach* chap. 465; Mandeville I 19; *Hortus sanitatis* V, 23; Leonardi II, 7, 34; *Liber secretorum* II, 1, 15; Ragiel 6; Solomon 18; *Phisice* 21.

Betyl: This name comes from Hebrew and means "house of God." It is also used to designate black stones, aeroliths, and thunder stones (see *ceraunia*). The *omphalos* of Delphi, the *kaaba* of Mecca, and the "black stone" (*lapis niger*) of Rome are betyls. In the Bible, a *betyl* is a standing stone whose origin goes back to Jacob's dream (Genesis 28:10–15). Jacob rested his head on a stone, contact with which gave him a divine vision while he slept. On awakening, he remembered the ladder that had appeared in his dream, stood the stone upright, poured oil over it, and gave it the name of beit El, meaning "dwelling of God." This is but one form of the worship of stones allegedly inhabited by spirits, a worship that is amply attested during the Middle Ages. Between 443 and 452, the Council of Arles (c. 23) condemned those who worshipped stones; in 506, the Council of Agde forbid the swearing of vows to stones; and in 567, the Council of Tours criticized those who performed acts incompatible with church rules near stones (c. 23). The Synod of Toledo mentions those who revere stones (c. 11) in 681. The *Admonitio generalis,* issued in 789, informs us that people were building fires and performing certain practices around stones (cap. 65). In the tenth century, the *Law of the Northumbrian Priests* condemned those who gathered around stones (c. 54).

These prohibitions targeted the use of stones as altars, "as if some deity lived within," deities that became dwarves, elves, and spirits. The *Kristni Saga* (Saga of Icelandic Christianization, chap. 2) provides solid evidence: "In Gilja [in northwest Iceland] stood the stone to which Kodran's folk had made their sacrifices and in which, it was said, dwelt, their tutelary deity."

In the *Þorvalds þáttr viðförla* (The Tale of Thorvald the Far-Travelled), which offers a variation on the same theme, the spirit is called "seer" (*spámaðr*), undoubtedly because it predicts the future.

We should recall that the church was unable to eradicate these practices and rites, which were often connected with fertility, so it Christianized them. The most obvious example of this can be seen with the Christian symbols covering some Breton menhirs, such as the Stone of the Twelve Apostles in Trégunc, the name of which was already attested as early as 713.

📖📖 Henri Lammens, "Le culte des bétyles et les processions religieuses chez les Arabes préislamites," *Bulletin de l'Institut français d'archéologie orientale*, vol. 17 (1920): 39–101; Pierre Saintyves, *Pierres magiques: béthyles, haches-amulettes et pierres de foudre, traditions savantes et traditions populaires* (Paris: Emile Nourry, 1936).

Bezoar: This term of Persian origin (*pâd zârh*) means "antidote" and "counter-poison." It can designate either a stone with this name or the stone-like concretions formed in the bodies of various animals, notably in the bile of the basilisk, and which were granted all manner of marvelous properties starting from the thirteenth century.

Von dem ORIENTALIſchen BEZOAR.

Animal Bezoard Orientale

Lapis Bezoar Orient

Some lapidaries state that they were found in India and China and were the eyes of stags. It was also believed that this stone was found in the droppings of a stag that had eaten a snake. Bezoars expel venoms, neutralize poisons, and even give life. They were used to make Moon talismans which had the property to prevent the approach of reptiles. Alchemists used this name for the white oxide of antimony. The three varieties of bezoars listed by the *Lapidario* fall under the influence of the 9° to 11° of Gemini.

In *Le Malade imaginaire* (The Imaginary Invalid, Act I, Scene 1), Molière mentions bezoars. They procure courage and boldness.

✦ *lapis expellens venenum, besar, bezahar, bezaar;* MFr. *bezar;* MSp. *uezahar;* Ar. *albezard, bezahar(d), elbasifer, elbelgar, bulacar.*

📖 Luka ben Serapion 8 and 39; *De lapidibus preciosis* 8; Serapion c. 396 (*hager albesahar*); Pseudo-Mandeville 48; *Lapidario* 69–71; 279; *Picatrix* II, 10, 78; *Hortus sanitatis* V, 24; Leonardi II, 7, 36; *Poridat* 1; *Phisice* 79.

📖📖 Anton Deusing, *De unicornu et lapide bezoar* (Groningen, 1659); R. van Tassel, "Bezoars," *Janus* 60 (1973): 241–59.

Bezoars: It was thought that fish were also a source of stones and the *Kyranides* collection mentions several. The stone from the head of the hydra cured dropsy; stones from the head of the sea perch cured migraine and headaches if one was applied to the right side of the head and one to the left side. Ingested in a drink, the stones of the weever eased stones in the bladder. Hung around the neck, those of the glaucis healed eye inflammation; those of the gnaphis fish caused insomnia and, when eaten, nightmares. Worn around the neck, the stones of the eagle cure quartan fever, and those from the head of the comber cure afflictions of the head and neck as well as headaches. More curiously, one tradition says that stones from the head of the hake cause an erection when worn next to the right and left testicles. Another maintains that, when worn around the neck, the stone from the right side of this fish's head will cause an erection whereas if it is a stone from the left side, it will suppress it. We find comparable elements with the stone from the ostrich's stomach, when crushed and ingested in food or drink, it engenders high sexual desire; when worn hanging from the neck, it causes an erection and facilitates digestion. In the sixteenth century, we find the yellow and triangular carp stone that stops nosebleeds if brought close to that organ. When crushed into a powder, it heals kidney stones.

Bolus Armenus/Armenicus: This term is used to designate clay that is naturally red because of its iron-oxide content. It is used as a dessicant and for its blood clotting, fortifying, and astringent properties. It heals plague fevers, diarrhea, hemoptysis, and illnesses of the spleen and stomach. See *rabri*.

📖 Aetios II, 12 and 47; *Gart der Gesundheit* chap. 76; *Hortus sanitatis* V, 26; Leonardi II, 7, 37.

Boralus: Another name for coral according to some. It seems obvious that this is a misspelling for *corallus*.

📖 Bodl. Digby 13 18.

Borax: The *borax* is created in the head of a toad, hence its other name of *crapaudine*. There are three kinds: one is white bordering on gray, another is black, and the third is a burned color. Like the *draconite*, it has to be extracted while the toad is still alive. Swallowed, the *borax* will cleanse the intestines of excrement. If set inside a ring band that allows the finger to touch the stone, if the hand wearing it approaches a poison, the *borax* will heat the finger. There is a story about a cleric who, in his valet's presence, found a toad with a round lump on its head. He thought it had to be *crapaudine* and therefore captured the animal and imprisoned it inside the sleeve of his shirt. Once he returned home, however, he found nothing there. This is why this stone is thought to be good for prisoners.

✦ *nosa, nose, crapondinus;* MFr. *borraux, boreaulx, crapa(n)dine, pierre de boutereaul;* MHG *chroten stain;* MDu. *padden steen;* ME *crepaund;* Ar. *bûrak, tinkar.*

📖 Alexander Neckham v. 199ff. (described but not named); Avicenna II, 2, 706; Luka ben Serapion 46; *De lapidibus preciosis* 11; Thomas de Cantimpré 14, 12; Vincent de Beauvais VIII, 49; Albertus Magnus 2, 2, 2; Lapidary of King Philip 63; Konrad von Megenberg VI, 12; Jacob van Maerlant XII, 14; Volmar v. 462–83; Pseudo-Mandeville 45; *Hortus sanitatis* V, 27; Leonardi II, 7, 35; *Phisice* 67.

Bostrychites: Zoroaster gives this name to a black gem, one with white or blood-red veins that resemble a woman's hair. It is a variety of banded agate.

 📖 Pliny 37, 150 and 191; Meliteniotes v. 1140.

Botryitis: A black or wine-colored stone that, as its name indicates, resembles a grape.

 📖 Pliny 37, 150; Meliteniotes v. 1139.

Boussad: A name given to coral root by Arabs in the Middle Ages. This refers to the main trunk of coral from which large amulets are made. If a person wears one, it halts blood rage and removes dirt and reddened veins from the eyes.

 📖 Dimishqî II, 5, 9.

Brasmeuef: See *tarnif.*

Breastplate: In the Biblical book of Exodus (28:15–30), the breastplate of the high priest Aaron, the brother of Moses, was adorned with twelve stones:

> A sardonyx, a topaz, and an emerald shall form the first row. The second shall include a carbuncle, a sapphire, and a diamond. The third, an agate, a jacinth, and an amethyst. The fourth, a chrysolith, a carnelian, and a jasper. These stones shall be fixed in gold settings.

Added to the breastplate were the two sacred stones of Urim and Thummim from which oracles were received. It is thought that these two names designate two gems that served as clasps for the breastplate. The Vulgate gives these following stones: sardonyx, topaz, emerald;

carbuncle, sapphire, jasper; jacinth, agate, amethyst; chrysolith, onyx, beryl. Each row represents a cardinal virtue, in the following order: prudence, strength, justice, and temperance.

In the Hebrew tradition, the twelve stones are the emerald (barequet), the topaz (pit dah), the sardonyx or carnelian (odem), the aquamarine (yasfeh), the sapphire (sapir), the ruby or garnet (nofek), the amethyst (ahlamah), the agate (sebo), jacinth (lesem), the jasper (yahalom), the onyx (schoham), and the chrysolith (tarsis). The stones of the first row represent three of the children of Leah: Ruben, Simon, and Levi; the second Judah, another child of Leah, then the children of Jacob's concubine Balla: Dan and Nephtali; the third are the children of Zalpha, Leah's servant: Gad and Ascher, with jacinth representing Issachar, another of Leah's children. The fourth row consists of Zebulon, the child of Leah, and two children of Rachel: Joseph and Benjamin. The Christian lapidary incorporated this tradition with the addition of the twelve apostles:

Sardonyx	Matthew	Judah
Topaz	Peter	Simon
Emerald	Bartholomew	Ephraim
Ruby	Andrew	Ruben
Sapphire	Philip	Issachar
Jasper	James the Greater	Zebulon
Amber	Judas	Nephtali
Agate	Matthias	Dan
Amethyst	John	Gad
Chrysolith	Thaddeus-Simon	Asher
Onyx	James the Lesser	Benjamin
Beryl	Thomas	Manassus

Hildebert de Lavardin (1056–1133) was inspired by the *Psychomachy* of Prudentius (fourth century) for the relationship between stones and virtues but, borrowing from the above tradition, added that these twelve gems represented the twelve tribes of Israel.

William Durant (died 1296), the Bishop of Mende, wrote the *Rationale divinorum officiorum* in 1286, in which he describes the breastplate in the chapter "On the Vestments of the Ancient Law": "It is called *heen* in Hebrew, *logion* in Greek, and *rationale* in Latin . . . It was called the breastplate of judgment because it held the stones that let the Jews know God looked upon them with favor."

In the Middle Ages, a metal breastplate worn next to a cloth garment was modeled directly on that owned by the high priest. The breastplate was worn into the 1930s by the Archbishops of Paderborn, the Rhineland, and Krakow, Poland, as well as by the bishop of Toul, after having been widespread from the tenth to fifteenth centuries among the bishops who were members or neighbors of the Germanic Holy Roman Empire. William of Poitiers (born circa 1020) mentions it in his *History of William the Conqueror:* while discussing the English conquest, he describes the attire of Hugh, Bishop of Lisieux, and explicitly states that he wore the breastplate over his habit. The statue of Saint Sixtus, the first Bishop of Reims, at the trumeau of the central door of the north transept of the Reims cathedral (circa 1230), is wearing this breastplate, but instead of four rows of three gems, it is three rows of four.

 📖 Epiphanius, *De duodecim gemmis quae erant in veste Aronis,* in Conrad Gesner *De omni rerum fossilium genere . . .* (Zurich, 1565); Gossouin de Metz v. 1–26; Valérie Gontero, "Un syncrétisme pagano-chrétien: la glose du Pectoral d'Aaron dans le Lapidaire chrétien," *Revue de l'histoire des religions* 223/4 (2006): 417–37; M. Salvat, "Du Pectoral d'Aaron aux lapidaires médicaux: l'infini pouvoir des pierres," in *Nature et encyclopédies,* ed. Denis Hüe (Le Mesnil-Brout: Association Diderot, 1992).

Brome, Breme:

Still called *vinly,* this is a Venus stone for which there are two species, one white and the other red. When thunder growls, it falls from the heads of "sea snails." Cameos are made from these. This appears to be a deformation of the name *brontea.*

 📖 *Phisice* 83.

Brontea: Brontea looks like a turtle's head; it is thought to have fallen with the thunder, hence its name. If we can believe what is said about it, it extinguishes objects set aflame by lightning.

This is a Venus stone that comes in a black variety and a red one. In the fifteenth century, it was believed that it fell from the heads of "sea snails" during thunderstorms, and it is said that these were often adorned with an image called "*camahuz*" (cameo). The Brontea protects against all the perils of water.

✦ *brontia, brontes, bronia;* MFr. *breme.*

📖 Pliny 37, 150 and 176; Isidore of Sevilla 16, 15, 24; *Summarium Heinrici* VI, 6, 8; Meliteniotes v. 1140; Vincent de Beauvais VIII, 32; Leonardi II, 7, 40; *Phisice* 83.

📖📖 Pierre Saintyves, *Pierres magiques: béthyles, haches-amulettes et pierres de foudre, traditions savantes et traditions populaires* (Paris: Emile Nourry, 1936).

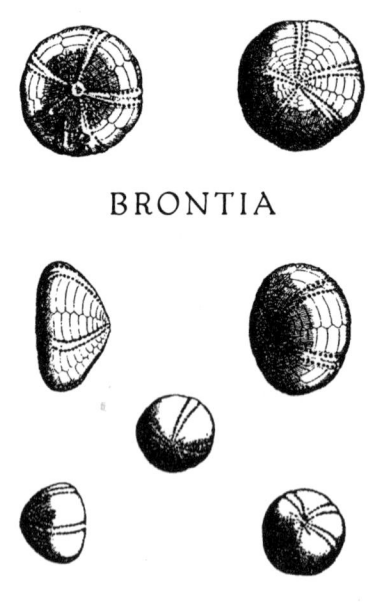

BRONTIA

Bubera: See *adamas.*

📖 *Vocabularius ex quo* b 222.1.

Bucardia: This is a gem resembling a bull's heart, which is only found in Babylon. It is most likely a fossil.

 📖 Pliny 37, 150; Meliteniotes v. 1139.

Burning Stone: According to La Relation d'Élysée (Elysaeus' Report; late twelfth century), there is a stone in India that releases an intense heat. It is placed at the southern door at one of Prester John's palaces and none could enter unless they had the aid of other stones to fight its heat. We should note that a freezing stone was located at the north entrance with the opposite effect.

 📖 Prester John (in Zarncke, 126).

Burtine: One of the Middle French names for amber. See *succinum*.

 📖 *Phisice* 77.

C

Cadmitis/Cadmia: *Cadmitis* (calamine) only differs from *ostracitis* by the blue blisters that sometimes surround it. See *ostracites*.

 📖 Pliny 37, 151; Dioscorides V, 84; Meliteniotes v. 1157.

Calaminaris: An opaque, yellow stone from which an eyewash is made by crushing it and mixing it with vinegar.

 📖 Leonardi II, 7, 72.

Calco: An abbreviation of *c(h)alcosmaragdus*. See *smaragdus*.

 📖 *Vocabularius ex quo* c 26.1.

Callaica: A stone that somewhat resembles sapphire but is not as dark, and which verges on the color of the water at the ocean's edge. During the Middle Ages, no distinction was made between this stone and the *callaina*.

 ✦ *callayca, caldaicus, gallaica, callais;* MSp. *Anglezia.*

 📖 Pliny 37, 151; *Summarium Heinrici* VI, 4, 8; Meliteniotes v. 1158; *Hortus sanitatis* V, 28; Leonardi II, 7, 57; *Poridat* 4.

Callaïs/Callaina:

The *callaïs* is pale green in color. It is found among the inhabitants of the Caucasus, where the Sacians and the Dacians live. This stone is noteworthy in size, but its surface is heavily pitted and contains many impurities. The variety found in Carmania is much cleaner and more beautiful in appearance. In both lands it is found on inaccessible, frozen cliffs. The most highly valued are emerald in color; it will lose its color if dropped in oil, essences, or pure wine. Some authors claim it can be found in Arabia, in the nest of a bird called the *melancoryphus*.

📖 Pliny 37, 110; Meliteniotes v. 1158.

Calophagus: See *sarcophagus.*

✦ MHG *calof.*

📖 Konrad von Megenberg VI, 18.

Calorite:

A stone that is as green as the sap from the herb. The magicians say that it can be found in the belly of a bird called the *scilla*. If placed in an iron setting, *calorite* is good for magical spells.

📖 Leonardi II, 7, 67.

Calx:

Limestone (*calx*) is employed frequently for medical purposes. It should be fresh lime that has not been dampened. It is an attractive stone with caustic and solvent properties, and it prevents the spread of serpiginous ulcers. It is mixed with vinegar and rosewater to treat this affliction, which is then tempered with wax and rose oil—this promotes the scarring of these sores. A combination of pork lard and liquid resin in honey is a remedy for sprains and scrofula sores.

📖 Pliny 37, 110; Hildegard von Bingen IV, 25; Avicenna II, 2, 148; Luka ben Serapion 22a; *De lapidibus preciosis* 19; Vincent de Beauvais XIII, 10; *Hortis sanitatis* V, 30.

Camaeus: This term designates *cameo,* most often called *gamaheus* from which the French word *gamahée* is derived. It is sometimes confused for sardonyx. It is a white stone with a blue border. Gervase of Tilbury, who wrote his *Otia Imperialia* between 1209 and 1214, believed these were naturally carved stones depicting the image of Moses with the serpent staff, or that of the sacrifice of Isaac, or other signs of divine omnipotence. He put forth the following etymology: "They take their origin—*caput*—from the admirable God—*manhu* is an exclamation of admiration in Hebrew."

Paracelsus believed that *cameos* were natural talismans permeated with the force of the stars, and their designs were all so many clues to the many ways they could be used. See *gamaheus, kauman.*

✦ *cama, capmahu;* MFr. *cama, cachmahief, camabieus.*

📖 Alphabetical Lapidary 29; Gervase of Tilbury, *Otia Imperialia* III, 28; Bartholomaeus Anglicus XVI, 57; *Picatrix* II, 10, 2.

Cambnitis: see *capnitis.*

📖 Leonardi II, 7, 65 (*cambnitis = kabrates*).

Cantharias: A stone that contains an image of a scarab on the inside. It takes its name from the Greek *chantharos,* "beetle."

✦ *cantarus;* MHG *winstein.*

📖 Pliny 37, 187; *Vocabularius ex quo* c 100.

Capnias: In the Middle Ages, no distinction was made between *capnias* ("smoked" quartz), which was believed to be a smoky quartz, and *capnitis.* See *capnitis.*

📖 Pliny 37, 128.

Capnitis: A name for smoky jasper. One lapidary says it comes from Macedonia and the Media. It helps women conceive and give birth. See *iaspis* and *kabrates.*

✦ *cantharias, cantarus;* MHG *winstein.*

📖 Pliny 37, 151; Aetios II, 35, Dioscorides V, 142; Damigeron 23; 46; Bodl. Digby 13 47; Meliteniotes v. 1158; Alphabetical Lapidary 19; *Phisice* 38.

Carbunculus: The carbuncle, which etymologically means the "little coal," is given this name by virtue of its resemblance to fire. However, it suffers no ill effects from flames, and for this reason some dubbed it *acaustoi*. There are three kinds: the balas ruby, the garnet, and the ruby (*balagius, graatus, rubinus*); all these names are often used to designate the carbuncle and as substitutes for its name.

Von dem Carbunckel.

There are two distinct species, the Indian and the Garamantic, to which are added the Ethiopian and Alabandic stones. These are further subdivided into male and female carbuncles, with the brilliancy of the male being stronger than that of the female. Among male carbuncles, there are some whose fire is brighter and others that are darker. The most highly valued are the *amethystizontes*. According to Marbode, there are twelve species, one of which is *anthrax*. The carbuncle has the property of illuminating the night as if it were day, which has given rise to the expression found in many medieval romances, "It changed night into day." It also serves as a light source in the underground palaces of the dwarves. In *The Thousand and One Nights,* Aladdin's lamp has a carbuncle for its light source. Heinrich der Glîchezäre gives Reynard the fox carbuncle eyes (*Reinhart Fuchs* v. 91692).

Reminiscent of the Alexandrian lighthouse, the carbuncle shines at the top of towers, such as that of Argos in the *Romance of Thebes*

(v. 2633 ff.) and on the "tower of the maidens" in *Floire et Blancheflor* (v. 1823ff.).

It is said that the carbuncle will expel poisonous air or vapors. Aelian (Claudius Aelianus) states in his *On the Nature of Animals* (VIII, 22) that a stork healed by a certain Heracleus brought him a carbuncle as a token of its gratitude, and he therefore deduced that this stone was not to be found in a dragon's skull. The Low German romance of *Reynard the Fox* (*Reynke de Vos,* v. 4897 ff.) says that the carbuncle cures those who are ill; protects from fire, water, captivity, and poisons; and gives one victory over one's enemies and even converts them into friends.

Circa 1350, Konrad of Hamburg made it the symbol of the Virgin Mary's eternal glory in a poem entitled *Anulus,* in which he offers Mary a ring with twenty gemstones. But Publius Syrius (around 85–43 BCE) had already quoted the saying *"Probitis est carbunculus"* (Probity is the carbuncle) in his *Sentences.* For clerics, the carbuncle represented the wine of the Last Supper, Christ's blood. According to the Koran, this stone illuminates the Fourth Heaven. It also illuminated Noah's Ark. In Spanish astrology, it is the symbol of the sun.

If one engraves on it an image of Athena holding a heron in her right hand and a helmet in her left, it permits one to triumph over all foes and rivals; it makes one friendly. According to the *Kyranides,* a lizard can also be found carved on it. Imprinted with the image of a dragon, the carbuncle is effective against paralysis and trembling limbs; it provides good sense and reason.

This stone has become the stuff of legend, and we learn from the *Romance of Thebes* (twelfth century) that the *guivre* or *vouivre* ["wyvern"—*Trans.*], like in Marcel Aymé's book, wears a carbuncle on its forehead (v. 4511–28), and the same is true of the women serpents in the *Romance of Alexander* (III, 1450 ff.). In Renaut de Beaujeu's *Bel Inconnu* (Beautiful Stranger), the *guivre* is described like this (v. 3127ff.): "Then he [the hero] saw a wardrobe open from which emerged a guivre that spread as much light around it as a lit candle, illuminating the entire hall with the glow it cast, a light rarely beheld;

its mouth spit fire. It was enormous, gigantic, and its chest was larger than a barrel of mead; its large eyes shone like two big carbuncles." The word *guivre* comes from *vipera,* but it is actually the asp that is described as wearing a precious stone in its brow; Albertus Magnus asserts this in his treatise on animals. Asps, vipers, and other snakes have often been considered equivalent to dragons, so it is likely that the *guivre*'s carbuncle can be traced back to the legend about *draconite.* The *Physiologus,* the most famous bestiary of the Middle Ages, in fact includes a passage from the chapter "De aspide," that describes enchanters gathering before the cave where a dragon is dwelling to use magic charms to compel it to come out, which brings to mind the story Herodotus relates about *draconite.* Brunetto Latini (circa 1220–1294) tells us: "The asp bears the very brilliant precious stone called carbuncle. When an enchanter seeks to steal it, he speaks his words. The animal hears them and sticks one ear in the ground and covers the other with its tail so that it becomes deaf and cannot hear the conjuration." The German translations of Mandeville's *Voyages* mention an island on which reside cruel women who have precious stones in their eyes; their nature is such that if they look at someone with rage, they slay him "just like the basilisk," but some incunabula actually speak of two pupils in the eyes. It so happens that in Middle High German, the word for pupil is "eye-stone" (*augstein*).

Jordan Catalani (circa 1321) writes this about deepest India: "There are, in fact, dragons in great quantity there, which bear luminous stones on their heads called carbuncles. These animals recline on golden sands and become quite large, and they project from their mouths a most foul and fetid breath, which resembles a huge cloud of smoke pouring from a fire. These animals gather together at a given moment, beat their wings, and begin rising through the air. And then, through the judgment of God, as they are so heavy, they tumble into a river flowing out of paradise and die there. All regions are always quite alert to dragon season, and when they see that one has fallen, they wait seventy days before going down to find the dragon's bones, now freed of its flesh. It is then that they salvage the carbuncle that is rooted in the bone of its skull."

In heraldry, the carbuncle is a piece taking up the field of the escutcheon, symbolizing a precious stone in the form of a circle and projecting eight radii that terminate in fleurs-de-lys.

✦ *carbunculum, carbun;* MFr. *scherbuncle, escarboucle, charboucle, charbucle;* MHG *carbunkelstein, carfunkelstein, kerbunkel, klarfunckels, clarfingkels.* Synonyms: *anthrax, rubith, rubinus/rubith, balasius, granat.*

📖 Pliny 37, 92–98; Solin 28, 1; Epiphanes 4; Isidore of Sevilla 16, 14, 1; Marbode 23; *Summarium Heinrici* VI, 5, 12; Hildegard von Bingen IV, 14; Old English lapidary 11; *Kyranides* 2, 10; Lambert de Saint-Omer 55, 26; Jacques de Vitry cap. 91; Lapidary of Marbode, 1st Romanesque translation XXIII; Lapidary in prose 51; 2nd Lapidary in prose 15; Alexander Neckham v. 242ff.; Bodl. Digby 13 17 and 47; *De lapidibus preciosis* 12 (*carbunculus = rubinus balausto*); Cambridge lapidary v. 585–98; Wolfram von Eschenbach 482, 24–483, 5; 741, 14; Arnoldus Saxo 13; Bartholomaeus Anglicus XVI, 26; Thomas de Cantimpré 14, 13; Vincent de Beauvais VIII, 51–52; Albertus Magnus 2, 3, 1; Brunetto Latini I, 138; Konrad von Megenberg VI, 13; Jacob van Maerlant XII, 15; Saint Florian v. 373–88; Volmar v. 125–36; Jordan Catalani §106–7; *Secrez* 3, 1; *Liber ordinis rerum* 129, 4; Closener ca 265; *Hortus sanitatis* V, 29; *Liber defota anima* v. 2934–3045; Leonardi II, 7, 42: Pseudo-Mandeville 1; *Phisice* 1.

📖📖 Theodore Ziolkowsky, "Der Karfunkelstein," *Euphorion* 55 (1961): 298–326; Thierry Miguet, "L'escarboucle médiévale, pierre de lumière," *Marche romane* 29 (1979): 37–60; Valérie Gontero, "La clarté de l'escarboucle dans les romans antiques," *PRISMA* 17 (2001): 57–71.

Carchedonia: The ancients used this word to not only designate chalcedony, but also a fairly common variety of a cloudy, dull, white quartz, which could sometimes have a slight bluish tinge. *Carchedonius lapis* was taken from Egypt, India, Persia, and from the land of the Nasamones, a Libyan people living to the south of greater Syrtis.

📖 Pliny 37, 92–98; Isidore of Sevilla 16, 14, 5; Lambert de Saint-Omer 55, 66; Meliteniotes v. 1160.

Carcinias, Carcina: "Crab stone" is a brittle, veined gem the color of an ocean crayfish and similar to the fire that kills it. It is found in the mountains of the Nasamones, whose natives believe the stones are produced by divine rain showers, and in the outskirts of Thebes, in Egypt. They cannot be engraved but drinking vessels are made from them.

 📖 Pliny 37, 187; Isidore of Sevilla 16, 15, 18; Meliteniotes v. 1158; Leonardi II, 7, 85.

Caristeus: A green gem resembling a shrimp, the sight of which is beneficial for the eyes.

 📖 *Hortus sanitatis* V, 31; Leonardi II, 7, 71.

Carniz: A heavy, white stone found in the island of Sanna(?). It expels poison and head pains and restores reason to the deranged, but it is harmful to pregnant women.

 📖 *Phisice* 76.

Carscinif: See *tarnif.*

Caspia Gemma: Name for Caspian jasper.

 📖 Pliny 37, 115.

Cassidoine: See *chalcedonius.*

 📖 Pseudo-Mandeville 17 and 38.

Caste Coq: This stone is found in the head of a rooster who has been chaste for a year. If it is slain at that time, this stone will be found. Whoever carries it in his hand will be invisible. It procures victory in all locations. It is a variant of *alectory.* See *alectorias.*

 📖 Pseudo-Mandeville 51.

Castologalue: According to the medieval lexicons, this would be the name for alum.

📖 *Vocabularius ex quo* c 220.

Catochitis: A stone native to Corsica. It holds the hand that touches it like gum, which is simply the interpretation of its name.

✦ *cathochiten, catochites, cathotices.*

📖 Pliny 37, 152; Solin 3, 4–5; Old English lapidary 19; Vincent de Beauvais VIII, 27; Meliteniotes v. 1159; Leonardi II, 7, 63.

Catotriptis, Catopyritis: A white stone found in Caradoccia that had the property of reflecting images, as its name implies.

📖 Pliny 37, 152; Meliteniotes v. 1160.

Cautaine, Cautame: This stone is ruby-colored but is thicker and tends to be blacker. It is no bigger than a dove's egg and glows at night like a carbuncle. It is found in Libya. It both elevates its bearer in rank and conversely prevents a man from falling from the estate he already possesses; it also permits the acquisition of honors.

📖 Pseudo-Mandeville 49; *Phisice* 80.

Celicolus: See *belioculus*.

📖 Leonardi II, 7, 87.

C(h)elidonius: The "swallow's stone" is a small, unformed variety of agate that is similar to the asp. According to Pliny, there exist two varieties: one black and the other red but both with the color of the swallow on one side. The black one permits the success of one's undertakings, soothes the noxious humors, and provides protection from animals. Water that it has been washed in gives comfort to the eyes. If it is wrapped in a linen cloth followed by a saffron-colored one, this cloth will multiply its virtues, destroy fevers, and purge the body of bad humors. Placed in the mouth, it makes you invisible; placed on the mouth with honey, it provides the gift of prophecy on the fifteenth day of the moon and on the new moon during a day, or before sunrise, during its waning; or the others from the first to sixth hour. The red stone cures lunatics, epileptics, and those lost in a rage or frenzy, as well as those who suffer from diurnal lethargy. This stone gives loquacity and grace, and makes one amiable and amusing if carried in the left pocket wrapped in clean linen, or on the left shoulder. Wrapped in cloth or calf hide and carried beneath the left armpit, it protects from folly, old illnesses, and torpor. *Chelidonia* is under the jurisdiction of the 19° of Gemini.

When hung from the right arm, *chelidonia* stones cure people with liver complaints and protect one from coughs, head colds, inflammation of the uvula, tonsillitis, and ophthalmic conditions.

✦ *celidonia, celidonius, celydonius, gorgia;* MFr. *celidoine, celidon(n)e;* MHG *elidonie, celidôn, swalben stain;* MSp. *piedra de la golondrina;* Heb. *memirum, memirem.*

📖 Pliny 37, 152; Isidore of Sevilla 16, 9, 6; Kerygma 47; Aetios II, 56; Dioscorides II, 56; Damigeron 10; 52; Marbode 17; *Kyranides* 3, 39; *Summarium Heinrici* VI, 4, 21; Lambert de Saint-Omer 55, 41; Avicenna II, 2, 490; Lapidary of Marbode, 1st Romanesque translation XXII; Lapidary in prose 4; 2nd Lapidary in prose 17; Alphabetical Lapidary 22; Alexander Neckham v. 219 (not named but described); Bodl. Digby 13 11; *De lapidibus preciosis* 16; Cambridge lapidary v. 415–52; Wolfram von Eschenbach 791, 11;

Arnoldus Saxo 16; Thomas de Cantimpré 14, 17; Vincent de Beauvais VIII, 53; Albertus Magnus 2, 3, 5; Brunetto Latini I, 169 (talks about the herb with the same name); *Lapidario* 79; Lapidary of King Philip 30; Konrad von Megenberg VI, 17; Jacob van Maerlant XII, 21; *Secrez* 3, 16; Volmar v. 412–29; Saint Florian v. 511–34; *Secrez* 1, 14; Mandeville I 21; Pseudo-Mandeville 22; *Vocabularius ex quo* c 312.1; *Liber ordinis rerum* 129, 19; Closener ce 32; *Hortus sanitatis* V, 33; *Liber defota anima* v. 6196–6247; Leonardi II, 7, 44; *Liber secretorum* II, 1, 23; *De virtutis lapidum* II, 16; *Phisice* 23.

M. Richard, "Les chélidoines ou pierres précieuses de Sassenage," *Bulletin de l'Académie delphinale* 5ᵉ série, 2 (1908): 11–29.

Ceminez: A stone native to the island of Charandin (Serendib?). It is naturally cold and damp, and is governed by the 19° of Scorpio. It is the same color as sapphire but opaque. It was called the "weeper" because it would invade the person who held it with strong feelings of grief and sorrow. If reduced to a powder and blended with plant sap, it healed cuts.

✦ MSp. *llorador.*

Lapidario 290.

Cenchritis: This stone resembles grains of millet scattered here and there.

Pliny 37, 188; Meliteniotes v. 1123.

Cenchron: This name was given to a kind of diamond the size of a grain of millet. See *adamas (I)*.

✦ *cencidii.*

Pliny 37, 57.

Cepocapites: A white stone with veins that all converge in a single point. It is also called cepitis.

✦ *cepolatitis, cepolames, cepot(h)atites, cepites.*

📖 Pliny 37, 152; Meliteniotes v. 1160; Leonardi II, 7, 66.

Ceponides: A gem that is found at Atarna on Aeolia (northwest coast of Asia Minor), which was once a city and is today a town. It is transparent and comes in a variety of colors, and sometimes looks like glass, crystal, or jasper. Even the ones that are tarnished are so brilliant that one can see oneself in them as if in a mirror.

✦ *cepionidus.*

📖 Pliny 37, 156 (cetionides); Leonardi II, 7, 68.

Cerachates: This name literally means "yellow agate" that is the color of wax; see *achates*.

📖 Pliny 37, 139; Meliteniotes v. 1162.

Ceramitis: A stone that has the color of earthenware.

📖 Pliny 37, 152; Meliteniotes v. 1161.

Ceraunia, Ceranitis: The "lightning stone" or "thunder stone" is a crystalline stone with a blue reflection that can be found in Carmania or Germania, depending on the authors, and in Spain. The ancients differentiated two other varieties of ceraunia, a black one and a red one, in India and Lusitania, resembling axes. Among these stones, the ones that are black and round are called betyls and are considered sacred. Through their assistance, cities and fleets can be captured. The ones that are long are called ceraunias. It is claimed that another extremely rare form of ceraunia exists, which is much sought after by magicians for their practices—it is only to be found in places that have been struck by lightning. There are two kinds: the Germanic, which resembles crystal but with red and blue shades; and the Spanish, which is red like pyrope. It protects one from lightning and drowning, protects sailors from storms, gives victory in the courtroom and on the battlefield, and provides one with good sleep and pleasant dreams. "Lightning does not strike him who bears a ceraunia with respect, nor a house or property where this stone has been stored. Anyone who travels by boat on a river or the sea shall not be drowned by storm or struck by lightning," says Marbode. Its zodiac sign is Sagittarius. However, "if one finds the names of God carved onto a ceraunia, it offers protection in the places where storms occur, and these engraved stones give their owners power and victory over their enemies."

According to Notker, who echoes Martinus Capella on this point, the *ceraunia* is governed by Leo and its month is August. A shaggy goat is engraved on it, according to Damigeron.

In Iceland, the *ceraunia* is called "thunderstone" (*skruggusteinn*) and it is said that its owner can see the whole world.

In mineralogy, *ceraunia* or *ceraunite* is nephrite or actinolate jade. Until recent times, it was placed in sheepfolds to protect the flocks. See also *lychnis*, for which *ceraunius* is another name, according to the *Kyranides*.

✦ *ceraunius, ceraumus, cerauninus, ceravinus, ceraolus, betannus, teranus*; MFr. *ceramon, ceraune, cheronne, creanie, selustre, teranus, theramius, veramius*; MHG *ceráuns, ceraune, cirion, donr stain*; MDu. *donresteen*.

📖 Pliny 37, 132; 134 sq.; 176; Solin 20, 15; Isidore of Sevilla 16, 13, 5; Damigeron 12; Marbode 28; *Summarium Heinrici* VI, 5, 11; Lambert de Saint-Omer 55, 93; Meliteniotes v. 1161; Lapidary of Marbode, 1st Romanesque translation XXVIII; Alphabetical Lapidary 20; Lapidary in prose 23; 2nd Lapidary in prose 37; Alexander Neckham v. 329; *De lapidibus preciosis* 20; Cambridge Lapidary v. 703–36; Wolfram von Eschenbach 791, 6; Arnoldus Saxo 15; Bartholomaeus Anglicus XVI, 32; Thomas de Cantimpré 14, 21; Vincent de Beauvais VIII, 55; Albert the Grand 2, 3, 4; Lapidary of King Philip 44; Die Krone v. 8280–84; Konrad von Megenberg VI, 21; Jacob van Maerlant XII, 27; *Secrez* 3, 18; Volmar v. 430–49; Saint Florian v. 638–63; Closener ce 105; *Hortus sanitatis* V, 32; *Liber defota anima* v. 6144–95; Pseudo-Mandeville 30; Leonardi II, 7, 53; Ragiel 17; *Phisice* 34.

📖📖 Pierre Saintyves, *Pierres magiques: béthyles, haches-amulettes et pierres de foudre, traditions savantes et traditions populaires* (Paris: Emile Nourry, 1936).

Cerinus: The name of a beryl that is wax-colored, hence its name.

 📖 Pliny 37, 77.

Ceritis: All we know about this stone is that it was the color of wax, hence its name.

 📖 Pliny 37, 153; Meliteniotes v. 1163.

Cetionis: A name of a transparent stone found in Atarna in Aeolia.

 ✦ *cepionides, cetionides.*

 📖 Pliny 37, 156.

Ceturius: This stone was said to be hardened whale sperm; it is red shading into gold.

 📖 Lambert de Saint-Omer 55, 40.

Chalazias: A white stone that takes its name from the Greek word for hailstone. It both resembles and has the hardness of the diamond. It is said that it retains its cool temperature when placed in fire. It is useful against fevers, snakebite, and scorpion stings, the Pseudo-Orpheus says, and it brings coolness to a patient burning with fever. If carried, it eases the hot passions, lust, and anger. It is also a stone that reveals the future to its bearer.

 The Lapidary of King Alfonso speaks of a "stone of cold" (*piedra del frio, mazintarican* in Arabic) that must be identical to *chalazias*. Prester John counts this stone among the five wonderful gems of his land and tells us that it is by nature so cold that it freezes everything within a radius of ten miles. A second stone produces heat, a third is blunted, the fourth illuminates the night and must be a carbuncle, and the fifth spreads darkness in the middle of the days, again in a ten-mile radius.

 In Ulrich von Zatzikhoven's *Lanzelet* (end of the twelfth century) *chalazias* is called *galazia* and it is "noble and of high price. Even if left within a fire for a year, it will not become hot. He who bears one will never fall into poverty and no evil spell can harm the people, men and women, who surround him" (v. 8525ff.).

> ✦ *chalacia, chaladias, chalatias, calazias, calazyas, chaezias, chalazius, calatia, chalazites, galacia, gallasia, gelasia, gelasius, gelasen, galatia(s), gelatia, gelathya;* Fr. *gelace, gelange, galayse, galatine;* Sp. *galacior, piedra del frio.*
>
> 📖 Pliny 36, 157; 27, 189; Solin 37, 16; Isadore of Sevilla 16, 13, 4 and 36; Kerygmes 24; Pseudo-Hippocrate 17; Pseudo Dioscoride 2, 152; Marbone 37; Lambert de Saint-Omer 55, 49; 55, 91; Meliténiote v. 1188; Lapidary of Marbone, 1st Romanesque translation XXXVII: Alphabetical Lapidary 48; lapidary in prose 54, 54; *Lapidaire de Cambridge* v. 959–966; Arnoldus Saxo 40; Prester John E § 9 (Zarncke); Bartholomaeus Anglicus XVI, 51; Thomas de Cantimpré 14, 33: Albert le Grand 2, 7, 3; *Lapidario* 206; Konrad von Megenberg VI, 40; Saint-Florian v. 565–610; Psellos 24; Closener ge 5; *Liber secretorum* II, 1, 38; *De virtutis lapidum* II 24; *Hortus sanitatis* V, 62; *Phisice* 41.

Chalcedonius, Carchedonius:

Chalcedony, a crystallized quartz and amorphous silicate blend, grows in India and resembles a flame or else is pale gray according to the ancients, but in the Middle Ages it was also said to be white or blue. When pierced through with a hole and worn around the neck or finger, it allows an individual to triumph over anything. Hung from the neck, it is effective against phantasms and the hallucinations caused by melancholy and allows one to prevail in all causes. Sometimes the same results can be obtained if one wears chalcedony on the finger simultaneously with emery. When carried since childhood, it prevents drowning if shipwrecked. It bestows eloquence and is useful in judgments, for if you show it to your adversary, it will help you win the court case. It renders one pleasant, easily understood, capable of achieving anything, and of overcoming shipwrecks. It is also effective against venoms, offers protection from fire and water, and delivers one from storms. It must be set in gold. The woman who gets married and owns a chalcedony will always keep her spouse's love and both will be humble and retain their faith. However, the stone will lose its virtues if a false oath is sworn on it, although the same thing is said of jasper. Lastly, we should note that the person who wears chalcedony, onyx, and sardonyx together will have good morals and habits.

Von dem Calcedoni.

In the Christian lapidary, chalcedony represents the strength of the faithful who serve discreetly, hiding their kindness and good works. When they go out, their kindness makes them luminous. They refuse praise and their preaching draws sinners like rubbing chalcedony attracts wisps of straw. Konrad of Hamburg made it the symbol of the Virgin's charity in a poem entitled *Anulus*, written circa 1350, in which he offers Mary a ring with twenty different gemstones.

Chalcedony is etched with an image of an armed Mars, or a virgin in a long dress holding a laurel branch, or an Athena on foot holding a heron in her right hand and a helmet in her left. If this stone is worn after it has been consecrated, it gives one the power to triumph over all foes and rivals.

If it is kept in a money-box, a chalcedony with an engraving of a stag or billy goat has the power to increase wealth.

If you find an image on a chalcedony of a man with his right hand raised toward the sky, it has the power to resolve civil wars and to bring health to its owner, protect him on the roads, and keep pernicious incidents from befalling him.

✦ *chalconeus, calcedonius, calcydonius, carchedonia, calidi, carsydonius;* MFr. *calcedonie, calcidoine, chalcydoine, calcedoine, cassidoine, casadoine, caucedoin(i)e, falcidoine, calcedonne, ccarsydoyne, marcedoine;* MHG *kalcedonius, kastedonius, calcedonie, calcidôn;* OE *chalcedony, calsydonye, salkessyne;* MItal. *calcidonia.*

📖 Theophrastus 25; Pliny 37, 52f.; 104; 115; Solin 15, 23; Dioscorides V, 99 (gives *larbason* and *platyophthalmon* as synonyms); *Kerygma* 29; Damigeron 27 and 33; Marbode 6; Hildegard von Bingen IV, 12; Old English lapidary 3; Lambert de Saint-Omer 54, 3; 55, 3; 55, 17; Lapidary of Marbode, 1st Romanesque translation VI; Alphabetical Lapidary 30; Lapidary in prose 9; *Sidrac* 15; Alexander Neckham v. 145ff.; Bodl. Digby 13 8 and 26; Gossouin de Metz v. 453–59; *De lapidibus preciosis* 13; *De la vertu des tailles* 31; Wolfram von Eschenbach 791, 3; *Liber lapidarii* 14; Arnoldus Saxo 12; Bartholomaeus Anglicus XVI, 28; Thomas de Cantimpré 14, 14; Albertus Magnus 2, 3, 2; Vincent de Beauvais VIII, 50; Lapidary of King Philip 15; Konrad von Megenberg VI, 14; Jacob van Maerlant XII, 18; Saint Florian v. 397–408; Volmar v. 572–93 (*caltzedodyon, kastedonius*); *Secrez* 3, 17; Mandeville I 15; *Vocabularius ex quo* c 20; *Liber ordinis rerum* 129, 18; Closener ca 48; *Hortus sanitatis* V, 28; *Libro di Sidrach* chap. 466; Leonardi II, 7, 43; *Liber secretorum* II, 1, 22; *De virtutis lapidum* II, 15; *Phisice* 17.

📖📖 Thomas Rogers Forbes, *The Midwife and the Witch* (New Haven, London: AMS, 1966), 64–79 (in the chapter "Chalcedony and Childbirth").

Chalcites: A copper-colored gem that must be a kind of malachite.

✦ *chalcitis, calcitis.*

📖 Pliny 37, 117–19; Dioscorides V, 115; Isidore of Sevilla 16, 15, 9; Lambert de Saint-Omer 55, 84; Leonardi II, 7, 84.

Chalcophonos: This is a black stone that clinks like brass when struck—the etymological interpretation of its name is "that which sounds like brass." It is thus a phonolite, and stage performers were advised to carry them as they gave one a sweet, melodious voice and prevented one from becoming hoarse. In his description of the Grail Palace in remote India, Albrecht von Scharfenberg (thirteenth century) said that the two bells there were made of *chalcophonos*.

> ✦ *chalcophthongos, calcophanes, calthosanus, calthosamus, chatophonus, calthofanus, calleoponos, galcophon, chalcofungos, calofanos, chelconphongos, calofagus;* MFr. *calcofoine, calcofonie, salcofane, kalcéphane, alcaferne, alcarferne, aleaferne;* MHG *calcofôn, kalcosan, kalcosam, dakasam.*
>
> 📖 Pliny 37, 117–54; Solin 37, 22; Isidore of Sevilla 16, 15, 9; Marbode 53; Meliteniotes v. 1187; Lapidary of Marbode, 1st Romanesque translation LIII; Lapidary in prose 49; 2nd Lapidary in prose 34; *De lapidibus preciosis* 17; Cambridge lapidary v. 1253–60; Wolfram von Eschenbach 791, 12; Arnoldus Saxo 14; Bartholomaeus Anglicus XVI, 59; Thomas de Cantimpré 14, 18; Vincent de Beauvais VIII, 50; Albertus Magnus 2, 3, 3; Lapidary of King Philip 69; Jacob van Maerlant XII, 22; Volmar v. 502–11; Saint Florian v. 718–25; Closener ca 93; *Hortus sanitatis* V, 28 and 32; Leonardi II, 7, 56; *Phisice* 57.

Chalcosmaragdus: This is the emerald of Cypress, whose surface is mottled by coppery veins. According to Theophrastus, Egyptian books reported that a king of Babylon sent an Egyptian sovereign an emerald as a gift that was four cubits long and three cubits wide.

> 📖 Pliny 37, 74; Solin 15, 26; Isidore of Sevilla 16, 7, 3; Meliteniotes v. 1187.

Chelonia: This is the eye of the Indian tortoise, "the most wonderful of all the stones," says Pliny the Elder. The magicians swear that this stone, placed on the tongue after the mouth has been rinsed out with honey, will ensure one the power of divination for an entire day, if this is done at the full or new moon. It must be done before sunrise if the moon is waxing and from dawn to noon at other times. During the Middle Ages, this stone was confused with the *chelonitis*.

📖 Pliny 37, 155; Lapidary of Marbode, 1st Romanesque translation XXXIX (*De chelonite*).

Chelonitis: A red-and-green gem that resembles a tortoise (Gk. *chelone*). It allegedly has the power to calm tempests, when a *chelonitis* stone sprinkled with gold spots is cast with a *scarabeus* (scarab beetle) into boiling water, it will instead raise a storm. Carried under the tongue, it permits one to foretell the future, but this power only manifests on the first day of the lunar month when the moon is waxing, and on the twenty-ninth day when it is waning. It has no fear of fire. It gives milk to women, and if tied to the thigh of a woman in labor, she will give birth quickly. Animals carrying it will be healed of tinea, as well as other diseases. Carried on one's person with a peony root, the *chelonitis* brings success.

✦ *celonite, cenolite, celiconites, celidanius, ceronites, celontes, chelonia, cephalicus;* MFr. *c(h)elonite, ceronite, colonice;* MHG *celidôn, sneckenstain.*

📖 Pliny 37, 155; Isidore of Sevilla 16, 15, 23; Damigeron 11 and 57; Marbode 39; *Summarium Heinrici* VI, 6, 7; Alphabetical Lapidary 21; Meliteniotes v. 1188; Lapidary of Marbode, 1st Romanesque translation XXXIX; Lapidary in prose 39; 2nd Lapidary in prose 28; Alexander Neckham v. 305ff.; Cambridge lapidary v. 977–1000; Arnoldus Saxo 17; Vincent de Beauvais VIII, 32 and 54; Albertus Magnus 2, 3, 6; Lapidary of King Philip 42; Konrad von Megenberg VI, 24; Saint Florian v. 876–89; *Hortus sanitatis* V, 34; Leonardi II, 7, 51; *Liber secretorum* II, 1, 17; *De virtutis lapidum* II, 34; *Phisice* 45.

Chelonitides: A stone that comes from tortoises other than the Indian tortoise. There are two kinds: one is similar to *chelonitis,* which magicians use to calm storms and to prophesize; the other is speckled with gold and will unleash a tempest when cast in boiling water.

📖 Pliny 37, 155.

Chernitis: This is a kind of sparkling or tree-like agate; it very much resembles two white hands clasping one another. This stone preserves the body without consuming it and spares it from putrefaction; the coffin of Darius is said to have been made of this substance.

✦ *chemites, gemytis, gemitis.*

📖 Pliny 36, 132; 37, 192; Isidore of Sevilla 16, 4, 24; Leonardi II, 7, 60.

Chlochitis: A dark and opaque green stone found in Arabia; it protects children from anger, polluted air, and the devil, and it protects its bearer from demons and misfortunes.

📖 *Phisice* 58.

Chloritis: This is a stone that is grass-green in color, which may be identical with the emerald green talc known as herbosa. It is a hydrated silicate. According to the magicians, it can be found in the crop or the belly of the wagtail; it is engendered with this bird. They recommend its setting be made of iron, in order to obtain certain wonders that it promises.

✦ *cloritis, chaloritis.*

📖 Pliny 37, 156; Meliteniotes v. 1187.

Choaspitis: This gem takes its name from the Choaspes River; it is green with golden highlights.

✦ *choaspites, coaspis.*

📖 Pliny 37, 156; Isidore of Sevilla 16, 7, 16; *Summarium Heinrici* VI, 4, 14; Lambert de Saint-Omer 55, 35; Meliteniotes v. 1189; Leonardi II, 7, 74.

Chryselectrum: This is another name for *succinum*, which is to say amber. Callistratus distinguished a new variety of it by calling a gold-colored amber *chryselectrum*, which offers the most pleasant hues in the morning light. This amber stone rapidly draws fire to itself and it will promptly ignite if near a flame. Worn around the neck it will heal fever and other illnesses. Ground and mixed with honey and rose oil, it heals the afflictions of the ear; crushed with Attic honey, problems with eyesight; taken alone as a powder or in water with mastic, it is good against stomach disorders. Finally, *chryselectrum* is of great use for imitating transparent gemstones, particularly amethysts. The name *chryselectrum* is also given to a stone verging on the color of electrum, but which is only attractive in the morning. The stones of Pontus are known for their lightness. Some are hard and red; others are soft and dirty in color.

Chryselectrae is the name for those chrysoliths whose color likens them to amber.

✦ *chryselectros, chryselecti, chruselectroe, cryselectroc, chrysolectri, crisoelectri, chrysoelectrus, criselectrus, criselectrius, crisolectus, crisolectrus;* MFr. *crosolectre, criselectre;* MHG *crysolecter.*

⌨ Pliny 37, 51 and 127; Isidore of Sevilla 16, 15, 3; Marbode 59; Psellos 22; *Summarium Heinrici* VI, 6, 3; Lambert de Saint-Omer 55, 70; Meliteniotes v. 1189; Lapidary of Marbode, 1st Romanesque translation LIX; Lapidary in prose 45; Cambridge lapidary v. 1323–38; Wolfram von Eschenbach 791, 20; Arnoldus Saxo 24; Albertus Magnus 2, 3, 13; Vincent de Beauvais VIII, 59; Konrad von Megenberg VI, 20; Jacob van Maerlant XII, 26 (*crisoletus*); *Hortus sanitatis* V, 36.

Chrysitis: This is another name for *phloginos*. An amulet is made from it by carving a bird on it that wears a round crown and has a sea bream at its feet. If one adds a small chrysanthemum root beneath it, it heals stomachache and kidney problems, and inversions of the uterus. See also *trisite* (which is sometimes a deformation of *chrysitis*) and *phlogitis*.

⌨ Pliny 36, 157 and 179 (*phlogitis* given as a synonym); Isidore of Sevilla 16,

4, 28; Dioscorides V, 62; *Kyranides* 1, 23; Alphabetical Lapidary 78; *Secrez* 4, 20; Leonardi II, 7, 77.

Chrysoberulli:
This is a beryl that is a bit paler, with a sparkle verging on that of gold. It is undoubtedly our *cymophane* or topaz.

✦ *chrysoberillus, crisoberillus.*

📖 Theophrastus 26; Pliny 37, 76; Isidore of Sevilla 16, 7, 6; *Summarium Heinrici* VI, 4, 4; Lambert de Saint-Omer 55, 27; Leonardi II, 7, 81.

Chrysocolla:
Still called *amphidames,* this Indian gem is blue-green in color and has magnetic properties. It is a natural hydrated copper silicate.

✦ *crisocollus.*

📖 Pliny 33, 86 and 37, 147; Isidore of Sevilla 16, 15, 7; Dioscorides V, 89; Pseudo-Dioscorides 2, 104; Lombard Dioscorides 115; Vincent de Beauvais VII, 103–4; VIII, 59; *Hortus sanitatis* V, 36; Leonardi II, 7, 58.

Chrysolampsis:
The *chrysolampsis* is a stone of Ethiopia that is pale by day and has the color of fire at night. It is a kind of topaz.

✦ *chrysolampis, chrysolansis, chrysolamsis, crisolapsis.*

📖 Pliny 37, 156; Isidore of Sevilla 16, 15, 4; *Summarium Heinrici* VI, 6, 4; Lambert de Saint-Omer 55, 71; Meliteniotes v. 1190; Arnoldus Saxo 25; Vincent de Beauvais VIII, 60; *Hortus sanitatis* V, 38; Leonardi II, 7, 76.

Chrysolithus:
This name designates either the topaz or the jacinth. *Chrysolithus,* natural magnesium and iron silicate, "resembles seawater with gold sparkles inside" and comes from Ethiopia. It blazes like fire in sunlight. It is placed under the patronage of the Moon, its zodiac sign is Leo, and its metal is gold. According to the Lapidary of King Alfonso, it is governed by the 2° of Gemini.

In the Bible, it is one of the twelve stones on the *rationale* or breastplate of the high priest Aaron (Exodus 28:15–30), and in the Christian lapidary, it represents the conduct of men of perfect wisdom and charitable individuals: it shines with the seven gifts of the Holy Ghost. Konrad von Hamburg made this stone the symbol of the glory of the miracles and the gift of wisdom of the Virgin Mary. This is one of the twenty gemstones on the ring he offers Mary in his poem *Anulus,* written circa 1350.

Set in gold, the *chrysolithus* acts like a phylactery. It affords protection from night terrors, in other words, nightmares. Pierced and threaded on the hair from a donkey foal or a pregnant ewe, or on a blue silk thread, it terrorizes and torments demons. It must be worn on the left wrist. When embedded in a gold setting, this stone repels phantasms, dispels madness, gives wisdom, and protects from fear. It heals alopecia and heart shudders, makes one gracious and friendly, prevents one from being suspected of malevolence, and helps one enter wherever he pleases. Carried in the hand of the plaintiff, the *chrysolithus* is effective in court cases.

According to Damigeron, the *chrysolithus* is the stone of the Moon. Free men wear it with an engraving of a seated Moon; the *chrysolithus* of freed slaves bears a cow; and that of slaves depicts a crescent moon.

A scarab with rays can also be etched on it, or Aphrodite, in which case it is helpful to women and procures great favor. An ass sculpted on a *chrysolithus* gives the power to predict the future. If a seated man holding a lit candle in his hand is found carved on one, this image brings wealth to its owner and it must be mounted onto the purest gold. If the image of a vulture is depicted, its power is to imprison demons and the winds, to contain and gather them together. It affords protection against evil spirits and their ravages in the place where it is found, and the demons obey the one bearing it.

It is said that the Egyptian King Nekraous, who lived in the time before the Deluge, had a dome constructed which on its top held: "a mirror of *chrysolithus* five spans in size, the clarity of which carried a very great distance."

✦ *chrysolitheos, crisolitus, chrisolicotus, crisolimus, crisolensis, chrysolie, cosolitus, crisoritus, petra asini;* MFr. *grisolite, crisolite, grisolythe, cristlice, trisolite;* MHG *crisolit, krisolit, crisolte;* ME *crysolyte;* MSp. *piedra del oro;* MItal. *crisolita.*

📖 Pliny 37, 126f.; Epiphanes 10; Isidore of Sevilla 16, 15, 2; Kerygma 37; Damigeron 47–48; Marbode 11; *Summarium Heinrici* VI, 6, 2; Lambert de Saint-Omer 54, 7; 55, 7; 55, 21; Meliteniotes v. 1121; Lapidary of Marbode, 1st Romanesque translation XI; Lapidary in prose 47; 2nd Lapidary in prose 5; Alphabetical Lapidary 23; *Sidrac* 10; Alexander Neckham v. 179ff.; *De lapidibus preciosis* 19 and 22; *De l'entaille des gemmes* 31; *De la vertu des tailles* 32; Cambridge lapidary v. 289–304; Wolfram con Eschenbach 589, 21; 791, 25; *Liber sigillorum Ethel* 7; *Liber lapidarii* 9; Gossouin de Metz v. 390–413; Arnoldus Saxo 22; Bartholomaeus Anglicus XVI, 29; Thomas de Cantimpré 14, 20 and 23; Vincent de Beauvais VIII, 60; Albertus Magnus 2, 3, 11; *Lapidario* 62; Lapidary of King Philip 10; Konrad von Megenberg VI, 23; Jacob van Maerlant XII, 24; Christian lapidary v. 545–72 and 1159–98; Volmar v. 235–54; Saint Florian v. 355–72; *Secrez* 3, 5; Pseudo-Mandeville 19 and 34; Mandeville I 18; Psellos 21; *Liber ordinis rerum* 129, 20; Closener cr 60; *Libro di Sidrach* chap. 463; *Liber secretorum* II, 1, 28; *De virtutis lapidum* II, 12; Ragiel; 48; Chael 6; Thetel 4; *Hortus sanitatis* V, 38; *Liber defota anima* v. 6088–6143; Leonardi II, 7, 49 and 50; *Phisice* 20 and 63.

Chrysopis: According to some, this is a pale stone that shines at night like a carbuncle, useful against paralysis and illnesses due to cold; it can be found in Libya and Ethiopia. According to others, it is a gem with the same properties as *chrysolampsis*. See *chrysolampsis*.

✦ *chrysoph, crisopis, chrysopastus;* MFr. *grisopitq*.

📖 Pliny 37, 156; Isidore of Sevilla 16, 15, 1; *Kyranides* 4, 66; *Summarium Heinrici* VI, 6, 1; Lambert de Saint-Omer 55, 77; Meliteniotes v. 1190; Bodl. Digby 13 24; Leonardi II, 7, 83; *Phisice* 64.

Chrysoprasus: *Chrysoprasus,* which is a variety of chalcedony, is the color of leek juice but its shades run somewhat to topaz and gold. It comes from Ethiopia, is good for the eyes, and renders its wearer graceful. It can be found because it glows in the darkness but pales beneath the light of day, which likens it to a stone in the Lapidary of King Alfonso that hides at day and reveals itself at night. In the Christian lapidary, the *chrysoprasus* symbolizes those who experience trials and hardships, yet remain charitable.

Konrad von Hamburg used this stone to symbolize the fervor of Mary's love for God and included *chrysoprasus* as one of the twenty gemstones on the ring he offers Mary in his poem *Anulus,* written circa 1350.

Whoever carries this stone overcomes his enemies; sees his wealth increase; and is protected from poison and treachery, fever and gout, sudden death, and the misdeeds of the devil.

For other references, see *crisoprassus.*

✦ *chrysoprasius, chrysoprassus, chrysoptasius, crisoprassis, crisopis, crisoffras;* MFr. *crisopras, crisopasse, crisopades;* MHG *crisopas, crisopast, crisopalt, crisops;* MItal. *grisopasa.*

📖 Pliny 37, 77, and 113; Solin 52, 62; Isidore of Sevilla 16, 7, 7; 16, 14, 8; Psellos 23; Lambert de Saint-Omer 55, 68; 54, 10; 55, 10; 55, 16; Hildegard von Bingen IV, 13; Old English lapidary 9; Meliteniotes v. 1189; Marbode Lapidary, 1st Romanesque translation XV and LX; Lapidary in prose 48; 2nd Lapidary in prose 24; *Sidrac* 14; Alexander Neckham v. 205ff. and 321ff.; Cambridge lapidary v. 347–58; 1339–50; Wolfram von Eschenbach 741, 6; 791, 27; *Liber lapidarii* 13; Gossouin de Metz v. 470–75; Bodl. Digby 13 24; Bartholomaeus Anglicus XVI, 27; Vincent de Beauvais VIII, 61; Albertus Magnus 2, 3, 10 and 14; Lapidary of King Philip 14 and 28; Jacob van Maerlant XII, 20; Saint Florian v. 535–40; Volmar v. 662–75; *Liber ordinis rerum* 129, 21; *Hortus sanitatis* V, 37; *Libro di Sidrach* chap. 470.

Chrysopteros: The name for a kind of topaz.

📖 Pliny 37, 109.

Chrysotix: The stone with the "golden hair" procures dignity and worth.

📖 Orpheus v. 292–305; Kergymes 10; Pseudo-Hippocrates 35.

Cimedia, Chimedia: See *cinediae.*

📖 Bodl. Digby 13 46.

Cimilanitus: This gem is found in the Euphrates River; it is the color of marble with a gold or yellow pupil in its center.

📖 Leonard II, 7, 75.

Cinediae, Cinedios: This name is used to designate three stones found in the fish of the same name, two in the head and one in the tail. One is a dull black and the other is brilliant and called "dragon stone" (*dracontius lapis*). The magicians assert that it foretells conditions at sea, whether calm or stormy. It is the stone of Saturn. If one takes *cinediae* with a being that resembles you, he will serve you as a female. The *cinediae* is part of the adornment called the "belt of Venus," which is made of sinew holding gems like *lychnite* and diamond, with some of them engraved. The *lychnite* depicts an armed Mars, while the diamond shows Aphrodite with either thorns or roses at her feet.

Another more precise tradition describes *cinediae* as a long, soft, dull stone of which there are two varieties: one is reddish like dry clay, the other black, like the flaws in a sapphire. It is found in the heads of fish living in the rivers flowing out of heaven where they meet the sea. It protects against lightning and storms, resists adversity, and its bearer cannot die before confessing, which is why it is called the "holy stone." Placed on the tongue, it allows one to prophesize. Several stones prevent sudden death from occurring, thus allowing their owners time to make their last confessions. These stones are the *chrysolithus,* the *demath,* the *pyrophilus,* and the *tarnif.* For more on these stones, see their individual entries.

✦ cynaedia, cinaedia, chimedia, cimidia, kinedius, cimedia, cinedius, cinedies; MFr. *crimodée, erimodée;* MSp. *sendia.*

📖 Pliny 37, 153; Alphabetical Lapidary 28; Meliteniotes v. 1162; Bodl. Digby 13 46; Vincent de Beauvais VIII, 54; *Summarium Heinrici* VI, 4, 32; *Kyranides* 1, 10; Lapidary of King Philip 74; *Secrez* 4, 10; *Hortus sanitatis* V, 34; Leonardi II, 7, 55; *Poridat* 21; *Phisice* 86.

Circos: A gem that is the color of a kestrel or sparrow hawk.

  Pliny 37, 153; Meliteniotes v. 1163.

Cissitis: The transparent white surface of this stone has leaves of ivy running all over it.

  Pliny 37, 188; Meliteniotes v. 1162.

Clitoris: Mount Lileus produces this black stone, which is used to make earrings.

  Pseudo-Plutarch §28.

Clastecolz, Castrecoq: A stone that is found in the head of a rooster. When the chicks are nine days old, or once their sex can be determined, they are separated from their mother and kept virginal for one or three years, depending on the manuscripts (which also say this about the *alectory* stone), then they are killed so the stone can be obtained. If carried in a closed hand, that person shall be invisible; furthermore it shall give one victory in all places. It is said that the cock should emerge from an egg that is hatched in March. It seems that the *clastecolz* was "manufactured" from the *alectorias*.

  Lapidary of King Philip 77; Pseudo-Mandeville 51.

Clupea Stone: A stone similar to a grain of salt found in the head of the clupea, a fish living in the Saône or Arar Rivers. It is a sovereign remedy against quartan fevers if applied to the left side when the moon is waning.

  Pseudo-Plutarch §2.

Clydros: See *enhydros*.

  De lapidibus preciosis 29.

Cochlis: An artificial gem manufactured in Arabia with large stone blocks that are cooked in honey for a period of seven days and seven nights.

 Pliny 37, 193f.

Cock Stone: A bezoar. See *alectorias*.

Cocrice: A white stone with a red tip that is the size of a broad bean. It is found on an island in the Indian Ocean, between two mountains. It heals corneal opacity, and banishes poisons and the venom from animal bites. Legend claims that it can be obtained in the following manner: sections of goat are covered with honey and cast below the mountain. The *cocrices* stick to the honey and are carried off when predator birds fly away with the goat meat. Men then hunt these birds to claim the stones. The same technique is used for other stones. See *otriche*.

✦ *ocrice, cotrice, coccrite, crocisee, corisse.*

 Sidrah 23; *Libro di Sidrach* chap. 476.

Collurus: A white and sea-green colored stone that resembles a sapphire and is good against all attacks (*injurias*). Its bearer "will never be turned down by his lord," and he will achieve all his desires.

✦ *collyria;* MFr. *collire.*

 Damigeron 38; Alphabetical Lapidary 31; Bodl. Digby 13 29.

Collotes: Stones from the Nile that swallows collect after the flood crests. They were used for building the Chelidonian wall that prevents this land from being ravaged by floods. They have unspecified magical properties.

 Pseudo-Plutarch §15.

Colue: This is a yellowish stone that is clear like sapphire, except for the fact that it borders on being white. It sparkles like the water of the sea in sunlight. It soothes the wrath of princes and diverts misfortunes and adversity.

 Phisice 87.

Conte: A pale yellow or red stone, engendered by the breath of the whale. It preserves health, sharpens memory, and banishes sorrow and melancholy. It is one of the Middle French names for amber. See *electrum, succinum, hanon*.

 Phisice 87.

Cophron: This stone is found in the Maeander River. If it is cast in someone's lap, he will immediately become enraged and slay one of his relatives. But after having calmed the "Mother of the Gods," he will be healed of his madness.

 Pseudo-Plutarch §5; *De mirabilibus auscultationibus* §167.

Corallachates: A variety of agate that is quite abundant in Crete; it is scattered with specks of gold like the sapphire. See *achates*.

✦ *choralichates, chrorolloachates, sollochates.*

 Pliny 37, 139 and 153; Meliteniotes v. 1163.

Corallis, Coraliticus: A vermilion stone found in Syene and India.

 Isidore of Sevilla 16, 5, 9; *Summarium Heinrici* VI, 3, 7.

Corallium: Coral is also called *gorgonios*, in connection with the legend of the Gorgon. The myth says that it was born from the drops of blood falling from Medusa's head into the sea while Perseus was carrying it. It was next believed to be a plant that was white as long as it remained in the water but which turned red and hard when removed from it. Dimishqî tells us it can be found near Sicily, Algiers, and Ceuta.

Coral is used to make amulets (Lat. *gestamina*) that are useful for many things and has been shown to be salutary for those who carry it. "It drives lightning, squalls, and storms far from boats, houses, or the fields in which one carries it. It banishes the demonic shades and witches (or the ghosts) of Thessaly (*Thessala monstra*); it provides easy beginnings and favorable outcomes," says Marbode of Rennes. "It drives monsters away, including the devil," the *Rosarius* asserts. Pulverized and sown with wheat, it prevents the flails from striking the laborers. Attached with the hide of a seal to the top of a boat's mast, it counteracts the winds and waves. When enclosed in sealskin, it protects from lightning, demons, brigands, dangers, evil spells, and nocturnal encounters. Coral lightens the mood, renders the soul communicative, restrains hemorrhaging, and protects from epilepsy. Worn next to an oozing, rheumy eye, it will remove the pain and cause the rheum to vanish. Crushed, it removes tartar from the teeth and strengthens the gums. Sprinkled over a wound, it will cause it to scar and prevent it from becoming infected by protecting it against the influences of air and water.

Von dem Corallen.

Dimishqî distinguishes coral from coral root (*bourad*), the latter being used to make large amulets. If coral is worn it halts the impetuosity of the blood and removes dirt from the eyes and the redness from their veins. Coral dulls scorpion stings and is good against the bite of the asp. It protects one from enemies in battle, as well as enchantments, potions, and spells. At sea, it offers protection against storms and pirates. It protects the fields from the burning sun, hail, caterpillars, grasshoppers, and ants. It stems the blood, expels madness, and bestows wisdom; it is good against storms and the perils of the sea.

For the anonymous fourteenth-century Dominican author of the *Rosarius,* the coral represented Mary, the "tree of life" that bore Jesus.

If a Gorgon or its forequarters is engraved on it, or the animal of Hecate, either the common rat, the dog, or the cow in Greco-Egyptian magic, it then gives protection against drugs, lightning, and evil spirits. It spares one from grief and, when placed in the house, it will expel spirits and ghosts. Carved with Hecate or the Gorgon, it protects from storms, lightning, wind, and enchantments, and it grants victory. A man holding a sword in his hand carved on a piece of coral has the power to protect the place where it is located from lightning, and to keep its owner safe from vices and enchantments. As support to the Venus talisman, coral sends mice fleeing.

✦ *corallus, corallius, curallis, curallium;* MFr. *coral;* MHG *coralle, coreal, korall, grallen, corel;* MSp. *coral;* MDu. *coreal;* Ar. *margan, besed/bassad, bresilis;* Heb. *margan, almogim.*

📖 Pliny 32, 21; 37, 153; Solin 2, 43; Isidore of Sevilla 16, 8, 1; Orpheus v. 510ff.; *Kerygma* 20; Nautical lapidary 28; Pseudo-Hippocrates 1; 41; Dioscorides V, 121; Damigeron 7; Marbode 20; Meliteniotes v. 1121; *Summarium Heinrici* VI, 4, 15; Lambert de Saint-Omer 55, 37; Pseudo-Dioscorides 2, 189; Lombard Dioscorides 148; Luka ben Serapion 53; Avicenna II, 2, 124; Marbode Lapidary, 1st Romanesque translation XX; Alphabetical Lapidary 18 and 26; Lombard 148; Lapidary in prose 17; 2nd Lapidary in prose 20; Alexander Neckham v. 237ff.; *De l'entaille des gemmes* 51; Bodl. Digby 13 10; *De lapidibus preciosis* 14; Cambridge lapidary v. 539–64; Wolfram von Eschenbach 791, 4; Arnoldus Saxo 19; Bartholomaeus Anglicus XVI, 33; Thomas de Cantimpré 14, 15; Vincent de Beauvais VIII, 56–57; Albertus Magnus 2, 3, 8; *Lapidario* 41–42; *Picatrix* II, 10, 62; Lapidary of King Philip 21; Konrad von Megenberg VI, 15; Jacob van Maerlant XII, 19; Saint Florian v. 487–510; Volmar v. 360–71; *Secrez* 3, 15; *Vocabularius ex quo* c 1026; *Liber ordinis rerum* 129, 11; *Rosarius* 1; Mandeville

I 25; Closener co 304; *Liber secretorum* II, 1, 18; *De virtutis lapidum* II, 10; *Poridat* 12; *Liber defota anima* v. 5642–5749; *Hortus sanitatis* V, 43; *Gart der Gesundheit* chap. 130; *Phisice* 28.

Coranus: A white stone that is harder than the marble of Paros.

📖 Isidore of Sevilla 16, 4, 31; Leonardi II, 7, 82.

Coribas, Corybas: This crow-colored stone can be found on Mount Mycenae; those who carry it need not dread any monstrous vision.

📖 Pseudo-Plutarch §17.

Colve: A clear, yellow stone that resembles sapphire, but which is whiter. It soothes the anger of princes and diverts court trials, adversity, and all things harmful.

📖 Lapidary of King Philip 75.

Corneolus: Pale and dark, and red in color, the carnelian, a variety of translucent agate, worn on the finger or hung from the neck, calms anger, purifies the flesh, and stops blood flow, especially that of women. According to Dimishqî, it is found in the Sana of Yemen and there are five types: blue, white, black, red, and one that is the same color as a date. The best is the one that has the color of the jacinth. According to the Arabic tradition presented by Belenus, its planet is Jupiter. Carnelian gives patience and resignation to those who wear it as a ring or otherwise; it strengthens eyesight, enlivens the soul, and gives one a venerable air and good character. Women should like this stone as "it gives them comfort against their illnesses and makes them pleasant and beloved." A man looking at a woman should be engraved on it, and the woman's hair should be down to her waist: a woman touched by this ring will do your will.

If one engraves on it a basilisk fighting a bull-headed dragon, or man, above, this stone will procure victory over wild animals.

If one finds the image on a carnelian of an adorned man or one holding a beautiful object, it has the power to halt bloodshed and lead to honors.

A man with a sword in hand carved into a carnelian has the power to protect the place it is found from storms and lightning, and to keep its owner free of enchantments and vices.

If one finds carved on a carnelian the image of a seated man looking upward, with a woman standing before him, with thick hair falling to her waist, its power will be to subject the will of others and compel obedience, and one will gain the benevolence of all; when engraving this stone, add a little of amber and of turpentine, or place it on betony and amber, and mount it in gold that is equal in weight to the stone.

If a man holding flowers in his hand is depicted on a carnelian and this stone is fixed into a tin ring, and if the ring was made on the day of the Moon or the day of Venus, on the first, eighth, or twelfth hour, then the person touched with this ring will obey you.

Whoever finds a depiction of a bearded man on a carnelian and fixes it to a tin ring during the revolution of the moon, either on the day of Venus at the first moon or the eighth moon, will bend to his will all persons who touch this ring.

✦ *cornelionus, corneol, cornelius, cornelio;* MFr. *corneole, cornel(l)ine, corniel, cornil, corneline, cornelyne, cornoligne, corgnieule, cornouille;* MHG *corneol, corniol, corniel, sorniol, kermel, carinel, carniol;* ME *cornelynes;* MDu. *corangeline;* Ar. *aliaza, haalkhec;* Heb. *alekszani.*

📖 Marbode 22; Hildegard von Bingen IV, 23; Alphabetical Lapidary 24; Lapidary in prose 18; 2nd Lapidary in prose 11; Alexander Neckham v. 244ff.; Luka ben Serapion 5; *De lapidibus preciosis* 5 and 21; Bodl. Digby 13 28; *De l'entaille des gemmes* 29 and 41; *De figura* 11; Dimishqî II, 5, 2; Marbode Lapidary, 1st Romanesque translation XXII; Wolfram von Eschenbach 791, 13; Serapion c. 400 (*hager salachil*); *Liber sigillorum Ethel* 5 and 20; Cambridge Lapidary v. 573–84; Arnoldus Saxo 20; Bartholomaeus Anglicus XVI, 34; Albertus Magnus 2, 3, 9; Thomas de Cantimpré 14, 22; Vincent de Beauvais VIII, 58; *Lapidario* 123–25; 247 (*alaaquic*); *Picatrix* IV, 2, 36; 4, 65; Lapidary of King Philip 38; Konrad von Megenberg VI, 22; Jacob van Maerlant XII, 23; *Secrez* 3, 12; Saint

Florian v. 479–86; Volmar v. 372–77; Leonardi II, 7, 46; Pseudo-Mandeville 25 and 40; Ragiel 10; 13; Chael 4; 17; 31; Hermes 13; Solomon 4; 27; *Hortus sanitatis* V, 44; *Phisice* 29.

Corsoïdes: This stone, which is gray or with gray-white veins, had the color of an old man's hair. It helps against pains of the nape of the neck, dropsy, and inflammation of the inguinal glands, according to the *Lapidary of Orpheus*. Blended with honey, the *corsoïdes* heals burns; crushed with garlic, it is a remedy against scorpion stings; and reduced to a powder and dissolved in wine, it arrests the effects of asp venom.

✦ *corsides, corsites, corsnides.*

📖 Pliny 37, 153; Pseudo-Hippocrates 39; *Kerygma* 19.

Corvia: A red stone that originates in a crow's egg that hardens after the calends of April. It increases wealth, brings honors, and permits the prediction of future events. The *corvia* is sometimes confused with the *corvina* (whose name designates two stones found in the head of the fish of the same name), which are white, gibbous, and opaque. They must be removed from the head of the living fish during a waxing moon; they will then have the property of suppressing pain.

It was said in the Middle Ages that if one touched iron with the crow stone, it changed into silver, that it could open locks, and it gave victory in court cases.

On the shores of the Baltic, there is a commonly held tradition about the crow stone. It is as big as a quail's egg, smooth, and grayish-blue in color. It can be found in the nests of crows, which bring it from the Jordan. It gives wealth, happiness, victory in court, invulnerability, invisibility if one puts it in their mouth or pocket, and finally it will open locks. A good many of its properties are those of the serpent egg. In fifteenth-century Germany, the following legend was common: if the eggs of a crow were cooked and placed back in the nest, the crow would fly to an island in the Red Sea and bring back a stone with which it would touch the eggs to immediately restore their freshness.

In Estonia, the *corvia* is used in a drink to fight illness, and people swear that it bestows wealth and good transactions and gives the ability to understand the language of cranes. In Pomerania, the stones can only be found in the nests of crow couples that are one hundred years old.

In Iceland, it is called *lausnarsteinn*, "stone of deliverance," because it eases childbirth. It is enough to place the stone on the belly of the woman giving birth, but as there are two stones, one male and the other female, only the second one has this ability.

We should finally note that in Norway it is called "victory stone" (*sejerstenen*).

✦ *corvina, corvina lapis*; MFr. *pere de corf, pierre del crot, cormux, corvine.*

📖 Lapidary of King Philip 72; Leonardi II, 7, 54 and 64; Anglo-Norman lapidary 13; *Phisice* 84.

📖📖 Jón Árnason, *Íslenzkar Þjóðsögur og Æventýri* (Leipzig: J. C. Hinrich, 1862–1864); Aukusti Vilho Rantasalo, *Einige Zaubersteine und Zauberpflanzen im Volksaberglauben der Finnen*, FFC 176, (Helsinki: Suomalainen Tiedeakatemia, 1959), 3–15.

Cos: The "sharpening stone."

✦ MFr. *queux*; MHG *wetz stain*; MSp. *piedra de aguzar*; Ar. *faischur*; Heb. *kisur.*

📖 Dioscorides V, 167; Isidore of Sevilla 16, 3, 6; Luka ben Serapion 54; Bartholomaeus Anglicus XVI, 23; *Lapidario* 250; Konrad von Megenberg VI, 27; Closener co 369; *Hortus sanitatis* V, 45.

Cotoice: See *cocrice*.

Crane Stone:
The Middle Ages were well acquainted with the story that maintained the crane would hold a stone in one of its claws to prevent itself from falling asleep. Conrad of Muri (1206–1281) echoes this tradition in his work. Another tradition informs us that cranes use stones

for ballast when facing the wind during their migration. After they have crossed the sea, they get rid of them. The authors reporting this have relied on the accounts of sailors who have often described stones falling down on them, or nearby to them, from the sky.

 Solin 10, 12; Brunetto Latini I, 163.

Crapaudine: In 1644, Anselm Boëtius de Boodt informed us: "The stone of the toad that some call *borax, chelonite,* or *crapaudine* from the French word *crapaut* and others *garatroine,* is called by the Germans *Crotenstein.* For it is a vulgar rumor that they are spit out by old toads; whereas others believe it is the skull . . . Some call it *bactachite,* others *brontia* or *ombria.*" The confusion of the *crapaudine* with the various other stones that can be found in the present dictionary is quite apparent. Only *borax* and *batrachites* are alternate names for this stone.

 Anselme Boetius de Boodt, *Le Parfait Joaillier ou Histoire des pierreries,* Lyon, 1664, 385f.

Crasmuez: See *tarnif.*

Crateritis: This is a gem whose color falls somewhere between that of the *chrysolith* and the *electrum.* It is extremely hard.

 Pliny 37, 154; Meliteniotes v. 1164; Damigeron 34.

Crasmif: See *tarnif.*

Crimodee: See *cinediae.*

Crisanterinus: A fragile gem whose color tends toward yellow. When hung from the necks of consumptives, it heals them. When hung from a child's neck, it banishes toothache.

 Leonardi II, 7, 61.

Crisolamsis: See *chrysolampsis.*

 📖 *Summarium Heinrici* VI, 6, 4; Leonardi II, 7, 6.

Crisopilon: The name for a kind of sapphire.

 📖 Leonardi II, 7, 80.

Crisoprassus: According to a later tradition, this is a green Indian gem that confers grace upon its wearer, brightens the eyes, and heals paralysis and sprains. See *chrysoprasus.*

 ✦ *crisopasius, crisoprasius, crisopasion, crysoprasyon, crysoprassen, crisopressus, crispassus;* MFr. *crizopas, crisopras, grisopars.*

 📖 Marbode 15 and 60; *Summarium Heinrici* VI, 4, 5; VI, 5, 14; *De lapidibus preciosis* 15; Arnoldus Saxo 21 and 25 Thomas de Cantimpré 14, 16; Konrad von Megenberg VI, 16; VI, 26; Mandeville I 20; Pseudo-Mandeville 21; Volmar 36; Leonardi II, 7, 48; 59 and 73; Closener cr 6.

Crocallis: A gem with the shape and color of a cherry.

 📖 Pliny 37, 154; Meliteniotes v. 1164.

Crocias: A stone named after a certain saffron-colored reflection that it possesses.

 📖 Pliny 37, 191; Meliteniotes v. 1164.

Crycalla: See *crocallis.*

 📖 Lambert de Saint-Omer 55, 81.

Cryphios: This stone is found on Mount Ida, but it is only seen when the mysteries of the gods are celebrated.

 📖 Pseudo-Plutarch §12.

Crystallus: It was once believed that the crystal was hardened ice. It was condensed by a hard freeze. Or it may at least be because it is found where the winter snows are iciest, hence the name it bears in Greek (*krustallos* = ice). The best cautery is a crystal ball receiving the rays of the sun. Attached at the level of the kidneys, it heals those who are suffering here. It enlivens the soul but fatigues the eyes and disrupts the strength of the nerves and eyes. It procures the favors of the gods and grants prayers. It is cold when taken out of the fire, but it will set fire to dry resinous wood, says Orpheus. Reduced to a powder and given to wet nurses, it increases their milk; it is sometimes necessary to add honey. If the stone has lost its virtue, it must be touched by a crystal then "it will confess the sin that caused it to lose its power." It is the stone of Sagittarius and the month of December; according to the Arab tradition represented by Belenus, its planet is the Moon.

It is used to make one of the talismans of Venus, which gives good fortune in commerce, makes the fortune of whoever devotes himself to its pursuit, and makes women love you. It may bear a variety of engravings. One depicts a woman holding a bird in one hand and a fish in the other; this crystal is therefore useful to fishermen and bird-catchers. If one carves on a crystal a man with the face of a lion and the feet of an eagle, holding on to a two-headed dragon sticking out its tail, and the man is holding a staff with which he strikes the beast's heads, he will compel the obedience of men and spirits and multiply his fortune. Another similar tradition concerns a crystal with a carving of a lion head or two-headed dragon with a small tail, or a man with a staff in his right hand, which is striking the lion head or the dragon's heads. This stone must be set on *aurichalque* [a copper alloy], placed on top of musk and amber. If you carry this on your person, all shall obey you and your wealth shall increase. This stone should be imprinted in wax and the seal then given to the person of your choice; he or she will then have the same powers.

A crystal or white jacinth on which is skillfully carved a bareheaded woman who has tousled her hair with her hands, and a man in front of her watching her from hiding so that she will do his will. The owner of this stone must keep it chastely and take twelve times its

Von dem Criftallen.

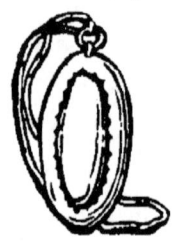

weight in gold to make a ring with a small piece of aloe wood beneath it. Whoever holds the ring in which this stone is set shall be found pleasing by any woman that lays eyes upon him; she will be unable to forget him. And she to whom he has made a request, if touched on the arm or hand with this ring, shall grant his wish immediately. If one finds the image of a griffin in a crystal, it will have the supreme power of filling the breasts with milk. This crystal must be set in archal (brass) or silver.

One should engrave the image of a lion-faced man with eagle claws on the crystal; the man shall have a two-headed dragon with its tail extended at his feet. This man should have a staff or wand in his hand to strike the head of the dragon. He who bears this stone will win the disposition of either sex, obtain the obedience of the spirits, increase his resources, and gather immense riches. This crystal should be mounted in brass atop musk and amber.

If a man seated on an eagle with a wand in his hand is depicted on a Vulcan stone or a crystal, and if this stone is mounted on a gold or copper ring, the person who sees this ring on the day of the Sun (Sunday) before the rising of that star, shall defeat and overcome all his enemies; if he sees it on Jupiter's day (Thursday), he shall win the war, and all will obey him of their own free will. It is necessary, though, that this ring's owner dress in white and abstain from eating pigeon.

Whoever finds the image of a woman with a bird in one hand and a fish in the other on the stone should know that it helps catch birds; it must be mounted on silver.

A virgin, a young girl, or even a torch carved on crystal possesses the power to protect eyesight.

Among the marvels recorded by Ibrahim Ibn Wasif Shah in the tenth century was the story of how, when Alexander the Great made his journey to the Land of Darkness, he saw an island with a crystal castle in the center of it that cast a glow above the neighboring sea. He sought to go ashore, but an Indian philosopher prevented him, saying, "any man who sets foot on this isle loses consciousness, is unable to leave, and dies there." It is specified that the castle is illuminated by candelabras that never go out. This brings to mind another stone, asbestos. This island is undoubtedly the one that al-Huwârizmi called the "Shining Castle" in his *Book of the Map of the World* (*Kitâb Sûrat al-ard*), which dates from the eleventh century. In the *Lanzelet* that Ulrich von Zatzihoven wrote toward the end of the twelfth century, the fairy (called an *Undine*) that kidnaps the hero dwells in a castle whose round earthwork was a crystal (v. 209–211). In *The Crown* (*Diu Crône*), an Arthurian romance written by Heinrich von dem Türlîn around 1230, Gawain reaches a castle surrounded by a crystal wall seventy-eight feet high, behind which mellifluous voices can be heard (v. 14272–283). In the popular Czech book *Stillfried und Bruncwig*, which dates from the sixteenth century, there is a crystal mountain simply called Karbunkulus. This motif crops up in numerous folktales; one of those collected by the Brothers Grimm (no. 197) mentions a crystal ball that breaks evil spells.

✦ *chrystallus, cristallus;* MFr. *crestail, cristal;* MHG *christallen, cristallar;* MSp. *cristal;* MDu. *kerstale;* Ar. *billaur, elicina.*

📖 Pliny 37, 23–29; Solin 15, 29–31; Isidore of Sevilla 16, 13, 1; Orpheus v. 171–90; Kerygma 1; Pseudo-Hippocrates 2; Marbode 41; Notker I, 42; *Summarium Heinrici* VI, 5, 8; Lambert de Saint-Omer 55, 89; Hildegard von Bingen IV, 20; Meliteniotes v. 1125; Psellos 12; Luka ben Serapion 42; Dimishqî II, 5, 6; XXXIX XLI; Lapidary in prose 40; 2nd lapidary in prose 31; Alphabetical Lapidary 25; Alexander Neckham v. 309ff.; *De lapidibus preciosis* 18; *De l'entaille des gemmes* 32; 46; *De la vertu des tailles* 37; 38; *De figura* 4; *Liber sigillorum Ethel* 8; Cambridge lapidary v. 1015–32; Arnoldus Saxo 23;

Bartholomaeus Anglicus XVI, 31; Thomas de Cantimpré 14, 19; Vincent de Beauvais VIII, 63; *Lapidario* 186; *Picatrix* II, 10, 44; 58; 61; 65; 76; 79; III, 1, 4; Lapidary of King Philip 26; Konrad von Megenberg VI, 19; Albertus Magnus 2, 3, 12; Jacob van Maerlant XII, 25; *Secrez* 3, 11; Pseudo-Mandeville 44; Saint Florian v. 860–75; Volmar v. 187–96; *Vocabularius ex quo* c 1137; *Liber ordinis rerum* 129, 6; *Hortus sanitatis* V, 39; Leonardi II, 7, 47; Closener cr 66; *Liber secretorum* II, 1, 19; *De virtutis lapidum* II, 11; *Poridat* 29; *Phisice* 47.

📖📖 Christa Tuczay, "Die Kunst der Kristallomantie und ihre Darstellung in deutschen Texten des Mittelalters," *Mediaevistik* 15 (2002): 31–50.

Curiallachaten: The *coralchate* resembles coral spattered with specks of gold.

📖 Pliny 37, 139; Solin 5, 26; Melitenotes v. 1163.

Curquemaf, Curcremaf, Curquemans: See *turcois*.

Cylindrus: This stone is found on Mount Cronius and every time Jupiter thunders, it rolls in terror down from the top of the mountain. It is no doubt *ceraunia*.

📖 Pliny 37, 20; Pseudo-Plutarch §19.

Cyamas: A black stone that when broken produces something similar to a broad bean.

✦ *cymea, cimea, cimata, clymata*.

📖 Pliny 37, 188.

Cyanea, Cyanus: Lazulite is a blue gem spattered with gold specks. The most beautiful *cyanea* is that from Scythia, next is that from Cypress, and finally that of Egypt. It is also divided into male and female stones.

✦ *cyanica, cyaneus, cyanos*.

📖 Pliny 37, 119; Dioscorides V, 91; Isidore of Sevilla 16, 9, 7; *Summarium Heinrici* VI, 4, 23; Lambert de Saint-Omer 55, 42; Pseudo-Dioscorides 2, 106; Leonardi II, 7, 70.

Cytitis, Cysitis: This stone is found in the vicinity of Coptos. It is white and seems to have a stone inside it that makes a noise when shaken. It is therefore a geode.

📖 Pliny 37, 154; Meliteniotes v. 1165.

Cymbra: Hiding behind this name is the ambergris that is "born from the whale." A Paris manuscript states: "The amber comes from this sea beast; however, there are those who declare it is born at the bottom of the sea. Others say that it is the foam of the whale, that enormous fish." Ambergris is by nature dry and warm, and varied in color. It is good for the stomach and all the viscera. It also procures joy. When ingested in a drink, it retards the appearance of the signs of aging. Another tradition says that ambergris is engendered by the breath of the whale and that it can be found at the bottom of the sea and at the mouth of rivers. It guards the virtues of the body, sharpens memory, and banishes sorrow and melancholy.

In *The Thousand and One Nights,* a shipwreck casts Sinbad onto a mountainous island during his sixth voyage. The stones are crystals, rubies, or other gems and "there is also a sort of fountain of pitch or bitumen that runs into the sea, which the fishes swallow and then vomit up again, turned into ambergris; and this the waves throw up on the beach in great quantities."

✦ *lambra;* MFr. *conte.*

📖 Alphabetical Lapidary 27; *Phisice* 85.

Cymedra: See *cinediae.*

📖 Lambert de Saint-Omer 55, 51.

Cytherins: This French name is the distorted form of *citrinus,* an abbreviated form of *hyacinctus citrinus,* designating a kind of jacinth. This "much gracious" stone is found in India. It must be set in gold. In the fifteenth century, people spoke of "yellow crystal" that was compared with "*safyr citrin.*" If one wears this stone around the neck or on the finger, one will be able to go everywhere safely, acquire honor and fortune, and be sheltered from evil spells. See *hyacinthos*.

📖 3rd Lapidary in prose 14; *Phisice* 48.

Cysteolithos: A yellow-and-white stone that is found in sea sponges. It is good against bile stones if drunk with wine. Fastened around the necks of children, it will heal their coughs.

📖 Leonardi II, 7, 62.

D

Daphnea: Zoroaster considered daphnea a remedy against epilepsy, and a French lapidary says:

> *Qui cette pierre portera,*
> *Jamais diable ne lui nuira*
> *Ni fluxum sanguinis n'aura,*
> *Ni hydropique sera.**

♦ dapnia, daphnion, daphinion, daphnius, daphnich(os), danich; MFr. dapimon.

📖 Pliny 37, 157; Damigeron 32; Alphabetical Lapidary 33; Meliteniotes v. 1143; Bodl. Digby 13 30.

De Capitis: This is a stone that is found in the head of the kite (or vulture), as is indicated by the title of the section of a Brussels manuscript (*De lapide capitis milvi*) and the *Phisice*: "the stone found in the head of the

---

*Translation: Whoever shall wear this stone / Never devil shall harm / Nor ever suffer the bloody flux / Nor be afflicted by dropsy.

escoufle [kite]." It is therefore a bezoar. It is black and reddish brown. It is highly valued by merchants and sailors because he who wears one can never be deceived about merchandise; in addition, it attracts buyers. It may be identical to the *quanidros* (see *quanidros*).

 📖 Lapidary of King Philip 87; Pseudo-Mandeville 64; *Phisice* 106.

Demath, Del Mach: It is alleged that this stone was discovered in the Garden of Olives when Christ was buried. Nicodemus and Joseph washed the Lord's wounds, and Nicodemus cast the bloodstained water on the stones on the ground there. They immediately changed color. All possess the virtue halting of blood flow, facilitating childbirth, and healing fevers and illness if one drinks the water in which they have been washed. They clear the eyes, provide protection from evil spirits and sudden death, procure divine grace, and increase devotion. It is possible that the name for this stone is a distorted version of that of hematite, which is suggested by the spelling "*mathice*" that has been detected in a manuscript.

 📖 Pseudo-Mandeville 67; *Phisice* 106.

Demonius, Deimonis: A bicolor gem resembling an *iris:* Johannes von Caub conflates the two stones with one another. It is good against fever, expels poisons, gives shelter to its bearers from their enemies, and gives them victory.

 📖 Meliteniotes v. 1191; Arnoldus Saxo 26; Albertus Magnus 2, 4, 1; Vincent de Beauvais VIII, 63; Konrad von Megenberg VI, 28; *Hortus sanitatis* V, 48; Leonardi II, 7, 88.

Dendrachates: This is an arborescent agate, or *eupetalos,* that contains diaphanous portions inside and a honey-colored part and another part the color of wax on the outside. It is found in the Indus. It renders one persuasive, enterprising, and ingenious and gives its bearer prosperity. It is also considered capable of easing thirst and sharpening eyesight, as well as healing intermittent fevers and poisoning. In Rome, it was the stone of gardeners and cultivators, and when it was attached to the arm or the plow, it would ensure a bountiful harvest. Carved on it would be a standing Hermes holding a purse in his left hand and a book in his right hand, with a cynocephalic creature (ape) at his feet, holding his hands as if in prayer.

 📖 Pliny 37, 139; Orpheus 3–4; Kerygma 3 and 41; Meliteniotes v. 1144; Marbode Lapidary, 1st Romanesque translation II.

Dendritis: White *dendritis* buried beneath a tree that one desires to chop down will ensure that the blade of the axe will never be blunted. To make an amulet of this stone, a peak over a sea dragon should be carved on it; when combined with grass from this peak, it allows one to compel the obedience of wild animals and find success in all undertakings: men will love you and listen to you. According to Notker, the *dendritis* is the stone of Libra and the month of October.

 ✦ *dentris.*

 📖 Pliny 37, 192; Kerygma 41; Pseudo-Hippocrates 29; Notker I, 41; Meliteniotes v. 1143; *Kyranides* 1, 4; *Secrez* IV, 4.

Derondor: See *diadochos.*

Diacodos: See *diadochos.*

Diadochos: In Greek, this word means the "replacement." This stone, which is similar to beryl, is used in hydromancy—"*Diadochos* is good for those who seek to divine secrets through water, and no stone is better than this"—because it causes the images of demons to appear in the water. It is very potent in necromancy but because it is a sacred stone, it will lose its power if it touches a dead person.

 If the figure of a standing man is carved on a *diadochos,* holding an offering in his right hand and a serpent in the other, with an image of the sun over his head and a lion sleeping at his feet, and if it is affixed to a lead ring with a little mugwort and fennel root, and if you then wear this ring to the river's edge and invoke evil spirits, the latter shall respond to your questions.

✦ *diadochuus, dyadochen, diacodos, diacoda, diacodus, dyadotos, dyadotus;* MFr. *diacodos, diadocode, dyadique, dyadice, dyascotos, siadocus;* MHG *diadochío, dÿadotes.*

📖 Pliny 37, 157; Damigeron 5; Marbode 57; Alphabetical Lapidary 32; Lapidary in prose 43; Meliteniotes v. 1144; Lapidary of Marbode, 1st Romanesque translation LVII; *De lapidibus preciosis* 25; Cambridge lapidary v. 1293–1310; Wolfram von Eschenbach 791, 28; *Liber sigillorum Ethel* 23; Arnoldus Saxo 27; Bartholomaeus Anglicus XVI, 36; Thomas de Cantimpré 14, 26; Vincent de Beauvais VIII, 64; Albertus Magnus 2, 4, 2; Lapidary of King Philip 53; Konrad von Megenberg VI, 31; Jacob van Maerlant XII, 30; Volmar v. 682–709; Saint Florian v. 726–43; *Hortus sanitatis* V, 49; Leonardi II, 7, 89; Closener di 9; *Phisice* 61.

Diane, Dyane: A clear stone, similar to a fingernail (like onyx), that can be found on the islands of the Indian Ocean and develops in the stomach of fish over a three-hundred-year period. It is then cast ashore by the sea where it is found. It possesses hemostatic properties and helps the eyes.

✦ MItal. *diana.*

📖 *Sidrac* 18; *Libro di Sidrach* chap. 471.

Dieu Amant: French spelling for diamond. See *adamas (I)*.

Dionysias: A hard, black gem with red patches. It imparts the flavor of wine to water in which it is steeped and its odor is generally believed to offer protection against inebriation.

✦ *dionysia;* MFr. *dionise, dionisie;* MHG *djonîsîâ, dÿonisia.*

📖 Pliny 137, 157; Solin 37, 18; Isidore of Sevilla 16, 4, 7; 16, 11, 8; Marbode 58; Lambert de Saint-Omer 55, 58; Alphabetical Lapidary 34; Lapidary in prose 44; Meliteniotes v. 1145; Bodl. Digby 13 31; *De lapidibus preciosis* 24; Cambridge Lapidary v. 1311–22; Lapidary of Marbode, 1st Romanesque translation LVIII;

Sidrac 18; Wolfram von Eschenbach 791, 10; Arnoldus Saxo 28; Bartholomaeus Anglicus XVI, 35; Thomas de Cantimpré 14, 25; Vincent de Beauvais VIII, 64; Albertus Magnus 2, 4, 3; Lapidary of King Philip 54; Konrad von Megenberg VI, 30; Jacob van Maerlant XII, 29; Saint Florian v. 734–43; *Poridat* 24; *Phisice* 62.

Diphryges: A variety of pyrite.

✦ *difrigus, friguus.*

📖 Pliny 34, 135; Damigeron 58 and 63; Pseudo-Dioscorides 2, 143; Lombard Dioscorides 129.

Diphyes: This describes a dual stone that is black and white, male and female, with a simple line separating the characteristics of the two sexes.

✦ *diffyes, diphres, diaspes, dipses.*

📖 Pliny 37, 157; Damigeron 56; Meliteniotes v. 1114.

Doctus Lapis: Another name for *chrysolite*.

📖 Leonardi II, 7, 93.

Donatides: This is a stone that resides in the head of an old rooster that can be obtained in the following manner. The rooster's head is placed in an anthill and after the ants have devoured the flesh and brain, the *donatides* can be found. It grants victory and makes it possible to obtain what one requests of princes. It is also called *radianes*—see *radaim*—and may be identical to the *doriatides*.

📖 Pseudo-Mandeville 59.

Doriatides: A sparkling black gem found in the head of the murex after ants have eaten it. Some claim that it comes from the head of a chicken, like the *radaim*. It is good for granting one's wishes. See also *donatides*.

📖 Leonardi II, 7, 92.

Dracontia, Draconitis: *Dracontia* or *draconitis* is diaphanous white, resists polishing or carving, and comes from the brain of dragons, but "will not become a gem unless the head is cut off while the beast is still alive, because otherwise the animal will spoil it out of spite when it feels itself on the verge of death," the ancients say. Consequently, the dragon is decapitated while sleeping. Sotacus, who writes that he saw this stone at a king's residence, says that those who hunt it travel by two-horse chariot and, when they catch sight of the dragon, they release stupefying drugs and decapitate the animal after it has fallen asleep. If it is worn on the left arm, one will vanquish all one's enemies. Camillo Leonardi believes it is the same stone as the *dentritis,* the *draconius,* and the *obsianus.*

Herodotus recorded the following legend (*Histories* III, 8–9):

> The pupil of a dragon's eye is a blazing stone . . . This is how the Indians capture it: they embroider magic symbols on a scarlet cloth and place it in front of the beast's lair; these symbols are a charm that causes a sleep through which the dragon's eyes are overcome, whereas otherwise they are unyielding. To obtain this slumber, the Indians say many incantations that cause the dragon to stick his neck from his hole and fall asleep under the influence of the magic signs. The Indians then hurl themselves upon him while he remains immobilized, killing him with axes, cutting off his head, and taking the stones found there. Our heroes say that a mountain of brightly colored stones can be found in the dragon's head, stones with a

thousand hues and mysterious properties, similar to those possessed by the ring of Gyges [i.e., it makes one invisible].

Fra Mauro (circa 1385–1460) also mentions *draconite*, without naming it: "There are several dragons with a stone in their foreheads; they cure illness. When the inhabitants wish to slay the dragons, they make a huge fire in the bushes of the mountains. The thick smoke kills the beasts, then their heads are chopped off and the stones removed."

✦ *dracontitis, dracontites, dracontias, drachonitis, draconitides, drachontos, draconius, dentrites;* MFr. *dracomde;* MHG *drachenstain.*

📖 Pliny 37, 158; Solin 30, 16; Isidore of Sevilla 16, 14, 7; Kerygma 49; Lambert de Saint-Omer 55, 67; Meliteniotes v. 1146; Alphabetical Lapidary 35; *De lapidibus preciosis* 23; Thomas de Cantimpré 14, 24; Vincent de Beauvais VIII, 63; Albertus Magnus 2, 4, 4; Lapidary of King Philip 85; Konrad von Megenberg VI, 29; Jacob van Maerlant XII, 28; *Vocabularius ex quo* d 562.1; Pseudo-Mandeville 63; Closener dr 76; *Hortus sanitatis* V, 47; Leonardi II, 7, 90; *Liber secretorum* II, 1, 40; *Phisice* 101.

Dragon Stone: A bezoar. See *dracontia*.

Dre Concides:

Although the name is obviously a distorted form of *draconitis* (see *dracontia*), Mandeville's description of the stone is quite different. It is born from the encounter of several snakes that join their heads together and blow; it is therefore what is called a serpent's egg, *ophites serpentarius* in 1643, or a "viper's knot." It is black with a little white in the middle, inside of which a snake can be seen. It is effective against venom and keeps it bearer safe from the bites of venomous snakes and reptiles, and one can even grab serpents barehanded without fear and without getting hurt.

During the first century CE, Pliny the Elder reported this:

There is a sort of egg in great repute among the Gauls (*ovarum genus in magna fama Galliarum*), of which the Greek writers have made no mention. A vast number of serpents are twisted together in summer, and coiled up in an artificial knot by their saliva and slime; this results in a ball called a "serpent's egg" (*anguinum*). The druids say that it is tossed in the air with hissings and must be caught in a cloak before it touches the earth. The person who thus intercepts it, flies on horseback; for the serpents will pursue him until prevented by a river that makes a barrier between them and him. This egg, though bound in gold, will swim against the current. And as the magicians are cunning to conceal their frauds, they pretend that this egg must be obtained at a certain age of the moon. I have seen that egg, as large and as round as a common-sized apple, in a chequered cartilaginous cover, and worn by the druids. It is wonderfully extolled for the winning of lawsuits, and for access to kings. It is a badge that is worn with such ostentation, that I knew a Roman knight, a Vocontian, who was slain by the stupid emperor Claudius, merely because he wore it in his breast when a lawsuit was pending.

This is what was said of the serpent's egg in the Middle Ages: it would be found where snakes gathered to hold court with their king. Whoever carries this round or oval stone, which is the size of a phalange, is assured of winning any court case. Carried in the mouth or a pocket, or on the skin, it makes one invisible and it will open any locks it touches. The serpent's egg heals the diseases of both men and livestock, and it accompanies its owner to the tomb. In Bohemia, the *ophites serpentarius* was reputed to protect against poison, the plague, and spells. See *dracontia* and *ophites*.

📖 Pliny 29, 52; Pseudo-Mandeville 63; *Phisice* 102.

📖📖 G. Chauvet, "Ovum anguinum," *Revue archéologique* 1 (1900): 281–85; Aukusti Vilho Rantasalo, *Einige Zaubersteine und Zauberpflanzen im Volksaberglauben der Finnen,* FFC 176 (Helsinki: Suomalainen Tiedeakatemia, 1959), 16–35.

Drinyllus Stone: This stone, which looks like sardonyx, is found on Mount Drinyllus near the Euphrates. Stepped in lukewarm water, it cures weak eyesight.

📖 Pseudo-Plutarch §21.

Drosolithus: A gold-colored gem named after the dew. It was also called *Iovis gemma,* "Jupiter's gem." Fire causes it to render a liquor similar to perspiration.

✦ *drosolithos, drusolithos, droselitus, droseritus, proselitus, chrysolithus.*

📖 Pliny 37, 170; Isidore of Sevilla 16, 12, 2; *Summarium Heinrici* VI, 5, 4; Meliteniotes v. 1145; Alphabetical Lapidary 74; Vincent de Beauvais VIII, 63; *Hortus sanitatis* V, 48; Leonardi II, 7, 91.

Dryitis: A stone that takes its name from the tree trunks; it burns like wood.

✦ *driyt(h)es, drytis.*

📖 Pliny 37, 188; Meliteniotes v. 1145.

Dryops: This stone provides a good crossing for those traveling at sea.

📖 Nautical lapidary 4.

Dyamas: See *adamas (I).*

✦ MHG *demant.*

📖 Volmar v. 294–345; *Vocabularius ex quo* d 30.8; *Secrez* 3, 21; Closener di 17.

E

Eagle Stone: A bezoar. See *aetites*.

Echistes: Another name for the *aetites*.

✦ *ethyces*.

📖 Lapidary of King Philip 35; Leonardi II, 7, 111.

Echitis: The name for this stone is formed from the Greek word meaning "viper," a reptile whose color it shares. It protects from serpents, gives light to the eyes, relieves headaches, and restores lost vitality.

✦ *echites, echyten, echidnes*.

📖 Pliny 37, 187; Solin 37, 17; Isidore of Sevilla 16, 15, 18; Orpheus 15; Kerygma 15; Marbode 25; *De lapidibus preciosis* 27; Meliteniotes v. 1151; Konrad von Megenberg VI, 33; Pseudo-Mandeville 27; Closener ec 3; Leonardi II, 7, 112.

Ecisopase: See *chrysoprasus*.

Ectenius: This stone is helpful to hunters and bird-catchers.

📖 Bodl. Digy 13 42.

Efestes, Effestin, Efestitis: See *hephaestitis*.

📖 *Hortus sanitatis* V, 53; Leonardi II, 7, 107.

Elaphoceratitis: The "stag horn" increases hair growth and procures understanding in marriage. It gives its bearer long life and mutual love, and it grants harmony to young married couples. Charred and thinned with wine and applied to the gums, it consolidates wobbly teeth; charred and washed, it heals dysentery and stomach problems in general. Crushed in oil, it will make hair grow back.

📖 Orpheus v. 244–59; Kerygma 4, Pseudo-Hippocrates 31.

Elatrest: A white stone that grows in Africa. Its nature is such that it cannot be heated. In the Lapidary of King Philip, it is no doubt *chalacias* (*gelace* in Middle French).

📖 Lapidary of King Philip.

Eldor: In the Spanish sea there is a stone that grows during a certain time of the year and detaches from the shore; it is created by the pounding of the waves and is called *eldor*. Alexander the Great discovered it when he reached the Land of Darkness. It is light in weight and floats on the surface of the sea at night, but when the sun rises, it plunges back beneath the waves. The Macedonian used it during his campaigns to surprise his enemies and defeat them. It is very likely pumice stone; see *pumex*.

✦ *lapis qui occultatur de die et apparet de nocte.*

📖 Luka ben Serapion 35; *Aristoteles de lapidibus* 376, 12ff.

Electioni: For Leonardi (II, 7, 10), this is another name for jayet or jet (*gagates*).

Electrepe: See *heliotropium*.

Electrides: According to Pliny the Elder, this is the name for amber in Brittany.

 Pliny 37, 35.

Electrum: A name for amber taken from the Greek *elektron*, which is called this because the Sun bears the name of Elector. Its creation is explained as follows: When Phaeton was struck by lightning it caused his sisters to weep so greatly they were changed into poplar trees. Every year their tears produced *electrum* on the shores of the Eridanus River, which is thought to be the Po River. Demostratus calls amber *lyncurion* and claims it comes from lynx urine and that the male urine produces a fiery red stone, while the urine of females produces one that is white and not as strong. Others have called it *langurium*. The Germanic peoples called it *glessum*, and it is for this reason that the Romans, when the Germanicus had a fleet in this area, gave the name of Glessaria to one of the islands, which in the language of the barbarians was called Austravia. When rubbed, amber attracts straw. See *succinum*.

 Pliny 4, 30, 2; 37, 33 and 127 and 152; 184f.; Lambert de Saint-Omer 55, 38; Meliteniotes v. 1154; Psellos 9; Bartholomaeus Anglicus XVI, 38.

 Eckhard Meineke, *Bernstein im Althochdeutschen,* Studien zum Althochddeutschen 6 (Göttingen: Vandenhoeck & Ruprecht, 1984).

Elidros: See *enhydros*.

 Closener el 29.

Eliotropia: See *heliotropium*.

✦ *electropia, elitropie, elytropius, elitropia, elitropus, elecoprius, elotropia, eliotrapia, alotropie, aldropi, latroe, alocripq;* MHG *sunnenwendl.*

📖 Marbode 29; *Summarium Heinrici* VI, 4, 10; Lambert de Saint-Omer 55, 29; Bodl. Digby 13 7; *De lapidibus preciosis* 28; Arnoldus Saxo 30; Thomas de Cantimpré 14, 29; Albertus Magnus 2, 5, 2; Konrad dvon Megenberg VI, 34; Volmar v. 450–61; *Secrez* 3, 10; Saint Florian v. 780–811; Leonardi II, 7, 94.

Elonia: According to Camillo Leonardi, this would be another name of the *siritis*.

📖 Leonardi II, 7, 79.

Elopsitis: A stone that is not at all beautiful but which has sovereign virtues against headaches and migraines, if one attaches it to his or her person.

📖 Leonardi II, 7, 108.

Emathites: See *haematitis*.

✦ *emathisten, emathitis, emathittes, ematites;* MHG *emathîtes.*

📖 Kerygma 22; Marbode 32; *Summarium Heinrici* VI, 2, 13; Bodl. Digby 13 33; *De lapidibus preciosis* 26; *De la vertu des tailles* 47; Lombard Dioscorides 153; Arnoldus Saxo 31; Alphabetical Lapidary 40; Wolfram von Eschenbach 791, 10; Thomas de Cantimpré 14, 27; Albertus Magnus 2, 5, 3; Konrad von Megenberg VI, 32; *Vocabularius ex quo* e 133; Leonardi II, 7, 95.

Emerald: See *smaragdus*.

📖 Pseudo-Mandeville 7 and 32.

Encardia: Also called *ariste, encardia* comes in three varieties: the first is black with a figure in relief on it that resembles a heart, the second is green and has the shape of a heart, and the third is all white except for the black heart it bears. It is said to come from Spain.

✦ *enariste, encariste, etariste, excardia, in arcadia.*

📖 Pliny 37, 159; Meliteniotes v. 1147.

Enchanted Stone:

During his travels in the Far East, Marco Polo reported that soldiers of the Grand Khan were unable to slay eight men with their swords, or decapitate them, because of the precious stones they carried. They were stripped of their clothing and the discovery was made that each had a stone sewn under his skin beneath the right arm. This stone was so strongly enchanted and held such power that as long as they had it on their person, they could not perish by fire nor even be harmed by it. The barons had the men beaten to death with cudgels, after which they took their stones.

📖 Marco Polo, chap. CLXI.

Enhydros, Enhygros:

This stone is always perfectly round, smooth, and white, and resembles rock crystal. But when it is shaken a liquid can be heard moving within it, much like the yolk of an egg. It constantly exudes drops that are good for fever but never diminishes in size. For Marbode of Rennes, it is a stone that is continuously weeping tears. It should be noted that *enhydros* is also one of the names for the hydra in the Middle Ages.

✦ *enidros, enidrus, elidros, elider, elidron, etnydros, erudros, exidros;* MFr. *enidros, enidre, enydires, evidre, oyndros;* MSp. *endios.*

📖 Pliny 37, 190; Solin 37, 24; Isidore of Sevilla 16, 13, 9; Marbode 46; Lapidary in prose 45; Meliteniotes v. 1146; Alexander Neckham v. 299ff.; Cambridge lapidary v. 1129–48; Wolfram von Eschenbach 791, 18; Arnoldus Saxo 32; Bartholomaeus Anglicus XVI, 42; Thomas de Cantimpré 14, 30; Albertus Magnus 2, 5, 5; Marbode Lapidary, 1st Romanesque translation XLVI; Lapidary of King Philip 46; Konrad von Megenberg VI, 37; Jacob van Maerlant XII, 34; Saint Florian v. 672–81; *Hortus sanitatis* V, 53; Leonardi II, 7, 97; *Poridat* 28; *Phisice* 53.

Enorchis: A white gem whose fragments look like testicles when split in half.

 📖 Pliny 37, 159; Meliteniotes v. 1147.

Epignathion: There is no description of this gem that has been left to us. We do know that it requires the engraving of a hoopoe with a fish beneath its claws and that it must be set completely in gold and carried in a state of purity. It prompts diabolical apparitions, and one should not use it at night otherwise one shall see true phantasms or ghosts (*fantasmata*).

 📖 Damigeron 66.

Epimelas, Epymelas: A white stone whose surface casts a black reflection; this is merely the interpretation of its name.

 📖 Pliny 37, 161; Isidore of Sevilla 16, 9, 10; Lambert de Saint Omer 55, 53.

Epistites: This is the spelling that numerous authors have used to transmit their knowledge about the "Vulcan stone" (*hæphaeistes*). The gem is a fiery red. It cools molten bronze and drives grasshoppers away as well as clouds, hail, and tornadoes. It calms seditions and gives its bearer safety, and it should be placed over the heart. If it is cast into boiling water, it stops it from boiling and cools the water. See *hephaestitis*.

 ✦ *epistides, epitusdes, epistrites, epistuten, epischuten, epyscutes;* MFr. *espuytes, epistite.*

 📖 Marbode 31; Alexander Neckham v. 289ff.; Bodl. Digby 13 6; 44; Arnoldus Saxo 33; Marbode Lapidary, 1st Romanesque translation XXXI; Bartholomaeus Anglicus XVI, 43; Vincent de Beauvais VIII, 70; Albertus Magnus 2, 5, 4; Konrad von Megenberg VI, 35; Saint Florian v. 758–79; *Hortus sanitatis* V, 55; Leonardi II, 7, 98.

Erimodeus: See *cinediae*.

Erotylos: A gem that is also known by the names *amphicomos* and *hieromnemon*. It is praised by Democritus for the art of divination.

✦ *erythilos, erichilos.*

📖 Pliny 37, 160; Meliteniotes v. 1149.

Erysthallis, Erithallis: A white stone that reveals red tints when viewed at an angle.

📖 Pliny 37, 130; Dioscorides IV, 88; Meliteniotes v. 1149.

Estimion, Exmisson: A sparkling, brilliant, gold-colored stone with white reflections at its extremities. This is nothing other than *hormesion*.

📖 Leonardi II, 7, 100.

Eumeces: The Bactrian stone that resembles flint. Put under the head of the bed, it gives nocturnal visions that have the characteristics of oracles. It is a key to dreams.

✦ *eumeges, eumethes, eumetres, eumetis, emites.*

📖 Pliny 37, 160; Meliteniotes v. 1149; Leonardi II, 7, 103–4.

Eumithres: This gem is leek-green in color. The Assyrians call it the "gem of Belus," their most sacred god. It is much sought after for use in superstitious purposes.

✦ *eumerges, eumetres, eumetis, emites.*

📖 Pliny 37, 160; Meliteniotes v. 1150; Leonardi II, 7, 106.

Eunophius: Another name for *aetites*.

📖 Leonardi II, 7, 109.

Eupetalos: This stone, which is sometimes considered to be identical to the arborescent agate (*dendrachates*), appears in four colors: blue, fiery red, vermilion, and apple-green. It is a variety of jasper.

 📖 Pliny 37, 161; Orpheus v. 230f.; Kerygma 3; Meliteniotes v. 1150.

Eureos, Euneos: This stone resembles an olive pit and is streaked like a sea shell and moderately white. It is undoubtedly a fossil.

 📖 Pliny 37, 161; Meliteniotes v. 1146 and 1151.

Eusebes: This is said to be the stone from which the seat in the temple of Hercules in Tyre was made. The singular characteristic of this seat was that only the pious were able to rise easily from it. The converse of this can be found in the Arthurian legend with the perilous seat in which only the chosen few can sit without danger.

 📖 Pliny 37, 161; Meliteniotes v. 1150.

Evanthus: This is a gem used to make an amulet as follows: "In order to be loved, gracious, known to all, and dreaded by all, take the stone called *evanthus* and carve upon it the belly and quills of a sea urchin, its tail and its head(!) as if all were attached, then place beneath it some rocket root and a nightingale tongue, and set it all in gold or silver, and wear it. You will be beloved and given a warm welcome, and not only by men; devils and wild animals will flee your presence."

 📖 *Kyranides* 1, 5; *Secrez* 4, 5.

Evax: See *zignites*.

Exacolitus: See *hexecontalithos*.

 📖 *Summarium Heinrici* VI, 5, 6; *Hortus sanitatis* V, 52; Leonardi II, 7, 99, and 101.

Exhebenus: A beautiful white gem that goldsmiths use to burnish gold. It is said to be "holy and divine, and good medicine." It is used in a drink with wine to cure certain afflictions.

✦ *exebonos, exebenius, ebenus.*

📖 Isidore of Sevilla 16, 9, 11; Damigeron 8; *Summarium Heinrici* VI, 4, 33; Alphabetical Lapidary 39; Meliteniotes v. 1147; Bodl. Digby 13 32; Cambridge lapidary v. 1351–66; *Hortus sanitatis* V, 53; Leonardi II, 7, 102.

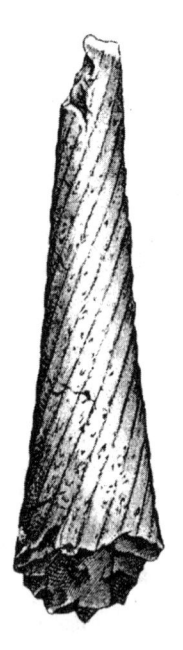

CERATITES LAPIS

F

Faihâr: A stone found in the East; it is transparent and has the color of jacinth. It destroys magic charms. If one drinks the equivalent of two barley grains of this stone, it heals madness and possession.

📖 Qazwînî (Ruska, 88).

Falconos, Falcones: For Johannes von Caub and Leonardi, this is another name for orpiment (*auripigmentum*) and arsenic. The lapidaries only examine it from the alchemical perspective. It is a "spirit" that, when calcinated, becomes black, and when sublimated, white. Counterfeiters use it to make copper look like silver.

📖 Arnoldus Saxo 36; Albertus Magnus 2, 6, 1; *Hortus sanitatis* V, 56; Leonardi II, 7, 116.

Fedus: See *medius*.

📖 Bodl. Digby 13 36.

Femur Stone: Giraldus Cambriensis, in his *Itinerarium Cambriae* (Journey through Wales; II, 7) says a bone that resembles a human femur can be found on an Irish island. It has the property of always returning to its original location after having been moved. Count Hugh of Slopesbury heard about this stone and had it bound fast with solid iron chains and cast into the sea. At dawn the next day it was found at its habitual place; he therefore forbid anyone from moving it. Giraldus added that if someone makes love by it or in its vicinity, the stone will immediately secrete large drops.

It should also be noted that in the *Historia Britonum* by Nennius (eleventh century), the author mentions a cairn in the land of Buelt, at the top of which is a stone that has the footprint of Cabal, one of King Arthur's dogs. If someone removes a stone from the cairn and carries it for the space of one day and one night, it will reappear on top of the pile the next day.

Fenicites: See *phoenicitis*.

 Alphabetical Lapidary 42.

Feripendamus: See *peridonius*.

 Liber secretorum II, 1, 5; *De virtutis lapidum* II, 4.

Fésteinn: See *livestock stone*.

Festinus: Another name for *hephaestitis*, from which the following talisman is made: "Take the *festinus* stone, also known as the Vulcan stone, and engrave upon it a flamingo with a scorpion at its feet, add a piece of sea holly root, and set all of it in gold or silver when the sun is in the sign of Scorpio, and keep this ring [this talisman] for it is the most precious jewel in existence against venom for whomever wears it. It works against all enchantments, witchcraft, and the evil visions that come at night when sleeping or keeping vigil. It is effective against the stones that cause the pissing of blood, and against bladder and kidney diseases. This ring must be made when the sun is in the sign of Scorpio, and kept safe, for it is very valuable." See *hephaestitis*.

 Secrez IV, 7.

Filacterium, Filaterius: Another name for *chrysolithus*. It is suggested for use as an amulet (phylactery).

   📖 Arnoldus Saxo 37; Albertus Magnus 2, 6, 2; *Hortus sanitatis* V, 53; Leonardi II, 7, 113.

Flammat: This stone is only mentioned by Volmar (thirteenth–fourteenth century) who devotes four verses to it. He who wears it shall never be tricked by merchants, nor deceived by anything else for that matter. It is undoubtedly amber.

   📖 Volmar v. 636–49.

Focarius Lapis: The "cook's stone"; another name for pyrite for the lexicologists Twinger and Closener (fifteenth–sixteenth century).

   ✦ *focaris, focares;* MHG *furstein.*

   📖 Isidore of Sevilla 16, 4, 5; Closener fo 3; pe 158.

Fongites, Flongites: See *phlogitis.*

   📖 *Hortus sanitatis* V, 56; Leonardi II, 7, 115.

Foringe: See *sorige.*

Frigius: See *phrygius.*

   📖 *Summarium Heinrici* VI, 2, 7; Lombard Dioscorides 150; Alphabetical Lapidary 41; Bodl. Digby 13 34; Leonardi II, 7, 117.

Fulmonius: See *memnonius.*

   📖 Bodl. Digby 13 35.

G

Gaenidea: See *paeanitis.*

📖 Pliny 37, 180.

Gagas: See *gagates.*

📖 *De lapidibus preciosis* 31.

Gagates: This is jet or jayet, sparkling pure black stone that is smooth, light, porous, and fragile, and will attract straw to it when rubbed. It has scarcely any difference from wood. It is a kind of fossilized lignite. There are also yellow and pale gray varieties. Jet comes from the bottom of the sea, according to a later tradition, and attaches itself to the hulls of ships from which it cannot then be detached. There is an odd thing about this stone: water sets it on fire and oil extinguishes it. When on fire, it drives away snakes and dispels hysteria. Its smoke "destroys devils" and is used to diagnose epilepsy when it is heated and held under the patient's nose. It restores women's periods and drives off serpents. As a decoction in wine, it heals toothache; mixed with wax, scrofula. Steeped in water, it strengthens the gums, and if a pregnant woman drinks this water, she will give birth.

Dioscorides used jet fumigations against epilepsy and Galen employed it in a plaster to heal wounds. Jet puts snakes to flight, opposes demons, destroys enchantments (*desfeit sorceries et charmes*), and can used as a stone to test chastity. There is no lock that jet cannot open. One legend maintains that Hercules wore a talisman made of jet.

Magicians used this stone in the practice of axinomancy (a divination method using an axe—it would be heated red-hot before the jet was placed on it) and swore that the stone would not burn if what the party desired was destined to occur. It also identifies virginity. It is crushed into a powder that is steeped in water. The water is then filtered and given to the girl being tested. If she is a virgin, she will be unable to urinate.

If you find the image of a proud, naked man on a *gagates,* along with the image of a well-dressed man holding a cup in one hand and a blade of grass in the other, it should be known that this stone has the power to bring relief to all persons who fall prey to fever, if you wear it on your person for three days. A piece of jet carved with a squill flower and worn in a ring protects against scorpion stings.

✦ *agastus, galerites, tabrites, lapis qui extinguit in oleo;* MFr. *jaiet, jayet, gaiet, gaiès, ghayet, galgate, geect, sayete, jades, gayde, laes, gagence;* MHG *gagâtes, aitstain, prennstain, bernsen, perlstain, permel;* ME *geete.*

📖 Pliny 36, 141f.; Solin 22, 11–12; Isidore of Sevilla 16, 4, 3; Aetios II, 24 and 34; Damigeron 20; Marbode 18; Orpheus v. 474ff.; Kerygma 17; Pseudo-Hippocrates 40; Dioscorides V, 128; Pseudo-Dioscorides 2, 146; Lombard Dioscorides 155; *Summarium Heinrici* VI, 2, 2; Meliteniotes v. 1123; Avicenna II, 2, 417; Lapidary of Marbode, 1st Romanesque translation XVIII; Alphabetical Lapidary 47; Avicenna II, 2, 324; Lapidary in prose 16; 2nd Lapidary in prose 21; Bodl. Digby 13 5; *De lapidibus preciosis* 31; Meliteniotes v. 1123; Cambridge Lapidary v. 453–82; Wolfram von Eschenbach 791, 15; *Liber sigillorum Ethel* 21; Arnoldus Saxo 38; Bartholomaeus Anglicus XVI, 49; Thomas de Cantimpré 14, 32f.; Vincent de Beauvais VIII, 22; Albertus Magnus 2, 7, 1; *Lapidario* 3; Lapidary of King Philip 25 and 47; Konrad von Megenberg VI, 39; Jacob van Maerlant XII, 37; Saint Florian v. 571–610; *Secrez* 3, 28; *Vocabularius ex quo* g 4; Leonardi II, 7, 123; Closener ga 7; *Liber secretorum* II, 1, 39; *De virtutis lapidum* II, 17; *Hortus sanitatis* V, 58; *Phisice* 24.

Gagatromeus:

A multicolored gem that resembles the hide of a roe deer; it grants victory if worn. "Hercules and Alcides were defeated every time they did not carry it on them," the texts state, forgetting that Alcides was one of the names of Hercules.

✦ *gagatronica, gagacromeon, gargatramea, gachatrameos, galgatromeus, gegatrom, geratrom, gelatromeus, bagates, agatromeus, agastus;* MFr. *gagatromé, gagatroméé, gagatromen, gagatoine, gagatroyne, galgataine;* MHG *gagâtromes, gickros, sycros, giticas, gythyros.*

📖 Damigeron 41; Marbode 27; Alphabetical Lapidary 45; Lapidary in prose 21; 2nd lapidary in prose 26; Wolfram von Eschenbach 791, 2; Bodl. Digby 13 37; *De lapidibus preciosis* 35; Cambridge lapidary v. 689–702; Lapidary of Marbode, 1st Romanesque translation XXVII; Arnoldus Saxo 39; Thomas de Cantimpré 14, 36; Albertus Magnus 2, 7, 2; Lapidary of King Philip 43; Konrad von Megenberg VI, 42; Jacob van Maerlant XII, 41 (*garotromeus*); Volmar v. 520–43; Saint Florian v. 541–54; *Secrez* 3, 28; Pseudo-Mandeville 27; Closener ga 8; Leonardi II, 7, 120; *Liber secretorum* II, 1, 24 (*gagatronica, bagates*); *De virtutis lapidum* II, 25; *Hortus sanitatis* V, 61; *Phisice* 33.

Gagites: See *aetites*.

📖 Pliny 10, 12.

Galacia: See *chalazias*.

Galacides: Another name for emerald. See *smaragdus*.

📖 Leonardi 11, 7, 133.

Galactitis: The "milk stone," from the Greek gala, is a milky white quartz that is found in the Nile and Achelous Rivers. *Galactitis* is always uniform in color, either that of milk or ash. The ancients gave it a dozen different names: *anactitis, leucogea, leucographitis, synectes, lithargum, gabatite, galbanites, lethargus (letheus), craterites, synechitis,* and *synnephitis*. In a thirteenth-century Anglo-Norman lapidary, these names became *mantiten, legraciten, smaragon, galbanicen, senechiten,* and *litargun*. This stone is ruled by Gemini. Crushed and added to water, it remarkably resembles milk in both taste and color. It is said to produce much more milk in nursing mothers and when attached to the necks of children with a string of blue wool, it produces a great deal of saliva, and it dissolves when placed in the mouth. It is also said to steal memory. Its wearer will find that the sovereigns of his country look kindly upon him. Crushed into a powder and mixed with brine, it will give good lactation to goats and ewes. It is helpful for eye sores and discharges if crumbled and smeared on the afflicted areas with water. It facilitates childbirth if attached to the leg of the woman in labor. Some call *galactitis* the emerald surrounded by white veins. In addition to its primarily medicinal properties, galactitis resists the evil eye and spells; whoever wears one will never be bewitched. Worn as an amulet around the neck, it protects children from wicked looks and enchantments, or else it can win you the friendship of men and dogs; finally, it grants victory.

For the twelfth-century Dominican author of *Rosarius*, *galactitis* represents the gentle piety of the Virgin Mary.

✦ *galaritides, galactides, galaricides, galatrides, gallantes, galaxias, galaxia, elebron, orachites, senochiten, graffites, galbates, lacteus lapis, leucographitis;* MFr. *galatine, galatade, callastida, alatide, alactide;* MSp. *galantes;* Ar. *alazal almares, zarocan.*

📖 Pliny 37, 162; Solin 7, 4; Isidore of Sevilla 16, 4, 20 and 10, 4; Aetios II, 14 and 17; Orpheus v. 191–229; Kerygma 2; Pseudo-Hippocrates 28; Dioscorides V, 132 and 134; 146; Lombard Dioscorides 159; Damigeron 34; Pseudo-Dioscorides 2, 150; Marbode 42; *Summarium Heinrici* VI, 2 18 and VI, 4, 28; Lambert de Saint-Omer 55, 48; Avicenna II, 2, 407; Lapidary of Marbode, 1st Romanesque translation XXXIX; Alphabetical Lapidary 46; Lapidary in prose 46; 2nd Lapidary in prose 32; Meliteniotes v. 1124; Alexander Neckham v. 315ff.; *De figura* 17; Cambridge Lapidary v. 1033–76; Wolfram von Eschenbach 791, 17; Arnoldus Saxo 41; Bartholomaeus Anglicus XVI, 50; Thomas de Cantimpré 14, 35; Vincent de Beauvais VIII, 5 and 73; Albertus Magnus 2, 7, 4; Lapidary of King Philip 48; Jacob van Maerlant XII, 40; *Lapidario* 61; Psellos 8; *Rosarius* 3; Leonardi II, 7, 119; Closener ga 21; *Poridat* 17; *Hortus sanitatis* V, 59; *Phisice* 49.

Galatia, Galatias, Gelacia: See *chalazias*.

📖 Pliny 37, 84; 121; 130; 173; *Summarium Heinrici* VI, 4, 29 and 5, 10; Lapidary of Marbode, 1st Romanesque translation XXXVII.

Galatides: A white translucent stone resembling an acorn that is as hard as diamond. It is so cold that fire cannot warm it. It curbs lust and anger. It is a remedy for all disorders caused by the heating of the body.

✦ *galactica, gelatia;* MFr. *galatude.*

📖 *Hortus sanitatis* V, 61; Leonardi II, 7, 121.

Galaxias, Galaxia: Called galactites by some, this gem is bisected by white or blood-red veins.

📖 Pliny 37, 162; Dioscorides V, 134; Meliteniotes v. 1142; Leonardi II, 7, 132.

Galertides: See *galactitis.*

📖 *De lapidibus preciosis* 34.

Galigus: A red and green stone the size of a hazelnut, which was called saigre in the sixteenth century. It was polished and set within a tin or lead ring. The woman who wore it could understand the hearts and thoughts of men and vice-versa. "It makes one friend to the heart of ladies and maidens, and women as well as men." If saigre is washed in white wine and this is then given to one's enemy to drink, your foe will love you. Whoever possesses saigre will be rich in material goods.

📖 *Phisice* 107.

Gallaica: A stone that resembles the argyrodamus, but a little dirtier; gallaica stones are found two by two or three by three.

✦ *callaica, gallerica.*

📖 Pliny 37, 110; Solin 20, 14; Isidore of Sevilla 16, 7, 10; Lambert de Saint-Omer 55, 28; Meliteniotes v. 1141.

Gallerica: See *gallaica*.

 📖 Leonardi II, 7, 125.

Gamaheus: The name for this stone was coined from the Arabic *kamaa* (relief), and indicates natural figures on stones. *Gamaheus* therefore relates to various gems such as agate and jasper. During the thirteenth century, this name was used to designate a stone with a white center encircled by black. It increases the bearer's wealth and renown. It should not be carried into battle on penalty of being defeated. Some lapidaries say it is the same as sardonyx. Paracelsus believed that *gamaheus* stones were natural talismans.

In 1394, Louis of Orleans founded the Canahieu, an order of knighthood whose members received a cameo depicting a porcupine as their insignia. See *camaeus, kauman*.

 ✦ *gamaho, kauman, kanmanu;* MFr. *camaheu, camahieu, camabieus, cachmahief, pierre de Ysrahel;* MHG *kammahu, kamman, gaman, kamachet*.

 📖 Volmar v. 636–49.

Garamantides: Another name for the *sandastros*.

 📖 *Hortas sanitatis* V, 59; Leonardi II, 7, 31.

Garatides: See *gelachide*.

Garatronicus: See *gagatromeus*.

 📖 Leonardi II, 7, 120.

Gasidana: See *aetites*.

Gassinnades, Gessidane: This stone comes from Media; it is the color of orobus and looks as if sprinkled with flowers. It can also be found in Arbelu. It is said that this stone conceives, and the admission of this conception can be wrested from the stone by shaking it. This conception lasts three months. The name is sometimes given as a synonym for *ethyces*.

 📖 Pliny 37, 163; Meliteniotes v. 1142; Leonardi II, 7, 127.

Gecolitis: See *tecolithos*.

 📖 *De lapidibus preciosis* 33; Lapidary of Marbode, 1st Romanesque translation LV; Jacob van Maerlant XII, 39.

Gelachide, Garatide: A blackish stone. It makes those who wear it friendly, gracious, and gentle. Placed in the mouth, it permits one to pronounce fair judgments, to form a clear opinion, and to know what others think of you.

Doctors perform the following experiment: in a place swarming with flies, they smear honey all over a person's body and have him hold this stone in his hand. If the flies and bees do not sting him, then it is a true *gelachide/garatide*. This experiment is the same as that for *hieracitis;* there is therefore good reason to believe *gelachides* is a deformation of that name. See *hieracitis*.

 📖 Lapidary of King Philip 48; *Hortus sanitatis* V, 60; Leonardi II, 7, 122.

Gelasia, Gelacia: See *chalazias*.

 📖 Alexander Neckham v. 283ff.; *De lapidibus preciosis* 32; Jacob van Maerlant XII, 38; Closener ge 5.

Gelatrest: See *elatrest*.

Genatides: See *donatides*.

Genninille: A stone found in the knee of the female kite, as indicated by the title of a section heading in a Brussels manuscript: *lapis de genu milve*. And the *Phisice* states, "The stone that is found in the knee of the kite." It restores love between married couples if glanced at quickly. It is small and it brings peace.

 📖 Lapidary of King Philip 88; Pseudo-Mandeville 65; *Phisice* 104.

Geodes: The stone earns this name because it contains dirt on the inside. It is excellent for ophthalmic concoctions and is also used for afflictions of the breasts and testicles.

 📖 Pliny 36, 140.

Geochitis: See *hieracitis*.

 ✦ *gerarchites, gerattides, garatides, gerachidem, beratiden.*

 📖 Alexander Neckham v. 288; *Liber secretorum* II, 1, 29; *De virtutis lapidum* II, 29.

Gerades: A brilliant red gem whose virtue is to protect men from aggressive birds.

 📖 Leonardi II, 7, 124.

Geranitis: This stone bears this name because its appearance is reminiscent of a crane's neck. It is a variety of agate.

 📖 Pliny 37, 187; Bartholomaeus Anglicus XVI, 52; Meliteniotes v. 1141.

Giant's Dance: The standing stones of Stonehenge have a legend that was vouched for and shaped early on by Geoffrey of Monmouth, Gervase of Tilbury, and others. In Hibernia (Ireland), mysterious stones possessing healing powers stood on Mount Kildare. Giants had brought them from the depths of Africa in an earlier age, placing them in their baths and thus healing their illnesses. They also mixed them with herbs to dress their wounds. Merlin the Enchanter brought them to Great Britain and placed them in their current site and stood them upright by means of magic spells.

📖 Geoffroy of Monmouth, *Historia regum Britaniae* chap. 128; Gervase of Tilbury, *Otia imperialia* III, 28.

Glossopetra: This stone looks like a human tongue. It is not engendered, or so it is said, in the earth, but falls from the sky during the lunar eclipse, and is essential for the practice of selenomancy [divination by the moon —*Trans.*]. This stone has the property of silencing the winds. In fact, it is a fossil that has been identified as the teeth of the Carcharodon megalodon, a Cenozoic era shark, and with the large triangular teeth of sharks.

Some ancient authors have confused the *glossopetra* with the *ceraunia,* believing it was the "dart of a lightning bolt," which is why it was called *donderkeil* (thunderstone) in German.

✦ *gulosus.*

📖 Pliny 37, 164; Solin 37, 19; Isidore of Sevilla 16, 15, 17; *Summarium Heinrici* VI, 6, 5; Meliteniotes v. 1143; *Hortus sanitatis* V, 62; Leonardi II, 7, 129.

📖📖 Caspar Bartholinus, *Dissertatio de glossopetris* (Copenhagen, 1704); Epistola itineraria XXIX, "De glossopetris et chelidoniis" (Wolfenbüttel, 1734); Fabio Colonna, De glossopetris dissertatio (Rome, 1616).

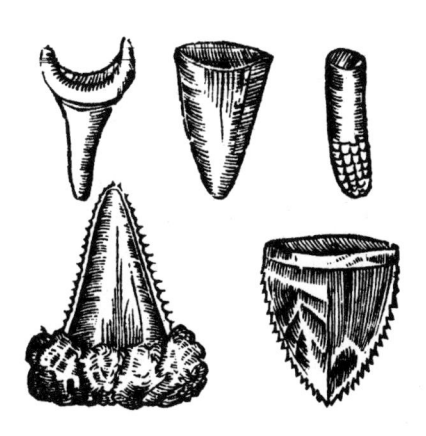

Gnathus: Engraved with an image of a diver (bird) on a fish of the same name, this gem provides truthful visions in bed. If an owl holding a glaucus fish in its claws is carved on it, and it is worn after the eyes of this fish have been enclosed beneath it, by abstaining from pig meat and all impurities, on the advent of darkness, one will appear to be a noble man inspired by the gods. During the day, everything one says will be believed.

 📖 *Kyranides* 1, 3; *Secrez* 4, 3.

Gogolitus: See *tecolithos*.

 📖 Closener go 2.

Goniaea: According to the magicians, *goniaea* helps us get revenge upon our enemies.

 ✦ *geniana, gemana, goone, gome, gonitea*.

 📖 Pliny 37, 164; Meliteniotes v. 1140.

Gorgias: Another name for coral or for *celidonius*. See *gorgonia* and *corallium*.

 ✦ *gorgonias, gorgia*.

 📖 Solin 2, 43; Leonardi II, 7, 45.

Gorgonia: The *gorgonia* is nothing other than coral, which has been given this name because while it is soft in the ocean, it becomes as hard as stone once it hits the air. The magicians declare it fights typhoons and lightning. *Gorgonia* has an effect on dreams, repels phantasms or ghosts, protects a house from lightning, and also protects against drugs, evil spirits, and grief. It dispels enchantments and banishes miasmas. Engraved with the image of a rat, dog, or the forefront of a gorgon, *gorgonia* protects one from the wrath of teachers.

✦ *grogias.*

📖 Pliny 37, 164; Meliteniotes v. 1142.

Grail, Graal: See *lapsit exillis.*

Grammatica Smaragpo:
This is how the lapidaries designate an emerald engraved with letters used for an amulet. The name indicates these are "Ephesian characters," one of the names for the magic signs used in the glyptic crafts.

📖 Leonardi II, 7, 26.

Granatus:
The garnet is a translucent red stone that is hot and dry. It is considered to be a variety of carbuncle or even a jacinth. There are two kinds, the red and the violet. It is supposed to rejoice the heart and banish sorrow, comfort the elderly, quench thirst, and to be good against all venomous animals. If one finds the image of a Lion on it, or an Astrolabe, in other words the constellations of the same name, skillfully carved on a garnet, the stone will have the power to preserve the body's health, honors, and spare its owner all illnesses. It also procures honors and protects its owner from the dangers of traveling.

Another carving is mentioned, that of Poseidon with a trident in his right hand and a dolphin by his right foot, but its virtue is not known.

✦ MFr. *granat, grenaz, grenat, garnaden;* MHG *grana(t);* Ar. *elzedi, albuzedi.*

📖 *De lapidibus preciosis* 30; Avicenna II, 2, 320; Luka ben Serapion 4; *De lapidibus preciosis* 4; Serapion c. 399 (*hager albuzedi*); Thomas de Cantimpré 14, 31; Albertus Magnus 2, 7, 7; *Picatrix* II, 10, 5; III, 3, 31; Lapidary of King Philip 23; Konrad von Megenberg VI, 38; Jacob van Maerlant XII, 36; Volmar v. 676–81; *Secrez* 3, 4; Mandeville I 8; Pseudo-Mandeville 10; *Liber defota anima* v. 2824–79; *Hortus sanitatis* V, 60; Ragiel 3; Solomon 9; Leonardi II, 7, 118; *Phisice* 9.

Green Jasper: Green jasper keeps one in good health and provides assurance, if it is kept chastely. It heals fever and dropsy, helps women in childbirth, makes its owner amiable and brave, and banishes ghosts. It must be set in silver. Various engravings are used to make talismans and amulets from this stone.

A stone engraved with the bust of a head prevents death at sea; otherwise a stag, a huntsman, dogs, or a Hare (the constellation of this name, i.e., Lepus in the Southern hemisphere) will cure lunatics, epileptics, those in a frenzy, and also affords protection from demons. "If the image is depicted on this stone of a man standing with firm footing and broad shoulders with a pouch of herbs hanging around his neck, know that this is useful for fever sufferers and will give them relief. A doctor who carries it will successfully identify illnesses, recognize the proper remedies, and provide good potions. It is useful against hemorrhoids and menstrual flow, and in all cases involving the loss of blood, which it will arrest immediately."

If an Aquarius has been carved on green jasper and carried on one's person, it will bring you profit in transactions, and merchants will seek your counsel. If a cross is carved on it, it is said to be able to prevent its owner from drowning. "If a green jasper is topped by the bust of a head, set it in a ring of gold or silver, bear it on your person, and you shall escape all deaths. Write the following letters upon the ring: B.B.P.P.N.E.N.A., and your body shall be spared from all illnesses, especially fever and dropsy, and the stone will offer you great assistance in hunting birds. And you shall be reasonable and congenial in all things, in times of war and in times of peace, this stone aids women to conceive and give birth; it brings peace and harmony and other good things to those who bear it. These latter should be of fair and honest conduct," says a lapidary attributed to Solomon.

 Lapidary of Marbode, 1st Romanesque translation IV; *De l'entaille des gemmes* 39; *Liber sigillorum Ethel* 17 and 24; *Lapidario* 20; Hermes 2; 4; Thetel 3; Solomon 2.

Grisoletus: See *chrysolithus*.

 📖 *Hortus sanitatis* V, 61; Leonardi II, 7, 130.

Grogius: See *corallium*.

 📖 Leonardi II, 7, 128.

Guers: A pale-red stone that is by nature hot and dry to the second degree and possesses astringent qualities. It is used for skin disorders; Avicenna also mentions red blotches as well as scurf patches, impetigo, and itching. It is good for cuts and ulcers. As a drink, it eliminates wastes from the body.

 📖 Avicenna II, 298.

Gulosus: See *glossopetra*.

Gurgum: See *lyncurium*.

 📖 Paris, National Library of France, French ms. 2009, folio 47 r°.

H

Haemachates: A variety of agate that is brown or red in color. It protects the eyes, and if dissolved in wine or water, is good against snakes. See *achates*.

📖 Pliny 37, 139; Solin 27, 25.

Hail Stone: See *chalazias*.

Haematitis: This is the "blood stone" whose name derives from the Greek αἱμα. The most beautiful hematites come from Ethiopia, but they can be found in Arabia and Africa as well. This stone, which is a ferruginous or reddish blood color, is found in mines. When burned, it looks like minium. It is burned in the same manner as Phrygian stone, but it cannot be extinguished with wine. Pulverized and saturated with wine, it will create a flame taller than the height of a man. It is claimed that it will reveal the treacherous designs of barbarians. Crushed and made into eyedrops, it facilitates one's knowledge and amorous relationships. It banishes blindness and reputedly cures all disorders of the eyes, the eyelids, the liver, and sexual diseases as well. It is recommended for the success of petitions addressed to rulers and is good in court cases and judgments. It guides human destinies.

Hematite improves formulations that include saffron. It is helpful against snakebite and grants victory in battle.

There is another kind of hematite called *menui* by the Indians and *xanthos* by the Greeks. It is a tawny color shading toward white. When ingested in a drink, it stops blood loss. People vomiting blood also drink it mixed with pomegranate juice. It is effective against bladder problems. It is drunk in wine to combat the wounds made by serpents. Mixed with sardonyx upon an inebriated man, it will make him sober. Hematite is useful for hunters trying to capture wild animals. It is used to manufacture one of the Sun talismans that protect its bearer from epilepsy.

Dimishqî attributes to it a powerful force of attraction that is increased when steeped overnight in the blood of a recently slain goat; it loses its properties if rubbed with garlic or smeared with saliva from an empty stomach. It will drive ants away if placed on an anthill. If the stone is worn in a ring, one's business affairs will meet with success. If a pregnant woman wears a hematite, she will have an easy childbirth; the same is true for an animal.

Magicians place it under the patronage of Mercury, its metal is lead, and its zodiac sign is Aries. Acording to Damigeron, freed men wore it with an engraving of Mercury sitting on a stone.

Engraved with a sword-wielding man sitting on a dragon, hematite makes it possible to see all the evil spirits that dwell in the limbs of man; one will also know where to find treasure. This engraving has the following variation: if one finds on a hematite the image of a man standing over a dragon, with a sword in hand, it should be set in a ring of lead or iron, and all the spirits that dwell in darkness shall obey you, revealing where treasures are located and how to find them.

A hematite on which is carved a spirited, foaming horse ridden by a black man holding a scepter has the power to give might to a king and bring about its owner's return in grace. It must be fixed upon an equal weight of gold and silver.

It should be noted that the French spelling *amatiste* for *haematitis* has caused many researchers to confuse this stone with amethyst.

✦ *aemathites, hematites, aematitis, ematites, emathites, emathytes;* MFr. *ematite, amatiste, mathice;* MHG *ematîtes, blotsten, blutstin;* Ar. *sedinech, scedenegi, sedine, sedina.*

📖 Pliny 36, 144; 37, 169; Solin 30, 34; Isidore of Sevilla 16, 8, 5; 16, 4, 16; Orpheus v. 642ff.; Kerygma 22; Pseudo-Hippocrates 3; Damigeron 9; Dioscorides V, 126; Pseudo-Dioscorides 2, 144; Avicenna II, 2, 241 and 665; Lapidary of Marbode, 1st Romanesque translation XXXII; Lapidary in prose 36; Dimishqî II, 6, 1; Alexander Neckham v. 293ff.; *Liber sigillorum Ethel* 6; Bodl. Digby 13 33; Cambridge lapidary v. 827–74; Wolfram von Eschenbach 791, 10; Bartholomeaus Anglicus XVI, 40; Vincent de Beauvais VIII, 68; Psellos 3; *Lapidario* 213; *Picatrix* II, 10, 4; 54; III, 3, 28; Jacob van Maerlant XII, 31; *Liber ordinis rerum* 129, 31; Chael 5; *Hortus sanitatis* V, 51; *Gart der Gesundheit* chap. 173.

Halasius, Halastus: See *balagius.*

📖 Saint Florian v. 389–96.

Hammites:
A stone that resembles fish roe; there is one variety that is said to consist of nitrate, yet is incredibly hard.

📖 Pliny 37, 167; Isidore of Sevilla 16, 4, 29.

Hammochrysos:
A gem that looks like sand mixed with specks of gold. Its description is simply a commentary on the name of the stone.

✦ *ammochrysus, amochrisus.*

📖 Pliny 37, 188; Solin 37, 13; Isidore of Sevilla 16, 15, 5; Lambert de Saint-Omer 55, 78; Leonardi II, 7, 140.

Hammonis Cornu: According to Pliny the Elder, the "horn of Ammon," ammonite, is one of the most revered gems of Ethiopia.

Gold in color and resembling a ram's horn, it is said to give prophetic dreams. It is a fossil that was considered magical because it came from a dragon (see *dracontia*). When a cow gives less milk than usual, this stone would be placed in the milk bucket.

Ammonite was also called *brontia, ombria,* and *ovum anguinum* (serpent's egg) from the Middle Ages into the Renaissance.

✦ *hamonis, hammonitis.*

📖 Pliny 37, 167; Leonardi II, 7, 136.

📖📖 Johann Jacob Reiskius, *Dissertatio de Cornu Hammonis,* 1688.

AMMONIS CORNV AVPEVM

Haneset: According to John Mandeville, this is the Indian name for diamond. See *adamas (I)*.

📖 Mandeville 2.

Harpax: See *succinum*.

Hanon, Hanom: This stone is created from the whale excrement that is swallowed by sea shrimp. It is nourished on water. Placed on a set of scales uncovered, it weighs nothing, but if covered with dirt, it weighs as much as lead. It renders people invisible and preserves bodily strength. This is yellow amber that has been confused with ambergris.

 📖 Pseudo-Mandeville 52; *Phisice* 90.

Helemetiz: An artificial stone that Aristotle is supposed to have created for Alexander the Great. It is composed of hellebore, white incense, lead, bones from a pig's hind feet, mandrake, lime, orpiment, and human blood. It is effective at preventing hail, rain, and snow.

 📖 *Picatrix* III, 10.

Heliotropium: Heliotrope, a green chalcedony with red patches today known as blood jasper or girasol, can be found in Ethiopia, Libya, Africa, and Cypress. It is leek-green in color and streaked with red veins. When placed in the rays of the setting sun, its reflected color is that of blood. Mandeville says its origin is from sea shrimp that have ingested "whale excrement." According to adepts of magic, when mixed with the plant of the same name (*solsequium*) or chicory, and with the help of certain incantations, heliotrope will confer invisibility on its bearer, and it is said that the famous ring of Gyges carried this stone. It preserves the body's force and causes water to boil, forming a small cloud. It summons rain, puts an end to nice weather, and gives the gift of prophecy, health, and long life. It obtains praise and renown, expels poisons, stops blood discharge, and prevents being fooled. Its powers are heightened if used with the herb of the same name and the correct spell. It is consecrated with the help of incantations (*carmine legitimo*) and characters, about which the lapidaries offer no details.

 According to Damigeron, this is the Sun stone; freemen wore it with a radiant sun engraved upon it, freed slaves had the head of a sun upon theirs, and slaves' heliotrope bore the image of an altar surmounted by a torch.

If the image of a bat is carved onto a heliotrope, it gives its owner power over demons, and it is useful for incantations.

According to Notker, who is repeating Martianus Capella on this point, heliotrope is the stone of Virgo and the month of September.

✦ *heliotropia, heliotropius, heliotropio, elitropia, eliotropia, elytropia, eleutropius, elentropio, eleytropius, eitropia;* MFr. *eleütropius, elyotropie, elyotrope, elpotroppe, oliotropie;* MHG *elitrôpîe, eljotrôpîâ, aldropi, alotropie, aldropy, latroe, abotropy, alotroppyge, sunnenwendel;* MSp. *elcutropia;* MItal. *girasole.*

📖 Pliny 37, 165; Solin 27, 36; Dioscorides IV, 190; Isidore of Sevilla 16, 7, 12; Damigeron 2; Notker I, 41; Meliteniotes v. 1153; Lapidary of Marbode, 1st Romanesque translation XXIX; Alphabetical Lapidary 37; Lapidary in prose 24; 2nd Lapidary in prose 19; Cambridge lapidary v. 737–74; Wolfram von Eschenbach 791, 7; Bartholomeaus Anglicus XVI, 41; *Liber secretorum* II, 1, 20; *De virtutis lapidum* II, 13; Lapidary of King Philip 33; Jacob van Maerlant XII, 33; Poridat 10; Pseudo-Mandeville 52; Ragiel 9; *Hortus sanitatis* V, 54; *Phisice* 35.

Hendemotuz: One of the artificial stones allegedly created by Aristotle for Alexander the Great. This one is composed of lead, bronze, molten iron, white and yellow sulfur, magnesium, diamond, gazelle's fat, horse's marrow or brain, sparrow's blood, pig bones, borax, and orpiment. The *hendemotuz* suppresses desire for women in men.

 📖 *Picatrix* III, 10.

Hepatites: This is the name for a kind of hematite, according to Socatus. It is called *hepatites* when raw and *militites* when calcined. It is good for burns.

 📖 Pliny 36, 147.

Hepatitis: A gem that heals liver diseases. Its name is coined from the Greek name for this organ.

 📖 Pliny 36, 147; 37, 186; Meliteniotes v. 1153.

Hephaestitis: Although it is radiant, this "Vulcan stone" found in Corycus, Cilicia, and in the sea has the property of mirrors to reflect images. It can be recognized immediately by putting it in boiling water, which it shall instantly turn cold. It heats cold water and, when exposed to the sun, sets dry wood alight. *Hephaestitis* protects the field from hail and grasshoppers, a property it shares with *lychnis*. The Vulcan stone is comparable to pyrite.

Worn over the heart, this stone provides security and curbs sedition and discord. The man who wears a *hephaestitis* on his left arm can sneer at all hardships and troubles. "The *hephaestitis* banishes far from the fruits of the earth swarms of grasshoppers, sterile clouds, and the harmful blows of hail . . . it keeps its bearer in safety when danger threatens. These stones should be carried (*esse gerondus*) on the chest at heart level," says Marbode of Rennes.

A hoopoe and a scorpion are engraved upon it; combined with the herb eryngo, the stone is a phylactery that sends nocturnal phantoms fleeing, dispels fascinations, and does good for those suffering from bile or kidney stones.

✦ *haephaestites, hefaeititis, hepesthitis, hepistitis, hephestionis, ephestis, epibretes, terristites, lapis Vulcani*; MFr. *epistite, epythiste, espite, epistes, aspitite, espuyte, aspice*; MHG *epistîtes*.

📖 Pliny 37, 166; Isidore of Sevilla 16, 15, 15; Damigeron 15; Meliteniotes v.1154; Marbode 31; *Kyranides* 1, 7; Lapidary in prose 35; Alphabetical Lapidary 38; Bodl. Digby 13 44; Cambridge lapidary v. 805–26; Wolfram von Eschenbach 791, 6; *Secrez* 4, 7; Lapidary of King Philip 36; *Liber secretorum* II, 1, 21 and 42; *De virtutis lapidum* II, 24; *Hortus sanitatis* V, 53 (efestes) and 55 (epistites).

Herbosa: According to Damigeron, the "herb stone" is the stone of Jupiter. Freemen wear it with Jupiter seated on an eagle, the freed men with an eagle hovering over a river, and slaves with an eagle holding a crown in its claws. According to R. Halleux and J. Schamp, *herbosa* might correspond with Pliny the Elder's *chloritis* (37, 156).

📖 Damigeron, *De lapidibus et eorum sculpturis* 7.

Herillicus: A naturally dry and cold stone that heals the body. Crushed into a powder and drunk in water, it is good against headaches; it cures baldness when the head is washed with this blend.

✦ *berillica*.

📖 Alphabetical Lapidary 16.

Herinaceus Lapis: A stone with the color of the tips of goshawk wings.

+ *herimac(h)ius, herinnachius.*

📖 Alphabetical Lapidary 50; Bodl. Digby 13 52.

Hermu Aedoeon: This stone is called "the sex of Hermes" because of the genital parts that it displays against a sometimes white, sometimes black, or sometimes pallid background, with a gold circle surrounding it.

+ *hermuredocon, hermeodes.*

📖 Pliny 37, 166; Meliteniotes v. 1148.

Hexecontalithos: The "stone of sixty colors" is a harlequin opal and is effective against colic and intestinal disorders if drunk after dissolving it in wine. It is found in the land of Troglodytica.

+ *hexaxontalithos, exacontalitus, exocontalitus, exacolit, exolicetus, exocontalitus, hexeconta;* MFr. *exacontalite, arecontadilles, arocondatiles, crocondatille;* MSp. *estanliço.*

📖 Pliny 37, 167; Isidore of Sevilla 16, 12, 5; Marbode 38; Lambert de Saint-Omer 55, 88; Meliteniotes v. 1148; Lapidary of Marbode, 1st Romanesque translation XXXVIII; Lapidary in prose 55; Cambridge lapidary v. 969–76; Arnoldus Saxo 34–35; Bartholomeaus Anglicus XVI, 44; Konrad von Megenberg VI, 36; Albertus Magnus 2, 5, 6–7; *Poridat* 25; *Hortus sanitatis* V, 50 (*exacontalitus*) and 52 (*exacolitus*); *Phisice* 42.

Hieracitis: It name means "falcon stone" and its appearance is reminiscent of the kestrel. Pliny says: "[this stone] is entirely covered with mottled streaks, resembling a kite's feathers alternating with black ones." To identify it, this stone is placed in the mouth, then smeared with milk and honey and exposed to flies and wasps. If these insects do not touch it, it is clearly a *hieracitis*. This black stone must be carried in the mouth; it brings favor and esteem, makes its bearer pleasant and friendly, lets you know what others think of you, makes you irresistible to women, and grants you great sexual prowess.

The *hieracitis* should be engraved with a goshawk above a sea frog, also with magic letters, and mounted on a ring made from magnetic stone. This stone is governed by the 26° of Aries.

✦ *hieracites, ieracitis, geracites, geraciten, gerarchyten, gerarchites, geranites, garatides, gerattides, gratices, gelaticum, yrachiten, jerachites;* MFr. *gerachite, geratique, geratice, genatides, genachille, yerachite, noire;* MHG *jerachites, geraite, meraîte, serate, berate, erutes;* MSp. *buitreña;* Ar. *abietityz.*

📖 Pliny 37, 167 and 187; Isidore of Sevilla 16, 15, 19; Kerygma 48; Aetios II, 30; Damigeron 26; Marbode 30; *Kyranides* 1, 22; Meliteniotes v. 1156; Lapidary of Marbode, 1st Romanesque translation XXX; *Alphabetical Lapidary* 65; Lapidary in prose 4; 2nd Lapidary in prose 29; Wolfram von Eschenbach 791, 7; *Lapidario* 26; Cambridge lapidary v. 775–804; Arnoldus Saxo 42; Bartholomaeus Anglicus XVI, 52; XVI, 102; Vincent de Beauvais VIII, 75; Albertus Magnus 2, 7, 6; Lapidary of King Philip 27; Konrad von Megenberg VI, 43; Jacob van Maerlant XII, 35; Volmar v. 484–501; Mandeville I 24; Pseudo-Mandeville 24; *Hortus sanitatis* V, 64; Leonardi II, 7, 135 (*hieracites* = *gelachides*); *Phisice* 27.

Hieromnemon: See *erotylos*.

📖 Pliny 37, 160ff.

Hismiris, Hysmeri: See *smyris*.

📖 *Summarium Heinrici* VI, 2, 22; Leonardi II, 7, 139.

Horcus: A synonym for *catimia*.

📖 Leonardi II, 7, 138.

Hormesion: This is one of the most delightful stones to look at: the color of fire, it gives off golden rays, the tips of which cast a white light.

✦ *hormiscion, hormision, ermistion, estimion, exmisson.*

📖 Pliny 37, 168; Isidore of Sevilla 16, 14, 11; Damigeron 14; Meliteniotes v. 1174; *Hortus sanitatis* V, 50; Leonardi II, 7, 137.

Hulinhjálmsteinn: This dark-red stone is called the "helmet of invisibility" in Iceland. In order to make oneself invisible, it must be kept beneath the left arm while holding the *sögusteinn* (saga stone) in the left palm. See also *náttúrusteinar, saga stone.*

📖 Jón Árnason, *Íslenzkar Þjóðsögur og Æventýri* (Leipzig: J. C. Hinrich, 1862–1864).

Human Stone: See *pyrophilus.*

Hyacinthizontes: This is the name given to an Indian gem that is akin to amethyst or resembles crystal. It has the characteristic of turning darker when touching hair.

✦ *hyacintizon, iacinctizonta chrysoprasi.*

📖 Pliny 37, 77; Solin 52, 63; Isidore of Sevilla 16, 9, 4; Kerygma 27; *Summarium Heinrici* VI, 4, 20; Lambert de Saint-Omer 55, 36; Alphabetical Lapidary 55.

Hyacinthos: Jacinths are a variety of zirconium silicate which is naturally white or red. It is produced in Ethiopia. Pliny the Elder tells us there are three kinds of this cold stone, "red, yellow, and pale blue," designated as *rubeus granatus, citrinus,* and *venetus saphirinus* or *aquaticus* (Middle French *jagonce rubis, balais, grenaz, citrin*). These denominations are sometimes used as names for this stone. According to one tradition, fish carry them for one hundred years in their bellies before expelling them. According to Notker, following the lead of Martianus Capella in this regard, it is the stone of Scorpio and the month of November. Placed beneath the tongue, it gives the power to predict the future. Jacinth is good for the eyes, offers comfort, banishes sorrow and idle suspicions, encourages liveliness and intelligence, and halts nosebleed and hemorrhages. Hung from the neck or worn on the finger, it offers protection when at sea and from pestilences on land, obtains consideration, and grants wishes. When worn on the finger or around the neck, it brings safety when traveling among strangers and a warm welcome for guests. Jacinth protects (*facit tutem*) travelers and roads. It is a good amulet (*tutamen*) against snakes and poisons. It renders its bearer amiable in the eyes of God and man, states a fifteenth-century lapidary housed in the Bodleian Library at Oxford, and according to Mandeville, it permits a man to go wherever he wishes in complete safety because nothing can happen to him and corrupted air will not harm him. Like garnet, it makes its bearer congenial to both God and man. The jacinth changes color in accordace with the weather, although the same is said of the balas ruby.

In around 393, Epiphanes informed us how Scythian jacinths were obtained from that land's deep, inaccessible mountain valleys. Men would cut the throats of lambs, skin them, and hurl their carcasses into the jumble of rocks where these stones would adhere to them. Eagles, drawn by the smell of the meat, would dive down on the lambs and carry them off to their nests, from where the men would be able to take the stones.

In the Bible, jacinth is one of the twelve stones on the *rationale* or breastplate worn by the high priest Aaron (Exodus 28:15–30), and in the Christian lapidary, jacinth symbolizes the angelic life. Konrad von Hamburg cites it as one of the twenty stones on the ring he offers the Virgin Mary in his poem *Anulus,* written circa 1350. It symbolizes the principle of active charity that Mary exemplifies.

If one carves on it the image of Poseidon holding a trident in his right hand and a dolphin at his right foot, this stone will spare those who practice commerce on the seas from storms.

If one carves on a white or red hyacinth a woman whose hair hangs down to her breasts standing in front of a man, this talisman will make you congenial to all and irresistible to women. They will do your will if touched by this ring. The white jacinth must be set in silver.

A lapidary mistakenly attributed to Solomon tells us: "If one carves upon a jacinth or crystal the image of a woman with hair down to her breasts, as well as a man who has just arrived beside her and is showing her some sign of affection, and this stone is set in gold, and if the stone bears amber, aloe, and that herb called polium [germander], the owner of this stone shall compel the obedience of all, and if you touch a woman with this stone, she will act in accordance with your will; and if you place it beneath your head when going to bed, you shall see all that you desire in your dreams."

If one finds on a white jacinth the image of a young, crowned man sitting on a four-legged stone—an engraving representing Jupiter wearing a crown—and a man is beneath one of these four legs, carrying the throne on his neck, and if the young man has a circle around his head and his hands outstretched toward the sky, then this stone should be set in a silver ring that is the same weight as the stone, and mastic and turpentine should be placed beneath the stone. This seal should be stamped in wax and given to the person of your choosing. Whether this individual carries the seal or the ring on his person, by his throat, or elsewhere, he should place himself in the presence of the king or another person of power, or in that of a tranquil sage, and this person shall obtain what they desire in all honesty.

The carved image of a horse with a crocodile painted on it and bearing a symbol on a white jacinth is helpful for plaintiffs. It gives its owner victory in the courtroom, bestows beauty upon him, the art of concession, and congeniality. It should be set in gold, for gold increases its properties. A siren holding a mirror in one hand and a bow in the other can grant invisibility.

The sea jacinth is used in magic. "If you find a sea jacinth depicting a woman who is half fish holding a mirror in one hand and a branch in the other, set it into a gold ring, cover the engraving with wax, and wear the ring on your finger. When you wish to turn invisible, hold the stone tightly inside the palm of your hand, and you shall obtain the desired effect."

In Wirnt von Grafenberg's *Wigalois,* an Arthurian romance written at the beginning of the thirteenth century, the coffin of a gentle lady is made in a jacinth on which a sapphire has been mounted. See *jargonce.*

✦ *iacinctus (aquaticus + saphirinus), jacinctus;* MFr. *jacinte, jacincte, jagunce, ortiche;* MHG *iochant, jachant, iacinctus, iacinkcht, jacint;* MItal. *jacinto, giarconsia;* Ar. *iacôt, iakût;* Heb. *odem.*

📖 Pliny 36, 198, 37, 125f.; Solin 30, 24 and 33; Epiphanes 6; Isidore of Sevilla 16, 9, 3; Kerygma 27; Marbode 14; Notker I, 41; *Summarium Heinrici* VI, 4, 19; Lambert de Saint-Omer 54, 11; 55, 11; Hildegard von Bingen IV, 2; Meliteniotes v. 1119; Lapidary of Marbode, 1st Romanesque translation XIV; Alphabetical Lapidary 52f.; Lapidary in prose 10; 2nd Lapidary in prose 12; Alexander Neckham v. 207ff.; Luka ben Serapion 3; *De lapidibus preciosis* 3 and 37; Bodl. Digby 13 3 and 43 (*iacinctus granatus*); *De lapidibus preciosis* 37; Wolfram von Eschenbach 791, 17; Serapion c. 398 (*hager iacot*); *De figura* 3 (*iacinthus albus*); 8 (*iacinctus cristallinus*); *Liber sigillorum Ethel* 4 (*iacinthus albus*); Cambridge lapidary v. 359–400; Arnoldus Saxo 44; Bartholomeaus Anglicus XVI, 54; Thomas de Cantimpré 14, 38; Vincent de Beauvais VIII, 76; Albertus Magnus 2, 8, 2; *Lapidario* 150 and 270 (yellow); 110 and 234 (red); Konrad von Megenberg VI, 45; Christian lapidary v. 133–60 (*jagonce grenat*); Lapidary of King Philip 22; Jacob van Maerlant XII, 43; Saint Florian v. 165–204; Volmar v. 161–86; Mandeville I 11; Pseudo-Mandeville 13; *Vocabularius ex quo* i 4; *Liber ordinis rerum* 129, 25; Closener ja 7; *Liber secretorum* II, 1, 43; *Poridat* 13; Chael 3 and 15; Hermes 10; *Hortus sanitatis* V, 65 and 108 (*iacinctus rubeus;* Ar. *hager albigedi, albuzedi*); Leonardi II, 7, 141; *Libro di Sidrach* chap. 469 (= *balascio*); *Phisice* 12 and 14.

Hyaenia:

This stone is said to come from the petrified eye of a hyena, and for this reason the animal is hunted. Placed beneath the tongue of a man, it will enable him to foresee the future and prevent him from being mistaken in his judgments.

✦ *hyaena, hiena, hyen(i)a, ihena, hymenia, hyenis, ena, yen, yena, bena;* MFr. *hyene, hyane, hiema, biemma;* MHG *hiennîâ.*

📖 Pliny 37, 168; Solin 27, 25; Isidore of Sevilla 16, 15, 25; Kerygma 53; Marbode 44; *Summarium Heinrici* VI, 6, 9; Lambert de Saint-Omer 55, 23; 55, 96; Lapidary of Marbode, 1st Romanesque translation XLIV; Alphabetical Lapidary 49; Meliteniotes v. 1186; Lapidary in prose 43; *De lapidibus preciosis* 41; Wolfram von Eschenbach 791, 20; *Liber sigillorum Ethel* 15 (*iacinctus marinus*); Cambridge lapidary v. 1103–116; Arnoldus Saxo 45; Bartholomeaus Anglicus XVI, 56; Vincent de Beauvais VIII, 32; Thomas de Cantimpré 14, 42; Albertus Magnus 2, 8, 1; Brunetto Latini I, 189; Lapidary of King Philip, Paris, National Library of France, French ms. 2009, fol. 9 v°; Latin ms. 11210, fol. 80 r° sq.; Conrad de Megenberg VI, 47; Jacob van Maerlant XII, 46; Saint Florian v. 664–71; *Liber secretorum* II, 1, 25; *De virtutis lapidum* II, 18; *Hortus sanitatis* V, 64 (*hyena*) and 68 (*jena*); Leonardi II, 7, 134; *Phisice* 51.

Hyetites: See *yetios*.

Hymus: The name of an unidentified stone in an early medieval lexicon.

📖 *Vocabularius ex quo* h 82.1.

Hyophthalmos: See *ægopthalmos*.

📖 Pliny 37, 187.

I–J

Iacincthus: See *hyacinthos*.

Iaspachates: The jasper-agate; it heals dropsy, quenches thirst, and keeps the body healthy and vigorous. See *iaspis*.

+ *phasphachates, phascates.*

📖 Pliny 37, 139; Kerygma 42; Aetios II, 37.

Iaspis: The name for jasper comes from the Assyrian *ashpu*, the Hebrew *jashpeh*. Several countries produce it: India has a jasper that resembles emerald; the island of Cypress has a hard jasper that is a full sea-green color; Persia has a sky-blue jasper that is called *aerizuse* for that reason; the jasper from the Caspian Sea also looks like this. The jasper on the banks of the Thermodon is blue, while that of Phrygia is purple, and jasper from Cappadocia is a sad bluish-purple that has no radiance. It is claimed to cause the milk remaining in the teats of camels to flow, dispel pain and heart palpitations, delay sperm, and cleanse the blood of dysentery, reduce pollutions and banish lust, and, according to Heinrich von dem Türlîn, heal lovesickness. The one who wears jasper is never subject to accident and whosoever girds their body with it will fulfill all their wishes. Jasper is a male stone, while jasmer (Eastern jasper) is female.

According to Marbode of Rennes, there are seventeen different kinds of jasper (a number that varies in the texts), but the best is translucent green. When carried, it repels or heals fevers and dropsy, and it facilitates childbirth but also has contraceptive virtues! When blessed, it makes one gracious and powerful and drives off dangerous phantasms. However, Mandeville says women should not wear jasper because it will make them sterile. With the help of incantations, jasper can confer beauty, prowess, and invulnerability, eliminate fevers and dropsy, and retain the blood from wherever it is flowing.

Some believe the metal for jasper is gold and other authors say silver, but all are unanimous in saying it should be worn on the right side. It is explicitly stated that jasper should be worn chastely after it has been blessed and consecrated.

If one has worn jasper since childhood, he or she will be protected from drowning and ghosts. When jasper has bright red spots, it is called *dyaspre* and is quite valuable. It heals fevers and dropsy; it is good for women in labor as it facilitates childbirth; it provides safety, increases honors and valor, and heals the bites of venomous animals. Crushed into a powder, it curbs blood flow. It brings rain. It should be set in silver and worn on the right hand. In fact, "its virtue is greater in silver than in any other metal," says the 2nd lapidary in prose.

Jasper can be found in all the Christian lapidaries, where it represents the first foundation of the church and the young vigor of the faith; in the abbreviated versions, the only quality that is retained is its protection against thunder and lightning. In the Bible, it is one of the twelve stones on the *rationale* or breastplate worn by the high priest Aaron (Exodus 28:15–30). The Apocalypse (21:11) regards it as the noblest of all gems. Konrad von Hamburg cites it as one of the twenty stones on the ring he offers the Virgin Mary in his poem *Anulus,* written circa 1350. It symbolizes the faith of the Virgin Mary.

Jasper was heavily employed in the glyptic arts. A depiction of a man, specifically Mars, on a piece of jasper, with a shield in his left hand and an idol in his right, or any kind of weapon, and with vipers in place of his feet, the head of a cock or lion, and a breastplate, enables its owner to battle his enemies and obtain victory, and it protects him from poison: this is the depiction on the Abrasax stone.

If one carves a kestrel rending a snake and places the head of an iulian fish underneath the stone, then puts all of this on one's chest, it gets rid of stomach pain, stimulates appetite, and provides good digestion.

If a hare is carved on it, meaning the constellation of that name, no diabolical shade will be able to harm you; if it is a dog, it protects against dropsy, venom, and dog bites. Wearing a jasper adorned with an image of a hare that does not correspond to its celestial symbol protects a person from attack by demons and spirits and prevents the demonic shade from doing harm.

A jasper that depicts an armed Mars, or a virgin wrapped in a toga with a laurel branch in hand, makes its owner powerful and capable of anything, and it grants protection from violent death, drowning, and adversity. Thanks to this stone, the bearer will not be tormented by the demon; he will be powerful, and obtain all he desires.

Whoever owns a jasper engraved with a stag or with hunting hounds will never by afflicted by the devil for as long as he wears this ring. Someone possessed by a demon will be freed once he holds this stone.

A depiction on a jasper of a man wearing a bouquet of herbs around his neck grants the power to identify and recognize illnesses. This stone also curbs blood flow from wherever it might originate; it is said that Galen owned a jasper like this and always carried it with him.

A wolf carved on jasper protects from guile and prevents one from spouting wild claims.

Decorated with the image of a hunter, jasper confers the power to treat the possessed and the frenzied. Adorned with the image of a horse or a wolf, it relieves fever and holds in blood.

A jasper with an image of an emperor with head held high brings the love of all creatures, and its possessor will obtain all he desires.

Jasper on which is depicted a man with a palm drawn on the hand will obtain power and the grace of princes.

According to Notker, who follows Martianus Capella here, jasper is the stone of Pisces and the month of March.

✦ *jaspis, jaspen, hyaspidis, lapis;* MFr. *jaspe, jaspres, japes, japhes, jaffes, jaispe, laspes, lapes;* MHG *jaspîs, jaspe, jaspant;* ME *iasper;* MItal. *iaspes, diaspro;* Ar. *yzf.*

📖 Pliny 37, 115–18; Isidore of Sevilla 16, 7, 8; Orpheus v. 267–79; Kerygma 6; Pseudo-Hippocrates 32; Aetios II, 17 and 36; Damigeron 13; *Kyranides* 1, 9; Dioscorides V, 142; Pseudo-Dioscorides 2, 160; Lombard Dioscorides 169; Marbode 4; Hildegard von Bingen IV, 10; Psellos 10; *Summarium Heinrici* VI, 4, 6; Old English Lapidary 1; Lambert de Saint-Omer 54, 1; 55, 1; 55, 14; Dimishqî II, 5, 5; Alphabetical Lapidary 51; Lapidary in prose 4; 2nd Lapidary in prose 4; *Sidrac* 6; Alexander Neckham v. 167ff.; Bodl. Digby 13 4; *De lapidibus preciosis* 36; Cambridge Lapidary v. 129–46; *De l'entaille des gemmes* 13–14; *De figura* 12; 13; Wolfram von Eschenbach 791, 13; *Liber lapidarii* 5; Gossouin de Metz v. 250–81; Arnoldus Saxo 43; Bartholomaeus Anglicus XVI, 53; Thomas de Cantimpré 14, 37; Vincent de Beauvais VIII, 77; Albertus Magnus 2, 8, 6; *Lapidario* 21–24 (five varieties); Lapidary of King Philip 6; Diu Crône v. 8271–74; Konrad von Megenberg VI, 44; Christian lapidary v. 381–416 and 981–1012; Jacob van Maerlant XII, 42; Saint Florian v. 69–98; Volmar v. 265–85; *Secrez* 3, 13; 4, 9; *Liber defota anima* v. 4080–4165; *Liber ordinis rerum* 129, 26; Mandeville I 13; Pseudo-Mandeville 15 and 33; *Vocabularius ex quo* i 29; Closener ja 36; *Poridat* 6; Thetel 2; 5–9; Solomon 13; 17; 43; *Hortus sanitatis* V, 66; *Libro di Sidrach* chap. 459; Leonardi II, 7, 142; *Phisice* 14.

Iasponyx: The name for one of the many kinds of jasper.

📖 Pliny 37, 118.

Icterias: The color of this stone resembles livid skin and for that reason was thought to be an excellent remedy for jaundice (*icteria*). Another stone of this name is even paler in color, and a third looks like a green leaf. It is broader than the others, weighs almost nothing, and has livid veins. A fourth variety is the same color, but the veins are black. It is governed by the 30° of Scorpio.

✦ *ictericis;* MSp. *sanador de ictericia;* Ar. *zarmiquidez.*

📖 Pliny 37, 170; Alexander Neckham v. 245ff.; *Lapidario* 211.

Idachites: This is another name for the *enhydros* stone. It is the stone of Aquarius and the month of February. See *enhydros*.

✦ *ydachites, hydatides.*

📖 Notker I, 42; Bartholomaeus Anglicus XVI, 101; Closener id 4.

Idaei Dactyli, Idaeus: These stones are found in Crete; they are iron-colored and shaped like a human thumb. They are common fossils called belemnites. In Germanic belief, belemnites were regarded as the heads of elvish or dwarfish arrows, and called "elf shot" (*alpschoss, ælfshot*).

📖 Pliny 37, 170; Solin 11, 14; Dioscorides III, 140; Isidore of Sevilla 16, 15, 12; Meliteniotes v. 1156; Psellos 11; Leonardi II, 7, 144.

Ierarchites: See *hieracitis*.

📖 Leonardi II, 7, 151.

Indyarus: A white, acorn-shaped stone that counteracts poisons, resists enchantments, and heals calculus.

📖 *Phisice* 68.

Indicus: A reddish brown gem that exudes a purpurin-colored liquid. It is native to India and is good for treating dropsy.

✦ *indica, lapis indicus, lapis sindicus, senditicos;* MSp. *piedra indiana;* Ar. *elchendi;* Heb. *even hodu.*

📖 Pliny 37, 170; Dioscorides V, 92; Aetios II, 30; Luka ben Serapion 30; *De lapidibus preciosis* 26; *Aristoteles de lapidibus* 373, 34; 374, 27 (two Indian stones); Pseudo-Dioscorides 2, 107; Lombard Dioscorides 118; Meliteniotes v. 1157; *Physiologus* Y 26; Vincent de Beauvais VIII, 5; *Lapidario* 185; Leonardi II, 7, 146; Closener in 37.

Invisibility Stone: See *hulinhjálmsteinn.*

Ion: A sparkling, violet gem found in India.

📖 Pliny 37, 170.

Iovis Gemma: "Jupiter's gem" is very light, soft, white stone. It is also sometimes called *drosolithos* (dew stone).

📖 Pliny 37, 170; Leonardi II, 7, 148.

Iris: This extremely hard fossil stone, which is naturally dry, is found on a certain island of the Red Sea, some forty miles away from the city of Berenice. It is partially crystal, which some have seen as reason enough to call it "crystal root." It is not without reason that it has been given the name *iris:* when struck by the rays of the sun in a covered spot, it casts the shape and varied colors of the rainbow upon the nearest wall, and is constantly shifting in hue. Burned and crushed, it provides a remedy against the bite of the ichneumon [giant wasp]. Engraved with the image of an armed man with a bow and arrow, the *iris* protects its owner and whatever place he happens to be. A variety of this stone is called *leros.*

✦ *yris, yrim, irim, irisites, iritis, virites, jyrim, hirritis, hirricis, inris, tride;* MFr. *yris, hyrum, pris;* MHG *îris, regenpogen.*

📖 Pliny 37, 136; Solin 33, 20; Isidore of Sevilla 16, 13, 6; Damigeron 39; Dioscorides V, 127; Marbode 47; Lambert de Saint-Omer 55, 94; Meliteniotes v. 1157; Lapidary of Marbode, 1st Romanesque translation XLVII; Alphabetical Lapidary 54; Lapidary in prose 46; 2nd Lapidary en prose 22; Alexander Neckham v. 303f. (described but not named); *De lapidibus preciosis* 40; Cambridge Lapidary v. 1149–60; Wolfram von Eschenbach 791, 14; Arnoldus Saxo 46; Bartholomaeus Anglicus XVI, 55; Thomas de Cantimpré 14, 41; Albertus Magnus 2, 8, 3; Lapidary of King Philip 34; Konrad von Megenberg VI, 46; Jacob van Maerlant XII, 45; Saint Florian v. 682–95; *Secrez* 3, 14; *Liber secretorum* II, 1, 37; *De virtutis lapidum* II, 23; Ragiel 12; *Hortus sanitatis* V, 67; Leonardi II, 7, 143; *Phisice* 54.

Ischistos: Among the various kinds of schist, most advantageous is the one resembling saffron. In women's milk, it is particularly good for ulcerations of the cornea, quickly halts the prolapse of the eye, and cures scabies. The stone also halts hemorrhoidal discharge. It should be taken on an empty stromach for blood afflictions in a dosage of three drachmas triturated in oil. There is a variety called "white carbuncle" or "white pebble" with the property of countering phantasms and hallucinations. Its fusibility is highly praised and an incombustible garment can be made from its fibers that can be cleansed in fire, hence its other name: salamander feather.

✦ *iscistos, iscutos, iscultos, iscitus, icitos, istmos, sciscos, schistos;* MFr. *chiste.*

📖 Isidore of Sevilla 16, 4, 18; Damigeron 64; *Summarium Heinrici* VI, 2, 15; Lombard Dioscorides 154; *De lapidibus preciosis* 38; Thomas de Cantimpré 14, 40; Albertus Magnus 2, 8, 4; Jacob van Maerlant XII, 44; Leonardi II, 7, 145; Closener is 3; *Liber secretorum* II, 1, 26; *De virtutis lapidum* II, 35; *Hortus sanitatis* V, 68.

Iudaicus: The "Judah" or "Judea stone" is white, has the shape of an acorn, and bears inscriptions similar to letters. It heals abscesses; if blended and crushed with bladder stones it makes an eyewash that is good against corneal opacity. It resists poisons and enchantments.

Iudaicus designates something that has been identified as the spines of fossilized sea urchins.

✦ iudaica, indyarus, lapis agapis, lapis marinus, lapis liberans a glarea; MFr. judayq; Ar. eliude (deformed into elinde), hager alyeudi, jahudi.

📖 Isidore of Sevilla 16, 4, 12; Dioscorides V, 137; Pseudo-Dioscorides 2, 155; Lombard Dioscorides 164; Meliteniotes v. 1128; Luka ben Serapion 41; *De lapidibus preciosis* 29; *Aristoteles de lapidibus* 375, 6ff; Avicenna II, 2, 404; *Lapidario* 102; 109; Thomas de Cantimpré 14, 39; Albertus Magnus 2, 8, 5; *Picatrix* III, 3, 28; Leonardi II, 7, 147 (*iudaicus* = *cogolitus*); *Phisice* 68.

📖📖 Johann Petrus Wagner, *Dissertatio de lapidibus judaicis* (Halle and Magdeburg, 1724).

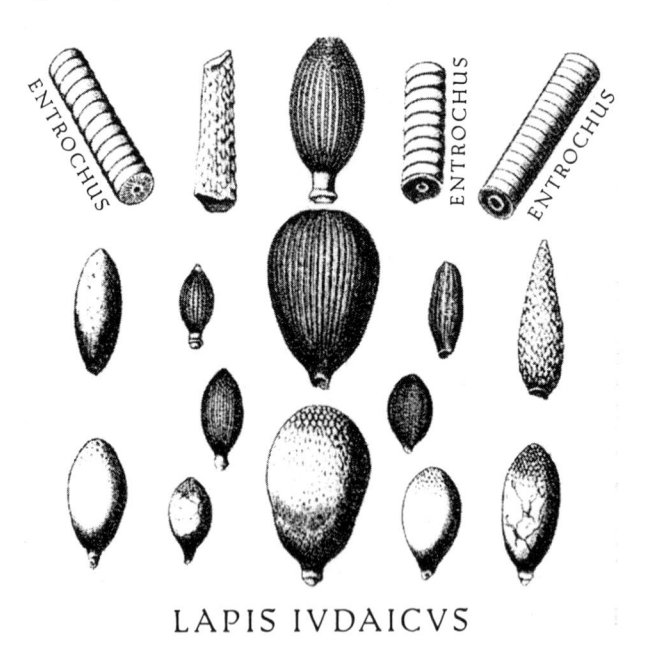

LAPIS IVDAICVS

Jacinctus: See *hyacinthos*.

Jacinctus Granatus: See *jargonce*.

📖 Bodl. Digby 13 23 and 43; *De l'entaille des gemmes* 37.

Jacunce Blanc: See *hyacinthos*.

 📖 *De l'entaille des gemmes* 28, 44 and 46; *De la vertu des tailles* 36 and 41.

Jaguntia, Jargoulce: See *granatus*.

 📖 Mandeville I (Amiens ms.) 1; Leonardi II, 7, 150.

Jakgan: A stone that never stays still unless someone touches it. It is good for heart palpitations; it is good for restless and sluggish limb. Hung from the neck, it prevents you from forgetting.

 📖 Qazwînî (Ruska, 88f.).

Jarknasteinn: Norse texts mention a stone whose name simply means "precious stone." It appears three times in the *Poetic Edda*. In the *Lay of Völund* (*Völundarkviða*, strophes 25 and 35), which tells the legend of Weland the Smith, this artisan slew the sons of Nidud to avenge his mutilation and fashioned precious stones of their eyes, which he gave to their mother. In the *First Lay of Gudrun* (*Gudrúnarkviða* I, strophe 9), the heroine compares her late husband Sigurd (Siegfried) to a precious stone set in a diadem. In the *Third Lay of Gudrun* (*Gudrúnarkviða* III, strophe 9), Gudrun must plunge her hand into a cauldron of boiling water to pull a gem out. She passes this ordeal and thereby proves to Atli (Attila) that she is not an adulteress.

Jargonce: In French, this term designates jacinth, but *La Fontaine de toutes sciences du philosophe Sidrac* (The Fountain of All Sciences of the Philosopher Sidrak), written after 1268, claims that concealed behind this name are sapphire, ruby, bais [balas], and garnet. In the manuscript tradition, it is repeated: "Jargonce is a stone called balas." There is also the jargonice grena (red jacinth), which is called "rubicund" because its color represents the red earth from which Adam was created. It is sometimes said that balas is the stone Saint John called jacinth in the Apocalypse. See *balagius*.

✦ *jagonce, jargance, jagoune, gargonce, laconce, largounce, jaguntia, jargoulce, sargonce, sargounce.*

📖 Paris, National Library of France, French ms. 1159, fol. 154; London, British Library, Harley ms. 4486 (fourteenth century), fol. 138 v°.

📖📖 Françoise Fery-Hue, "Sidrac et les pierres précieuses," *Revue d'Histoire des Textes* 28 (1998): 93–191; 30 (2000): 315–21.

Jasme: Oriental jade. It is claimed that it can cause the milk remaining in the teats of camels to flow. It banishes heart pains and palpitations, delays sperm ejaculation, and reduces nocturnal emissions. The bearer, by the grace of God, is never threatened by any accident, and whoever girds his body with it shall attain the goal he desires. The two stones jasme and jasper are found in copper mines; the first is male and the other female. Jasme has properties that bring forgetfulness to the lover, harden his heart, give assurance to reason, and calm the mind.

📖 Dimishqî II, 5, 5.

Jaspis: See *iaspis*.

Jon: An Indian stone of violet color.

📖 Leonardi II, 7, 149.

K

Kabrates: This is a stone similar to crystal that is certainly the same stone as the *kacabre*. It bestows eloquence, favor, and honor, protects from enchantments, heals dropsy and, according to Dioscorides, illness of the spleen. An image of an eagle carved in a *kabrates* or crystal gives its owner wealth, victory, and eloquence. It must be worn on the left arm. *Kabrates* represented the steadfast nature of the Virgin Mary to the anonymous fourteenth-century Dominican author of the *Rosarius*.

Some French lapidaries list this stone as *capnite*. See *capnitis*.

✦ *caprates, chabrates, tabrices, karabrattes;* MFr. *kabiate*.

📖 Alphabetical Lapidary 19; Arnoldus Saxo 48; Bartholomaeus Anglicus XVI, 58; *Vocabularius ex quo* k 1.2 (*kabrata* = *aquila*); *Rosarius* 2; *Liber secretorum* II, 1, 27; *De virtutis lapidum* II, 36.

Kacabre: The Arabic name for amber. This term was used in the West as a designation for jet and this stone was said to be effective against dropsy and to grant eloquence. According to Avicenna's classification, *karabe* is dry and hot by nature. It is good for the heart and the spirit. See *karabe* and *succinum*.

✦ *cacabre, carrabre, tabricu, cabices, kacabrates;* MHG *agestein*.

📖 Arnoldus Saxo 47; Albertus Magnus 2, 9, 1; Vincent de Beauvais VIII, 34; Closener ca 9; *Liber secretorum* II, 1, 39; *De virtutis lapidum* II, 17; *Hortus sanitatis* V, 69.

Karabe: The name for amber derived from the Arabic. This stone is governed by the 29° of Virgo. See *succinum* and *kacabre*.

📖 Avicenna II, 2, 404 and fol. 550 r°; *Lapidario* 150; *Hortus sanitatis* V, 70; Leonardi II, 7, 153.

Kauman: A name for *gamaheus*. Albertus Magnus describes it as a white or variously colored stone whose power originated in the marks to be found on it. See *gamaheus*.

✦ *kakman, kaman.*

📖 Arnoldus Saxo 49; Bartholomaeus Anglicus XVI, 57; Albertus Magnus 2, 9, 2; *Hortas sanitatis* V, 69; Leonardi II, 7, 152.

Kenne: Another name for the stone known as "stag's tear." It is effective against poisons. See *lacrimae cervinae*.

📖 *Hortas sanitatis* V, 69; Leonardi II, 7, 154.

Kezik: The "loadstone for vinegar" is a white stone; placed in a vessel full of vinegar it will draw the liquid into it until entirely saturated. As long as it contains vinegar it will boil without heat or fire.

 📖 Dimishqî II, 6, 15; Albertus Magnus II, 3, 6.

Kimedini: See *cinediae*.

 📖 Leonardi II, 7, 155.

Kinedius:
A very rare stone sometimes called opsianus (obsidian), which the Kyranides defines by "what comes later," "belated" (*serotinus tardus*). There are two kinds: one is opaque black; the other is black and shines like a mirror, which many seek unknowingly and is draconite (*dracontius*). Etched with the image of a woman and set in a ring when the moon and Saturn are in the sign of Virgo, the stone makes any woman who wears it chaste and pure. Another carving depicts an emasculated man holding his testicles in one hand and a knife in the other; it is set in a piece of gold jewelry with a little of the herb known as Venus' Belt and a little of the heart of the *kinedius* (a fish, a variant of the *limedi*), when the moon and Venus are in Virgo. The wearer of this ring will no longer experience any sexual desire.

 ✦ *occeano*.

 📖 *Kyranides* I, 10; *Secrez* 4, 10.

Kinocetus:
All we know of this stone is what Leonardi says: "It is not completely useless when demons are shaking you," which could refer to frenzy.

 📖 Leonardi II, 7, 156.

Kisserios:
The name for pumice stone in the Pseudo-Dioscorides. See *pumex*.

 📖 Pseudo-Dioscorides 2, 125.

Kurum: A stone that is white, red, yellow, or black and which divers bring out of the sea. When a person wears it around her neck, she will speak the truth and demons shall flee far from her presence. A piece the size of a grain of barley, crushed and drunk with a little aloe, is effective against joint pains and those of the bones and arteries.

 📖 Qazwînî (Ruska, 88).

L

Lacrimae Cervinae: The name of this stone appeared in the early Middle Ages in Johannes von Caub's *Hortis sanitatis* (*Garden of Health*). It was believed that stags ate reptiles to regenerate their strength and then dove in the water, where they stayed until they had eliminated all their venom. When they did this, they sweated drops similar to hazelnuts, which changed into stones with medicinal properties. See *kenne*.

◆ *cerui lacryma, kenne.*

📖 *Hortas sanitatis* V, 69.

Lacteus Lapis: See *galactitis*.

📖 Leonardi II, 7, 162.

Lagapis: A round stone that is dry and cold by nature and is good for wounds, as it draws out arrowheads and spear points.

✦ MHG *lagapen*.

📖 Konrad von Megenberg VI, 49.

Lambra: See *succinum*.

📖 Bodl. Digby 13 9; 50.

Lampus: Another name for amber in the tradition of the lapidaries translated from Arabic.

✦ Ar. *barkijj, elbarchi*.

📖 Luka ben Serapion 28; *Aristoteles de lapidibus* 373, 22ff.

Lantelius: See *odontolycius*.

📖 Alphabetical Lapidary 60.

Lapidary of the Twelve Stones: The biblical Apocalypse (21:18–21) describes the foundations of the heavenly Jerusalem as being made from twelve stones. In the Middle Ages, these constituted a small Christian lapidary, the *Cives cœlestis patriae* (Citizen of the Land of Heaven). Formerly attributed to Marbode of Rennes, this text is the work of Amatus of Monte Cassino, who wrote it in 1071 for the consecration of the new church. It was inspired by the *Psychomachia of Prudentius* (fourth century), which describes the new Temple built after the victory of the virtues over the vices, and by a hymn of the Venerable Bede (died 735) as well as his commentary on the Apocalypse. Each gem is given a symbolic interpretation, for example:

Sardonyx is of three colors:
It represents the inner man,
Humility makes it black;
Through it chastity finds its whiteness;
At the summit of honor
It blushes like the martyr.

The thirteenth strophe of the hymn condenses what is most necessary to know:

These precious stones
represent men of flesh;
the variety of their colors,
match the great number of virtues;
He who is illuminated by them
will be a citizen of the City.

The color of each stone was decisive for identifying its religious value. This lapidary is also known as the *Carmen de XII lapidibus*. The same gems do not always appear in these lapidaries, as there are some variations.

Sometimes we come across a simple list, as found in *Phisice*:

The name of the twelve stones that our Lord named to Moses the prophet.

The first is Sardonyx
The second Topasse [topaz]
The third Emerald
The fourth Ruby
The fifth Sapphire
The sixth is the Ligure stone
The seventh Acheta [agate]
The eighth Amatiste [amethyst]
The ninth Crysolite
The tenth Oniche [onyx]

The eleventh Jasper
The twelfth Beryl.

Numerous lapidaries modeled on the *Cives cœlestis patriae* saw the light of day, such as a poem by Hildebert of Lavardin (ca. 1056–1133), and were often inserted into commentaries, for example the *Expositio super Apocalypsum* by Bruno di Segni (died 1223), the abbot of Monte Cassino. Some of these twelve-stone lapidaries focused especially on their medicinal virtues. Later, the number of stones was slightly increased.

In Benedict's *Voyage of Saint Brendan* (early twelfth century), Brendan and his monks finally reach the lost island, that of paradise on earth. "They first spied a wall that rose to the clouds . . . It was erected by the King of Heaven . . . It was scattered with gems that cast a strong radiance: a great quantity of choice chrysoliths speckled with gold; the wall shone with topaz and chrysoprase, jacinth and chalcedony, emerald and sardonyx, bordered by richly glowing jaspers and amethysts; also contributing their light were shiny jacinths, crystals, and beryls."

Many poets were inspired by the hymn. In the *Romance of Troy* (v. 14631ff.; 14647–62), Benoît de Sainte-Maure, describing the chamber of beauty, mentions the twelve stones of the Apocalypse with the addition of carbuncle. Similar examples include Brun von Schönebeck, in his *Das Hohe Lied* (*The Song of Songs*; written 1275–1276); Henrich von Meissen, also known as Frauenlob (ca. 1250–1318), in his *Lay of Mary*; and the anonymous *Heavenly Jerusalem,* whose French text arranges the twelve stones into four groups of three representing the cardinal virtues. In Heinrich von Mügeln's work, the twelve stars of the crown of the woman who appears in the Apocalypse (12:1) are transformed into the twelve gems on the crown of the Virgin Mary: jasper, sapphire, emerald, chrysolith, asbestos, chrysoprase, agate, amethyst, carbuncle, topaz, and magnet (*Der Tum,* str. 132–43).

Many authors found inspiration in the Christian lapidary, chiefly for constructing metaphors. For example, the Virgin was described as a crystal, a "gem of clemency," and so forth. It should also be noted that the Pope Gregory the Great (died 604) attributed a gemstone to each of the angelic orders:

Sardonyx	Seraphim	Topaz	Cherubim
Emerald	Angels	Ruby	Archangels
Jacinth	The Virtues	Jasper	The Thrones
Sapphire	The empty thrones	Chrysolith	The Dominations
Agate	to which those who strayed	Onyx	The Powers
Amethyst	shall return to sit	Aquamarine	The Principalities

The romance writers picked up and expanded the biblical model. Heinrich von der Türlîn, for example, uses twenty-five stones in the description of Lady Fortune's palace at Ordohorht (*Diu Crône* v. 15664–721). This palace is constructed of sardonyx and jacinth, with emerald corners; columns of sapphire, onyx, and chrysolith; borders of beryls and jasper; and a diamond door topped by a ruby ciborium in which an *alectory* has been placed. The walls are highlighted with carnelians, amethysts, and coral, their foundations are made of *aetites* and agate, the two sides of the crenelations are covered with *ceraunia* and diamonds. *The Letter of Prester John* depicts the palace of this mythical sovereign in similar fashion, albeit more modestly.

📖 The Venerable Bede, *Explanatio Apocalypsis* II, 21, ed. Migne, Patrologia Latina 93, col. 194–204; Lambert de Saint-Omer, *Liber floridus*, chap. 54; Richard de Saint-Victor, In Apocalypsin VII, 6, ed. Migne, Patrologia Latina 196, col. 870–75; Gossouin de Metz v. 27–56; Brun von Schönebeck, *Das hohe Lied*, ed. Arwed Fischer (Tübingen: Georg Olms, 1893); *Die kleineren Dichtungen Heinrichs von Mügeln*, ed. Karl Stackmann, DTM 50–51 (Berlin: Akademie Verlag, 1959); Frauenlob (Heinrich von Meissen), *Leichs, Sangsprüche, Lieder*, ed. Karl Bertau und Karl Stackmann, vol. 1 (Göttingen: Vandenhoeck & Ruprecht, 1981); *Himmlisches Jerusalem*, ed. Erich Henschel and Ulrich Pretzel, in *Die kleinen Denkmäler der Vorauer Handschrift* (Tübingen: Niemeyer, 1963), 94–123; Christoph Gerhardt, "Zu den Edelsteinstrophen in Heinrichs von

Mügeln, 'Tum,'" *Beiträge zur Geschichte der deutschen Sprache und Literatur* 105 (1983): 80–116.

📖📖 Anselmo Lentini, "Il ritmo Cives caelestis patriae e il De duocecim lapidibus di Amato," *Benedictina* 12 (1958): 15–26; John M. Riddle, ed., *Marbode of Rennes (1035–1123) De lapidibus*, (Wiesbaden: Steiner, 1977), 118–29; Anselm Salzer, *Die Sinnbilder und Beiworte Mariens in der deutschen Literatur und lateinischen Hymnenpoesie des Mittelalters. Mit Berücksichtigung der patristischen Literatur. Eine literarhistorische Studie* (Darmstadt: Wissenschaftliche Buchgesellschaft, 1967 [1893]).

Lapes: See *iaspis*.

Lapides Lanceæ: These are often still called "arrow stones" (*lapides sagittarii*) and "witches arrows" (*sagittas lamiarum*), or "elf shot" and "dwarf shot" (*ælfshot, dvergshot*). This name refers to the invisible projectiles that witches—and some creatures from folklore—can shoot to harm men and animals. Ancient authors identified this with *ceraunia*.

Lapis Fulgureus: See *lychnis*.

Lapis Humanus: See *pyrophilus*.

Lapis Lazuli: This stone, a sodium aluminum silicate chloride with sulfur and lime, comes from Phrygia and is sky blue, speckled with gold. It cures melancholy and quartan fever if drunk with dew. It is also said to rejoice the soul and to strengthen eyesight, and it is useful against epilepsy. It is also a contraceptive. Lapis lazuli is used to manufacture the Moon talisman: if this talisman is plunged into a liquid that is then given to two individuals to drink, they will fall in love and become inseparable.

✦ *lapis azurii, azurius, lasulius, lazul, lasul(i)us, lazolus, zumemelazoli, zimeni ella zuri, zunich;* MFr. *pierre de l'azur, zumet;* MHG *lazur stain;* Ar. *lâzurd, lezawarz, lezanarz, alazar lâzuard, hager alzenard, smid.*

📖 Epiphanes 5; Luka ben Serapion 12; Avicenna II, 2, 57 and fol. 550 r°; Alphabetical Lapidary 61; Bodl. Digby 13 2; Vincent de Beauvais VIII, 108; Lapidary of King Philip 84; Konrad von Megenberg VI, 81; Dimishqî II, 5, 10; *De lapidibus preciosis* 12; *Picatrix* II, 10, 6; 57; 75; 77; III, 3, 17; 31; IV, 8, 29; Pseudo-Mandeville 62; *Liber secretorum* II, 1, 35; *De virtutis lapidum* II, 22; *Poridat* 3; *Hortus sanitatis* V, 71; *Gart der Gesundheit* chap. 241; Leonardi II, 7, 174; *Phisice* 100.

Lapis Loquax: In his *Itinerarium Cambriae* (Journey through Wales; II, 1), Giraldus Cambrensis (Gerald of Wales, Gerald de Barry, circa 1145–1223) reported the existence of a strange stone in Ireland: if a corpse were placed upon it, the cadaver would start speaking and give oracles. King Henry II went there and placed his foot upon the stone, whereupon it shrieked indignantly: "You are not the sovereign destined to conquer Ireland! Merlin did not speak your name." See *Lia Fáil*.

Lapsit Exillis: The name of the Grail in Wolfram von Eschenbach's *Parzival*. Contrary to Chrétien de Troyes, this author described it as a stone of unsurpassed beauty that overshadowed all earthly wonders. A Toledo pagan, Flegetanis, whose father was an Arab, discovered the name of this gem when studying the stars. It bestowed food and drink, and sight of it restored the freshness of youth. The patient who looked at it could not die during the entire following week. It was by virtue of this stone that the phoenix consumed itself and became ash. The owners of the Grail are of divine origin and every Friday a white dove would deposit a host on the stone. It was so heavy that no sinner could ever lift it, no pagan could catch sight of it, and the road leading to the castle where it was kept could only be found by chance, for it hid from anyone looking for it. This castle is Munsalvaesche, the "Wild Mountain" that is home to a temple whose guardians are Templars and virgins. This is where the stone was kept.

The name of the Grail has given rise to all kinds of interpretations: *lapis berillis, betillis, elixir, exilii/exulis, exilis, ex celis, ex illex, e(x) silice, sextilis, lapsus exilliens, textilis, erilis, electrix; aspis exilis, absite (apsyctos) exilli(e)s;* the stone of the phoenix nest; amber; Solomon's stone, the Shamir; the pearl; the Shechina of the Kabbalah; the cornerstone of Zion; the Philosopher's Stone; the stone of paradise (in the legend of Alexander); the *zimur* (Prester John); the Kaaba.

A curious fact: the world's second-largest diamond, which weighs 995.2 carats and was discovered in South Africa, is called Excelsior.

✦ *jaspis exilix, jaspis exsilix, japsis, and silix.*

📖 Wolfram von Eschenbach 468, 1ff.; 469, 7ff.

📖📖 Joël H. Grisward, "Des Scythes aux Celtes. Le Graal et les talismans royaux des Indo-Européens," *Artus* 14 (1983): 31–34; Felix Karlinger, *Der Graal im Spiegel romanischer Volkserzählung* (Vienna: Praesens, 1996); Philippe Walter, *Galaad, le pommier et le Graal* (Paris: Imago, 2004); André de Mandach, *le Roman du Graal imaginaire*, G.A.G. 581 (Göppingen: Kümmerle, 1992); Faugère Annie, *Les origines orientales du Graal chez Wolfram von Eschenbach, Etat des recherches*, G.A.G. 264 (Göppingen: Kümmerle, 1979).

Lauraces: The name for stones that are effective in treating migraines and other headaches.

📖 Leonardi II, 7, 172.

Lepidotes: With its varied colors, this stone resembles fish scales. It heals nerve pain.

VERTIX

BASIS

BASIS   VERTIX

LEPIDOTES ALIVS

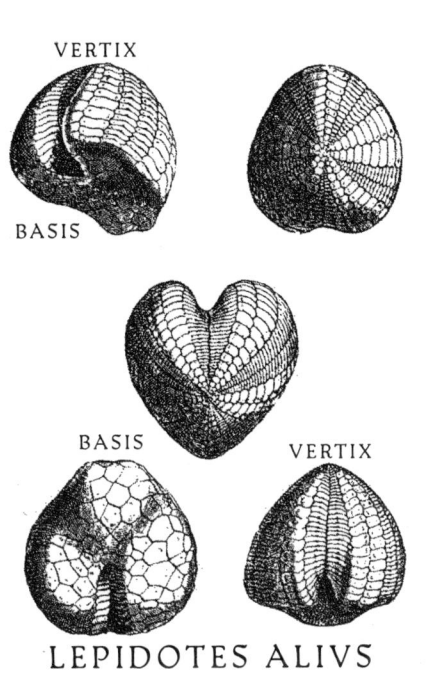

✦ *lepidotis, lepedotis.*

📖 Pliny 37, 170; Orpheus v. 287ff.; Meliteniotes v. 1165; Leonardi II, 7, 169.

Leontios: A gem that resembles lion hide.

📖 Pliny 37, 190.

Leros: A stone whose crystal is bisected by a white patch and a black patch. See *iris*.

✦ *ieros, eiros, erros, ros zeros.*

📖 Pliny 37, 138.

Lethargus: Another name for the galactite to which is attributed the ability to remove memory.

✦ *letheus, lithargum.*

📖 Orpheus v. 191–229; Kerygma 2; Damigeron 34.

Leucachates: White agate. Those from Bohemia were particularly valued, according to Hilarius Salustius, who wrote on this subject in 1717.

📖 Pliny 37, 137; Meliteniotes v. 1166.

Leucochrysus: This name designates a chrysolith with white veins or specks.

✦ *leucochrysos, leuchochryses, leuchochrysa, leocrisus, leochrysus.*

📖 Pliny 37, 128; 172; Isidore of Sevilla 16, 15, 6; Lambert de Saint-Omer 55, 79; Leonardi II, 7, 165.

Leucogea: Another name for galactite.

✦ *leucogagea, leucea, leuca.*

📖 Pliny 37, 162.

Leucographitis: Another name for "milk stone." See *galactitis*.

✦ *leucographitia, leucografitis, leucographides, leciamgraphiris.*

📖 Pliny 37, 162; Aetios II, 16; Pseudo-Dioscorides 2, 152.

Leucophthalmus, Leucoptalmus: A sparkling black-and-white stone that looks like the eye of a wolf, hence its name. This stone is certainly identical to the lycophthalmus—lyco read as leuco—but some have put forth the hypothesis that it is an opal.

✦ *leuco obthalmos, lycophthalmos.*

📖 Pliny 37, 171; Leonardi II, 7, 163.

Leucopoecilos, Leucopetiles: The name for a white stone mixed with golden red specks.

📖 Pliny 37, 171; Meliteniotes v. 1166.

Leucostyctos: Another name for porphyry.

📖 Leonardi II, 7, 176.

Lia Fáil: The mythic, phallus-shaped stone that the Tuatha Dé Danann, the "People of the Goddess Dana," allegedly brought to Ireland with other talismans, and which they placed at the center of the country. When a king sets foot on this stone, it begins shouting, thus demonstrating the legitimacy of the new ruler. It reputedly guaranteed a long reign, rejuvenated the king, and protected Ireland. But Cú Chulainn, the hero of Celtic epics, split the stone in half with a blow from his sword because it failed to shout under the foot of his adopted son Lugaid, and since that time it has remained silent. Lia Fáil has an exact correspondence with the Greek *omphalos*.

This stone was discovered by chance. One morning, Conn Cétchathach stepped on a stone on Tara hill. The stone let out a cry that could be heard throughout Ireland and at the very same instant he was swallowed up by a dense fog. A prince of the fairies stepped forth and predicted the future of a green Ireland to Conn. See also *lapis loquax*.

📖 Jan de Vries, *La religion des Celtes* (Paris: Payot, 1963), 248ff.; Joël H. Grisward, "Des Scythes aux Celtes: Le Graal et les talismans royaux des Indo-Européens," *Artus* 14 (1983): 31–34.

Libanochrus, Labanochros: A stone that resembles incense but exudes a fluid similar to honey.

📖 Pliny 37, 171.

Licania: See *lyncurium*.

📖 *Liber secretorum* II, 1, 19.

Life Stone: See *lífsteinn*.

Lífsteinn: This "life stone" appears in the *Saga of Kormak Ögmundarson* (chap. 12); it gives its owner luck and allows him to swim better than his rival.

In Iceland, the "life stone" could bring back the dead and restore the health of those on their deathbeds. It is found where the shadow falls and the earth has been overturned. It causes no harm to its bearer.

📖📖 *Kormáks Saga,* ed. Theodor Möbius (Halle: Weisenhaus, 1886); *Íslenzkar Þióðsögur og Æventýri* (Leipzig: J. C. Hinrich, 1862–1864).

Lignyzon: An Indian carbuncle whose sparkle is duller than those of other countries.

✦ *liuizonia, lithizonta, lithiconia, licitiona.*

📖 Pliny 37, 94.

Ligurias: See *lyncurium*.

📖 *Summarium Heinrici* VI, 4, 16; *De lapidibus preciosis* 42; Lapidary of Marbode, 1st Romanesque translation XXIV; *Liber lapidarii* 6; *Vocabularius ex quo* l 328; 291; Jacob van Maerlant XII, 48; Saint Florian v. 611–34; Leonardi II, 7, 167; Closener li 64.

Limacie: The "turtle stone," which appears here as "*limacia* stone" (Middle French translates it as *chelon*), takes its name from the fact that it is found in the head of this animal. It should be extracted as soon as it is seen. It is small and white, and semitransparent, similar to a human fingernail. It is said to banish fever if worn around the neck.

📖 Leonardi II, 7, 161.

Limoniates: A green stone reminiscent of emerald, but paler and less transparent.

  Pliny 37, 172; Meliteniotes v. 1168; Psellos 1; Leonardi II, 7, 166.

Limphicus: Camillo Leonardi states that the limphic stone possesses great virtue. If it is shown to an epileptic, it will heal him. Wrapped in linen that has been folded twelve times, it protects against ophthalmia, coughs, headaches, and present and future sore throats.

  Leonardi II, 7, 170.

Linourgos: The *linourgos* is quite pale in color and found near the Achelous River. If it is cast on linen, it immediately—through a kind of sympathy—takes on its form and whiteness and becomes a cloth that is as fine and delicate as a spider web.

  Pseudo-Plutarch §24.

Liparea: A Libyan stone with marvelous powers. Following a lengthy ceremony described by the Pseudo-Orpheus, *liparea* will provide knowledge of the future and make it possible to understand the cries of birds and the howling of four-legged creatures. It is very useful in the magical arts, and the magicians of Egypt and Babylon pacified serpents and dragons with it. Those who ingest it become seers. When used in fumigation, it causes all wild beasts to leave their lairs; it will attract game animals to any hunter who carries this stone. *The Letter of Prester John* mentions its virtue without naming the stone, but it does say how to use it. It needs to be attached with the sinews of dragons and carried behind oneself.

> ✦ *lippares, lipparis, luperius, lyparea, lupparea, li(p)paria, litarea, leparaios, lipercoli, le pero;* MFr. *lipparie, liparée, lyparie, syppere, eyaperea, dyparea, lipparre, syppere;* MHG *lipparêâ.*
>
> 📖 Pliny 37, 172; Orpheus v. 691ff.; Kerygma 23; Isidore of Sevilla 16, 15, 22; Marbode 45; Meliteniotes v. 1178; Psellos 1375; Lapidary of Marbode, 1st Romanesque translation XLV; Lapidary in prose 44; Wolfram von Eschenbach 791, 24; Prester John §46.19 (Wagner, 451); Cambridge Lapidary v. 1117–28; Arnoldus Saxo 51; Bartholomaeus Anglicus XVI, 61; Thomas de Cantimpré 14, 43; Vincent de Beauvais VIII, 32; Albertus Magnus 2, 10, 2; Lapidary of King Philip 56; Jacob van Maerlant XII, 47; Closener li 109; *Liber secretorum* II, 1, 33; *De virtutis lapidum* II, 19; *Hortus sanitatis* V, 75; Leonardi II, 7, 160; *Phisice* 52.

Lithargyrum: *Lithargyrum,* which literally means "stone of silver," was used as a "regenerative and consolidating vulnerary," to borrow the phrase of medieval doctors. It is cold by nature and heals festering wounds and scars. Attached to a wound, it immediately cauterizes it. The physician Guy de Chauliac (ca. 1298–1368), for example, called *lithargyrum* the "shit of lead"; French lapidaries meanwhile described it as "escume de plum et d'argent" (foam of lead and silver). Mineralogists today call it lead protoxide.

+ *lithergireum, litargirus, litigerum, litigerus;* Ar. *merdasengi, marechet.*

📖 Lombard Dioscorides 113; Avicenna II, 2, 471; Alphabetical Lapidary 59; *Hortus sanitatis* V, 73; *Gart der Gesundheit* chap. 242.

Litos: Another name for magnet. See *magnes*.

📖 Leonardi II, 7, 175.

Livestock Stone: According to Icelandic belief, the livestock stone (*fésteinn*) is a white stone that is somewhat rough and quite thin at one end. It is found in the bodies and on the tongues of sheep. It must be hidden to work, but no one says what purpose it serves.

There is another variety whose color is almost black or hazel; it floats on the sea and should be concealed in a white cloth.

📖 Jón Árnason, *Íslenzkar Þióðsögur og Æventýri* (Leipzig: J. C. Hinrich, 1862–1864).

Lizard Stone: A bezoar. See *sauritis*.

Locoptalmos: See *lycophthalmos*.

📖 Lambert de Saint-Omer 55, 74.

Lunarius: Another (and rather rare) name for *selenite*.

📖 Leonardi II, 7, 177.

Luperius: See *liparea*.

📖 *Liber secretorum* II, 1, 33.

Lupi Dens: See *odontolycius*.

📖 Alphabetical Lapidary 60.

Lychnis:
A flame-colored stone, still called "divine stone," which owes its name to the luster it displays under the light of a lamp, which is quite pleasing. Some believe it is a balas ruby. It is found in the vicinity of Orthosia, throughout all of Caria, and in neighboring localities, but the most highly valued are those that come from India. Some have called it a "deadened carbuncle." When warmed by the sun, or by rubbing it between the fingers, it will attract chaff. It can also be found in the Hydaspes River, according to the Pseudo-Plutarch. When the moon is waxing, it is sought out by the sound of flutes in the nests of storks, where, it is believed, these birds place it to fertilize their eggs and keep snakes away. The *Kyranides* calls this stone *lapis fulgureus* and *keranitis* (*ceraunius*). Carved with the image of an armed Mars, it possesses magic powers. According to Notker, who repeats Martianus Capella's observation, the *lychnis* is the stone of Gemini and the month of June.

Lychnis banishes hail and other plagues that menace the fields; it helps water retain its coolness, even when placed in a cauldron on the fire. If the cauldron is cold, it will cause it to boil (properties that are reminiscent of *hephaestitis*). Fire will never burn where it is housed.

Worn around the neck, *lychnis* protects every place it touches from vermin; it protects against sorrow and languor, grants the power of prophecy, and heals the discharges of blood by women.

✦ *lychynites, lychinites, lychines, lychynes, lychynis, lychius, lygdinus, lichinis, lignis, lignites, letites, licnis, leniten, lithiten;* MFr. *letite.*

📖 Pliny 36, 14; 37, 103f.; Solin 52, 58–59; Philostratus II, 14; Pseudo-Hippocrates 33; Isidore of Sevilla 16, 14, 4; Kerygma 7; Damigeron 28; Pseudo-Plutarch §1; Notker I, 39; Psellos 13; *Summarium Heinrici* VI, 5, 13; Meliteniotes v. 1119; Alphabetical Lapidary 56; Vincent de Beauvais VIII, 79; *Hortus sanitatis* V, 74; Leonardi II, 7, 157; 168 and 173.

Lycophthalmos: The "wolf's eye," an agate with orbicular layers, is quadricolored: blood red mixed with flame red, around a center that is black, surrounded by white like the eye of a wolf.

✦ *hyophthalmos.*

📖 Pliny 37, 187; Isidore of Sevilla 16, 15, 20; Lambert de Saint-Omer 55, 74; Leonardi II, 7, 163.

Lydius: Another name for the touchstone (*coticula*) found in the Tmolus River.

📖 Pliny 33, 126.

Lygdinus, Ligdinus: An glaring white stone, *lygdinus* is found in Paros, never in a size large enough to make more than a goblet or plate. It was used for the preservation of perfumes. It was first discovered in Arabia.

📖 Pliny 36, 62; Leonardi II, 7, 171.

Lyncurium: *Lyncurium* or ligure stone is, according to the legend, the product of lynx urine and a kind of earth that the animal uses to cover its urine immediately as he is jealous of the use men get out of it. It has the same hue as the fire-colored *succinum,* and is sometimes spotted with black and sometime spotted red like a ruby, but it does not glow at night. It lends itself to engraving: it attracts leaves, chaff, copper filings, and iron flakes. Ingested as a drink, it removes stones from the bladder, and drunk in wine or even worn as an amulet, it cures icterus and diarrhea, quenches thirst, and possesses hemostatic properties. This is how the romance *Ruodlieb,* written in Latin and dating from the end of the eleventh century, describes the genesis of *lyncurium,* which it calls *ligurius*:

> A precious stone is born from the urine of the lynx, the *ligurius,* which sparkles like a precious carbuncle. May those who would

learn how to do this heed my words. Have four iron nails forged and drive them deep inside a large tub, so deeply that no one could pull them back out. Drill a hole with a borer in the middle of the tub. Place the beast inside, even if it balks, and tie its feet to the nails, then wind a chain around its neck and attach it above so that the animal is unable to lower his head to rid himself of his bonds. Give the lynx enough to eat and drink; the drink should be a strong, sweet wine that will get him inebriated and force him to urinate. He should even piss unknowingly. You will collect the urine flowing out the hole in the tub in a bowl. If the lynx does not urinate, it will die. In this case, skin it and carefully open its belly. Remove its bladder, make a hole in it with a thin needle and express its contents into a very clean bowl, then pour it into a copper vessel the size of a pea and into containers with the capacity of a hazelnut. Bury these containers and let them rest for fifteen days in the earth. When you dig them up, you shall see that all the drops of urine have condensed into gems that shine in the darkness like a flame. (v. 99–127)

It was also believed that *lyncurium* came from animals called *langures* or *langes,* which dwelt by the banks of the Po River. "Whoever drinks of this stone, shall be healed of stomachache," states one lapidary. *Liguria* protects all houses from ill fortune and heals women of belly disorders. One lapidary declares that it is the anaphrodisiac of prostitutes.

Having been seen in the past as a yellow amber, a peridot, and a rose of the sands(!), the ligure stone is today thought to be a kind of jacinth or tourmaline, or even a belemnite.

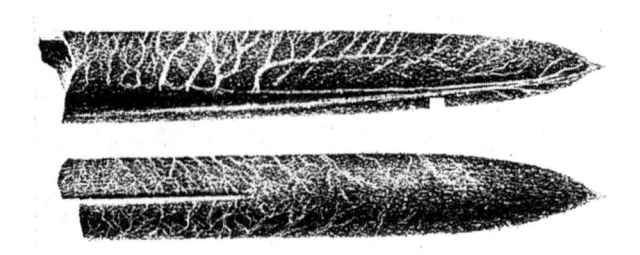

✦ *lyncurius, lynguros, lyngurium, lygurium, liguros, ligurius, lingurius, lincis, lyncis, ligure;* MFr. *ligurie, liguire, liguerres, sigurre;* MHG *luchs stein;* MItal. *liguria.*

📖 Pliny 37, 52; Solin 2, 38–39; Epiphanes 7; Isidore of Sevilla 16, 8, 8; Damigeron 31; 43; Marbode 24; Dioscorides II, 81; Pseudo-Dioscorides 2, 100; Hildegard von Bingen IV, 19; Lambert de Saint-Omer 55, 39; Meliteniotes v. 1168; *Kyranides* 1, 11; Lapidary of Marbode, 1st Romanesque translation XXIV; Lapidary in prose 19; Alphabetical Lapidary 57–58; 2nd Lapidary in prose 35; Cambridge lapidary v. 599–620; Gossouin de Metz v. 282–319; *Sidrac* 7; Wolfram von Eschenbach 791, 15; Arnoldus Saxo 50; Conrad von Mure (1210–1281), *De naturis animalium* v. 1253f.; Bartholomaeus Anglicus XVI, 60; Thomas de Cantimpré 14, 44; Vincent de Beauvais VIII, 80; Albertus Magnus 2, 10, 1; Brunetto Latini I, 190; Konrad von Megenberg VI, 48; Christian lapidary v. 417–70 and 1013–68; Saint Florian v. 611–34; Pseudo-Mandeville 26; Psellos 1; *Liber ordinis rerum* 129, 27; *Libro di Sidrach* chap. 460; Leonardi II, 7, 158 and 159; *Hortus sanitatis* V, 72 (*lincis*) and 75 (*ligurius*); *Phisice* 30.

Lysimachos, Lisimacus:
A stone that resembles Rhodes marble with gold veins. It is polished to rid it of its flaws.

📖 Pliny 37, 172; Leonardi II, 7, 164.

M

Macedonius: The diamond found in Philip's gold mines was called "Macedonian." It was about the size of a cucumber seed. The Macedonian stone has the ability to grow another stone inside it. If a woman possesses it, she will not experience the pains of childbirth.

 📖 Pliny 37, 57; Alphabetical Lapidary 64.

Machaera: The machaera stone, which is similar to a knife, is found on Mount Berecynthus (Phrygia). If someone finds it during the "Mother of the Gods" celebration, he will be sent into a rage.

 📖 Pseudo-Plutarch §7.

Magnasia: A black stone used by glassblowers because fire melts it and it purifies the glass with which it is blended.

 ✦ *magnosia*; Ar. *magnisijâ, almagnicia*.

 📖 Luka ben Serapion 25; Avicenna II, 2, 476; *De lapidibus preciosis* 22; *Aristoteles de lapidibus* 372, 5ff.; *Picatrix* IV, 8, 29; Leonardi II, 7, 186; *Hortus sanitatis* V, 79; *Phisice* 93.

Magnes: This stone was called magnes after the name of the individual who discovered it on Mount Ida. This Magnes is said to have made his discovery when leading his cattle to pasture there and the stone adhered to the nails in his shoes and the iron of his shepherd's crook. In the Middle Ages, it was called the "mariner's stone" starting in the twelfth century, at the time when Alexander Neckham (1157–1217) and Guyot de Provins (1190) both described the compass as a needle floating over a wheel. In the fifteenth century, it was called "the stone of heaven, or alternately the mariner's stone, because it demonstrates the parts of the sky by means of a needle."

There are five different kinds of magnet (magnetite): the Ethiopian, that of Magnesia, the Boetian from the region of Hyettus, the magnet from the outskirts of Alexandria in Tross, and finally the magnet from Magnesia in Asia. The primary distinction between magnets is their sex, male or female, with the second greatest difference being their color. The ones from the Magnesia that borders Macedonia are a reddish black; those from Boetia are more red than black; and those from Tross are black and female, and consequently without any power of attraction. The worst of all is the magnet from Magnesia in Asia: it is white, does not attract iron, and resembles pumice stone. Experience has shown that the bluer the magnet, the stronger its power, or so say the ancients. The Ethiopian variety is deemed the best of all and is bought for its weight in silver. Smeared with garlic, the magnet loses its virtues but it will recover them if bathed in ram's blood. The properties of the magnet are often confused with those of the diamond; this confusion came about due to the name *adamas* being used for both stones. According to the Arabic tradition presented by Balenis, its planet is Mercury. Poets often compare the magnet to the sirens' song, as both possess an irresistible power of attraction.

Men of the Middle Ages even believed in the existence of a magnetic mountain somewhere in the East or elsewhere (the locations proposed varied greatly). *The Voyage of Saint Brendan,* written down circa 1150, informs us that the Mountain of the Magnet rises near the Sluggish Sea, meaning the "coagulated sea," which is in fact a mythical image of an ice floe. Pliny was one of the first to speak of two such mountains near the Indus: one attracted iron; the other repelled it. The Greek geographer Ptolemy (second century) mentions the Magnetic Mountain near the Maniole Islands, on the maritime route between India and the unknown territories south of the Equator at 142° longitude and 2° latitude. He says that Indian navigators allow no iron objects onto their boats for fear of being pulled to this mountain. *The Marvels of India*, a treatise written around 950 by Buzurg Ibn Sharijâr, says this: "A sailor told me that between Khanfu, which is the main city of China Minor, and Khômdan, the principal city of Greater China, the larger of the two and where lives the Grand Baghpur, there is a freshwater river with a strong current that is wider than the Tigris of Basra. Magnetic mountains are found at certain points along this river, making it so none will sail this river with a ship that contains iron for fear of being attracted by these mountains, so strong is their power. The horsemen who travel through these mountains do not shoe their mounts."

The Arab encyclopediast Kazwînî (1203–1283) echoes this legend: "The Magnetic Mountain is located near Egypt. It is a mountain on which can be found the magnet that attracts iron; all the boats used to navigate this sea are built without iron out of the fear this mountain inspires." The mention of Egypt should not be misunderstood: Kazwînî is referring here to islands in the Red Sea. Goethe mentions this legend in *The Sorrows of Young Werther* (letter of July 26), as does Jules Verne in his *An Antarctic Mystery (The Sphinx of the Icefields)*, where there appears "a magnetic cliff that causes the adventurers to suffer a shipwreck by tearing all the metal from their ships.

In *The Thousand and One Nights* (story of the third calendar), Agib's vessel is drawn toward the Black Mountain that "is a magnet mine."

In *The Romance of Eneas*, the twelfth-century adaptation of Virgil's *Aeneid*, it is said that the walls of Carthage were constructed of magnets, "a very hard stone that by nature attracts all armed men" (v. 432ff.).

The magnet serves as a touchstone for conjugal fidelity, and the belief assumes the following form: "If this stone is placed beneath the head of a sleeping women, the majority of lapidaries claim, it will cause her to roll over immediately into her husband's arms if she is chaste. But if she is an adulteress, the terrible fear of her nightmares will cause her to fall out of bed." The magnet creates fraternal understanding, bestows the gift of persuasion at assemblies, and grants the realization of all wishes on the part of the gods. It reconciles couples and gives grace, persuasion, and judgment. With honeyed wine or milk, it brings relief to sufferers of dropsy; in powdered form, it heals burns. Its attracting property has given rise to the following metaphor: "Like the magnet attracts iron, Jesus Christ pulls us out of Hell."

Thieves or enchanters (depending on the source) use the magnet to rob houses by proceeding as follows. When they enter a house, they place burning coals at the four corners and sprinkle the house with powdered magnet. This causes those sleeping there to be so tormented by nightmares that they flee the premises, letting the scoundrels steal whatever they like! If one puts magnet powder on the fires burning at the four corners of the house, its occupants will flee because it gives them the impression the house is about to collapse upon them.

The magnet is quite potent in magic and, if consecrated with ad hoc charms or characters (magic symbols), it will cause ghosts to appear. It is the stone of the "wondrous witch" Circe.

Engraved with an image of Aphrodite pulling a man toward her by a panel of his garment with her left hand and displaying an apple in her right, the magnet will ensure that harmony rules among couples, friends, and brothers; it bestows eloquence and provides persuasion and dignity.

If one finds carved in a magnet the image of a naked man standing with a naked girl, whose hair has been tied around her head, to his right, and this man has his right hand on the young girl's neck while his left is on the chest, while he is looking into the face of this young girl with her own eyes downcast, this stone should be set in a ring equal in weight. Beneath this stone should be placed the tongue of a hoopoe, myrhh, alum, and a bird-tongue's weight of human blood. No one who sees this ring shall be able to resist its owner, whether in war or any other context. No thief or wild beast can enter a house in which this stone is found.

And an epileptic will be cured who drinks the water in which this stone has been steeped. This magic spell has the following variation:

> He who possesses the magnet on which is engraved a man holding a maid, both being nude and the maiden's thick locks wrapped around

her head, and the man embracing the maid with his right arm and looking at her while she has lowered her eyes; if he wishes to wear this gem, he needs must take twelve times its weight in iron, then he should know he must place beneath it a grain of hops, a little alum, and three drops of human blood: the ring is then good and will annihilate his true enemies. As long as he wears this ring, all his enemies must dread him and are unable to resist him, and he is victorious in all great battles. As long as he wears this ring on his finger, no thief has the skill to wreak mischief upon him, or any evil spirits; and no dog will bark at him. If the world was full of his enemies, he would still suffer little harm. This stone should be protected from contact with blood when worn, otherwise it shall lose its power.

An image of a man in armor sculpted on a magnet gives the power to fight enchantments and brings its owner victory in war. "Make an imprint of this ring in red wax, hang it around a dog's neck, and as long as this stone remains at this place, it will never bark. Any person who carries this seal among thieves, enemies, and dogs will be spared by their ill attentions," claims the lapidary of Solomon.

The owner of a magnet adorned with the image of a bull or calf can go where he pleases in all safety and no anxiety; he is also freed of all enchantments and artifices and transfers them to another object.

If we believe the ancient accounts, magnets were used to perform miracles. The architect Dinochares built the dome of the temple of Arsinoe in Alexandria with magnetic stone so that the iron statue of this princess could appear there suspended in the air. A curious text from the end of the twelfth century titled *La Relation d'Élysée* (Elysaeus' Report) describes the tomb of Saint Thomas in India, which is "suspended in the air by virtue of four precious stones called adamans. One is placed in the pavement, another in the roof, the third in one corner and the fourth in the other. These stones attract iron: the one below does not allow the sepulcher to rise, the one above does not let it descend, and those at the corners prevent it from moving here or there." A French lapidary reports there was an image of Muhammed that floated in the air like this by virtue of magnets and that men regarded it as a great miracle and worshipped it like a god. This motif appears at the very beginning of the thirteenth century in the *Chanson de geste of Quatre Fils Aymon* (Aymon's Four Sons ; v. 9613–16), and a century later in that of the *Bastard du Bouillon* (v. 1364–66) with one oddity: the statue is made of gold. The author did not realize that magnet does not attract this metal! See also *segulsteinn*.

✦ *magnet, magnetes, magneten, magnetis, magnessa, magniten, mangneta, magnesia, qini*; MFr. *magnete, man(n)et(t)e, mennate, mangue(t), aymant, athemaunte*; MHG *magnat, magnet, mangnât, mannet, nadilstein, agestein*; ME *loadstone*; MSp. *iman*; OIc. *leiðarsteinn*; Ar. *elbeneg, mâ(g)natas, magnatis*.

📖 Pliny 36, 126–30; Solin 57, 27; Isidore of Sevilla 16, 4, 1f.; 16, 13, 3; Orpheus v. 306–43; Kerygma 11; Pseudo-Hippocrates 36; Aetios II, 25; Damigeron 30; Dioscorides V, 148; Lombard Dioscorides 157; Marbode 19; *Summarium Heinrici* VI, 2, 1; Hildegard von Bingen IV, 18; Old English Lapidary 13; Lambert de Saint-Omer 55, 92; Avicenna II, 2, 474; Luka ben Serapion 15; *De lapidibus preciosis* 15 and 44; Lapidary of Marbode, 1st Romanesque translation XIX; Alphabetical Lapidary 62; Meliteniotes v. 1122; Jacques de Vitry cap. 9; Lapidary in prose 16; 2nd Lapidary in prose 18; Alexander Neckham v. 330; *De lapidibus preciosis* 44; *De la vertu des tailles* 43; *De l'entaille des gemmes* 47; *De figura* 10; Wolfram von Eschenbach 791, 21; Serapion c. 394 (*hager almagnitos*); Arnoldus Saxo 52; Bartholomaeus Anglicus XVI, 63; Thomas de Cantimpré 14, 45; Vincent de Beauvais VIII, 19–21; Albertus Magnus 2, 11, 1–2; Guillaume Le Clerc v. 3357ff.; *Lapidario* 1; *Picatrix* II, 10, 2; Lapidary of King Philip 31; Konrad von Megenberg VI, 50; Jacob van Maerlant XII, 1 and 50; Volmar v. 594–635; *Secrez* 3, 20; Saint Florian v. 451–78; *Liber defota anima* v. 6300–6409; *Vocabularius ex quo* m 51; *Liber ordinis rerum* 129, 12; Closener ma 41; Mandeville I, 23; Pseudo-Mandeville 23; Psellos 14; Leonardi II, 7, 185; *Liber secretorum* II, 1, 2; *De virtutis lapidum* II, 1; *Hortus sanitatis* V, 77; *Gart der Gesundheit* chap. 342; *Phisice* 25.

📖📖 Claude Lecouteux, "La Montagne d'Aimant," in *La montagne dans le texte médiéval: entre mythe et réalité*, ed. C. Thomasset, D. James-Raoul (Paris: Université Press–Sorbonne, 2000), 167–86, with bibliography and texts.

Portrait of Roman emperor Caracalla, amethyst intaglio, ca. 212 CE.
Photo by Marie-Lan Nguyen/Wikimedia Commons

Reclining satyr, Etruscan ca. 550 BCE.
Photo by Marie-Lan Nguyen/Wikimedia Commons

Ptolemy II and Arsinoe III carved from Indian sardonyx. Photo courtesy of Creative Commons

The Ottonian Lothair cross. Photo courtesy of Creative Commons

Warrior supporting dying comrade, ancient Roman intaglio, first century CE. Photo by Marie-Lan Nguyen/Wikimedia Commons

The Punishment of Tityus,
a rock crystal by Giovanni Bernardi (Public Domain)

Sapphire, from Konrad von Megenberg,
Buch der Natur, Heidelberg, ms. p. 300

Allectorius, Yris, from the *Hortus sanitatis*, end of the fifteenth century

Frontispiece from the *Hortus sanitaris*, Mainz, 1491

Ca. crlj.

Yris. Ysidorus. Yris apud arabiam nascitur in mari rubro coloris cristallini sexangulata. dicta ex argumento yris. Nam sub tecto pensa sole species z colores celestis arcus in proximo parietes ymitatur. Plinius Optima yris est que maximos facit arcus similimosq; celestibus.

Yris, from the *Hortus sanitatis*, end of the fifteenth century

Jeweller, frontispiece of the
chapter on stones in the *Hortus sanitatis*

Magnet of Bone: This is a magnet that pulls bone toward it when placed close to it. According to Aristotle, it is yellow, rough to the touch, and comes from the land of Balkh [Persia].

 📖 Dimishqî II, 6, 8; Arnoldus Saxo 26; Vincent de Beauvais VIII, 39; Albertus Magnus II, 3, 6; *Lapidario* 37.

Magnet of Copper: This is a yellow stone that is a mixture of dust and trash. It attracts copper when placed near it.

 📖 Dimishqî II, 6, 5; *Aristoteles* 369, 32ff.; Arnoldus Saxo 26; Vincent de Beauvais VIII, 39.

Magnet of Cotton: Aristotle called this "cotton stone." It is produced of saline substances on the seashore. It is white, and if placed near cotton, it will become attached to it. The same holds true for cloths of blended linen.

 📖 Dimishqî II, 6, 10.

Magnet of Fingernails: Aristotle called this "fingernail stone." According to him, it is mixed with dust and soft to the touch. When passed over a fingernail, it tears it off, and it attracts nail clippings to itself. Despite its softness, this stone cannot be scratched by iron or diamond, but it will crack if blood is poured on it.

 ✦ *lapis attrahens ungues;* Heb. *hatsprnim.*

 📖 Luka ben Serapion 22; *De lapidibus preciosis* 18; *Aristoteles de lapidibus* 370, 29ff.; Dimishqî II, 6, 10; *Lapidario* 140.

Magnet of Fish: A veritable gift of providence for the fisherman, when placed in the water this stone attracts fish so strongly that nothing can drive them away. The texts inform us there is no need for any net or line; the fish can be taken by hand.

 📖 *Aristoteles de lapidibus* 368, 34ff.; Prester John §46.18 (Wagner, 450).

Magnet of Gold: There is only a single mention of this loadstone in a list of singular magnets in the Arabic Aristotle. According to Dimishqî, it is the diamond.

> *Aristoteles de lapidibus* 368, 31f.; Luka ben Serapion 16; Dimishqî II, 6, 2; *Liber defota anima* v. 6312–14; *Lapidario* 15.

Magnet of Hair/Fur: According to Aristotle, this stone resembles first and foremost a tuft of hair and only after touching it will one see that it is a stone. It pulls hair off like quicklime when passed over an animal's body, and if spread over the ground, this stone will gather hair together.

> Luka ben Serapion 21; *De lapidibus preciosis* 17; Aristoteles 370, 11ff.; Dimishqî II, 6, 9; Arnoldus Saxo 26; Vincent de Beauvais VIII, 39; Albertus Magnus II, 3, 6.

Magnet of Lead: This is a horrid-smelling stone that is fusible and malleable. When a speck of it is tossed in with six drachmas of lead, it changes them into silver.

> Dimishqî II, 6, 6; Arnoldus Saxo 26; Vincent de Beauvais VIII, 39; Albertus Magnus III, 6.

Magnet of Meat/Flesh: According to Aristotle, there are two kinds: one is an animal and the other a mineral. The animal, known as a "sea hare," is a shellfish. When any kind of animal is thrown toward it, it bonds with it so strongly that it cannot be torn away, although no blood can be seen flowing from the wound. The other kind, the stone, when brought near a living animal will attract its flesh more strongly than it will a corpse.

> Luka ben Serapion 20; *De lapidibus preciosis* 16; Dimishqî II, 6, 7; Arnoldus Saxo 26; Vincent de Beauvais VIII, 39; Albertus Magnus II, 2, 11; *Lapidario* 64.

Magnet of Men: See *bahit*.

Magnet of Quicksilver: This is gold, according to Dimishqî.

📖 Dimishqî II, 6, 3.

Magnet of Silver: According to the Arabic Aristotle, it is a white stone mixed with red that reverberates like tin when touched. It can draw silver to itself from a distance of five cubits, even when the silver is securely fastened in place.

📖 Luka ben Serapion 17; *Aristoteles de lapidibus* 369, 17ff.; Dimishqî II, 6, 4; Arnoldus Saxo 26; Vincent de Beauvais VIII, 39; Albertus Magnus III, 6; *Lapidario* 96; *Liber defota anima* v. 6316ff.

Mâhâni: A light-yellow colored stone that is native to Persia. Burned and applied to hemorrhoids, it cures them. Whoever uses it as a seal is protected from terror, worries, and grief.

📖 Qazwînî (Ruska, 88).

Malachites: See *molochitis*.

📖 Leonardi II, 7, 183.

Marcedoine: This is the name Gossouin de Metz (v. 453–59) gave to chalcedony, of which he only retained the color (murky white); it bestows eloquence and the ability to plead one's case well.

Marchasita: Two kinds or marcasite are mentioned: silvery and golden. It can take on the color of any metal. It was well known to the alchemists.

📖 Luka ben Serapion 24; Avicenna II, 2, 475; *De lapidibus preciosis* 21; Albertus Magnus 2, 11, 3; *Lapidario* 172–74; *Picatrix* II, 10, 2; 8 (silvery); III, 3, 31; IV, 8, 29 (golden); *Hortus sanitatis* V, 79; Leonardi II, 7, 187.

Margarita: The pearl was considered to be a stone and almost all of the lapidaries discuss it. Isidore of Sevilla called it the "first among the white gems" (*prima candidarum gemmarum*). There are a variety of legends about the generation of pearls. In classical antiquity, they were believed to be the tears of Venus. A similar motif turns up in the Finnish *Kalevala,* in which they were created by the tears of Väinämöinen. This is what Marbode, Bishop of Rennes, had to say about them:

> Oysters open to the heavens at certain times in order to collect the dews that come from them; from this they create small balls of a brilliant white. The more dew absorbed by the oyster, the bigger the pearl. But if the heavens are in an upheaval, if there is thunder and lightning, the oysters become scared, scattering and closing after expelling the pearls, as if they had aborted them.

According to some lapidaries, morning dew creates white pearls, while evening dew produces red ones. Pearls soothe anger and melancholy; provide joy, peace, and harmony; give comfort to the heart and eyesight; give good memories; and are effective against inflammation of the blood and other fluids, leprosy (meselerie), and stomach problems. One of the *Sidrach* manuscripts states that a person who is in the habit of eating them will never die a sudden death or from poison.

Konrad von Hamburg made the pearl the symbol of the perfection of the Virgin Mary, and it was one of the twenty gems on the ring offered the Virgin in his poem *Anulus,* written circa 1350.

For his part, Ovid tells us that the stag sacred to the nymphs of the fields around Carthea wore one in his brow (*Metamorphoses* X, 14f.).

In Middle French, the pearl is called *oignon* (onion) with the following justification: "The *marguerite* or pearl is called onion because it possesses several garments and shirts, one over the other, like an onion." The interpretation is based on the homonymy between Latin *unio, union,* and *oignon*.

✦ *unio, bacca, perla, perna;* MFr. *marguerite, oignon, perle;* MSp. *margarita;* OE *eorscanstân (also designates topaz), gim, gimstân;* OIc. *gemsteinn;* Ar. *aljofar, adestaten, hager albalo.*

📖 Apocalypse 21:21; Pliny 9, 106–23; 36, 5; 37, 12; and various other places; Solin 53, 23–29; Marbode 50; Hildegard von Bingen IV, 21; *Summarium Heinrici* VI, 4, 25; Lambert de Saint-Omer 55, 45; Lapidary of Marbode, 1st Romanesque translation L; Lapidary in prose 48; *De lapidibus preciosis* 43; Luka ben Serapion 1; Serapion c. 397; Pseudo-Hugues de Saint-Victor II, 35; Dimishqî II, 7; Arnoldus Saxo 53; Bartholomaeus Anglicus XVI, 62; Vincent de Beauvais VIII, 81–83; Albertus Magnus 2, 11, 4; Lapidary of King Philip 19; Jacob van Maerlant XII, 49; Volmar v. 512–19; Pseudo-Mandeville 14; *Vocabularius ex quo* m 166; *Liber ordinis rerum* 129, 9; Closener ma 173; *Hortus sanitatis* V, 78; *Gart der Gesundheit* chap. 243; Leonardi II, 7, 178; *Poridat* 14; *Phisice* 13.

📖📖 Friedrich Ohly, "Tau und Perle," in *Schriften zur mittelalterlichen Bedeutungsforschung* (Darmstadt: Wissenschaftliche Buchgesellschaft, 1974): 274–92, and "Die Geburt der Perle aus dem Blitz," ibid., 292–311; Odo Casel, "Die Perle als religiöses Symbol," *Benidiktinische Monatsschrift* VI (1924): 321–27.

Margul:

This is an opaque, hot, moist stone that is difficult to carve and which comes from the source of the Nile in the Mountains of the Moon. It is governed by the 5° of Gemini and is especially good for young married men lying with their wives as it causes the virile member to grow.

📖 *Lapidario* 65.

Marvelous Stone (I):

This stone swims to the surface of the water when the sun is shining and dives back beneath the waves when the sun is setting or obscured by clouds. If hung around their necks, it has the property of causing animals to howl ceaselessly day and night.

✦ *lapis qui occultatur de nocte et apparet de die;* Ar. *haġar 'aġib.*

📖 Luka ben Serapion 36; *Aristoteles de lapidibus* 377, 10f.

Marvelous Stone (II): The Sea of Darkness (in other words, the ocean) tosses onto its shores a stone of little weight that cannot tolerate sunlight and which dives into the water when it appears. When hung from the neck, it prevents animals from baying. Alexander the Great discovered this and had it hung around the necks of the horses and other animals of his army, which permitted him to surprise and defeat his enemies. In a Hebrew manuscript from Munich, it is called "stone of the West," and it is gathered from the sea along with pearls. When a piece with the weight of six barley grains is hung around a horse's neck, it will be unable to neigh, as Alexander demonstrated. A fifteenth-century manuscript in the National Library of France (French ms. 2017, folio 62, v°) contains the same legend concerning Alexander, but here it involves two stones, one red and the other white, and the weight has changed: it is now a dram's worth that should be hung around the horse's neck.

+ Ar. *ḥaġar 'aġib;* Heb. *even min hama'arav.*

📖 Luka ben Serapion 35; *Aristoteles de lapidibus* 376, 30–377, 9.

Marvelous Stone (III): A German *fabliau* dating from the thirteenth or fourteenth century, *Der Jungherr und der treue Heinrich* (The Young Nobleman and Loyal Heinrich), tells how a young nobleman saw a bird holding a stone in its beak one day. The bird deposited it on the grass and began singing wonderfully before perching in a tree. The nobleman took the stone, "which gleamed like a carbuncle," and immediately felt as if he were flying like a bird. Shortly before this, the text expressly mentions that the young man could metamorphose into a bird. In the events that follow, the stone helps him to visit his lover.

📖 "Der Jungherr und der treue Heinrich," ed. Friedrich H. von der Hagen, in *Gesamtabenteuer,* vol. 3 (Stuttgart and Tübingen: J. G. Cotta, 1850): 197–255.

Meciena: According to the Lapidary of King Alfonso, this "Chaldean" name is glossed as "weeping stone" because the person wearing it is always sorrowful and grief-stricken.

If a *meciena* is placed in the bed of a sleeping person, it will have the same effect. It is found in the Indian isles, on the banks of the Careth. By nature it is hot and moist, and governed by the 20° of Capricorn.

📖 *Lapidario* 291.

Meconites: A gem that resembles a poppy and whose juice is as sweet as honey.

✦ *melonites, meconitetis, meconio*; MFr. *melanice*.

📖 Pliny 37, 173; Solin 37, 22; Isidore of Sevilla 16, 15, 20; Meliteniotes v. 1170; Thomas de Catimpré 14, 47.

Medius, Medea: According to some, the *medius* stone is black; according to others, it is green. Its discovery is attributed to the legendary sorceress Medea. It has gold-colored veins and secretes a saffron-colored fluid that tastes like wine. Its zodiac sign is Taurus. Dissolved, it is used for medicinal purposes. It is good against chronic gout, blindness, and nephritic colic. It restores vigor. Black *medius* dissolved in water and drunk causes fatal vomiting, and this blend causes the skin to peel. Blended with mother's milk and the powder of the green whetstone, it restores sight to those who have lost it. But if you wash your forehead with water in which *medius* has been dipped, you will lose your sight. Soaked in the milk of a ewe that has had only one male lamb, or a woman who has given birth to one son, and then placed in a box made of silver or glass, the *medius* will soothe gout as well as those who are gripped by frenzy.

To make an amulet from it, an image of Venus should be engraved upon it, under whose protection is placed a bream or mormyrid (fish), while she stands beneath a mulberry branch that is turned upward, and then enclose it in a pillbox. This amulet is useful against hemorrhoids and bleeding in the nose. If the branch is pointing toward the ground, it makes a phylactery that is effective against coughing up blood, nosebleeds, and hemorrhages.

✦ *media, medo, medos, medus, metus, medicos, midicos, medoria, fedus;* MFr. *mede, medux;* MHG *mêdus, meden.*

 Pliny 37, 173; Isidore of Sevilla 16, 11, 4; Damigeron 21; Marbode 36; Meliteniotes v. 1170; Lapidary of Marbode, 1st Romanesque translation XXXVI; Alphabetical Lapidary 44; Lapidary in prose 38; *Kyranides* 1, 12; Alexander Neckham v. 275ff.; Bodl. Digby 13 36; *De lapidibus preciosis* 47; Cambridge Lapidary v. 921–58; Wolfram von Eschenbach 791, 29; Arnoldus Saxo 54; Bartholomaeus Anglicus XVI, 67; Thomas de Cantimpré 14, 48; Vincent de Beauvais VIII, 85; Albert le Grand 2, 11, 5; Lapidary of King Philip 41; Konrad von Megenberg VI, 52; Jacob van Maerlant XII, 53; Closener me 25; *Liber secretorum* II, 1, 8; *De virtutis lapidum* II, 7; *Hortus sanitatis* V, 84; Leonardi II, 7, 179 (*medus*) and 188 (*medeae*).

Melas: This "black stone," also called *syrtis,* contains tiny stars. It is effective against the threats of enemies, damage, evil spells, potions, and incantations; it repels hatred and illness and provides the plaintiff with the appropriate words as well as success and victory. It permits the realization of one's plans. This stone is both consecrated and used only when the moon is waning, from the seventeenth to the thirtieth day. *The Greek Romance of Alexander* by the Pseudo-Callisthenes (§II, 36, 4) mentions black stones that Alexander's soldiers gathered from a river: the men who grabbed one turned black and only regained their normal color once they had gotten rid of the stone.

The *Hortus sanitatis* in French cites a black stone called *atramentum,* though without providing any detail.

📖 Damigeron 40; Alphabetical Lapidary 63.

Melichloros, Melichrus:
A stone named after the two colors in which it is found: one is yellow, the other is like honey. Nothing more is known about it.

✦ *melichrous, molochros, melecros, melithron.*

📖 Pliny 37, 191; Dioscorides V, 133; Isidore of Sevilla 16, 7, 15; Damigeron 75 (*meletinus*); *Summarium Heinrici* VI, 4, 13; Lambert de Saint-Omer 55, 34; Meliteniotes v. 1169.

Melichrysus:
The name of this stone designates a chrysolith whose color is quite similar to that of honey. It comes from India. Although hard, it is said to be fragile and worthless.

✦ *melectrysus, elichrysus.*

📖 Pliny 37, 128; Isidore of Sevilla 16, 15, 6; Lambert de Saint-Omer 55, 80.

Melitite:
A stone that takes its name from honey. Crushed and mixed with wax, *melitite* heals pituitous eruptions, blotches on the body, and throat ulcerations; it banishes skin ulcers and, used as a pessary in wool, pains of the womb.

📖 Isidore of Sevilla 16, 4, 26; Dioscorides V, 15; Lombard Dioscorides 160; Bartholomaeus Anglicus XVI, 64; Leonardi II, 7, 191.

Melonites:
See *meconites.*

📖 *De lapidibus preciosis* 46; Thomas de Cantimpré 14, 47; Jacob van Maerlant XII, 52.

Memnonius, Memnonia: "Memnon's stone" banishes prepared poisons, illnesses, langor, terrors, and enmities. It makes its bearer trustworthy, sincere, eloquent, steadfast, modest, and invincible, and it facilitates his encounters with everyone. If he is shipwrecked, he will save himself by swimming.

> ✦ *memninius, fumonius.*
>
> 📖 Pliny 37, 173; Damigeron 4; Alphabetical Lapidary 43; Bodl. Digby 13 35; Meliteniotes v. 1170.

Memphites: This stone gets its name from the Egyptian city of Memphis. It possesses the power to make heat like wood. Crushed, mixed with water, and given to patients to drink, it will desensitize them to cauterization or amputation.

> ✦ *memphytes, memphyten, memfites, menfites, mensites;* MFr. *menophite.*
>
> 📖 Pliny 36, 56; Isidore of Sevilla 16, 4, 14; *Summarium Heinrici* VI, 2, 11; Dioscorides V, 140; Pseudo-Dioscorides 2, 158; Lombard Dioscoridse 167; Meliteniotes v. 1128; *De lapidibus preciosis* 45; Bartholomaeus Anglicus XVI, 65; Thomas de Cantimpré 14, 46; Vincent de Beauvais VIII, 27; Albertus Magnus 2, 11; Lapidary of King Philip 66; Konrad von Megenberg VI, 51; Jacob van Maerlant XII, 51; *Secrez* 3, 25; *Vocabularius ex quo* m 301.1; Leonardi II, 7, 184; *Liber secretorum* II, 1, 9; *De virtutis lapidum* II, 8; *Hortus sanitatis* V, 83; *Phisice* 70.

Meroctes: See *molochitis.*

> 📖 Bartholomaeus Anglicus XVI, 68.

Mesomelas, Meromelas: A gem bisected by a black line, in conformance with its name. Nothing at all is known about this stone.

> 📖 Pliny 37, 174; Isidore of Sevilla 16, 11, 6 and 12, 2; Lambert de Saint-Omer 55, 57.

Midriosus: A stone that can allegedly make its bearer invisible if consecrated with the appropriate charms. It appears mainly in the legend of Prester John. It was also called *Ydoneus* because it could be found in a river with this name. Its creation is due to a misreading of Latin abbreviations meaning "in the nest" (*in nidis*). It is an eagle stone. See *aetites*.

✦ *nudiosi, nucliosi, nadyosis, indiosi, riridiosi, nodosi, radiosi, nides, ydonici.*

📖 Prester John §29 (Zarncke; Wagner, 359, 369, 375, 415, 445; Anthony, 337).

Militites: See *hepatites*.

Mirâd: A marvelous red stone, which is dry and warm by nature, and found in southern lands. If it is born in northern regions, it is naturally cold and dank. Qazwînî says that in Greek it is called *sarutatis*, "flying stone," because it is created by vapors rising from the earth. If one takes this stone, one can compel the obedience of demons who will offer to fulfill your every wish.

📖 Qazwînî (Ruska, 88).

Mithrax: This gem comes from Persia and the mountains bordering the Red Sea. It comes in a variety of colors and displays diverse reflections when exposed to sunlight.

✦ *mirthridax, mitridas.*

📖 Pliny 37, 173; Isidore of Sevilla 16, 4, 22; *Summarium Heinrici* VI, 2, 20; Meliteniotes v. 1171.

Mitrydax: See *mithrax*.

📖 Isidore of Sevilla 16, 4, 22; *Summarium Heinrici* VI, 5, 3; Leonardi II, 7, 190.

Molaris Lapis: A synonym for *pyrites*.

📖 Pliny 36, 136f.

Mole Stone: See *aspalachites*.

Molochitis: Malachite is a copper hydroxide carbonate that is still called melonite and is described as a green stone whose color is darker and duller than that of the emerald. The name malachite comes from mauve, a color it sometimes possesses. It is found in Arabia. It is good for making tablets and is endowed with a natural medicinal virtue that makes it suitable for protecting children—those still in the cradle, some texts say—against the dangers that threaten them, mainly evil spells, and this stone protects its bearer from accidents. It is said to soften gold. It is also used to make Venus talismans, which protect against leeches. Malachite also keeps one safe from lightning and night terrors.

The anonymous Dominican author of the fourteenth-century *Rosarius* said malachite represented the Virgin Mary.

There are several varieties of this gem. The one that is a diaphanous black is known as *promnion;* the ruby-colored one is called *alexandrinum,* and the one that is the same hue as carnelian is the *cyprium.* It can be found in India, Galatia, near Tyre, and in the Alps.

✦ *molochites, melochides, melochites, malachites, melonites, meroctes;* MFr. *melochite, melocite, melocete, malaquite, malachite, maliada;* MHG *melochîtes;* MSp. *melozio;* Ar. *eidhenegi, dhaneg, dehenc, dehenech, cimetît;* Heb. *alzahng.*

📖 Pliny 37, 114; Solin 33, 20; Isidore of Sevilla 16, 7, 11; Marbode 54; *Summarium Heinrici* VI, 4, 9; Pseudo-Dioscorides 2, 152; Lambert de Saint-Omer 55, 32; Luka ben Serapion 7; *De lapidibus preciosis* 7; Lapidary of Marbode, 1st Romanesque translation LIV; Lapidary in prose 51; Cambridge lapidary v. 1261–72; Wolfram von Eschenbach 791, 28; Arnoldus Saxo 55; Albertus Magnus 2, 11, 6; *Picatrix* II, 10, 6; 64; 78; IV, 8, 28; *Poridat* 9; *Rosarius* 4; *Hortus sanitatis* V, 82.

Molotius: See *morochthos*.

📖 Isidore of Sevilla 16, 4, 32.

Monogrammos, Monogramma: A variety of chalcedony known as *plasma*.

📖 Pliny 37, 118.

Moon Stone: It is pale white with red, or black, or sometimes yellow veins. It illuminates the night like the full moon. Sometimes it only glows at certain times and under specific constellations. It preserves the virtues of the body, protects from storms, heals lunatics, and help win honors. See *selenite*.

📖 Mandeville I 10; Pseudo-Mandeville 12; *Phisice* 11.

Mormorion, Morion: There are several different kinds of this stone. The stone from India is transparent and deep black in color, and it is also called *pramnion,* which brings to mind one of the names for malachite. There is also the variety from Alexandria that has a mixture of the color of rubies, and the one from Cypress shares the color of *sarda*. This seems to have been a form of marble, since the authors say it is good for making tombs.

📖 Pliny 37, 173; Meliteniotes v. 1169 (*marmaros*); Leonardi II, 7, 189.

Morochthos: This would be chalk for whitewashing; when cut, it releases a milky fluid.

✦ *meroctes, morochthe, moroptos, moroctius, molotius, moroxos.*

📖 Pliny 37, 173; Dioscorides V, 134; Lombard Dioscorides 161; Meliteniotes v. 1128 and 1171; Pseudo-Dioscorides 2, 152; Bartholomaeus Anglicus XVI, 68.

Mucul, Mucula: This is the name given by the Persians to *thelycardios*. See this name.

📖 Pliny 37, 183.

Murmur, Murmus: This is a stone that mice carry into their nests in order to give birth more easily. It is white, resembles a hailstone, and is good for pregnant women. It increases its bearer's wealth and bestows grace on him.

📖 Pseudo-Mandeville 54; *Phisice* 79 (unnamed) and 91.

Mutil: Still called aquileus "eagle" and "break glass," this iron-colored stone is square and breaks glass and other stones. Rogues have a great liking for it as they can stain it with dragon's blood (a mixture of tannin and resin) and then rub it over their hands and faces, giving themselves the appearance of leprosy.

📖 Lapidary of King Philip 81; Pseudo-Mandeville 55; *Phisice* 92.

Muytes: All we know about this bezoar is that it is extracted from the rat. This stone appears in the sixteenth-century book *Le Parfait Joallier ou Histoire des pierries* (The Perfect Jeweler, or the History of Stones) by Anselm Boëtius de Boodt (1550–1632).

Mynda/Modon: A brilliant white stone found in the Tigris River. It provides protection against the attacks of wild beasts.

📖 Pseudo-Plutarch §26; De mirabilibus auscultationibus §159.

Myrmecias: A black gem that displays wartlike protrusions and bumps; perhaps it is identical to myrmecites.

📖 Pliny 37, 174; Meliteniotes v. 1171.

Myrmecitis, Myrmecites: A stone that contains "the image of an ant rampant," hence its name.

📖 Pliny 37, 187; Solin 37, 22; Isidore of Sevilla 16, 15, 19; Meliteniotes v. 1171.

Myrrhitis: This stone, which is found in Persia, has the same color as myrrh and scarcely appears to be a gem; when rubbed it releases a perfume-like scent that smells like nard. It is an antidote for people who have been poisoned and is a great means of attraction, especially for women.

✦ *myrritis, murritis, mirites.*

📖 Pliny 37, 174; Solin 37, 10; Isidore of Sevilla 16, 7, 14; Kerygma 46; *Summarium Heinrici* VI, 4, 12; Lambert de Saint-Omer 55, 33; Meliteniotes v. 1171; Leonardi II, 7, 182.

Myrrina: Murrhine was understood as being a liquid substance that would solidify under the effect of heat. The best came from Carmania (Kirman or Carmana today). It was used for eating and drinking vessels and they were quite expensive. Nero bought a murrhine cup for more than one million sesterces.

📖 Pliny 37, 18–22; Isidore of Sevilla 16, 12, 6; *Summarium Heinrici* VI, 5, 7; Lambert de Saint-Omer 55, 87; *Hortus sanitatis* V, 82; Leonardi II, 7, 181.

Myrsinitis: This stone is the color of honey and smells like myrtle, to which its name refers.

📖 Pliny 37, 174; Meliteniotes v. 1172.

N

Narcissitis: When crushed, this moderately green and marbled stone releases the odor of narcissus, hence its name. It bears the sign of Mars. Whoever uses the *narcissitis* shall triumph over all.

 📖 Pliny 21, 25; 37, 188; Damigeron 44; Meliteniotes v. 1172.

Nasamonites: This stone has the color of blood with black veins. Its name indicates it comes from the land of the Nasamons, a word sometimes used to designate a savage people of Africa and sometimes the Numidians.

 ✦ *nassonites, nassamonites.*
 📖 Pliny 37, 175; Solin 27, 43; Meliteniotes v. 1171; Leonardi II, 7, 194.

Náttúrusteinar: The name, which literally means "stones with natures" (i.e., stones possessing powerful, supernatural virtues), was a general term for magical and marvelous stones in medieval Iceland. In addition to the stones that guarantee victory (*sigrsteinar*), which appear rather frequently in the fourteenth- and fifteenth-century legendary sagas (e.g., the *Þorsteins saga Víkingssonar* [Saga of Thorstein, Son of Viking], chap. 16), we also find stones that make it possible to change one's appearance and grant other magical powers.

For example, in the *Nikulás saga leikara* (Saga of Nikulás Leikari), King Nikulás of Hungary had come into the possession of some stones and a man reveals their powers to him:

> That red stone has the power that if you have it with you in battles, then you will gain victory; and you will never become poor with whatever you have. And poison may not harm you, and no evil spell may affect you. And this is the nature of the blue: cold may never harm you, and you will not grow tired swimming. And fire will not scathe you, and no magic. That is the nature of the green stone: if you enclose it in your hand, then no one may see you wherever you have gone. And you may adopt those human shapes for any destiny that you wish, and obtain the love of those women whom you wish to choose. You seem to me a more daring, bold man than any example to be found.

In the *Þorsteins þáttr bæjarmagns* (Tale of Thorstein House-Power; chap. 3 and 10), a dwarf offers a black stone to a hero who rescued his daughter from the clutches of an eagle. When concealed in the hand, it makes one invisible. The dwarf then gives him a steel point and another triangular stone that is white in the middle, red on the other side, and has a yellow border (*Hallrinn var þríhyrndr. Hann var hvítr í miðju, en rauðr öðrum megin, en gul rönd utan um*). If the steel point is stuck in the white part of the stone, it causes a hailstorm; in the yellow, a blazing hot sun; and in the red: fire, embers, and a shower of sparks. If the stone and the point are thrown, they return of their own accord when called (*hann kemr sjálfr aptr í hönd þér, þegar þú kallar*).

In the *Jökuls þáttr Búasonar* (Tale of Jokul Buason; chap. 3), the hero receives a ring in which a stone is set; when slipped onto the finger it turns one invisible. A little later (chap. 5), Jokul says he knows how to craft a helmet of invisibility (*hulinshjálmr*).

In the *Nítíða saga* (Saga of Nitida; chap. 1), an invisibility stone works on large objects: "the maiden-king [*meykóngur*] took a supernatural stone and quickly waved it over the ship and the heads of all who were on board." Another episode (chap. 3) relates, "The queen Nítíða then looked into another supernatural stone so that, whether she sat or stood, nobody could see her". There are also *náttúrusteinar* that confer the ability see things that are far away (chap. 3): "Now it is to be said of the maiden-king that she looked into her supernatural stones every day to see throughout the world if Vikings were coming to attack her kingdom. She saw where King Ingi sailed, and that, late one day, he came to France."

Also appearing in various texts are the *fésteinn* (livestock stone), a bezoar; the *lausnarsteinn* (releasing stone = *corvia*), used to facilitate childbirth; and the *sögusteinn* (saga stone), a "speaking stone" that permits divination and can be found in a wagtail's nest during the month of May. It is worn around the neck, wrapped in a blood-soaked scarf. Other stones allow the possessor to perform magic, for example to bewitch a princess who one wishes to wed, and also to bewitch those who would otherwise hinder her kidnapping. In Iceland, the *ceraunia* is called "thunderstone" (*skruggusteinn*) and it is said that its owner can see the whole world.

A short lapidary can be found in the *Hauksbók* written by Haukr Erlendsson (died 1334) that lists seven stones (*ematistes, crisopatius, gerathises, magnetis, adamantes, allectorius celidonius*) along with their magical properties.

See also *corvia, hulinhjálmsteinn, lífsteinn, livestock stone, saga stone, sólarsteinn, segulsteinn, wishing stone.*

📖 *Ajax saga frækna*, ed. H. Erlendsson and Einar Þórðarson, in *Fjórar Riddarasögur* (Reykjavík: Einar Þórðarson, 1852); *Gibbons saga*, ed. R. I. Page, Editiones Arnamagnaeanae B 2 (Copenhagen: Munksgaard, 1960); *Hauksbok udgiven efter de Arnamagnaeanske Handskrifter No. 371, 544 to 675, (quarter) samt forskellige Papirshandskrifter af det Kongelige Nordiske Oldskrift-Selskab* (Copenhagen: Thiele, 1892): 227–28; *Jökuls þáttr Búasonar*, in *Kjalnesinga saga*, ed. Jóhannes Halldórsson, Íslenzk Fornrit 14 (Reykjavík: Hið íslenzka fornritafélag, 1959); Keren H. Wick, *An Edition and Study of Nikulás saga leikara* (Dissertation, University of Leeds, 1996);

Nitida saga, ed. Agnete Loth, in *Late Medieval Icelandic romances,* Editiones Arnamagnaeanae B 24 (Copenhagen: Munksgaard, 1962); Sheryl McDonald, "*Nítíða saga:* A Normalised Icelandic Text and Translation," *Leeds Studies in English* 40 (2009): 119–45. *Rémundar saga Keisarasonar,* ed. Sven Grén Broberg, SUGNL 38 (Copenhagen: Møller, 1909–1912); *Þorsteins saga Víkingssonar,* in *Fornaldarsögur Nordrlanda,* ed. Carl Christian Rafn, vol. 2 (Copenhagen: Popp, 1829); *Þorsteins þáttr bæjarmagns,* ed. Guðni Jónsson, in *Fornaldar sögur Norðurlanda,* vol. 3 (Reykjavík: Íslendingasagnaútgáfan, 1950).

📖📖 Jón Árnason, *Íslenzkar Þióðsögur og Æventýri* (Leipzig: J. C. Hinrich, 1862–1864), Frederik L. Grundtvig, *Løsningsstenen* (Copenhagen: Schønberg, 1878), 154–55 (*lífsteinn*); 164–65 (invisibility); 217–18 (transportation by virtue of stone and runes).

Nebride, Nebritis:
Sacred to Bacchus, this gem earned its name because of its resemblance to the stag skin (*nebrides*) worn by that god. Its name covers two stones, one of which is black. It enables one to hear the gods. *Nebrides* removes the pain of snakebite, banishes asps, and inspires the wife's desire for her husband.

✦ *nebridum, nebrium, nebride, nebrice, neurites, nebrites, norites.*

📖 Pliny 37, 175; Orpheus v. 748ff.; Kerygma 24; Pseudo-Hippocrates 16; Meliteniotes v. 1173.

Nemesitis, Nemessitis:
The "stone of destiny." Its magical properties stem from the engravings it bears. If an image of Nemesis standing upon a wheel is carved on this stone, or her feet trampling on a bull, while holding a cubit-rule in her left hand and a wand in her right, and if one wears it on one's finger, it is useful against demonic phantasms in dreams, nightmares, and in children's fears, according to the *Kyranides.* The old French version is even more detailed:

> Engrave the image of a maid on the *nemecite* stone, with her feet resting on a fixed wheel and who is holding cubit-rule in her left hand and a wand in her right. Beneath this stone place a little pilot

fish and the herb *nécya* [MFr. *nokia*], then set the entire combination in a gold or silver ring when the sun is in the sign of Scorpio. Know that his ring possesses an extremely wonderful property: if you give it to someone who is possessed, the demon will immediately admit his presence and flee and the individual will be restored to his good senses and virtue. It is good against dreams and the fantasies to which those possessed by demons fall prey, and against the fears of small children, and against all evil events that occur at night . . . It is necessary for the bearer to abstain from sin.

Undoubtedly in conformance with its name, *nemecitis* indicates to its wearer the number of years he is destined to live and the place of his death!

📖 *Kyranides* 1, 13; *Secrez* 4, 11; Leonardi II, 7, 195.

Nicolus:
A bicolored stone that is yellow on the surface and black within, and sometimes all black. It is considered to be a kind of chalcedony. It gives victory to its bearer and makes him congenial to all. In the sixteenth century, the lapidaries said it was onxy or sardonyx.

📖 Leonardi II, 7, 193.

Nicomar, Nycomar:
Another name for alabaster and the marble family; the stone is described as being cold and white. It preserves perfumes and prevents the odor of corpses from becoming too strong, and was therefore used to make funerary monuments and vases. Spices were kept fresh in it. Reduced to a powder, it cured illnesses of the chest and the udder. It was also said to enable love to be preserved and to grant victory. See *alabastrum*.

✦ *nychomas, nic(h)omai, incomar*; MFr. *nichonias, nichomas*.

📖 Arnoldus Saxo 57; Albertus Magnus 2, 12, 2; Lapidary of King Philip 82; Pseudo-Mandeville 56; *Liber secretorum* II, 1, 30; *De virtutis lapidum* II, 39; *Phisice* 94.

Nilion, Nilus: This gem has a dull luster that is fleeting and that becomes invisible when stared at. Its color is that of a smoke-colored topaz, or sometimes with a tint like honey. According to Juba, it is produced on the banks of the Nile in Ethiopia, which is how it gets its name. Sudines says that it can also be found in the Siberus, a river in Attica. It can be found in India and elsewhere in Attica as well.

📖 Pliny 37, 114; Meliteniotes v. 1174.

Nipparene: A stone that resembles the teeth of the hippopotamus. It bears the name of a city and a people in Persia.

📖 Pliny 37, 157; Meliteniotes v. 1173 (*niparios*).

Nisus: A stone found in the head of a toad. It is therefore *borax* or *crapaudine*. See *batrachites, borax*.

📖 *Hortus sanitatis* V, 87.

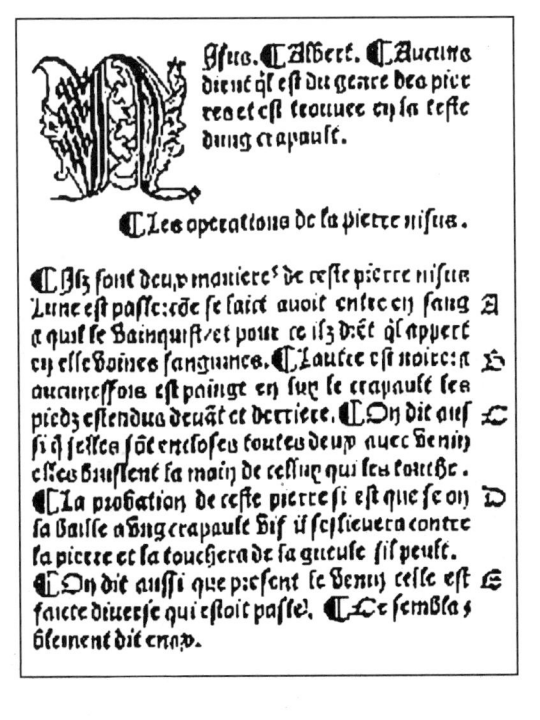

Nitrum: Natron, or niter (or in Avicenna's work *baurach armenus, mûruz,* and *altin alamen*), a form of saltpeter, is a pale and transparent stone effective against jaundice. Crushed into powder and blended with honey, it calms wrath and kills parasites.

 Isidore of Sevilla 16, 2, 7; Avicenna II, 2, 88 and 522; Bartholomaeus Anglicus XVI, 70; Arnoldus Saxo 56; Albertus Magnus 2, 12, 1; Konrad von Megenberg VI, 53; *Hortus sanitatis* V, 89; Leonardi II, 7, 192.

Nose: *Nose* can be either semiwhite with red veins running through it or black and sometimes marked with a toad with its legs spread. If two *nose* stones are contained in the presence of poison, they will burn the hand of whoever touches them. To identify it, it is necessary to put a living toad in the stone's presence: he will leap toward it and touch it if he can. According to Leonardi, *nose* is another name for alabastrite but other authors refer to it as *borax,* to wit *crapaudine,* which corresponds more closely to its description above. See *batrachites, borax.*

✦ *nisus, nosech, nusae.*

 Arnoldus Saxo 58; Albertus Magnus 2, 12, 3; Konrad von Megenberg VI, 55; Leonardi II, 7, 196.

Notia: Another name for the *ombria,* a stone that falls from the sky during storms. The stone takes its name from the Greek name for the south wind, *notos,* a rainy wind.

 Pliny 37, 176.

Nutill: See *mutil.*

O

Oangari: Another name for the "ass stone" (*asini lapis, petra asini*), which also designates the chrysolith. It forms a growth on the animal's forehead. The name is due to an error where a copyist read *oangari* as *oangri* (i.e., onager, wild ass). Another name found in French lapidaries is "stone of the ass's forehead." See this name and *asinius*.

 📖 Leonardi II, 7, 209.

Obsianus: Obsidian, a natural aluminum silicate called "volcano glass," "mirror of the Incas," and "Iceland agate," owes its name to its discoverer, Obsidius, or so it is said. It is deep black and sometimes transparent, but this is a dull transparency so if one were to be hung on the wall like a mirror, it would display the shadow instead of the image of objects. It has often been used for making jewelry. According to Pliny the Elder, it is found in India, the Samnium region (Italy), and Spain. It is useful for those traveling by sea or river. Accompanied by burning pine resin, incense, and lepidota, obsidian grants the gift of prophecy. The sun and moon are engraved on it. Benoît de Sainte-Maure recalled its properties when, in his *Romance of Troy,* he described the Chamber of Beauty (v. 17767ff.), but he adds that it regenerates and grants youth. Whoever wears obsidian shall never have nightmares, and anyone he curses shall die soon afterward.

✦ *opsianus, obsidius, obsius, obsiana, obsyontes, oprianus, obsidianum, obsidius lapis, absiamus;* Ar. *sabh, cysaban.*

📖 Pliny 36, 196f.; 37, 177; Kerygma 9; Pseudo-Hippocrates 34; Nautical lapidary 7; Isidore of Sevilla 16, 4, 21; Damigeron 25; Meliteniotes v. 1176; *Summarium Heinrici* VI, 2, 19; *De lapidibus preciosis* 13; Alphabetical Lapidary 68; Leonardi II, 7, 203.

Odontolycius:

The "wolf's tooth" is not described in the lapidaries, which limit themselves to describing its virtues. This stone brings luck to soldiers, hunters, and to all those who wish to steal something; it is very useful to thieves and hydromancers. It is a good amulet for children.

✦ *odontolicius, ondontolicio, adonzelicius, lontilimo, lantelius.*

📖 Damigeron 18; Meliteniotes v. 1175 (*odontoeides*); Alphabetical Lapidary 60; Leonardi II, 7, 212.

Oica, Olca: See *orca*.

📖 Pliny 37, 176; Isidore of Sevilla XVI, 12, 1; Leonardi II, 7, 212.

Okitokius:

This name refers to a pretty and resonant *aetites*. It is made into an amulet by carving a swallow on it with a scorpion at its feet, which is standing on the bembra fish.

📖 *Kyranides* 1, 25; *Secrez* 4, 22; Leonardi II, 7, 208.

Olea: See *orca*.

📖 Leonardi II, 7, 212.

Ombria: This is another name for the *ceraunia*, which some call *notia*. This stone is said to fall with rain and lightning bolts, like *ceraunia* and *brontea*. It is attributed with the same effect as the latter stone. The commentators add, however, that when placed on altars this stone prevents the offerings from burning. See *ceraunias, brontea,* and *notia*.

 📖 Pliny 37, 170; Meliteniotes v. 1174; Leonardi II, 7, 210.

OMBRIA

Önkesteinn: See *wishing stone*.

Onocardia: A gem that resembles a cochineal insect.

 📖 Pliny 37, 176.

Onyx, Onychinus: This name—which is sometimes used to designate Carmanian marble, sometimes alabaster, and sometimes chalcedony, and even some varieties of sardonyx—refers to a stone that has a white portion similar to a human fingernail, hence its name. A myth explains how it formed: one day, Cupid was clipping Venus's nails while she lay sleeping and the Parcae transformed these clippings into stone. Onyx also shares the color of the chrysolith, sarda, and jasper. Arabian onyx is black with white zones. It is supposed to heal head sores and help the secretion of drool and saliva in the children wearing it. There are several kinds of onyx among the Arabs (the *baqarânian, arwian,* Persian, and Abyssinian). It arouses sorrow and anxiety, renders the soul stubborn, and makes for wrathful and difficult moods. In thirteenth-century France, it was believed to make one quarrelsome. There is another kind of onyx that is tricolored: honey, black, and white. It will give one beautiful progeny if engraved with the image of Apollo and Artemis, and consideration and prosperity to its bearer when he advances through a crowd. A third onyx, which is white and translucent, should be carved with the circumvolution of a serpent with the forequarters or head of a lion and rays, in other words the image of the decan Chnoubis. When worn or carried, this stone will prevent stomach pains. It will increase the saliva of a child who wears one around his or her throat. A fourth onyx is black: it is useful for pregnant women and those who are breastfeeding. A three-headed Chnoubis should be carved on it. A scarab in the middle of an egg is engraved on the perileukios onyx; this talisman ensures a splendid progeny, high esteem, and prosperity. It should be set in gold for it to deploy its full properties. An onyx worn at the throat or on the finger will inspire sorrow, fear, nightmares, and disputes because it causes black bile to circulate, especially in the head, and it makes it possible to see devils. It is a malefic stone whose effects are countered by the presence of sardonyx. Whoever wears an onyx ring shall be sad, pensive, and melancholy; he will have deceitful bad dreams and experience litigation and scenes of discord. The stone is also used to make one of the Venus talismans, which protect a place from flies, and another that relieves children with stomachache.

Another tradition maintains that onyx is used in dream necromancy. To speak with a dead friend at night, it is necessary to wear onyx around one's throat or on a finger. Upon awakening, the dreamer will remember what the dead person needs.

If one finds an onyx with the image of a camel or two goats among myrtles, it has the power to summon demons, gather them together, and imprison them. If worn on one's person, it will cause terrible dreams.

If one sees an image on an onyx of a man standing and holding a weapon in his hand, this stone has the power to win for its owner the esteem of all kings and princes.

If a man wielding a sword in his hand is depicted on a small onyx (*onichilus*), it should be set in a ring of any kind. Its owner will be feared and loved, and he will receive the honor of the powerful and the rulers.

A stag or a viper carved on an onyx give its owner courage, calls demons together and sends them fleeing, and calms evil winds.

In the Bible, the onyx is one of the twelve stones adorning the *rationale* or breastplate of Aaron, the high priest (Exodus 28:15–30).

In the *Livre du Graal* (Book of the Grail; §111), when Bohort and Lionel arrive at the dwelling of King Claudias, the Lady of the Lake places a crown of flowers on Lionel's head, and hangs around his neck "a gold clasp embellished with many precious stones, which caused him to burn with the desire to commit a folly." This effect is attributed to the strength of the herbs and the stones of the clasp, and could very easily refer to the virtues of the onyx.

The *onichinus* provides extraordinary dreams.

✦ *onix, onycha, onica, onychites, onichitis, onichilus, onochinus, onocinus, onchinius, enichinus, enichius, orincles*; MFr. *onicle, onich, orniche, orache, oriches, orinches, enice, eniches, honice, honiche*; MHG *onichen, onich, honiche, onisse, orache;* ME *begantoneles (besant onicle), vnycle;* MItal. *onica;* Ar. *lesen, elgesha, elgeysa, goza, gahza, dschaza, aliaza, aliarzaha.*

📖 Pliny 36, 59–61; 37, 90f.; Kerygma 32–36; Isidore of Sevilla 16, 8, 3; Aetios II, 38; Dioscorides V, 135 and 139; Marbode 9; Hildegard von Bingen IV, 3; Old English Lapidary 6 (*onichinus*); Lambert de Saint-Omer 55, 25; *Kyranides* 1, 15; Meliteniotes v. 1120; Jacques de Vitry cap. 91; Lapidary of Marbode, 1st Romanesque translation IX; Alphabetical Lapidary 69–70; Lapidary in prose 46; 2nd Lapidary in prose 7; Alexander Neckham v. 163ff.; Luka ben Serapion 6; *De lapidibus preciosis* 5; 48–49; Bodl. Digby 13 41; Cambridge lapidary v. 267–76; Gossouin de Metz v. 432–45 and 460–69; *Sidrac* 11; *De la vertu des tailles* 49; *De l'entaille des gemmes* 48; Dimishqî II, 5, 4; Wolfram von Eschenbach 791, 3; Serapion c. 401 (hager aliazaha); *De figura* 16; *Liber lapidarii* 10; Arnoldus Saxo 59; Bartholomaeus Anglicus XVI, 72; Thomas de Cantimpré 14, 49-50; Vincent de Beauvais VIII, 87; Albertus Magnus 2, 13, 1–2; *Picatrix* II, 10, 2–3; 50; 63 and 66f.; III, 1, 5; III, 3, 28; Lapidary of King Philip 11; Konrad von Megenberg VI, 56; Jacob van Maerlant XII, 54 (*onichinus*) and 55 (*onix*); Saint Florian v. 331–54; Volmar v. 255–64; *Secrez* 3, 8; 4, 13; *Psellus* 15; *Vocabularius ex quo* o 209 and 209.2; Mandeville I 17; Pseudo-Mandeville 20 and 36; Leonardi II, 7, 197f.; *Liber secretorum* II, 1, 4; Ragiel 7; Solomon 10; *Hortus sanitatis* V, 91; *Libro di Sidrach* chap. 464; *Phisice* 19 and 71.

Opallios: In the opal is found the subtle flame of the carbuncle, the purplish gleam of the amethyst, and the sea-green color of the emerald, says Pliny the Elder. India produces a variety called *sangenon* and opal from Egypt has the name *taenites.* By virtue of its great beauty, many gave the irised opal the name of *paederos* or *paederota.* Opal is effective for eye maladies. For this reason, its name was quite quickly distorted into *ophthalmius.*

It is the trump for robbers, for it covers its bearer with a thick fog screening him from the view of those around him, thus making him invisible, and also increases his eyesight, which is why another name for the opal is "thieves' stone." If magic letters are carved on it, it will banish Hecate's phantasms, encourage the love of boys, and obtain the satisfaction of one's requests. The person who owns an opal can never be arrested or restrained by any bonds.

✦ *apalius, oppalius, oprallius, oppallius, optalius, optallion, ophtalius, ophtalmius, ostolamus, ostolanus, obtalmius, oltamius, astamus, ostenius, ostomus, ostola;* MFr. *optal, obtalmius, optal(l)ie, optalig, optal;* MHG *optallies, ostolan, openkas, optalias.*

📖 Pliny 37, 80f.; Orpheus v. 281–91; Kerygma 38; Pseudo-Hippocrates 23; Isidore of Sevilla 16, 12, 3; Damigeron 24; Marbode 49; *Summarium Heinrici* VI, 5, 5; Lambert de Saint-Omer 55, 86; Meliteniotes v. 1122; Lapidary of Marbode, 1st Romanesque translation XLIX; Alphabetical Lapidary 67; Bartholomaeus Anglicus XVI, 73; Wolfram von Eschenbach 791, 5; Arnoldus Saxo 60; Albert the Grand 2, 13, 3; Lapidary of King Philip 57; Saint Florian v. 850–59; *Liber secretorum* II, 1, 3; Volmar v. 544–57; *Hortus sanitatis* V, 90 (*obtalmius*) and 93 (*opalus*); Closener on 4 and 6; Leonardi II, 7, 199–200; *Phisice* 56.

Ophicardelon: This stone, whose name might mean "snake heart," is a black agate bordered by two white bands.

✦ *oficardelus, opycardelus, opphicardelus.*

📖 Pliny 37, 177; Leonardi II, 7, 207.

Ophiokoilos: This "stone of the serpent's belly" comes from Egypt. It protects its bearer from storms at sea.

📖 Nautical lapidary 6.

Ophites, Ophietis: The "snake stone" is helpful against venom, problems affecting the eyes, head, and ears, and it helps make one more apt to procreate. Its smoke drives away snakes and it has the power to conjure spirits who predict the future in the voice of an infant. Ophite is dark vermilion, cures the possessed and viper bites, kindles fire, and fuels the flame of a candle. It restores sight to eyes whose vision is disturbed. The Lapidary of King Alfonso mentions two: one governed by the 7° of Gemini and the other by the 12° of Libra.

Ophite, a rock whose texture falls midway between that of granite and porphyry, was once identified as being the same as serpentine.

✦ *ofites, pietra serpentaria;* MFr. *pierre de serpent;* Sp. *piedra de serpente;* Ar. *alazaracen, alazaracorem;* Chald. *bezaquid.*

📖 Pliny 36, 55; Orpheus v. 461ff.; Kerygma 12–13; Pseudo-Hippocrates 38; Isidore of Sevilla 16, 5, 3; Aetios II, 29; Dioscorides V, 143; Pseudo-Dioscorides 2, 162; Lombard Dioscorides 170; *Summarium Heinrici* VI, 3, 2; *Avicenna* II, 2, 416 (*lapis serpentis i. alazaracen*); Vincent de Beauvais VIII, 5 and 16; *Lapidario* 67 and 163; Lapidary of King Philip 86; *Hortus sanitatis* V, 95; Leonardi II, 7, 205.

Ophtalmus: See *opallios*.

✦ *obtalmicus, obtalius, olchanius.*

📖 Albertus Magnus 2, 13, 3; Saint Florian v. 850–59; *Liber secretorum* II, 1, 3; *De virtutis lapidum* II, 2.

Orachites: See *galactitis*.

Orca: A stone that displays a pleasing array of black, red, green, and white.

✦ *oica, olca, iolca, olea.*

📖 Pliny 37, 176; Isidore of Sevilla 16, 12, 1; *Summarium Heinrici* VI, 5, 2.

Orique: See *sorige*.

Oritis: A round stone that is either black or green with white patches, or like a grater on one side and smooth on the other. It is not transformed or heated by fire. To determine if the stone you have is truly an *oritis*, put it in a fire: if it is heat-resistant, it is an *oritis*. There are three varieties: one black, one green, and lastly one that is copper (reddish brown). The green stone is the best; when carried, it protects its bearer from a variety of mortal dangers. Rubbed with rose essence, it protects its bearer from adversity and the venomous bites of reptiles. Carried by a woman with an iron wand, it

prevents pregnancy, and if she is already pregnant, it will cause her to abort. *Oritis* also offers protection from wild animals. Crushed into a powder and drunk, this stone cures the bites of venomous animals. It is also another name for siderite (*sideritis*).

✦ *orithes, oristes, oriten, ortites, onites;* MFr. *oryte, orite, oriste, oricte, ariste, torites, corites, cornice, erides;* MHG *orîtes, orate, grîte, aristes, onides, enites, elyte.*

📖 Pliny 37, 176; Orpheus v. 419ff.; Pseudo-Hippocrates 37; Damigeron 16; Marbode 43; Meliteniotes v. 1173; Lapidary of Marbode, 1st Romanesque translation XLIII; Lapidary in prose 42; 2nd Lapidary in prose 30; Alexander Neckham v. 297ff.; Cambridge lapidary v. 1077–1102; Wolfram von Eschenbach 791, 18; Bodl. Digby 13; *De lapidibus preciosis* 51; Arnoldus Saxo 61; Bartholomaeus Anglicus XVI, 74; Thomas de Cantimpré 14, 52; Albertus Magnus 2, 13, 4; Lapidary of King Philip 49; Konrad von Megenberg VI, 58; Jacob van Maerlant XII, 57; Volmar v. 564–71 (*orate, aristes, onides, enites*); Closener or 42; *Hortus sanitatis* V, 94; Leonardi II, 7, 201; *Phisice* 50 and 69.

Ornicus: Another name for sapphire.

 📖 Leonardi II, 7, 211.

Orphanus: The "Orphan" is a single stone, hence its name, on the throne of the crown of the Germanic Holy Roman Empire. Wine-colored, it glows at night and keeps vigil over the royal honor. A legend passed down in an adventure romance entitled *Herzog Ernst,* which dates from the end of the twelfth century, tells how this unique stone came into the possession of Kaiser Otto I. During his underground voyage through an Indian mountain on a raft borne by the waves, Ernst spotted stones shining in the darkness and tore one from the rock wall with a blow of his sword. Upon returning to Bamberg, he gave it to the Kaiser as a gift of reconciliation, for he had been banished by the ruler. In the Vienna manuscript of *Herzog Ernst,* the stone is a carbuncle. The Orphan is frequently mentioned in the poems of the minnesinger Walther von der Vogelweide (thirteenth century) as a symbol of the empire. It should be noted that the Spanish crown held a magnificent pearl called the Orphan (*huefarna*) or Solitaire (*Sola*). It vanished in 1734, during a fire at the royal palace.

Lastly, *orphanus* (and *pupillus*) designated the round, milky-white opal that is called *augstein* in Middle High German.

 ✦ *orfanus;* MHG *weise.*

 📖 Albertus Magnus 2, 13, 5; *Hortus sanitatis* V, 92; Leonardi II, 7, 202.

📖 Thomas Ehlen, *Hystoria ducis Bauarie Ernesti*, ScriptOralia 96 (Tübingen: Narr, 1996); *Gesta Ernesti ducis,* ed. Peter Christian Jacobsen and Peter Orth (Erlangen: Universitätsbund Erlangen-Nürnberg, 1997); Brigitte Gansweidt, *Der 'Ernestus' des Odo von Magdeburg,* Münchener Beiträge z. Mediävistik und Renaissance-Forschung 39 (Munich: Georg Olms, 1989); Cornelia Weber, *Untersuchung und überlieferungskritische Edition des Herzog Ernst B,* GAG 611 (Göppingen: Kümmerle, 1994).

Orphites: See *ophites.*

📖 Closener or 57.

Ostolanus: See *oppalus.*

✦ *ostolamus, ostomus, ostolan.*

📖 *De lapidibus preciosis* 50; Thomas de Cantimpré 14, 51; Konrad von Megenberg VI, 57; Jacob van Maerlant XII, 56; Saint Florian v. 850–59; Closener os 18; 19.

Ostracios: Another name for *ostracite* or *cadmitis.* According to Damigeron, it is used to make talismans and amulets by carving a man with the head of a crocodile on it, with inscriptions on his hips and sides. *Ostracios* removes pain. Its zodiac sign is Capricorn.

✦ *ostracea, ostrateas, ostretea.*

📖 Pliny 37, 177; Dioscorides V, 146; Meliteniotes v. 1175; Leonardi II, 7, 206.

Ostracite, Ostragite: *Ostracite* resembles an oyster shell; one harder variety looks like agate—this variety is so hard that pieces of it are used to carve other stones. It is also used like pumice stone to buff skin. As a drink, it has hemostatic properties. Applied externally with honey, it heals wounds and soothes breast pains. Its zodiac sign is Capricorn and its planet is Saturn. *Ostracite* is another name for *cadmitis.*

✦ *ostracitis, ostracitin, ostraciten, osiracitim, ostrachitis, ostritis, ostriditis.*

Pliny 37, 139; 37, 151 and 157; Isidore of Sevilla 16, 4, 20 and 25; 16, 15, 16; Lambert de Saint-Omer 55, 73; Dioscorides V, 146; Pseudo-Dioscorides 2, 165; Lombard Dioscorides 179; Meliteniotes v. 1129; Vincent de Beauvais VIII, 26; *Hortus sanitatis* V, 94; Leonardi II, 7, 204.

Ostritis, Ostrites: A stone with the name and the appearance of the oyster, which is an etymological interpretation of the Greek *ostreon*. Crushed in wine, it is an analgesic.

 Pliny 37, 177; Orpheus v. 344f.; Kerygma 14; Meliteniotes v. 1174.

Otriche: The *otriche* is white and vermilion, and the size of a broad bean. It is presumably jacinth. If ailing eyes are touched with it for three or four days, it will heal them. Any poisoned prisoner who drinks water in which *otriche* has been placed will not be exposed to danger. Whoever carries it upon their person will not be attacked by vermin.

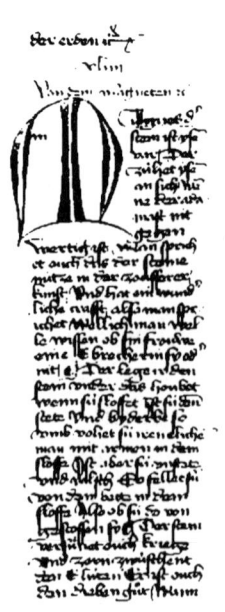

This stone is found on an island off the shores of India, between two mountains where the valleys are so deep that no man can dwell there. To obtain these stones, meat smeared with honey is cast to the bottom of these valleys. Birds then arrive to take it. The men then attack the birds, which drop the quarters of meat (to which the stones are now glued by virtue of the honey). A similar legend is told about diamonds, as can be seen in *The Second Voyage of Sinbad the Sailor*, as well as in the work of Epiphanes, where jacinth is the stone collected by this means, and in the work of the Pseudo-Aristotle.

✦ MFr. *cocrice, cotrice, coccrite, cosicre, cochrice, cocte, coctrise, corige, costerces, crise, ocric(h)e, cotoice, rocrice, socrice, sictote, tocrice;* MItal. *cocrice.*

📖 *Sidrac* 23; Mandeville 6 (Amiens manuscript); *Libro di Sidrach* chap. 476.

P

Paeanitis: Paeanitis, also called *gaeanidea*, is a stone that is born in Macedonia, near the monument of Tiresias. It resembles congealed water and is of the female sex. In fact, it is said that at certain times it conceives and engenders another stone that resembles it. It is a medication for women in childbed.

> ✦ *peanites, paeanitides, peanita, peaniten, peantes, peantides, paeanides, paonites, peanitus, peonites, peranites;* MFr. *peanite, pianite, peaniste, pionice;* MHG *pêanîtes, aniten, pestniten.*

> 📖 Pliny 37, 180; Solin 9, 22; Marbode 34; Lapidary of Marbode, 1st Romanesque translation XXXIV; Lapidary in prose 37; Cambridge lapidary v. 885-98; Wolfram von Eschenbach 791, 29; Arnoldus Saxo 63; Bartholomaeus Anglicus XVI, 79; Albertus Magnus 2, 14, 2; Konrad von Megenberg VI, 63; *Hortus sanitatis* V, 102; Leonardi II, 7, 216.

Paederos: This kind of opal is called *"sangenon"* by the Indians. This stone possesses the beauty of the opal, but its radiance is not as bright and it is rarely smooth. Its shade is sky blue and purple. The most sought-after *paederos* comes from India, while that of Egypt, called *syenite,* is in second place. Third place goes to the variety from Arabia, but it is coarse. The stone from Punt and Asia has the gentlest radiance and its very substance is softer than the stones from Galatia, Thrace, and Cypress.

Benoît de Sainte-Maure recorded a curious legend concerning this stone. In the River of Paradise, there was an apple tree whose fruits would harden over the years and become transformed into hard, strong stones that banish dementia (*Romance of Troy* v. 16883ff.). The *Letter of Prester John* appears to be familiar with this legend, but presents it in a later stage. Here a stone stands upright in a large plain. Out of this stone grows a tree with a leafless branch at its top from which dangles an apple. Whoever smells the aroma of this apple shall be healed if sick and find himself invigorated if already enjoying good health; also his thirst will be quenched and his hunger eased.

✦ *pederotes, pedoros, pedorus, podoros, podetos;* MFr. *pedoire, pedoretés.*

📖 Pliny 37, 129f. (= *opalus*); Solin 33, 22–23; Lambert de Saint-Omer 55, 44; *Summarium Heinrici* VI, 4, 26; Meliteniotes v. 1176; *De lapidibus preciosis* 52 (*perites vel pederotes*); Cambridge lapidary v. 1367–74; Prester John §E 31 and §96 D nn; *Hortus sanitatis* V, 103.

Palas, Pales: See *balagius*.

📖 Volmar v. 658–61.

Panchrous:
The "multicolored stone," sometimes called *taconites, paonites,* and *pavonnius lapis* ("peacock stone"), is a holy stone on which is engraved an image of Lato and Harpocrates and three greyhounds on the back. It is useful against all the magical arts. It is undoubtedly an irised hyaline quartz. The scribes of the medieval lapidaries distorted the word *panchrous* into *pantherus/panther.*

✦ *panchrus, pangrus, panchrodus, paonites.*

📖 Pliny 37, 178; Kerygma 45; Damigeron 37; Isidore of Sevilla 16, 12, 1; *Summarium Heinrici* VI, 5, 1; Lambert de Saint-Omer 55, 85; Bartholomaeus Anglicus XVI, 80.

Paneros: We know nothing about this stone except that it did not encourage fecundity and was also called *paneraston,* "entirely amiable."

📖 Pliny 37, 178; Meliteniotes v. 1177.

Pangonus, Panconus: A stone that is no larger than a finger in length; it cannot be mistaken for a crystal because it has a greater number of angles, which is a linguistic interpretation of the Greek *pan* + *gonia* ("all" + "angle").

Engraved with an eagle holding a leaf in its beak with a man's head looking at it, the *pangonus* set in gold will make a person rich, eloquent, and beloved by all.

📖 Pliny 37, 178; Meliteniotes v. 1176; Leonardi II, 7, 221; Hermes 5; Solomon 38.

Pantarbe: This is the extraordinary stone that Philostratus described as follows in his *Life of Apollonius of Tyana* (III, 46):

> However, about the stone which attracts and binds itself to other stones you must not be skeptical; for you can see the stone yourself if you like, and admire its properties. For the greatest specimen is exactly the size of this finger nail (here Apollonius points to his own thumb), and it is conceived in a hollow in the earth at a depth of four fathoms, but it is so highly endowed with spirit, that the earth swells and breaks open in many places when the stone is conceived in it. But no one can get hold of it, for it runs away, unless it is scientifically attracted; but we alone can secure, partly by performance of certain rites, this *pantarbe,* for such is the name given to it. Now in the night-time it glows like the day just as fire might, for it is red and gives out rays; and if you look at it in the daytime it smites your eyes with a thousand glints and gleams. And the light within it is a spirit of mysterious power, for it absorbs to itself everything in its neighborhood. And why do I say in its neighborhood? Why you can sink anywhere in river or sea as many stones as you like, and these

not even near to one another, but here and there and everywhere; and then if you let down this stone among them by a string it gathers them together by the infusion of its spirit, and the stones yield to its influence and cling to it in a bunch, like a swarm of bees.

Other authors say that the *pantarbe* guarantees fire to those that carry it. It is called the "gold magnet," as it possesses the property of attracting this metal from great distances. Others claim that it is the matrix for all precious metals.

 Philostratus, *The Life of Apollonius of Tyana*. English translation by F. C. Conybeare (London: William Heinemann, 1912).

Pantherus:
A multicolored stone found in Media that contains black, green, red, and so on. It steals the sight from one eye. Its bearer should, if he wishes to be victorious, look at it at sunrise. This stone arose from a distortion of *panchrous,* the "multicolored stone," whose name was gradually mangled because this mineral brought to mind the skin of this animal. Whoever wears this stone can never be vanquished.

✦ *pantheros, pateron, pantheron, panthera;* MFr. *panther(e), pantiere;* MHG *panthers, ponteron.*

 Marbode 51; Alphabetical Lapidary 71; 2nd Lapidary in prose 33; Alexander Neckham v. 351ff.; Wolfram von Eschenbach 791, 8; Bodl. Digby

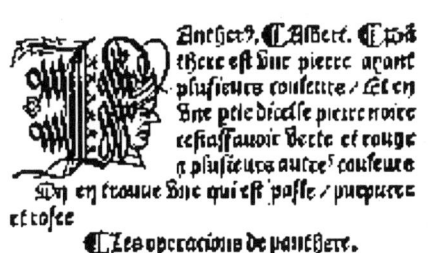

13 38; *De lapidibus preciosis* 53; Arnoldus Saxo 62; Lapidary of Marbode, 1st Romanesque translation LI; Thomas de Cantimpré 14, 54; Albertus Magnus 2, 14, 1; Konrad von Megenberg VI, 60; Jacob van Maerlant XII, 59; Saint Florian v. 696–709; *Hortus sanitatis* V, 97; Leonardi II, 7, 214; *Phisice* 43.

Pantilonos: The name for a stone that grows and shrinks with the waxing and the waning of the moon. It must be identical to selenite.

📖 *Vocabularius ex quo* p 84.8.

Paradise Stone: According to the cosmographical conceptions of the Middle Ages, the earthly paradise was located in various places: sometimes a mountain in the East, sometimes on an island in the Atlantic Ocean. The anonymous author of Alexander's *Journey to Paradise* (*Iter ad paradisum*), recycles the geographical fable of paradise as the source for four rivers (the Geon, the Physon, the Tigris, and the Euphrates), and therefore one could reach paradise by following them back to their source. For this reason, Alexander the Great retraced the course of the Ganges and reached the area preceding it, where he sought to pay tribute. Despite their careful search, his men could only find a small opening, at which one of them knocked. A voice asked them what they wanted, then told them to wait. The invisible being returned, and he gave the emissaries a precious stone of marvelous radiance and rare color, in color and appearance it resembled a human eye. "The inhabitants of this place would like your king to know this," he said. "You can regard this as a gift or as payment of a tribute. Take this stone which, out of love, we give you as a warning. It can furnish one purpose or all your desires, because you shall be freed of all pride once you have grasped its nature and wonderful properties. You shall also realize that neither you nor your people can remain here any longer, for if this river is stirred up, even if by merely a modest storm, your ship shall undoubtedly sink and you shall lose your lives. Return, therefore, to your fellows so as not to appear ungrateful toward the God of gods."

On his return to Susa, Alexander sought out an old Jewish scholar named Papas and asked him to explain the stone's nature. Papas placed the stone on one plate of a scales and a gold coin on the other. The stone went down, raising the coin. Another coin was added, then another, until an entire pound of gold—all that could fit on the scales—was added, but the stone did not even budge. Someone then said that an almost weightless feather could replace the pile of gold. Alexander was greatly amazed at this. Papas picked up the small scales onto which the gold had been piled and placed the stone again on one plate and covered it with a little dirt, then put one gold coin on the other plate, which was immediately raised up while the one with the stone went down. He then removed the coin and replaced it with the feather, and it weighed more than the stone. Alexander asked Papas to enlighten him and the elderly Jew told him: "What you saw there, my dear king, could not be called a city, nor is it one. It is a solid wall that no living creature can cross. The Creator of the universe made it to be the frontier for the souls of the just, once freed of their bodies, to await the resurrection of the flesh. They enjoy a restful existence in the cool shade, in conformance with divine will, but not for all eternity. According to their sentence, they will return into their bodies and live eternally in the company of their Creator. These souls aspiring to salvation have intended this stone to remind you of your good fortune, both to comfort you and to curb your wild ambition and indecent pride . . . today, dissatisfied with your own wealth and with foreign treasures, you suffer in the midst of your fellows and nothing sates you. By risking your life and not without wreaking havoc on others, you have wrongfully burdened yourself with the weight of foreigners' gold. In the proclamation of such lessons is hidden the reason for this wondrous occurrence; it is this that the nature of this stone reveals. In shape and color, it is truly the human eye: as long as it enjoys the light of life, it will be excited by the attack of desires and revel in the multiplicity of new phenomena and nothing can appease it because gold arouses an inextinguishable hunger. The more it acquires, the greater its desire to hoard: this is what the unexpected behavior of the marvelous weight teaches us. But once it is stripped of life and returned to the bosom of Mother Earth, the eye is unable to use or delight in anything; it can no longer ask for anything and nothing touches it, for it no longer feels anything. This is why even a light feather, which performs a use despite being weak, weighs more than the stone once it has been covered with earth. Thus, dear king, this stone represents you—you who have mastered wisdom, vanquished kings, and possess kingdoms, you who are master of the world."

In the Strasbourg edition of the *Romance of Alexander*, the old Jew recognizes the stone as the gem of youth and proves this to the Macedonian. In other traditions, a human skull takes the place of the stone.

This legend is based on the fact that the four rivers flowing out of the earthly paradise carry precious stones, a belief that finds its full expression in the *Letter of Prester John*, which mentions emeralds, sapphires, carbuncles, topazes, chrysoliths, onyx, beryls, amethysts, sardonyx, jaspers, and crystals. In *Floire et Blancheflor*, for example, the Euphrates, one of these four rivers, flows through the emir's garden, and sapphires, chalcedony, rubies, and so forth can be found in it.

📖 *Letter of Prester John* v. 233–46.

📖📖 Claude Lecouteux, *Mondes parallèles. L'univers des croyances au Moyen Âge,* Collection Champion classiques, Essais 8 (Paris: Champion, 2007), 25–33.

Paragonius: The term designates two stones, one black and one golden in color. *Paragonius* is the result of a spelling error, as it is in fact pyrite, as indicated by the *Lapidary of Solomon*. It can be made into amulets and talismans by being engraved.

If an image of a bird with a leaf in its beak, as well as the head of a man looking at this same bird, are depicted on a golden *paragonius*, and this image has been set in gold, one will be rich, fortunate, and respected by all.

If the engraving of a sea turtledove is seen on the paragon and this stone is set into a lead ring, none shall give offense to its owner; he will be valued by his elders and the great ones of the earth, and protected from drowning. Another manuscript offers the following variation: "If you find a turtle dove etched on a paragon, and you set this stone in a lead ring, its owner shall never be wounded or touched by sickness. And he will be honored by all men, particularly the elders." See *pyrite*.

◆ *paragonnius, peragone;* MFr. *orie paragone, pierete*.

📖 *De la vertu des tailles* 33 (*peragone noire*); 35 (*peragone dorée*); *De figura* 2; *Liber sigillorum Ethel* 26; Solomon 22–23; Leonardi II, 7, 226.

Parasius: See *prasius*.

📖 *De lapidibus preciosis* 54.

Pardalios: A stone that looks like panther hide.

📖 Pliny 37, 190.

Parius: The name for the white marble from the island of Paros. It is particularly useful for conserving all kinds of perfumes. In the Christian lapidary, it symbolizes chastity.

📖 Isidore of Sevilla 16, 5, 8; *Summarium Heinrici* VI, 3, 6; Bartholomaeus Anglicus XVI, 76.

Pausilype: This stone is found in the waterway of the Strymon, and brings grief.

📖 Pseudo-Plutarch §8.

Pavonnius Lapis: See *panchrous*.

📖 Leonardi II, 7, 224.

Peridonius: A fawn-colored stone that is good against sore throat. If one presses it in one's hand, one will burn oneself, although the same thing is said of asbestos in the *Letter of Prester John*.

◆ *peridon, feripendamus, veripendamus, perithes, parides*.

📖 *De la vertu des tailles* 44; *De figura* 6–7; Albertus Magnus, 2, 14, 3; Closener pe 149; *Liber secretorum* II, 1, 1, 5; *Hortus sanitatis* V, 99.

Perla: See *margarita* and *unio*.

✦ *perna;* MHG *berle, berlin, bernin;* MFr. *perle*.

📖 Cambridge lapidary v. 1181–1244; *De lapidibus preciosis* 1; *Picatrix* II, 10, 51; III, 1, 7; 3, 3; Jordan Catalani §71; *Vocabularius ex quo* p 410; Mandeville I 12.

Petra Asini: See *chrysolithus*.

Pharanites: See *amethystus*.

Phengites: This is a stone as hard as marble, white and transparent even in those parts where red veins can be seen, which is what earned it the name of *phengites*. Nero used this stone to rebuild the temple of Fortuna Seia, which he had enclosed within the precincts of his Golden Palace. Even when the doors and windows were closed, this stone provided light inside during the day, a light that was not transmitted from outside but which appeared to be enclosed within. See *phrygius*.

♦ *phingites, fingites.*

📖 Pliny 36, 163; Isidore of Sevilla 16, 4, 23; *Summarium Heinrici* VI, 2, 23; *Hortus sanitatis* V, 104; Leonardi II, 7, 114 and 115.

Philadelphos: A stone that is the color of a crow feather and has a depiction of a man. These stones are found on the slopes of the Haemus and Rhodope mountains. When they are separated from each other, if their name is spoken, they will disengage from their surroundings and reunite.

📖 Pseudo-Plutarch §9.

Philosopher's Stone: The Philosopher's Stone is the fruit of a long history, one based on traditions attributed to Aristotle that were picked up by the Arab alchemists and passed on to Europe by means of various treatises such as *De perfecto magisteris, la Practica lapidis philosophici,* the *Secret of Secrets* (*Sirr al-asrar,* tenth century; *Secretum secretorum*), and *The Emerald Tablet* attributed to Hermes (eighth century). Thanks to their translations into Latin, these texts were adopted by many authors including Roger Bacon (1214–1294) and Arnaud de Villeneuve (1238–1311 or 1313), and translated into the vernacular languages by John of Sevilla (twelfth century), Philip of Tripoli (thirteenth century), and Hildegard von Hünheim (twelfth century).

The philosopher's stone or *lapis physici* was defined as follows during the early Middle Ages: "It is a stone and it is not a stone" (*est lapis et non lapis*), an expression going back to Zosimos (third–fourth centuries). It gathers all of the four elements within itself to form a microcosm (*minor mundus*). By virtue of its round shape in likeness of the terrestrial globe, it was also called the "culmination of the egg" (*terminus ovum*) and the "egg of the philosophers" (*ovum philosophorum*). We are told that this stone contends with wind and water, emerges from the waves of an underground sea, and, according to the *Letter of Aristotle to Alexander on the Secret of Secrets,* commonly called *Writings on the Philosopher's Stone,* it has the ability to put an entire army to flight.

An anonymous sonnet, inserted in a manuscript now housed in the Library of the Arsenal in Paris, tells us:

> *It is a spirit body, first born of nature,*
> *Very common, very hidden, very vile, very precious,*
> *Conserving, destroying, good, and malicious,*
> *The beginning and end of every creature:*
> *Triple in substance, it is of salt, oil, and pure water,*
> *Which coagulates, collects, and drips in low places,*
> *Completely pure, oily dry, and half of the high heavens,*
> *Skilled at receiving all forms and figures.*
> *The sole art by Nature that to our eyes makes us see:*
> *It conceals an infinite power in its heart,*
> *Filled with the faculties of heaven and earth.*
> *It is hermaphroditic and gives increase*
> *To all in which it blends with equal measure,*
> *For which reason it enfolds all species.*

The philosopher's stone is regarded as the most perfected substance because it carries within it an admixture of extremely perfect elements. It transmutes other metals into gold at the end of complex operations. In the form of an elixir or beverage, it restores youth to the adept, prolonging his life indefinitely, and grants him the universal science, the knowledge of the reason behind all things, the total vision of past and future, and finally changes common stones into gems.

 Aristotle, "De practica lapidis philosophici," in *Ars aurifera* I (Basel, 1610): 232–39; "Aristotle, De perfecto magisterio," in *Theatrum chemicum* III (Strasbourg, 1659): 76–127; *De lapide philosophico*, V, 1660, 787–98; Mahmoud Manzalaoui, *Secretum Secretorum*. Nine English Versions, I (Oxford: Early English Texts Society, 1977); R. Steele, ed., "Secretum secretorum cum glossis et notulis," in Roger Bacon, *Opera hactenus inedita*, vol. 5 (Oxford: Clarendon, 1920).

 Mario Grignaschi, "La diffusion du *Secretum secretorum* (*Sirr-al-'Asrar*) dans l'Europe occidentale," *Archives d'Histoire doctrinale et littéraire du Moyen Âge* 55 (1980): 7–70; Martin Plessner, *Vorsokratische Philosophie und griechische*

Alchemie in arabisch-lateinischer Überlieferung. Studien zu Text und Inhalt der Turba philosophorum, ed. F. Klein-Franke (Wiesbaden: Steiner, 1975).

Phloginos: The etymological meaning of this stone is "flame-colored" and it is also called *chrysitis*. It resembles the ochre of Attica and is found in Egypt. It is undoubtedly identical to *phlogitis*.

✦ *philoginos.*

📖 Pliny 37, 179; Damigeron 77; Meliteniotes v. 1186; *Hortus sanitatis* V, 56; Leonardi II, 7, 228 (= *crisites*).

Phlogitis: All we know about this stone is that a flame, which does not reach the surface, seems to be burning inside it. See *chrysitis* and *phloginos*.

✦ *phlogitidis, flogates.*

📖 Pliny 37, 189; Isidore of Sevilla 16, 14, 9; Lambert de Saint-Omer 55, 63.

Phoenicitis: An unknown stone that owes it name to its resemblance to the date. The virtue of *phoenicitis* is that its bearer will experience no sorrow or behave badly when carrying it in his left hand.

✦ *Phœnicites, phenicites, fenicites.*

📖 Pliny 37, 180 and 189; Damigeron 42; Alphabetical Lapidary 42; Meliteniotes v. 1186; Leonardi II, 7, 227.

Phrinos: See *batrachites*.

📖 Kyranides 1, 21; Secrez 4, 19.

Phrygius: This stone is named for its land of origin. It is a porous, black mass. It is first soaked in wine and then scorched. The fire is kept hot with bellows until the stone is red hot, then it is extinguished with sweet wine. This operation is repeated three times. Is is used to dye cloth. As a decoction, it heals gout. Also see *phengites*.

📖 Pliny 36, 143; Isidore of Sevilla 16, 4, 9; Pseudo-Dioscorides 2, 141; Meliteniotes v. 1131; Vincent de Beauvais VIII, 25; *Hortus sanitatis* V, 104; Leonardi II, 7, 218.

Phrynites: This stone, which looks like a turtle, is extracted from the frog. It is helpful for attracting women if a certain prayer is spoken. *Phrynite* means "toad stone," *crapausine*. See *batrachites, borax*.

📖 Kerygma 52.

Phycitis: A stone that gets its name from its resemblance to a kind of seaweed.

📖 Pliny 37, 180.

Piropus: Depending upon the authors, this is the name for pyrophilus or for jet. See *gagates* and *pyrophilus*.

✦ MHG *brantstein, born stein, brünstain, prait stein, kachel;* MSp. *syropus, pardero*.

📖 *Vocabularius ex quo* p 626; *Liber ordinis rerum* 129, 14; Closener pi 92; *Poridat* 15.

Planitorium: This name designates a glowing stone.

 📖 *Vocabularius ex quo* p 677.1.

Platona, Platana: An unknown stone (*lapis quidam*) whose description in Middle High German, "a plain stone" (*eyn slicht steyn*), provides no additional information.

 📖 *Vocabularius ex quo* p 695.2

Podros: See *paederos*.

 📖 Leonardi II, 7, 220.

Polophos: This stone possesses the singular feature of changing color every day. Sometimes it is red, sometimes green, and sometimes yellow, and it shines at night like fire. It resembles a laughing mouth. Alexander the Great made his nobles wear it night and day for protection against attack by demons, for *polophos* sends them, as well as ghosts, fleeing. The stone also drives away wild animals—including lions, panthers, bears, and wolves—from wherever they may be lurking.

 ✦ Ar. *apôlôkus, failakûs*.
 📖 Luka ben Serapion 37; *Aristoteles de lapidibus* 377, 24.

Polygrammos Iaspis: A variety of jasper girded by white lines.

 📖 Pliny 37, 118.

Polythrix: A green stone "with many hairs"; it is said to cause hair to fall out.

 📖 Pliny 37, 190; Meliteniotes v. 1177.

Polyzonos, Polyzonas: This is the name for a black stone that is striped with several white zones. It brings about the meeting of many friends, generates business, and creates profit. If bound to your person, it will resolve illnesses and court proceedings.

📖 Pliny 37, 189; Solin 37, 23; Kerygma 44; Damigeron 55; Isidore of Sevilla 16, 14, 9; Meliteniotes v. 1177.

Ponatade: See *radaim*.

📖 *Phisice* 97.

Pontica: There are several different kinds of this stone. One is starred with drops that are sometimes the color of blood and sometimes that of gold; it is ranked among the sacred stones. Another kind has lines of the same color instead of stars. The last variety offers images of mountains and valleys. It is a kind of frothy agate.

📖 Pliny 37, 149; Isidore of Sevilla 16, 12, 4; *Summarium Heinrici* VI, 6, 10; Meliteniotes v. 1178; Leonardi II, 7, 215.

Porphyrites: This name designates a variety of andesite, a compact volcanic rock, which is dark red mixed with white crystals. A bird above a snail should be carved on it. Prepared during the waning of the moon, this stone can be used for an eyewash.

✦ *porphysites, prophirites.*

📖 Pliny 36, 57; 88; Isidore of Sevilla 16, 5, 5; *Kyranides* 1, 16; *Secrez* 4, 14; *Hortus sanitatis* V, 95; Leonardi II, 7, 219.

Praeconissus: A stone whose color resembles that of sapphire. It seems to have been born from a mistaken reading of Pliny the Elder, who spoke of a certain Stilon Praeconinus with respect to engraved emeralds (37, 9).

📖 Leonardi II, 7, 223.

Pramnion: See *mormorion*.

Prasius: An opaque green quartz that is sometimes called false emerald or plasma. This gem comes from India. A second type of prase can be distinguished from the ordinary stone because it is marked with blood-red dots, and a third has three white stripes. Chrysoprase is preferred to all of these. It is said that the prase is the womb for the emerald. It is good for eyesight and possesses some of the same properties—alas, unidentified—as emerald and jasper. The image of Taurus on a prase is said to thwart evil spells and earn a leader gratitude and recognition.

> ✦ *prassius, pransius, prasitis, praxus;* MFr. *prasie, prasme, pras(s)e, grasnis;* MHG *prasem, brasem.*
>
> 📖 Pliny 37, 113f; Isidore of Sevilla 16, 7, 4; Marbode 40; *Summarium Heinrici* VI, 4, 2; Hildegard von Bingen IV, 11; Lambert de Saint-Omer 55, 31; Marbode Lapidary, 1st Romanesque translation XXXIXXL; Lapidary in prose 56; Cambridge lapidary v. 1001–14; Wolfram von Eschenbach 791, 9; Arnoldus Saxo 64; Bartholomaeus Anglicus XVI, 77; Thomas de Cantimpré 14, 55; Albertus Magnus 2, 14, 4; Konrad von Megenberg VI, 61; Jacob van Maerlant XII, 60; Closener pr 7; Ragiel 14; *Hortus sanitatis* V, 98; Leonardi II, 7, 213; *Phisice* 46.

Prasme: The name for green agate, which in Arabic is *zavarget*. This stone is ruled by the 17° of Taurus, and it is the enemy of green jasper. Contemporary mineralogists consider it to be a kind of rock crystal that is green in color. See *achates*.

> ✦ MFr. *prisme, prime, plasma, fresme.*
>
> 📖 Cambridge lapidary v. 918–20; *Lapidario* 47.

Premonada: A red stone whose patronage is attributed to Mars.

> 📖 *Picatrix* II, 10, 4.

Promnion: See *molochitis*.

Psoritis: Still known under the names of porphyry and porous stone, *psoritis* mixed with the blood of a starling helps cure tertian and quartan fevers if the patient's face is daubed with said blood. Restless children who grind their teeth are given a *psoritis* engraved with three sand fleas beneath a green reed to carry.

✦ MFr. *cirico*.

📖 *Kyranides* 1, 24; *Secrez* 4, 21.

Pumex, Pumice: The pumice stone, which is still sometimes called "sea foam," is a volcanic variety of orthoclase feldspar. The most highly valued is pumice from Melos, Nisyros, and the Aeolian Islands. To be considered good, these stones should be white, not very heavy, and as dry and porous as possible. They should not release grit when rubbed. In medicine, they are invigorating and siccative after they have been fired three times, an operation performed with the purest charcoal. The fire is extinguished each time with white wine. Once this is done, they are washed, dried, and stored in the driest place available. A powder made from them is used especially for ophthalmic mixtures. They gently heal and correct ulcerations of the eye. There are those who prefer, after the third firing, to let them cool down slowly rather than extinguish the fire and triturate them in wine. They are also incorporated into plasters for ulcerations on the head or genitals. The best kinds of toothpaste are made with this powder. According to Theophrastus, people who are drinking wine on a bet take the precaution of ingesting some powdered pumice beforehand. If they fail to drink the entire flagon at once, however, they run a great risk, because this substance has such a coolant quality that if it is thrown into a fermenting vat, the fermentation will stop at once. If it is bound to the thigh of a pregnant woman, it will cause her to give birth, and if hung around a child's neck, he will stop coughing.

✦ *lapis vulcani, spuma maris; pumey;* MFr. *la pierre engendrée de l'escume de mer;* Ar. *famech, feni, cosseres, zebezalbar*.

📖 Pliny 36, 130; Lombard Dioscorides 134; 171; Isidore of Sevilla 16, 3, 7; Avicenna II, 2, 613; *Lapidario* 153–57 (five varieties); Pseudo-Mandeville 66; *Hortus sanitatis* V, 105; Leonardi II, 7, 225; *Phisice* 105.

Punicus: A stone found in the Aeolian Islands and of which there are two species. The best is white and is used in medicine. Dried and washed, it strengthens eyesight, purifies abscesses, and hastens the scarring process. Ingested before drinking wine, it will hinder intoxication. It is undoubtedly a kind of pumice stone. See *pumex*.

📖 Leonardi II, 7, 222.

Purpurites: Another name for porphyry, a red marble with white spots.

📖 Isidore of Sevilla 16, 5, 5; *Summarium Heinrici* VI, 3, 3; Closener pu 76; *Hortus sanitatis* V, 94.

Pyrite: In the Middle Ages, this name refered to a black stone with shades of fawn that could not be squeezed without it burning the hand of the person holding it. It is governed by the 16° of Sagittarius. Some lapidaries confuse pyrite and jet. Today a distinction is made between yellow pyrite, a natural metallic sulfur, and the white variety, which is marcasite. Its name became distorted and gave rise to *paragonius*.

Pulverized in water, pyrite is effective against evil spells. If put in holy water while making the appropriate oration, demons will appear who will not be able to refuse to answer questions put to them.

If the image of a dove or a vulture is seen on a pyrite, and the bird is carrying an olive branch in its beak, and this stone is set in a silver ring, everyone will invite you to banquets where the other guests shall keep their eyes fixed on you instead of eating, if you wear this ring on your right hand during the meal.

If a pyrite is embellished with the image of a horseman with a sword at his belt, holding the reins in one hand and a bow in the other, and if this stone is set into a gold ring, its owner will be victorious in battle and no one will be abe to resist him. And if someone steeps this ring in musk-scented oil and then dampens his face with this blend, all those who see him shall be scared and unable to resist him.

The image of a man holding a flower etched on a pyrite and mounted in a tin ring, and all this achieved at the fourth, eighth, or twelfth hour of a Monday or Friday, can compel the obedience of whoever he touches with it.

> ✦ *pirites, piritides, piriten, perites, perithes, petites, parides, piridan, perithes, virites, piridonidiud, paragonius;* MFr. *pyrite, pirite, berrite, piere, pierete, pirestes;* MHG *pirrîtes;* MSp. *piedra del fuego;* Ar. *hager al markasita.*
>
> 📖 Pliny 36, 137; Solin 37, 16; Isidore of Sevilla 16, 4, 5; 16, 11, 8; Damigeron 56; Marbode 56; Dioscorides V, 125; Pseudo-Dioscorides 2, 143; Lombard Dioscorides 151; *Summarium Heinrici* VI, 2, 4; Melteniotes v. 1129; Old English Lapidary 15; Lambert de Saint-Omer 55, 60; Marbode Lapidary, 1st Romanesque translation LVI; Alphabetical Lapidary 72–73 (*pyrites = gaiet*); Lapidary in prose 57; Alexander Neckham v. 347ff.; Cambridge lapidary v. 1283–92; Wolfram von Eschenbach 791, 22; *Liber sigillorum Ethel* 12; Bartholomaeus Anglicus XVI, 78; Thomas de Cantimpré 14, 53; Vincent de Beauvais VIII, 24; Albertus Magnus 2, 14, 3; 2, 19, 3; Konrad von Megenberg VI, 59; *Lapidario* 227; Jacob van Maerlant XII, 58; Saint Florian v. 812–23; Leonardi II, 7, 217; Chael 13; Hermes 9; Solomon 31; *Hortus sanitatis* V, 100; *Phisice* 60.

Pyrophilus, Piropholos:

This stone, still called "human stone" (*lapis humanus*), is red with a white streak. It comes from the heart of a man who has been poisoned. If this heart is kept in the fire without interruption for nine years, it transforms into a stone with marvelous properties. It protects its bearer from thunder and lightning, gives victory to kings and princes in battle, and offers protection from poison. Alexander the Great wore one, but when he was bathing in the Euphrates, a snake stole it and caused it to fall to the bottom of the river. It also protects its owner from sudden death.

Generally, *pyrophilus* stones are seen in pairs, a male and a female, and they catch on fire when brought close to each other. Heinrich von

Mügeln, a thirteenth-century German poet, goes so far as to state that possession of a *pyrophilus* will prevent death, a tradition repeated in other lapidaries. See also *terobolen*.

✦ *pyrophilis, prosilis, propholus, proppholus, t(e)erobolen, turrobolen;* MFr. *purphile;* MHG *kerobel, therobel, leutzstain;* MSp. *piedra del fuego.*

📖 Thomas de Cantimpré 14, 56; Albertus Magnus 2, 14, 5; *Lapidario* 227; Lapidary of King Philip 67; Konrad von Megenberg VI, 62 and 78; Jacob van Maerlant XII, 61; Filippo da Ferrara, *Liber de introductione loquendi* chap. 114; *Phisice* 72.

Q

Quanidros: Called "vulture stone" because it is found in the body of this bird, it will be the good fortune of its bearer if he is a goshawk hunter. It is good against all kinds of ills and will swell the breasts with milk. The *quanidros* is called *vulturis lapis* and "stone from the vulture's head" by other authors following a tradition in which the stone goes unnamed. See *vulture stone*.

✦ *quandros, quayndros, quaidros, quirindros;* MHG *geyrstain*.

📖 Arnoldus Saxo 66; Bartholomaeus Anglicus XVI, 84; Albertus Magnus 2, 15, 1; Pseudo-Mandeville 58; Konrad von Megenberg VI, 65; Leonardi II, 7, 230 (= *vulturis*); *Phisice* 96.

Quatique: See *amethystus.*

Quirin: This stone is called "the stone from the hoopoe's nest," as it is found there. It allows the revelation of secrets; all that is required is for it to be laid upon the chest of a sleeping individual. It cures fever and reduces fallacious visions. It is quite dangerous, however, for if the sleeper invokes the devil, he will appear at once.

> ✦ *quirinus, quirus, quris, quiritia, lapis de nido upuppe;* MFr. *quuris, qurins, iquisis;* MHG *wythopfen stain.*
>
> Damigeron 67; Arnoldus Saxo 65; Bartholomaeus Anglicus XVI, 83; Pseudo-Mandeville 57; Lapidary of King Philip 58; Konrad von Megenberg VI, 64; Saint Florian v. 744–49; *Hortus sanitatis* V, 106 (*quirin*) and 107 (*quirinus*); Leonardi II, 7, 229; *Phisice* 95.

Quiritia: See *quirin.*

> Albertus Magnus 2, 15, 2; *Liber secretorum* II, 1, 31; *De virtutis lapidum* II, 40 (*quiriti*).

R

Rabri: Still known as "Armenian death," this stone is good for bleedings and hemorrhages. It also limits discharges from the stomach.

- *ranius, rami, bolus armenicus.*
- Bartholomaeus Anglicus XVI, 85; Leonardi II, 7, 232.

Radaim: A shiny, black stone found in the head of a rooster, thus a bezoar. It is said that when rooster heads are left for the ants to eat, this stone will be found long afterward in the head of a male cockerel. It appears that it is capable of obtaining anything. It is identical to the *doriatides/donatides*. See also *alectorias*.

- *radaym;* MFr. *ponatade (from donatides), radian.*
- Arnoldus Saxo 68; Albertus Magnus 2, 16, 1; Leonardi II, 7, 231; *Liber secretorum* II, 1, 32; *De virtutis lapidum* II, 32 (*rodianus*); *Hortus sanitatis* V, 107; *Phisice* 97.

Radianes: See *donatides*.

- Pseudo-Mandeville 29.

Rain Stone: The Algeriche River in Turkestan (now the Wadi-al-Harluh) was the source for these stones, whose colors ranged from white and gray to black and multicolored. When rubbed together, they will cause rain to fall, which continues for as long as the stones are manipulated in this fashion.

 📖 *Picatrix* IV, 8, 6.

Ranius: See *rabri* and *bolus armenus*.

Ranni: A reddish brown stone considered identical to the *bolus armenus*. It is good for stomach constrictions and the bleeding caused by dysentery and women's periods. See *rabri* and *bolus armenus*.

 ✦ *ramai, ranius, ranno.*

 📖 Arnoldus Saxo 67; Albertus Magnus 2, 16, 2; *Hortus sanitatis* V, 107.

Rapondinus: A flawed spelling of *crapaudine,* which is also called *borax.* See *batrachites, borax.*

 📖 Leonardi II, 7, 86.

Raven Stone: A raven egg is taken nine days before the calends of April and cooked in water until hard. It is then put back into the bird's nest. The raven knows a stone that will restore the egg to its raw state when it touches it, and this stone helps its owner increase his wealth and earn the good will of all. See *corvia*.

 ✦ *pierre del crot, du corbiau.*

 📖 Lapidary of King Philip, Bern, Bibliothèque de la Bourgeoisie, ms. 646, fol. 79 r°; Paris, National Library of France, French ms. 2009, fol. 10 v°; Latin ms. 11210, fol. 82 r°.

Rayetanz: An artificial stone allegedly crafted by Aristotle for Alexander the Great. It consists of ruby, diamond dust, lead, magnesium, sulfur, gold, lion's brain, leopard's fat, wolf's blood, orpiment, and crocus. The person who wears it set in a ring will compel the obedience of both man and beast.

 📖 *Picatrix*, III, 10.

Rebis: The ruby. See *balagius, carbunculus,* and *rubinus*.

 📖 Vocabularius ex quo r 75.1.

Red Jasper: If it bears the engraving of a man seated on a fish with a peacock over his head, red jasper prevents the diners seated at one's right from becoming intoxicated, but if this stone is placed in the pocket of a person who eats using his right hand, he will not become full during a banquet.

 If one wears a piece of red jasper around the neck with the image of a helmeted man with his shield at throat level, wielding a sword and trampling on a snake at his feet, then this stone's owner will vanquish all enemies in battle, particularly if this battle began on the day of Mars [Tuesday]. The same engraving can be used on green jasper, although then the stone needs to be set in bronze.

 📖 *De la vertu des tailles* 42; *De l'entaille des gemmes* 27; *Liber sigillorum Ethel* 3; Chael 2; Solomon 29.

Reflambine: This stone is yellow, the size of a broad bean, and found in a river that travels through "Little India." It stops blood, cures rheum, and strengthens the limbs of its bearer. It also provides great strength to widows. "*Reflambine*" appears to be the result of a poor reading of *elambari*, the Arabic name for amber.

 ✦ *raflambine, refflaibine, reflamberine, jeflambine;* MItal. *reflabina*.

 📖 *Sidrac* 23; Mandeville I (Amiens ms.) 5; *Libro di Sidrach* chap. 475.

Reieben: See *t(r)esbut*.

📖 Avicenna II, 2, 592.

Resten: See *t(r)esbut*.

Rhamnos: The name for a kind of ruby.

📖 Pliny 27, 124.

Rhinoceros: This stone, also known as "unicorn horn" is found in the nose or horn of the rhinoceros. It banishes demons when worn. It is necessary to engrave an owl on it with a needle fish and add a little radish root. If this is secretly placed beneath someone's head, he will no longer be able to sleep.

📖 *Kyranides* 1, 17; *Secrez* 4, 15.

Rhoditis, Roditis: A stone that derives its name from its resemblance to a rose (Greek *rodon*).

📖 Pliny 37, 191; Isidore of Sevilla 16, 9, 8; *Summarium Heinrici* VI, 4, 22; Meliteniotes v. 1178.

Risolansis: See *chrysolampsis*.

Rodianus: See *radaim*.

Rosten: This is a small stone that is found in the head of a crab. It is sometimes white and sometimes bordering on yellow. It is not very hard and it is similar to the pupil of a fish that is cold and dank by nature. It is effective against scorpion and weasel bites if applied in a plaster. It is also said to be good against the bites of rabid dogs if crushed into powder and ingested as a drink. If the powder is incinerated, it strengthens teeth, dries out wounds, heals itching and wrath, and dries watery eyes.

◆ MFr. *resten;* MHG *reiben.*

📖 Bartholomaeus Anglicus XVI, 86.

Rubinus: During the Middle Ages, the ruby was known as the "lord of stones." The ruby is crystalline aluminum. Herodotus said that storks placed rubies in their nests to drive away serpents and aid in the hatching of eggs (*Histories* II, 14). In the Bible, it is one of the twelve stones that adorn the *rationale* or breastplate of the high priest Aaron (Exodus 28:15–30). Sick men and animals that drink water in which a ruby has been steeped will be healed "by the virtue that God has given to this stone." It is found in a river flowing from paradise and must be set in gold and worn on the left side. The ruby permits the acquisition and protection of lands, makes one devout, calms anger, and protects against seduction, procures grace and dominance over other people, protects from all peril and causes all melancholy to be forgotten, delights the individual, and comforts the heart. As a trituration, it heals ocular problems and dropsy. Finally, it safeguards the fruits of trees, vines, and the earth, and protects houses from lightning. It symbolizes chastity, loyalty, and boldness, and represents Jesus, but also excites anger and lust. Its prophetic power was still well known into the seventeenth century: if it loses its bright color, it is heralding some dire event.

Counterfeiting is certainly not only a modern phenomenon, and lapidaries also provided the means for testing the authenticity of stones. For the ruby, it is enough to drop it into a pot of boiling water. If it stops boiling, it is a true ruby.

Rubies were also used to make amulets and talismans. Engraved with the image of a scorpion, it protected the bearer from spider bites, or cured them.

If the image of the beautiful yet terrifying constellation of Draco is on a ruby or on another stone with a similar nature and power, its virtue is the increase of earthly possessions. It also brings its owner joy and health. A quarreling man engraved on a ruby brings honors and riches.

According to the Lapidary of King Alfonso, the ruby is called *bezebekaury* in Chaldean and its definition is "banisher of sorrow and bestower of good spirits." In fact, its bearer will witness the departure of all kinds of sorrow and it gives him a haven from the ills caused by the melancholy humors. This stone is dry and cold by nature, and governed by the 17° of Capricorn. The ruby is used to make the Sun talisman: if the stone is carved with one of the forms of this heavenly body, it prevents a person from being defeated.

In his *Book of the World Map* (eleventh century), al-Huwârizimi mentions what he calls the "peninsula of rubies" (*Gazirat al-Yâkût*), which actually refers to Ceylon (Sri Lanka), whose name in Sanskrit literature is *Ratna-dwipa*, "Isle of the Jewels." Jordan Catalani (circa 1321) mentions the king of Ceylon who owns two rubies, "one worn around his neck and the other on his hand, which he uses to clean his lips and beard."

John Mandeville indicates in his *Travels* that the king of the Nicobar Islands wears a ruby that is a foot in length and five fingers wide. When the people select their king, they give him this stone before leading him into the capital. The people see the gem and obey its wearer. It is therefore an insignia of sovereignty. See *balagius, carbunculus, epistites*.

✦ MFr. *rubi, rubinz, balayze;* MHG *rubyn, rubîne;* MDu. *rubijn;* MItal. *rubino;* Ar. *elantagar, alkarkahin, yakut;* Heb. *odem.*

📖 *De l'entaille des gemmes* 22; *Sidrac* 4; *Liber lapidarii* 3; Gossouin de Metz v. 162–203; Volmar v. 682–709; Wolfram von Eschenbach 791, 25; Christian lapidary v. 261–308 and 887–936; *Picatrix* II, 10, 51f.; III, 1, 6; 3, 31; Jordan Catalani §76; Jacob van Maerlant XII, 16; Mandeville I 1; Pseudo-Mandeville 2 and 42; *Libro di Sidrach* chap. 457; Leonardi II, 7, 233; Ragiel 1.

Runcanbon:

This name for a stone appears in a fourteenth-century lexicon. Its German translation as *agetsteyn* does not allow this stone to be identified, since this term is used to designate all igneous rocks and even the loadstone.

📖 *Vocabularius ex quo* r 445.4.

S

Saburna: The name of a crystal.

 📖 *Vocabularius ex quo* s 11.

Saga Stone: This stone, which is called *sögusteinn* in Iceland, is found in wagtail nests during the month of May. It should be carried in a bloodied scarf and held close to the right ear, if one wishes to learn something.

 📖 Jón Árnason, *Íslenzkar Þióðsögur og Æventýri* (Leipzig: J. C. Hinrich, 1862–1864).

Sagda: A green or black gem that is found in Chaldea or on Samothrace. It adheres to boats—behaving toward wood as magnets do toward iron—and drags them to the bottom of the sea.

 ✦ *sadda, saga, sarda, agada;* MFr. *sade, sarde, sayde, hadda, badda, balda, radas;* MHG *saddâ, saden.*

 📖 Pliny 37, 181; Solin 37, 8; Isidore of Sevilla 16, 7, 13; Marbode 35; *Summarium Heinrici* VI, 4, 11; Lambert de Saint-Omer 55, 30; Meliteniotes v. 1178; Marbode Lapidary, 1st Romanesque translation XXXV; Lapidary in prose 53; Alexander Neckham v. 273ff.; Cambridge lapidary v. 899–920;

Wolfram von Eschenbach 589, 21; 741, 7; 791, 9; Arnoldus Saxo 72; Albertus Magnus 2, 17, 3; Lapidary of King Philip 47; Konrad von Megenberg VI, 76; *Hortus sanitatis* V, 114; Leonardi II, 7, 244; Closener sa 38.

Saigre: See *galigus*.

Sambeti: Another name for diamond, according to Arnoldus Saxo. See *adamas* (I).

Samius: This stone comes from the isle of Samos and is used to polish gold. It can be recognized by its weight and white color. It is also used in medicine with milk for treating ulcerations of the eyes, as well as for chronic lacrimation. Taken internally, it is good for stomach disorders; it soothes dizzy spells and restores the mind after a shock. Some believe it is effective for epilepsy and painful urination. It is incorporated into medications called *acopes* (relaxants). When tied to the hand of a woman in labor as an amulet, it is claimed it will prevent abortion, but it provides the same effect when crushed and drunk. Worn on the left, it dries tears if crushed in milk and applied as eyewash.

> ✦ *sami, samis, saumus, samolithos.*

> 📖 Pliny 36, 152; Dioscorides V, 172; Pseudo-Dioscorides 2, 173; Isidore of Sevilla 16, 4, 13; *Summarium Heinrici* VI, 2, 10; Meliteniotes v. 1130; *De lapidibus preciosis* 59; Thomas de Cantimpré 14, 63; v; Albertus Magnus 2, 17, 6; Konrad von Megenberg VI, 72; Jacob van Maerlant XII, 67; *Hortus sanitatis* V, 112; Leonardi II, 7, 240; *Liber secretorum* II, 1, 46.

Samothratia: A stone of average beauty. Crushed and offered as a drink with satyrion, it stiffens the penis; hung around the neck, it provides good digestion and the desire to copulate.

> 📖 Leonardi II, 7, 250.

Sanctus Lapis: Another name for sapphire. See *saphirus*.

> 📖 Leonardi II, 7, 250.

Sandaracha: See *zandarakes*.

> 📖 Pliny 32, 39f.; Lombard Dioscorides 131; Avicenna II, 2, 627; Vincent de Beauvais VII, 102; *Hortus sanitatis* V, 22.

Sandasirus: See *sandrastos*.

> ✦ *sandasyrus, sandaresos, sandariso.*

> 📖 Pliny 37, 102; Isidore of Sevilla 16, 14, 3; Lambert de Saint-Omer 55, 65; Meliteniotes v. 1179; *Hortus sanitatis* V, 114.

Sandrastos: This is the stone known as aventurine. It is found in India, in a place called Sandaresus, and in southern Arabia. It seems to contain a shimmering fire of starlike sparks that look like drops of gold, which are always seen inside the stone and never on its surface. The male stones can be distinguished from the female by their vigorous and deep hues, which they impart to any neighboring objects. The radiance of the stones from India is said to cause harm to the eyes. The fire of the female stones is softer and could be described as lustrous rather than brilliant. There are some religious associations with this stone because of the rapport it has with the stars. In fact, their scintillating drops of gold resemble in arrangement and number the stars of the constellations of the Hyades, which is why the Chaldeans used it in their ceremonies.

✦ *sadasius, sandrisita, sandristae, sandasirus, garamantica.*

📖 Pliny 37, 100–102; Leonardi II, 7, 131 and 245.

Sandristae: Another name for the *sandrastos* stone.

📖 Pliny 37, 101.

Sanguineus: See *haematitis*.

📖 Leonardi II, 7, 252.

Saphirus: Until the thirteenth century, this name referred to the lapis lazuli that came from Libya and Turkey. The name sapphire is of Semitic origin and this gem is among those found on the high priest Aaron's breastplate. It is also one of the twelve stones of the heavenly Jerusalem (Apocalypse 21:19) and is mentioned by all the Christian lapidaries (see Exodus 28:18). The prophets even state that God's throne is made of sapphire (Ezekiel 1:26; Isaiah 54:11). For the church, sapphire was a symbol of purity and a bull promulgated by Innocent III, pope from 1198 to 1216, commanded cardinals and bishops to wear a ring adorned with this gem on their right hand (the one used to give a blessing). Some maintain that the Tablets of the Law given to Moses on Mount Sinai were made of sapphire, as was Solomon's seal, which gave one power over demons. In the Christian lapidary, it represents the heart of the simple folk whose life and behavior are enchanting to God, those who look toward the heavens and despise all earthly things, as if they did not live on earth. Konrad von Hamburg made the sapphire the symbol of the hope exemplified by the Virgin Mary in his poem Anulus, written circa 1350. It is one of the twenty gems on the ring he offers to Mary.

According to the texts, the sapphire is also named *sirites* or *sirtites*. God so loved the sapphire that he called it the "holy stone and gem of gems." It resembles a crystal-clear sky and is also called the "sacred stone." Sea-blue sapphires are regarded as male stones. The most beautiful come from Media. This gem invigorates the body, overpowers envy, vanquishes fear, and ensures that God looks favorably on one's prayers. It is used to restore peace and elevate thought. It prevents a man from being imprisoned—or, if he has this stone on his person, it can aid in his deliverance, for it opens locked doors and undoes all bonds. The prisoner should touch his shackles and the four sides of his cell with the stone.

The sapphire is useful to hydromancers, cools down inner zeal, and cleanses rheumy eyes, but for all this to work, the individual must be chaste. It heals abscesses, fortifies the body, and encourages reconciliations. According to Heinrich von dem Türlîn, it protects from poison and curbs lust.

The best sapphire is green. It inspires peace and harmony, purifies the mind, and compels devotion to God. It cools inner enthusiasms and is effective against headaches, eye taints, and bad breath. If the stone is touched several times it will heal the disease known in the Middle Ages as *noli me tangere* (touch me not), but this will shrink the stone. Crushed and drunk with milk, it heals all illnesses. According to the Arabic tradition passed down by Balenus, its planet is the Sun.

In the texts that derive from the Greek tradition, sapphire is under the patronage of Aphrodite, whose image is engraved on this stone to make it into an amulet. It bestows graciousness and victory at assemblies. A ram, a sheep, or an ostrich holding a hake can be carved on it. An astrolabe etched onto a sapphire has the power of increasing wealth and predicting the future. Aries, or the head of a bearded man, carved into a sapphire has the power of offering relief and freedom from numerous ills, for example prison and all forms of imprisonment. A sapphire with the image of a man desiring to play a musical instrument will elevate its owner to honors and earns him the favor of all. The image of an armored man, or a virgin wrapped in a toga holding a laurel branch in her hand, will protect its owner from danger, particularly that of drowning, if it is etched onto a sapphire.

When the *Romance of Alexander* describes the palace of the Indian king Porus, it mentions a vine hanging between the columns: its leaves and branches are gold and some of its grapes are crystals and pearls "as big as a man's thumb," and others are emeralds and sapphires. Over the course of his travels, Alexander catches sight of a sapphire rampart surrounding a round temple with one hundred pillars made from this same stone: one gem replaces the lamps and lights up the whole interior. In his *History of the Battles of Alexander the Great,* Leon of Naples (tenth century) mentions Mount Adam in Ceylon, the peak of which is reached by a staircase consisting of two thousand sapphire stairs. The ceiling of Prester John's room is also made of sapphire, with topaz stars.

Today's sapphire is a blue variety of corundum, and a distinction is made between the male stone or Eastern sapphire, a hyaline quartz, and the female stone, a transparent blue fluorite commonly known as the water sapphire, a blue variety of cordierite.

✦ *sapphirus, saphyr;* MHG *saffir, sapfir;* ME *saphyre;* MItal. *zaffiro.*

📖 Pliny 37, 120; Isidore of Sevilla 16, 9, 2; Aetios II, 38; Damigeron 14; Marbode 5; Dioscorides V, 139; Pseudo-Dioscorides 2, 157; Lombard Dioscorides 166; Hildegard von Bingen IV, 6; *Summarium Heinrici* VI, 4, 18; Old English Lapidary 2; Lambert de Saint-Omer 54, 2; 55, 2 and 22; *Kyranides* 1, 18; Meliteniotes v. 1120; Jacques de Vitry cap. 91; Marbode Lapidary, 1st Romanesque translation V; Alphabetical Lapidary 76; Lapidary in prose 3; 2nd Lapidary in prose 2; Gossouin de Metz v. 204–248; *Sidrac* 4; Alexander Neckham v. 135ff.; Bodl. Digby 13 27; *De lapidibus preciosis* 55; Cambridge lapidary v. 147–88; Wolfram von Eschenbach 791, 22; *Liber lapidarii* 4; Arnoldus Saxo 60; Bartholomaeus Anglicus XVI, 87; Thomas de Cantimpré 14, 57; Vincent de Beauvais VIII, 94; Albertus Magnus 2, 17, 1; Diu Crône v. 8263f.; Lapidary of King Philip 5; Konrad von Megenberg VI, 66; Jacob van Maerlant XII, 62; Volmar v. 137–60; Christian lapidary v. 309–80 and 937–80; Saint Florian v. 11–68; *Secrez* 3, 6; 4, 16; Psellos 16 and 18; *Vocabularius ex quo* s 45; 163.1; *Liber ordinis rerum* 129, 8; Mandeville I 4 (*esmeraude*); I 5; Pseudo-Mandeville 6 and 31; Closener sa 144; *Libro di Sidrach* chap. 458; *Liber secretorum* II, 1, 45; Ragiel 5; Solomon 7; *Hortus sanitatis* V, 109; Leonardi II, 7, 234; *Phisice* 5.

Sarcitis: *Sarcitis* resembles raw beef; nothing more is known about it.

📖 Pliny 37, 181; Meliteniotes v. 1181.

Sarcophagus: This stone that "eats away the corpses of the dead" is found in Assos in Troas. The dead bodies placed inside this stone are consumed, except for the teeth, in forty days (or thirty days, according to other authors). It transforms the mirrors, strigils, garments, and shoes buried with the dead into stone. There are stones of a similar nature in Lycia and in the East that when attached to the body will even consume the flesh of the living. A French lapidary provides a piquant etymology for its name: "The Greek *sarcos* means flesh; the French *arche*, coffin, meaning that the flesh is eaten by the stone coffin."

✦ *sarcofagus, calophagus;* MFr. *caconsage;* MHG *calof, leych stain (corpse stone)*.

📖 Pliny 2, 211; 28, 140; 36, 161; Isidore of Sevilla 16, 4, 15; *Summarium Heinrici* VI, 2, 12; Thomas de Catimpré 14, 62; Vincent de Beauvais VIII, 26; Albertus Magnus 2, 17, 2; Konrad von Megenberg VI, 71; *Vocabularius ex quo* s 163.1; *Hortus sanitatis* V, 112; Leonardi II, 7, 246; *Phisice* 75.

Sarda, Sardius:

This stone is carnelian or red sardonyx, a variety of chalcedony. India has three species of *sarda:* a red one, a second with the name *"pionia"* because of its thickness, and a third beneath which silver leaves are placed. The most highly valued come from the outskirts of Babylon. Indian *sarda* stones are transparent and the Arabic ones are more opaque. The French spelling *cardinie* is evidence of its confusion with sardonyx (*sardonicus*). This stone should be set in gold.

In the Christian lapidary, *sarda* symbolizes the martyrs that die for Christ.

According to Damigeron, freemen carry the stone with an etching of Mars carrying a trophy, freed slaves with an armored Mars, and slaves with one depicting the god's weapons.

Sarda provides protection against worms and wild beasts. Whoever wears one of these stones that is the weight of twenty barley grains at his throat or on his finger will see no frightful or terrible thing in his dreams, or have dread of any curses or evil spells. If Artemis on foot with a doe standing beside her is carved on this stone, it will make one courageous, vigorous, noble, and bold; it weakens adversaries and repels wounds. To be beneficial for women, the image of a grapevine entwined with ivy is also carved on it, or else the sun above four hens or above a *quadriga* [a chariot drawn by four horses] with a moon above two bulls.

✦ *sardis, sardonia;* MFr. *sarde, cardinie, grenaz;* MHG *sardîne, sarden;* MSp. *sardia*.

📖 Pliny 37, 186f.; Solin II, 27; Isidore of Sevilla 16, 8, 2; Damigeron 50; Marbode 10; Hildegard von Bingen IV, 7; Old English Lapidary 7; Lambert de Saint-Omer 54, 6; 55, 6 and 19; Meliteniotes v. 1124; Jacques de Vitry cap. 91; Lapidary in prose 47; *De lapidibus preciosis* 58; Cambridge lapidary v. 277–88; Gossouin de Metz v. 59–85 (*sarda,* garnet, and almandine are apparently the same stone here); *Sidrac* 1; Wolfram von Eschenbach 589, 22; Arnoldus Saxo 71; Bartholomaeus Anglicus XVI, 89; Thomas de Cantimpré 14, 60; 14, 67; Lapidary of King Philip 1; Konrad von Megenberg VI, 69; Jacob van Maerlant XII, 65; Volmar v. 578–89; Christian lapidary v. 706–750; Saint Florian v. 321–30; *Vocabularius ex quo* s 165–66; Leonardi II, 7, 237 and 259 (= *saphirus*); Closener sa 162 and 165; *Poridat* 11; *Hortus sanitatis* V, 110.

Sardachates: This lemon-colored stone with white bands, a *sarda*-agate, is good for keeping the wicked at bay and for finding love and good arguments. Whoever wears it will be friendly to all. It reconciles friends who are angry with each other if placed between them or if one holds it in his hand. It is consecrated by carving magic letters upon it.

📖 Kerygma 43; Meliteniotes v. 1180.

Sardinius: Another name for sardonyx based on the discovery of this stone near the city of Sardes.

📖 Albertus Magnus 2, 17,4.

Sardonyx: In the Middle Ages, this stone was defined as follows: Sardonyx is two stones, "*sarda* and onyx." There are five different kinds of *sard* or sardonyx, a variety of chalcedony—a hard, fine stone that has the white of the skin beneath the fingernail and the incarnadine red or brown of the *sarda* (*sardius, sardus*), to which some authors compare it. It can be found in India, Arabia, Libya, and Sodom. The Arabian sardonyxes are noteworthy for their fairly large and sparkling white circles, which shine from the fissures of the stone against its extremely black background. This background is the color of wax or horn in the Indian sardonyx, but also with a white circle. Sardonyx imparts a beautiful color to the face, curbs lust, makes one humble, lends boldness, and strengthens eyesight. It destroys curses and enchantments and makes one chaste and modest. Sardonyx is effective against the bloody flux. Some authors describe it as *sarda* (*sardius, sardus*). It should be set in silver.

In the Bible, this is one of the twelve stones found on the breastplate of the brother of Moses, the high priest Aaron (Exodus 28:15–30). In the Christian lapidary, sardonyx represents those who suffer the tortures of the Passion of the Christ in their own hearts, who have pure souls even though they see themselves as vile and black (in other words, as sinners). Konrad von Hamburg described this stone in his poem *Anulus* as the symbol of the Virgin's suffering at the foot of the cross. It is one of the twenty stones on the ring he offers Mary in this poem, which was written circa 1350.

If an image of a ram and Athena holding a heart is carved on this stone, it makes an excellent phylactery for the body; moreover, sardonyx grants success.

✦ *sardonix, sardonis, sardonicen, sardonius, sartonix, sardone;* MFr. *sardonis, sardoine, sardine, sardoyne, sardoynis, sardonie, sardonne, saridoine;* MHG *sardonîs, sardîne, sardon, sardoniß, sardonicen;* MItal. *sardonia*.

📖 Pliny 37, 86–89; Solin 33, 8–9; Epiphanes 1 and 12; Isidore of Sevilla 16, 8, 4; Kerygma 31; Marbode 8; Hildegard von Bingen IV, 5; Old English Lapidary 5; Lambert de Saint-Omer 54, 5; 55, 5 and 18; Meliteniotes v. 1120; Marbode Lapidary, 1st Romanesque translation X; Lapidary in prose 6; 2nd Lapidary in prose 8; Alexander Neckham v. 157ff.; Bodl. Digby 13 25; *De lapidibus preciosis* 57; Cambridge lapidary v. 247–66; Gossouin de Metz v. 446–52; Wolfram von Eschenbach 791, 12 and 26; *Liber lapidarii* 15; Arnoldus Saxo 70; Bartholomaeus Anglicus XVI, 90; Thomas de Cantimpré 14, 59; Vincent de Beauvais VIII, 33; Albertus Magnus 2, 17, 5; Lapidary of King Philip 16; Konrad von Megenberg VI, 68; Jacob van Maerlant XII, 64; Saint Florian v. 299–320; *Liber defota anima* v. 4332–443; *Secrez* 3, 9; *Vocabularius ex quo* s 184.1; *Liber ordinis rerum* 129, 22–23; Mandeville I 16; Pseudo-Mandeville 18 and 37; Leonardi II, 7, 238; Closener sa 164; *Hortus sanitatis* V, 111; *Libro di Sidrach* chap. 467; *Phisice* 18 and 73.

Sarutatis: See *mirâd*.

Sauritis, Saurites: A stone that is said to be found in the belly of a green lizard split asunder with a reed.

 📖 Pliny 37, 181; Kerygma 51; Isidore of Sevilla 16, 7, 13; Meliteniotes v. 1179.

Sayette: This name masks the black stone jet, which, when rubbed, attracts hairs and chaff. It burns in cold water, at which time its glow is effective against epilepsy, and oil extinguishes it. Its boiling water is good for dropsy sufferers. Powdered jet strengthens the teeth and the smoke from burning this stone will restore women's menstrual cycles. Jet sends evil spirits fleeing. See *gagates*.

 📖 Mandeville I, 22.

Scaritis: A stone that takes its name from the fish called "scarus" or "sarget." It is a fossil.

 📖 Pliny 37, 187.

Schistos: See *ischistos*.

 📖 Pliny 36, 144–48; Dioscorides V, 127; Meliteniotes v. 1130; 1184.

Scirites: The name for a kind of sapphire.

 📖 Anglo-Norman lapidary 23.

Scorpion Stone: See *scorpitis*.

Scorpitis: A stone that has either the color or the shape of the scorpion. It is undoubtedly a fossil.

 ✦ *scorpius, scorpios, scorpeta*.

📖 Pliny 37, 187; Orpheus v. 494ff.; Kerygma 18; Isidore of Sevilla 16, 15, 19; Meliteniotes v. 1181; Closener sc 110.

Scyenos: See *amethystus*.

Scyrius: On the island of Skyros there is a stone that is said to float on the water's surface if whole but will sink to the bottom when crumbled. In powdered form, it cleanses wounds of dead skin and heals tinea. One medieval lapidary switches Skyros with Syria!

✦ *symis;* MFr. *syrre.*

📖 Pliny 2, 233; 36, 130; *Phisice* 74.

Scyticis, Scithis: A variety of emerald that takes its name from the region in which it is found, Scythia. According to Notker, who repeats Martianus Capella on this point, it is the stone of Aries and the month of April.

📖 Pliny 37, 65; Notker I, 40

Sedeneg: See *haematitis*.

📖 Leonardi II, 7, 255.

Segulsteinn: This is the "stone for sailing" or "navigator's stone" or "compass stone," which is well known in Iceland and used for uncovering a thief. If the suspected individual's name is written on paper and the stone is placed beneath the name, the name of the guilty party will appear on the stone. There is also another method: the stone is blended into raw dough with wine from the mass, and this mixture is then cooked over a fire. This "bread" is then given to the putative thief; if his name appears on the bread, he is the criminal.

📖📖 Jón Árnason, *Íslenzkar Þjóðsögur og Æventýri* (Leipzig: J. C. Hinrich, 1862–1864).

Selenite: Opinions vary regarding *selenite*, which is the old name for calcium sulfate. It is diaphanous white with a reflection the color of honey, or can be red, white, and purple, or even green. It contains an image of the moon and grows or shrinks in accordance with the lunar phases. It is found in Arabia, Persia, and India. It is often confused with *chelonite*. Today it is considered to be argentine, a kind of feldspar. Other authors maintain that it is a green stone. It is capable of inspiring love and bringing relief to consumption. The two phases of the moon should be carved on it, and it should be worn around the neck. If enclosed in a gold capsule with parsley, it will make bees fertile. It allows pregnant women to carry to term, reduces swellings, reconciles lovers, and grants peace and harmony.

Placed under the tongue on the first and second days of the moon, it bestows prescience of the future. In fact, it only has this power for one hour during the rise of the new moon. It has it on the tenth day during the first and sixth hour. It is claimed to heal consumptives, protect thieves, and keep sea travelers safe, especially from storms, to increase personal properties, and to help obtain honors. Worn on the finger, *selenite* makes one worthy of honor and veneration and gives divine inspiration.

In the fifteenth century, the *Phisice* stated that *selenite* is sometimes black, sometimes green. It also said that it safeguards pregnancy and gives women a good labor and birth; it also bestows peace and harmony, reconciles lovers, shrinks welts, and heals those suffering from consumption. See also *moonstone*.

✦ *selenitis, salonites, solenites, sollentes, silente, silenites, sylenites, syleniten, sylonites, celonites, lapis lune;* MFr. *sylenite, silleniche;* MHG *silenistes, silenites;* ME *seleten;* Sp. *galantes, salentes.*

📖 Pliny 37, 181; Solin 37, 21; Isidore of Sevilla 16, 4, 6; Damigeron 36; Marbode 26; Dioscorides V, 113 and 141; Pseudo-Dioscorides 2, 159; Lombard Dioscorides 168; *Summarium Heinrici* VI, 2, 5; VI, 4, 31; Old English Lapidary 16; Lambert de Saint-Omer 55, 50; Meliteniotes v. 1127; Avicenna II, 2, 412; Marbode Lapidary, 1st Romanesque translation XXVI; Alphabetical Lapidary 75; Lapidary in prose 22; 2nd Lapidary in prose 25; Alexander Neckham v. 249ff.;

Bodl. Digby 13 39; *De lapidibus preciosis* 61; Cambridge Lapidary v. 667–88; Wolfram von Eschenbach 791, 1; Arnoldus Saxo 73; Bartholomaeus Anglicus XVI, 92; Thomas de Cantimpré 14, 66; Vincent de Beauvais VIII, 5; Albertus Magnus 2, 17, 7; Konrad von Megenberg VI, 74; Jacob van Maerlant XII, 69; *Vocabularius ex quo* s 780.1; Psellos 18; *Secrez* 3, 16; Leonardi II, 7, 239; Closener si 52; Pseudo-Mandeville 28; *Liber secretorum* II, 1, 6; *De virtutis lapidum* II, 5 Poridat 20; *Hortus sanitatis* V, 115.

Selustre: The name for *ceraunia* in Middle French.

    📖 *Phisice* 34.

Senochiten: See *galactitis*.

    📖 Leonardi II, 7, 253.

Serpent's Egg: See *dre concides*.

Serpent's Tongue: A stone of varied colors—whitish, black, or ash red—that changes color when carried in front of oneself. It resists venom, suppresses tongue embarrassment, and makes one a good speaker, with grace and honesty.

    📖 Lapidary of King Philip 79; Pseudo-Mandeville 53.

Sibiciosus, Sibinosus: A stone that is never described and about which we know nothing.

 📖 *Vocabularius ex quo* s 597.1.

Sicyonos: A blackish stone found in the Araxus River. When an oracle has ordained the sacrifice of a human victim, two young virgins place this stone on the altar of the tutelary deities. Barely is it touched by the priest's knife when it disgorges an immense quantity of blood. Immediately, those performing the rite leave while making great cries, taking the stone back into the temple.

 📖 Pseudo-Plutarch §25.

Siderites, Siderate: The "magnetic stone of the mountains" resembles iron. Siderite, which some authors treat as a diamond, has the metallic sheen of iron, weighs more than all the other stones, but differs from them on account of its properties: in fact, it can be broken by a hammer, and it can be pierced with another diamond. One of its varieties, found in Ethiopia, is called *sideropoecilos*. It maintains the discord between litigants, protects from snakebite, and if a woman wears one on her belt, she will become pregnant and have a happy birth. Siderite is used for divination in the following manner: the stone must be washed in pure water and wrapped in white linen. Once the lamps have been lit, then the siderite will answer your questions.

 📖 Pliny 37, 58; Solin 37, 23; Isidore of Sevilla 16, 15, 11; Dioscorides V, 13; Orpheus v. 346ff.; Kerygma 16; Damigeron 15; Meliteniotes v. 1122; Leonardi II, 7, 248.

Sincicetus: This stone cures dropsy. It is extracted from a freshwater serpent that should be hung head down for five days in a row, or seven nights, which one should go look at during the fifth hour of the night with a lantern while saying: "I am Adam, the protoplast of paradise.

Give me the stone that you have in your ear" (or, alternatively: "in your belly"). A vase of very pure water is placed above the reptile and the stone is tossed within, after which this water is boiled. The stone is then attached to the dropsy sufferer with bonds that completely encircle the patient for three or four days, or longer. According to legend, Alexander the Great sent this stone to his mother.

✦ MFr. *si(n)tique*.

📖 *Liber sigillorum Ethel* 25; Lapidary of King Philip, Paris: National Library of France, French ms. 2009, fol. 10 v° sq.; Latin ms. 11210, fol. 82 v°.

Sinerip: When worn at the same time as chalcedony, this stone will heal all fevers.

📖 Mandeville 15.

Sinodontitis, Sinodontide: *Synondontitis* is a stone that comes from the brain of a fish called the synodus, and is synonymous with the *corvine,* the stone found in another kind of fish. It has no connection with the crow (*corvus*). The name of this stone suffered from poor reading and transcription, which rendered it as *sincicetus,* and then in Middle French as *si(n)tique*. See these names.

📖 Pliny 37, 182; Leonardi II, 7, 260.

Si(n)tique: See *sincicetus*.

Siphinius, Sifinus: The Island of Siphnos produces this stone, which is used to make utensils for cooking or serving food. What is unique about this stone is that it darkens and turns hard when heated in oil, whereas normally it is quite soft.

📖 Pliny 36, 159; Leonardi II, 7, 247.

Siren's Stone: A stone that can be found in the bellies of sirens; it has the property of ensuring conception.

 📖 Pseudo-Mandeville 48.

Sirites: Another name for sapphire.

 📖 Leonardi II, 7, 256.

Sirtis: See *melas*.

Skruggusteinn: See *ceraunia*.

Smaragdus: The ancients used this name to designate the green quartz called peridot or false emerald that is used in jewelry-making. The Arabs, according to Juba, called emerald *chloran*. In Persia, there is a variety called *tanos* (perhaps *euclase*), and the name for the coppery variety from Cypress is *chalcosmaragdus*. Other varieties are known as *hermineus* and *limoniatis*. This is a clear translucent or yellow stone said to be found in the nests of griffins, where it was collected by the one-eyed people of Scythia, the Arimaspians. Another source for these stones was claimed to be the Phison, one of the rivers that flows out of Eden. This legend can be found in the biblical commentaries that are more or less inspired by the Venerable Bede's analysis of the Apocalypse.

 There are twelve species of emerald. The most renowned are Scythian emeralds, named after the land where they are found. None has a deeper color or fewer flaws, and the degree to which emeralds prevail over all other stones is the degree by which the Scythian variety prevails over all other emeralds. Bactrian emeralds, which are next-door neighbors by virtue of their land of origin, are likewise next in status. They are collected, it is said, in the fissures of rocks when the etesian winds are blowing. They then glitter on the ground, having been uncovered by the action of the winds, which greatly disturb the sands. But we are assured they are much smaller than those from Scythia. In third place is the Egyptian emerald extracted from the rocks in the hills surrounding Coptos, the city of the Thebaid. The other kinds of emeralds are found in copper mines.

According to the Arabic tradition, for which Balenis is the spokesperson, the emerald's planet is Mars. This gem gives rest to the eyesight. Hung from the neck, it expels demitertian fever, relieves madness and epilepsy, calms the lascivious impulses, and imparts chastity, for it does not tolerate sexual relations. When lying together, the man and woman should never wear this stone, for it "distracts and disturbs." In the Middle Ages, the emeralds would divert storms, banish evil spirits, increase prestige and eloquence, multiply wealth, and give joy while dispelling melancholy. It should be set in gold. It facilitates understanding and improves memory; it increases riches if worn at the throat, and it is good for divination because it grants the gift of prophecy when placed beneath the tongue. Those who wear it in a state of purity will see their wealth, words, and activities increase. According to Rabelais, this gem possesses erective virtues, which is the reason why Gargantua's codpiece was fastened "with two enamell'd clasps, in each of which was set a great emerald, as big as an orange."

Emerald is used in hydromancy. The stone should be carved with the image of Isis standing over the belly of a scarab, then pierced, a good fitting inserted, and worn on the finger. Those who know how to prepare and consecrate this stone will obtain all. It is necessary to carve a scarab on a diamond to do this. According to the *Lapidario,* the emerald is ruled by the 16° of Taurus and according to Notker, echoing Martianus Capella on this point, its month is May.

In the Bible, this stone is one of the twelve stones found on the high priest Aaron's breastplate (Exodus 28:15–30).

The emerald is used to craft Mercury talismans. Such a talisman frees one from prison, earns the excellent service of scribes and secretaries in commerce, ensures that no one can alarm or worry its bearer, and enables him to escape illness. The emerald also ensures that an individual will be feared and people will have nothing but good to say about him. It is also used to make one of the Moon talismans:

carved with a depiction of the moon and then imprinted upon a seal of incense, this stone provides good memory.

An emerald with an engraving of a man looking like a merchant bringing his merchandise to market, or the image of a man sitting beneath a centurion, will give wealth and victory and save its bearer from evil and desperate situations.

To obtain a divine phylactery, a harpy with a sea lamprey beneath its claws should be carved on this stone and a briar root placed underneath it. When this combination is worn, it banishes panic, terrifying visions, and all that affects lunatics; lastly, it heals colic.

It is said that Nero owned an emerald in which he gazed at his reflection and knew, by the power of the stone, what he wished to ask about. In Tyre, in the temple of Hercules, there was a pillar made from a single emerald; in Egypt, there were obelisks and a colossal statue of Serapis also made from a single emerald block.

When the *Romance of Alexander* describes the palace of Porus, the king of India, it mentions a grapevine that hangs between its columns. Some of the grapes on this vine were emeralds and sapphires. The altar in the temple of Helios was made from gold and emerald. The *Letter of Alexander to Aristotle* (§69) mentions the Jordan Valley being full of venomous serpents wearing emeralds on their necks, which collected the light of their eyes. This presumably softened the toxicity of their gaze.

Medieval Arabic literature speaks of a valley that a sage showed to Pharaoh Neharous; its slopes were covered with emeralds and topazes. In the city of Karmidah, there was an emerald statue on an amethyst pedestal. Among the things placed in Adam's tomb, there was "a green emerald tablet of dazzling color that cast yellow rays. When vipers looked at it, their eyes would melt." One of the treasuries of Egypt held "the emerald statue of a crow with red jacinth eyes."

In the Christian lapidaries of the Middle Ages, this stone represents faith in its fullness, which is never absent from pious works. They also repeated the legend that maintained emeralds were stolen from the griffins fought by the Arimaspians, who were often called Monoculi (one-eyed). This was accompanied by the following interpretation:

> By emerald, we mean those stones that are greener than all others and which, through the vigor of their faith, prevail over the infidels who are cold and dry for they lack all charity. The griffins guarding these stones represent demons, jealous of men with faith, which is a gem and a pearl, and they strive to drag them off; rightfully, they have been likened to griffins, beasts of both heaven and earth, inasmuch as they have been cast into hell for their behavior and who, soaring with pride like birds, have tumbled from the skies. Fighting them are the Arimaspians, that is to say, those who do not walk two paths, who are not of two hearts, and do not serve two masters but always keep their rectitude and the pearl of their faith that the demons seek to wrest from them, as they prevail over the latter with divine aid.

In his poem *Anulus* (written circa 1350), in which he offers Mary a ring adorned with twenty precious stones, Konrad von Hamburg made emerald the symbol of the Virgin's purity. The emerald later became the symbol of hope, the gem of wisdom and harmony.

A legend has it that when Lucifer rebeled against God, at the moment he was vanquished by Saint Michael, the emerald shining on his brow came off and fell to earth. It was later offered to Solomon by the Queen of Sheba and subsequently carved into a chalice. Nicodemus inherited it, then Joseph of Arimathea, and it became the Grail after the Last Supper.

The emerald is used in architecture. For example, in *Herzog Ernst* (Duke Ernst), a late-twelfth-century romance recounting fantastic adventures, the palace of the Men-Cranes had walls made from this gem (v. 2532ff.).

✦ *zmaragdus, smaragden, salaragdus;* MFr. *esmeraude, esmaragde;* MHG *smârât, simaragdus, smaragdus, smarakd, smarker, schmaractus, smareis;* ME *emerawde;* MSp. *meragus, esmeralda;* MItal. *smeraldo;* MDu. *marauden;* Ar. *zamorat, zabargad, zumurrud, alferuzegi;* Heb. *pit dah.*

📖 Tobit 13:21; Pliny 37, 62–74; Solin 15, 23ff.; Epiphanes 3; Isidore of Sevilla 16, 7, 1–2; Kerygma 26; Bede, *Explanatio Apocalypsis* III, 22 (Migne, Patrologia Latina 93, col. 198f.); Damigeron 6; Marbode 7; Notker I, 40; Hildegard von Bingen IV, 1; *Summarium Heinrici* VI, 4, 1; Old English Lapidary 4; Lambert de Saint-Omer 54, 4; 55, 4 and 13; *Kyranides* 1, 6; Meliteniotes v. 1120; Marbode Lapidary, 1st Romanesque translation VII; Lapidary in prose 5; 2nd Lapidary in prose 3; Alexander Neckham v. 153ff.; Luka ben Serapion 2; *De lapidibus preciosis* 2 and 56; Cambridge lapidary v. 189–246; Gossouin de Metz v. 113–61; *Sidrac* 3; Wolfram von Eschenbach 589, 22; 741, 7; 791, 21; *De la vertu des tailles* 30; Serapion c. 381; *Liber lapidarii* 2; Arnoldus Saxo 74; Bartholomaeus Anglicus XVI, 88; Thomas de Cantimpré 14, 58; Vincent de Beauvais VIII, 102; Albertus Magnus 2, 17, 8; Psellos 19; *Lapidario* 46; *Picatrix* II, 10, 3; 7; 68–72; 79; III, 1, 4; IV, 8, 2; Lapidary of King Philip 3; Konrad von Megenberg VI, 67; Christian lapidary v. 195–260 and 813–86; Jacob van Maerlant XII, 63; Volmar v. 105–24; Saint Florian v. 205–44; *Liber defota anima* v. 3634–3774; *Secrez* 3, 3; 4, 6; 30; *Liber ordinis rerum* 129, 16; *Libro di Sidrach* chap. 456; Leonardi II, 7, 235; *Vocabularius ex quo* s 750; Closener sm 1; *Liber secretorum* II, 1, 36; *Hortus sanitatis* V, 113; *Phisice* 6; Rabelais, *Gargantua* I, 8.

Smirillus, Smerillus: See *smyris*.

📖 Leonardi II, 7, 241.

Smyridos: See *smyris*.

 📖 Pseudo-Dioscorides 2, 166.

Smyris: Emery, a yellow (or black mixed with yellow) ferruginous stone, is used by jewelers to polish and shape all gemstones with the exception of jacinth and pearl. An emery stone on which is carved an armored horseman with a lance will bring its owner victory on the field of battle.

 ✦ *smirillus, smerillus, smyridos, hismiris, hysmeri;* MFr. *esmeril, esmera, smerip;* MSp. *esmeril;* Ar. *zumberic, sunbâdag, elsebada, sumbedig, alsubedehi, feruzegi;* Heb. *shamir.*

 📖 Isidore of Sevilla 16, 4, 27 (*smeriglius*); Dioscorides V, 147; Lombard Dioscorides 174; Luka ben Serapion 10; *De lapidibus preciosis* 10; Dimishqî II, 5, 7; *Lapidario* 39 (*zumberich*).

Smyrnites: The "myrrh stone" is green-yellow. It is an antidote for people who have been poisoned and a great charm for women, as men will fall in love with them because of the power of this stone.

 📖 Kerygma 46.

Socon, Socondion: See *amethystus*.

Soentre, Suentre: Another name for the *panthera* stone in the first version in Middle French of Marbode of Rennes' lapidary. See *pantherus, panchrous*.

Sögusteinn: See *saga stone*.

Sólarsteinn: This "sun stone," which should not be confused with the "gem of the sun," has been identified as a bimetallic crystal like aventurine, cordierite, tourmaline, and feldspar. Around 1360, its name was glossed as "*kristall*" accompanied by a modifier (*náttúra*) that refers to magical properties, such as those of attracting sunlight. In its round form, this stone is used to light fire, just like crystal and beryl, especially on Easter Eve in the context of consecrating the new fire. *Sólarsteinn* can be found listed in the inventories of Nordic churches from 1318 to 1408.

Taking on faith a description of it in the *Rauðúlfs þáttr* (Tale of Raudulf), a twelfth- or thirteenth-century Icelandic narrative, it was long believed that the Vikings used this stone as a compass. See also *náttúrusteinar*.

P. G. Foote, "Icelandic solarsteinn and the Medieval Background," *Arv* 12 (1966): 26–40.

Solis Gemma:

The "gem of the sun" is black with white veins, sometimes completely white, and sometimes blue; like that star, it projects a circle of dazzling rays. It has been identified as Eastern aventurine, a kind of feldspar, or as girasol. It is good for princes, as it gives them protection when they are a source of dread to their subjects; it increases wealth and dominions, protects the virtues of the body, and provides pleasure.

✦ MFr. *pierre de solea, pierre du souleil;* MSp. *sulgema*.

Pliny 37, 181; Solin 37, 20; *Summarium Heinrici* VI, 4, 30; Meliteniotes v. 1151; Bartholomaeus Anglicus XVI, 9; Leonardi II, 7, 243; *Poridat* 19; Mandeville 9; Pseudo-Mandeville 11; *Phisice* 10.

Somniferous Stone:

A bright-red stone that is brilliant and soft, and which glows at night and releases vapor or smoke during the day. If a dram's worth is placed around a man's neck, he will fall asleep and, when reawakened, will not regain his senses until the stone has been removed and taken away from his presence. The Arabic legend about Alexander the Great, as told by Ibrahim Ibn Wasif Shah, includes a similar stone, but it is black.

Ptolemy reports that in the Green Sea there are 27,000 islands, both inhabited and deserted. Among them is . . . an island in the middle of which sits a large pyramid made of a radiant black stone. No one knows what it holds, but around it are corpses and vast ossuaries. A king once visited this island; when he set foot upon the land, sleep took hold of his companions. They fell into a torpor, lost all strength, and could not move. Those who realized this in time hastily returned to their ship, but all those who stayed or lingered, perished.

According to the *Lapidario,* this hot, damp stone is found in the Red Sea near the isle of Alytuas. It is transparent vermilion that is fire resistant and hard to carve. Whoever carries a dram's worth on his person shall sleep for three days and nights.

✦ *lapis inducens somnum, lapis qui facit dormire;* MSp. *piedra del sueño;* Heb. *even sheyimshokh.*

📖 Luka ben Serapion 33; *De lapidibus preciosis* 31; *Aristoteles de lapidibus* 375, 22ff.; *Lapidario* 68.

Somnifugeous Stone:
This stone is governed by the 29° of Aries. It is black and naturally dry and hot. It is found in the West on a dark mountain. Whoever wears six drams' worth shall no longer be able to sleep.

✦ *lapis auferens somnum, lapis prohibens somnum;* MSp. *ahuyentador del sueño;* Ar. *bedunaz;* Heb. *sheyigrah hasheinah.*

📖 Luka ben Serapion 34; *De lapidibus preciosis* 32; *Aristoteles de lapidibus* 375, 34ff.

Sophron:
This stone that is carried by the Meander River has the distinct feature of triggering fury if thrown at someone's chest; this person will then slay a relative.

📖 Pseudo-Plutarch §5.

Sorige: This stone is found and guarded by large animals like dogs and *ichtyophages* (fish-eaters). It comes from paradise via a canal that feeds into an Indian river that crosses through a desert before forming a lake at the foot of the mountains. Animals are well aware of its properties and take it so that no one will find it. To obtain the *sorige,* men bring a maiden to the edge of the lake. She bares one of her breasts, the beast smells its odor and comes running, places its head in her lap, and falls asleep. The men then slay it and remove this stone from its mouth. This method for recovering the stone is based in large part on the legend of the unicorn. If we realize that the unicorn is nothing other than a mythical vision of the white rhinoceros of India, and that this animal has a stone with the same name under its horn, we can clearly see how the tradition of the *sorige* arose.

The stone is good for treating gout and whoever drinks its water for nine and a half days is protected the entire year. It is also good for stomachaches and the bodily humors, rabies, and vermin. It must be identical to the stone of the unicorn (the rhinoceros), as it can only be obtained with the help of a virgin.

✦ *serige, soride, sorinde, sorie, soringe, sorigue, corig(u)e, gorige, foringe, orique, sourige;* MItal. *sorige, sorgie.*

📖 *Sidrac* 19; Mandeville I (Amiens ms.) 2; *Libro di Sidrach* chap. 472 (called *turchiman* and *sorige*).

Sostoros: This stone was born from the misreading of a manuscript by a scribe. It is found at the bottom of the sea and climbs to the surface at dawn when it opens its mouth to swallow heavenly dew, and the rays of both sun and moon, engendering a pearl. In fact, *sostoros* represents the oyster!

📖 *Physiologus* Y 23.

Spanios: This "rare stone" is purple with a solar brilliance. Only the king of the Persians possesses it, for even when unetched it can achieve great things for its bearer. This stone has been identified as *lychnite,* but it may well also be the *atizoe* described by Pliny the Elder (37, 147).

📖 Kerygma 28.

Specularis: The "specular stone" is as transparent as glass, hence its name. It is listed among those that can be cut asunder most easily and is divvied up into layers that can be as thin as one likes. It can be found in Spain, Cypress, Cappadocia, Sicily, and Africa. The most preferred variety is from Spain. The ones from Cappadocia are quite large and delicate, but dull in appearance. Some believe that this stone is a fluid of the earth that congeals like crystal. There are three distinct varieties: one is as clear as glass, one is as black as ink, and one is yellow. The black variety is sometimes tinged with red. According to Albertus Magnus, this latter is called *orpiment* or *arsenic.*

It is quite possible that the specular stone inspired the description of marvelous mirrors—with the comparison resting on a linguistic basis (Lat. *speculum,* "mirror," genitive *specularis*)—such as those found in Wolfram von Eschenbach's *Parzival* and the *Letter of Prester John.*

✦ MFr. *speculayre;* MHG *spiegel stain.*

📖 Pliny 36, 160–62; Isidore of Sevilla 16, 4, 37; Thomas de Cantimpré 14, 65; Albertus Magnus 2, 17, 9; Konrad von Megenberg VI, 75; Pseudo-Mandeville 47; Leonardi II, 7, 257 (*specularis = phengites*); Closener sp 33; *Phisice* 78.

Speculum: See *specularis*.

📖 *Vocabularius ex quo* s 880.

Sphragides, Sphragis:
There is no difference between the stone called *sphragis* and jasper. It is only included in the domain of gems because it is good for making signets, which is what its Greek name is based upon.

📖 Pliny 37, 117.

Spinella:
The name for a variety of ruby that is a magnesium aluminate. The first mention of the name is undoubtedly to be found in the work of the Pisan doctor, Camillo Leonardi.

📖 Leonardi II, 7, 251.

Spongius:
Another name for *cysteolithos*.

📖 Leonardi II, 7, 254.

Steatites, Steatitis:
A stone that is the color of lion's fat, but more brilliant. Worn on the left arm, it brings victory.

📖 Pliny 37, 186; Damigeron 45; Meliteniotes v. 1183.

Stone for Testing Virtue:
In Ulrich von Zatzikhoven's *Lanzelet*, written toward the end of the twelfth century, the author mentions a stone called *eren stein*, "stone of honor" (or "honorability"), which has the property of being unable to tolerate contact with people of a larcenous or wicked bent (v. 5177ff.) A similar stone appears several years later in

Wigalois by Wirnt von Grevenberg (v. 1478 ff.), described in more detail. The stone is square, "bisected here and there by red and yellow stripes and the rest is of a blue purer than the glass of a mirror. It possesses a power that makes it so none who has committed an evil deed may lay their hand upon it." During the Middle Ages, this kind of stone was part of an entire complex of "detectors" of countless different properties, such as a cloak that adapts to the size of a person based on his purity or honesty. Among the other forms taken by this test, and following similar principles, are a glove, a crown, a harp, and a bridge. In the twelfth-century Anglo-Norman Arthurian romance *Lai du Cor* (Lay of the Horn; v. 39–51), there is a drinking horn that spills on the drinker who has committed some misdeed. It is decorated with beryls, sardonyx, and chalcedony, which are undoubtedly the source for its marvelous properties.

📖 Wirnt von Grafenberg, *Wigalois, le chevalier à la roue d'or,* text and translation by Claude Lecouteux and Veronique Lévy (Grenoble: ELLUG, 2001); *Viegoleis à la roue d'or,* trans. from the Danish by Anne-Hélène Delavigne and Claude Lecouteux (Paris: PUPS, 2000); Ulrich von Zatzikhoven, *Lanzelet,* text and translation by R. Pérennec (Grenoble: ELLUG, 2004).

Stone of Inachus:

This stone resembles a beryl and will turn black in the hand of anyone bearing false witness.

📖 Pseudo-Plutarch §16.

Stone of Israel:

Medieval authors gave this name to carved stones and stones with sigils, cameos, or intaglios. Visible on them are the four triads of the zodiac, the figurative depictions (*paranatellonta*) of the planets and constellations, for it is from the heavenly bodies that the stones receive their powers by means of the engraving:

> Honestete recorde la force et la vertu des pierres qui sont entaillées et de celles qui sont enlevées de naturelle enleveure. Moult est grant leur force dessus toutes autre; leur force leur est donnée de la divinité et du Souverain Seigneur. Le viel ancien sy ont moult grans vertus,

ce sont cil qui sont en hault entaillez, cils ont vertus sur toutes autres tailles (Paris: National Library of France, French ms. 2009, Hugues Ragot).*

The most widespread lapidary on engraved stones was that of Thetel (also known as Cethel, Gethel, Fethel, Techel, Techef, and Ethel), "the first sage to deal with carved stones," who has been identified as Saul Ibn Bishr or Zahel Benbris, a ninth-century Jewish author. He is found both in extenso or in extracts in the great thirteenth-century encyclopedias (Arnoldus Saxo, Thomas de Cantimpré, Vincent de Beauvais, Konrad von Megenberg) as well as in numerous poems dedicated to the engravings. One part of Thetel's lapidary was transmitted by Chael, an author about whom we know nothing, but this name may well be a deformation of Thetel:

> The extremely old scholar Chael, one of the sons of the sons of Israel, saw and had carved numerous images of the signs and planets when he was in the desert, and he perceived the great effect they could have. So that the power of these images would pass down to posterity, he wrote this book in which he lists them in the order of the many powers, so that they may be known; and that God be blessed for having placed such powers on earth for the salvation of the human race.

Another important author, Ragiel, or Raziel, wrote a *Liber de virtutibus et secretis,* and a *Liber institutionis,* still known as *Liber Razielis* (Sefer Raziel), the second book of which is the *Liber alarum* (Book of Wings), and the seventh and final book of which examines astrological images in its twenty-six chapters. At the end of the fifteenth century, his text was introduced in the following way:

---

*Translation: Honesty compels remembrance of the strength and power of the stones that are engraved (by man) and those carved naturally. The power of the latter surpasses that of the former, for it is given them by the divine Lord. According to an ancient [author] the powers of those carved in relief prevails over all other forms of carving.

Many have written on this subject (stones with sigils), especially the illustrious Ragiel in the *Book of Wings,* in which he has passed on perfect theories otherwise none would have a perfect understanding of magic. In fact, in the first wing of his work, he identifies these images and says that they possess many powers when found carved on the appropriate stones; but that they needs must be carried and kept with much care.

A second tradition goes back to the *De quindecim stellis* (Treatise of the Fifteen Stars) by Hermes, which was reworked by a certain Enoch.

Two Anglo-Norman lapidaries have partially or entirely translated these lapidaries from the Latin, but they seem to essentially derive from a work attributed to Solomon which, according to the manuscripts, included forty-seven to fifty-four headings. An examination of it shows it was a compilation in which we find extracts from the authors just cited, especially Ragiel. All of these lapidaries provide recipes for transforming stones into talismans by means of engraving. When stars are involved, their names are most often Arabic: Aldebaran, Algol, Alchimech Alaazel (Spica), and so forth.

 📖 Joan Evans, *Magical Jewels,* 239ff.; Joan Evans and Paul Studer, *Anglo-Norman Lapidaries,* 288ff.; Lynn Thorndike, "Traditional medieval tracts concerning engraved astronomical Images," in *Mélanges Auguste Pelzer* (Louvain: Université de Louvain, 1947), 217–74; Armand Delatte and Philippe Derchain, *Les intailles magiques gréco-égyptiennes* (Paris: Bibliothèque nationale, 1964); Nicolas Weill-Parot, *Les images astrologiques au Moyen Âge et à la Renaissance. Spéculations intellectuelles et pratiques magiques* (Paris: Honore Champion, 2001), chap. 8; A. Garcias Avilés, "Alfonso X y el Liber Razieli: imagines de la magia astral judia en el scriptorium Alfonsi," *Bulletin of Hispanic Studies* 74 (1997): 21–39; Claude Lecouteux, "Les pierres talismaniques au Moyen Âge," *Nouvelle Plume: Revue d'études mythologiques et symboliques* 1 (2000): 2–19; Claude Lecouteux, *Le Livre des amulettes et talismans* (Paris: Imago, 2004).

Stone of the Ass's Forehead: Sometimes the forehead of the donkey or wild ass swells and produces a stone that heals all bites of venomous animals and snakes.

 📖 Lapidary of King Philip, Paris, National Library of France, French ms. 2009, fol. 10 v°; Latin ms. 11210, fol. 81 v°.

Stone of the Caicus: By the Caicus River there grows a kind of poppy that produces stones instead of fruits. Some are black and resemble wheat seeds. The Mysians throw them into plowed soil. If the year is destined to be barren, they remain motionless where they fell, but if an abundant harvest is heralded, they leap like grasshoppers.

 📖 Pseudo-Plutarch §21.

Stone of the Nile: This stone resembles a broad or fava bean. Any dog that looks at it is unable to bark. It has the greatest virtue against evil spirits and makes it possible to free the possessed.

 📖 Pseudo-Plutarch §14; *De mirabilibus auscultationibus* §166.

Stone of Sipylus: A cylindrical stone is found on Mount Sipylus. Devout children that find it take it to the "Mother of the Gods" and henceforth commit no impious acts and cherish all their relations.

 📖 Pseudo-Plutarch §6; *De mirabilibus auscultationibus* §162.

Stone of the Tanais: There is a stone that looks like crystal and depicts a man that can be found in the Tanais River (the Don). It is used to name the successor of dead kings.

 📖 Pseudo-Plutarch §13.

Stone of the Three Magi: When Melchior, Balthazar, and Gaspard arrived at the side of the infant Jesus and gave him their presents, he gave them a small chest in return, telling them not to open it. Several days into their return journey they opened the chest and found a stone inside. They thought they were being played for fools and tossed the stone into a very deep well. Immediately, a blazing flame fell from the skies directly into the well, where it kindled an immense fire. The three well-chastened kings repented of their gesture, realizing that this stone was of great significance. They took some of this fire to their church and kept it burning, where it was worshipped as God. Behind this legend is the fact that the water in the well ignited this stone, which implies it was an *anthracitis*.

📖 Marco Polo chap. XXXI–XXXII.

Stone of Tmolus: There is a stone whose color changes four times a day that can be found on Mount Tmolus. The only ones who can find it are young girls who have not yet attained the age of reason. This stone protects nubile young girls from the outrages some may seek to commit against them. In the *Aye d'Avignon* (from the Doon de Mayence chanson-de-geste cycle; twelfth century), there is a ring that holds three stones, one of which prevents women from being raped (*desvirginee*; v. 2005–2013).

📖 Pseudo-Plutarch §4; *De mirabilibus auscultationibus* §174.

Stone of the Virgins: A stone from the Indus that protects the young girls who carry it from rape. We should note that in the *Aye d'Avignon* (v. 2005–2013) a chanson de geste in the Doon de Mayence cycle (twelfth century), a ring adorned with three precious stones protects women from rape.

📖 Pseudo-Plutarch §27.

Stuxites: Crushed and mixed with the herb satyrion, this stone will cause an erection of the penis. When worn around the neck, it gives good digestion and the desire to copulate. It so happens that the *samothratia* stone possesses the same peculiarity; this could well be another name for the same stone.

📖 Leonardi II, 7, 249.

Succinum: This is one of the Latin names for amber, which in Greek is *elektron*, from which the word *electrum* is derived. There are several kinds of *succinum*. The white possesses the best aroma, but neither the white *succinum* nor the wax-colored variety is very expensive. The most highly valued is the red *succinum*, especially when it is transparent; however its radiance should not be overly bright. When it has been given an invigorating heat by being rubbed with the fingers, it attracts chaff, dry leaves, and pieces of bark like a magnet attracts iron. Pieces of amber in oil burn with a clearer and more durable flame than wicks made from linen tow. When burning, it drives snakes away and its smoke helps achieve an easy birth. Worn as an amulet, it is helpful to infants. According to Callistratus, it is good at any age against folly and dysuria if ingested in a beverage or worn as an amulet. It is also claimed that amber in wine will inebriate the person drinking, making him pensive and sad.

A symbol of beauty and tenderness, amber is said to possess the power to heal goiters.

Various legends have arisen around amber. According to Ovid, it is the tears of the Heliads who were transformed into trees and are mourning their dead brother Phaethon (*Metamorphoses* II, 364ff.). A Christian legend says that amber was born from the tears shed by pine trees during the Flood. According to other traditions, they are the tears of sea birds. See *ambra, burtine, flammat, reflambine*.

✦ *succinus, suctinus, succinus, sucanus, sutenius, electonny;* MFr. *burtine, buctur;* MDu. *ambersteen;* OE *eolhsand;* MHG *prûngolt;* Ar. *anbarijj.*

📖 Pliny 37, 30–51; Solin 20, 9–13; Isidore of Sevilla 16, 8, 6–7; Luka ben Serapion 14; *De lapidibus preciosis* 60; Thomas de Cantimpré 14, 64; Albertus Magnus 2, 17, 10; *Picatrix* IV, 8; Konrad von Megenberg VI, 73; Jacob van Maerlant XII, 68; Pseudo-Mandeville 46; *Vocabularius ex quo* s 1232; Leonardi II, 7, 236; Closener su 127; *Phisice* 77.

Sun Stone: This is a round black stone with white and blue veins. It will emit a strong glow if put in water exposed to sunlight. The stone is useful for rulers and protects them from treachery, and increases their wealth and power. It provides pleasure and preserves health. See *solis gemma.*

📖 Mandeville I, 9; Pseudo-Mandeville 11; *Phisice* 10.

Surquemaf: See *turcois.*

Swallow's Stone: See *c(h)elidonius.*

Syenites: The name for this stone comes from Syene, the former designation for the city of Aswan. Syenite is a grainy plutonic magnetic rock that is pink or red in color.

📖 Pliny 36, 33 and 86.

Synnephitis: Another name for *galactitis.*

📖 Pliny 37, 162.

Synochitis, Sinoctide: A gem used in hydromancy to summon the dead. It is claimed that this stone retains the shadows of the infernal specters that have been summoned.

📖 Pliny 37, 192; Isidore of Sevilla 16, 15, 22; *Summarium Heinrici* VI, 6, 6.

Synodontitis: This stone comes from the brain of the fish called *synodus;* it is a bezoar, a stone of animal origin.

📖 Pliny 37, 182.

Syringitis: This stone, also known as *syrtilidis,* is hollow throughout like the space between the joints of a wisp of straw or a blade of wheat.

📖 Pliny 37, 182; Meliteniotes v. 1184.

Syrites: A small stone found in a wolf's bladder; it fits the classic definition of a bezoar.

📖 Pliny 11, 208.

Syrius: Another name for pumice stone. See *pumex.*

✦ *syrus, syris, sirius, surus.*

📖 Isidore of Sevilla 16, 4, 10; *Summarium Heinrici* VI, 2, 8; Thomas de Cantimpré 14, 61; Albertus Magnus 2, 17, 11; Lapidary of King Philip 68; Konrad von Megenberg VI, 70; Jacob van Maerlant XII, 66; Leonardi II, 7, 242; *Vocabularius ex quo* s 723.2; Closener si 143.

Syrtitides: A variety of carbuncle that comes from the coast of the Syrtes, as its name indicates, but it can also be found on the coasts of Lucania. It is the color of honey with saffron tints; inside, it contains faintly gleaming stars.

The man armed with this stone can thwart fraud and evil-doers and resist the wiles of other stones. This stone has the power to break the chains of those who are imprisoned.

✦ *syrtites, syrtius, syrtilidis, stircites.*

📖 Pliny 37, 182; Solin 2, 43; Isidore of Sevilla 16, 14, 10; Damigeron 22; Old English Lapidary 18; Lambert de Saint-Omer 55, 69; Meliteniotes v. 1183; *Hortus sanitatis* V, 115.

T

Taitis: This stone has the colors of the peacock; looking at it is good for eyesight and it possesses powers in proportion to its beauty. This stone is engraved with the image of a peacock holding a sea turtle and, beneath the stone, "AIO," which is the peacock's cry, then sealed beneath is a clover root. When carried, this phylactery brings victory and friendship, and leads to the reconciliation and enthusiasm of all. When asleep, it informs its owner about what he wishes to know. See also *taos* and *tartis*.

📖 *Kyranides* 1, 19; *Secrez* 4, 17; Leonardi II, 7.

Talc: Talc is the stone of the alchemists, Camillo Leonardi informs us. When incinerated, it produces a violent poison.

📖 Avicenna II, 2, 695; Leonardi II, 7, 265.

Tanos: This stone is classified as an emerald. It comes from Persia and is a disagreeable shade of green. It has a soiled color inside.

📖 Pliny 37, 74.

Taos: This gem has the colors of a peacock's feathers and the skin of an asp. It is undoubtedly identical to the *taitis*.

 Pliny 37, 187; Isidore of Sevilla 16, 15, 19.

Taphiusius: This is the name for one of the four varieties of the *aetites*. It is found in Taphius, near Leucadia, hence its name.

 Pliny 36, 151.

Tarnif: Depending on the sources, we have two different traditions. In the first tradition, the name *tarnif* refers to a white stone with a green stripe or border. The person who carries one can go fearlessly among his enemies and will be invisible to all for three days of the lunar month. But the *tarnif* only possesses this power for three days. The person who looks at the stone in the morning and in the evening cannot die suddenly; the person who carries one and is wounded shall not die that day. Its bearer is honored highly with people heeding his words and showing signs of their reverence to him. If placed beneath one's head when sleeping, one will see what he loves and what he hates in a dream. If it is placed over the feet of a sleeper, he will see everything he did over the last four years again.

In the second tradition, *tarnif* is found on an island in the Indian Ocean. The tide tosses it up on the beach. Fish will sense its presence, leave the water, and die. The men who pass by and see this realize that *tarnif* is there. They then hunt for it until they find it.

✦ *trasmif, craffinif, cramif, crasmir, carnif, carscinif, crasmif, crasinif, armif, eramif, irasmif, gra(s)mif, trasmif, brasmuef, crasmuez*; MItal. *cramis, grasimif.*

 Sidrac 20; Mandeville I (Amiens ms.) 3; *Libro di Sidrach* chap. 473.

Tartis: An extremely beautiful stone whose color is akin to that of the peacock. It is pleasant to gaze upon and its virtues are great.

 Leonardi II, 7, 266.

T(r)esbut: A stone that is found in the head of a crawfish. If soaked in cold water, it is effective against the bite of rabid dogs. In his translation of Johannes von Caub's *Hortus sanitatis* (Garden of Health), Jean Corbichon calls it *resten,* claiming it is referred to by Avicenna. The closest name to this in the latter author's *Liber canonis* (II, 2, 592) happens to be the *reiben/ runegi,* which "resembles a crab" (*cancer*).

 📖 Lapidary of King Philip 59.

Tecolithos: Galen called this stone "*judaicus*" (*iudaicos*). It looks like an olive pit and is not valued as a gem, but when rubbed or dissolved in water and drunk it will break and expel urinary stones. This is also the case with the stone called *melizlumen* in Chaldean, which the Lapidary of King Alfonso defines as a "stone that breaks the stone created inside a man," and which is governed by the 23° of Capricorn.

 ✦ *tecolithus, tegolitus, gegolitus, cegolit, cerogolit, celgelitus, cogolitus, cogolites, cegolitus, telitos;* MFr. *cegolite, gegolite;* MHG *cegôlitus.*

 📖 Pliny 37, 184; Solin 37, 12; Aetios II, 19; Marbode 55; Meliteniote v. 1185; Marbode Lapidary, 1st Romanesque translation LV; Lapidary in prose 42; Alphabetical Lapidary 77; Bodl. Digby 13 40; Cambridge lapidary v. 1273–82; Wolfram von Eschenbach 791, 16; Konrad von Megenberg VI; Arnoldus Saxo 1825; Thomas de Cantimpré 14, 34; Albertus Magnus 2, 3, 7; 2, 7, 5; *Lapidario* 264; Leonardi II, 7, 52; 267; 269; Closener go 2; *Phisice* 59.

Terebinthizusa: A variety of jasper that is sky blue or looks like crystal but is composed of several stones.

 📖 Pliny 37, 116.

Termidor: See *vermidor.*

Terobolen: This stone can be found in the *Physiologus* and in bestiaries. It owes its names to successive distortions of the word *pyrophilos.* In general, the name designates two burning stones, one male and the other female, that when brought together start a fire. They are used as the basis for a downright misogynistic Christian interpretation: a man should beware of women and not go near them so as to avoid being tempted by lust. See *pyrophilus*.

✦ *turrobole(i)n, thurobolen, chirobolos, cerobolim, piropolis, pirobolis, lapides igniferi.*

📖 *Physiologus* Y 3; Pierre de Beauvais 2; Guillaume Le Clerc v. 345–98; Pseudo-Hugues de Saint-Victor II, 19 [*chirobolos id est manipulos*].

Theamedes: This stone is found in an Ethiopian mountain not far from Zimiris. It is a mineral that rejects and repels all kinds of iron.

📖 Pliny 36, 130.

Thebanus: This is the name for a kind of marble speckled with gold dots that is found in Egypt. It is used to make eyewashes.

📖 Isidore of Sevilla 16, 4, 36; *Summarium Heinrici* VI, 3, 9.

Thelycardios: A stone that has the color of the heart. The Persians value it highly and call it *mucul*.

📖 Pliny 37, 183.

Thelyrrhisos: This stone is of an ashen or russet color but white at the lower part.

📖 Pliny 37, 183.

Thracia, Tracius: Depending upon the author of the text, this stone comes in either three varieties (one green, another that is of a more pallid color, and a third marked with drops of blood) or in two varieties (one a blackish tone, the other green and translucent).

📖 Pliny 37, 183; Isidore of Sevilla 16, 4, 8; *Summarium Heinrici* VI, 2, 6; Lombard Dioscorides 156; Leonardi II, 7, 263.

Thrasidyle: This stone can be found in the Eurotas River and looks like a helmet. It springs onto the bank when it hears the sound of a trumpet but dives back into the water as soon as it hears the name of the Athenians spoken aloud.

📖 Pseudo-Plutarch §16.

Thyites: This is a green stone that grows in Ethiopia, but which turns milky white when broken.

✦ *tyites, uibo.*

📖 Isidore of Sevilla 16, 4, 30; Dioscoride V, 154; Lombard Dioscorides 163.

Thyrsitis: This stone resembles coral. It should be engraved in the following two ways. One is to etch upon it the *thyr* bird (a falcon or kestrel) and Dionysius holding the thyrsus, and place an ivy or grapevine root beneath it. This stone is proof against drunkenness, wins the favor of all, and grants its bearer an invincible will. Carved with Dionysius holding a kestrel and enclosed beneath a large sage root, *thyrsitis* provides protection from danger and makes you invincible in the courts. The name of Dionysius is EVIRA SUB SICHI CHEIV EX III OIOO ACUL.

✦ *thirsitis, tirsis, tiersus.*

📖 *Kyranides* I, 8; *Secrez* 4, 8; Leonardi II, 7, 264.

Timictonia: A stone that resembles an asp.

📖 Pliny 37, 187.

Tinkar: Another name for *crapaudine*. See *borax*.

📖 Avicenna II, 2, 706.

Tonatides: See *donatides, radaim.*

Topazos: This name actually refers to the peridot while the topaz is a natural aluminum fluosilicate. Legend says that this green, translucent gem was discovered by troglodytic pirates, who landed on an Arabian isle called Cytis and unearthed topazes when uprooting plants in search of food. Juba claims that Topazos Island is in the Red Sea, one day's sailing from the continent. Surrounded by fog and often sought by navigators, it has taken the name it bears from this circumstance, for in the troglodyte language *topazin* means "to look for." Topazes are also found near Alabastrum, a city of Thebais. Two varieties of this stone are distinguished: the *prasoides* and the *chrysopteron,* which resembles chrysoprase. One is similar to pure gold; the other is lighter in color. Topaz calms the raging waves, helps treat hemorrhages, and is effective against attacks of madness. It banishes curses from the house, cools boiling water, heals the liver and also varicose tumors, curbs anger, and reduces lust. The man who bears this stone remains chaste. It bestows love and happiness, makes its bearer charming to those around him and a better orator in his speeches, ensures substantial profits in trade, cures ophthalmia, and gives one a good memory. It is effective in hydromancy. It should be set in gold for all its virtues to be deployed. It makes a person rich, eloquent, but no felon will own a topaz for long.

It is also a meteorological stone: when the moon is rainy, the topaz releases a bad smell or darkens in color, but when good weather is coming, it is clear and glowing.

It is one of the twelve stones on the breastplate of the high priest Aaron (Exodus 28:15–30). In the Christian lapidary, it represents the contemplative life and those who love God and their neighbor. In the *Anulus,* written circa 1350 by Konrad von Hamburg, is it the symbol for the profound nature of the Virgin's contemplation and it is one of the twenty gems on the ring the author offers Mary.

If an image of Poseidon in a harnessed chariot is etched on this stone, and he is holding the reins in his left hand and a blade of wheat in his right, with Amphitrite above the chariot, the topaz bestows love and property and is effective in hydromancy. Carved with a falcon, it procures grace, charity, and love, and gives nobility to its bearer; it disposes a king or prince to increased benevolence.

A crowned man rising through the air depicted on a topaz will render its owner as good, obliging, and esteemed by others, and it will bring him honors and consideration.

✦ *topazius, topazion, topadium, thopazius, topatius, tobasius, thopayus, toutpasse, tompase, tospasse, capasius, copasius, kaspasinus, caspasianus;* MFr. *topacïus, topas(se), topaze, topace, thopache, thopasche, estoupace, topaç, toutpase, ethopace, copace, compac;* MHG *topaß;* ME *topace;* MItal. *topazio.*

📖 Pliny 37, 107ff.; Pseudo-Hippocrates 23; Epiphanes 2; Isidore of Sevilla 16, 7, 9; Orpheus v. 280ff.; Kerygma 8; Damigeron 29 and 54 Marbode 13; *Summarium Heinrici* VI, 4, 7; Hildegard von Bingen IV, 8; Old English Lapidary 10; Lambert de Saint-Omer 54, 9; 55, 9; 55, 24; Meliteniotes v. 1119; Jacques de Vitry cap. 91; Marbode Lapidary, 1st Romanesque translation XIII; Lapidary in prose 9; 2nd Lapidary in prose 2; Alexander Neckham v. 193ff.; *De lapidibus preciosis* 62; Cambridge lapidary v. 329–46; Gossouin de Metz v. 86–112; *Sidrac* 2; Wolfram von Eschenbach 589, 20; 791, 30; *Liber lapidarii* 1; Arnoldus Saxo 75; Bartholomaeus Anglicus XVI, 96; Thomas de Cantimpré 14, 68; Vincent de Beauvais VIII, 106; Albertus Magnus 2, 18, 1; Konrad von Megenberg VI, 77; Jacob van Maerlant XII, 70; Volmar v. 87–104; Saint Florian v. 245–60; *Liber defota anima* v. 4646–753; Christian lapidary v. 161–94 and 751–812; *Secrez* 3,

2; 4, 8; Psellos 25; *Vocabularius ex quo* t 389; t 392; t 388; *Liber ordinis rerum* 129, 15; Closener to 21; Mandeville I 6; Pseudo-Mandeville 8 and 35; *Libro di Sidrach* chap. 455; *Liber secretorum* II, 1, 7; *De virtutis lapidum* II, 6; Ragiel 2; Solomon 14; Leonardi II, 7, 261; *Phisice* 7.

📖📖 René Cadiou, "L'île Topaze. Le fragment du Lithognomon de Xénocrate d'Ephèse," in *Mélanges Desrousseaux* (Paris: Hachette, 1937), 27–33.

Tophus: This is tuff, a soft stone that has very little durability. However, it is the only building stone available in some localites, for example Carthage in Africa. Sea air erodes it, the wind pounds it into dust, and rain detiorates it, according to what the authors tell us.

- ✦ MHG *dugstein*.
- 📖 Pliny 36, 166; *Vocabularius ex quo* t 393; Closener to 23.

Trapendanus: This name refers to a variety of pyrite.

📖 Leonardi II, 7, 268.

Tresbut: A stone by this name appears in the Lapidary of King Philip, which that says it can be extracted from the head of the crawfish. Pulverised and steeped in cold water, it is good against snakebite and scorpion stings.

📖 Lapidary of King Philip, Paris, National Library of France, French ms. 2043, folio 148 r°.

Trichrus: This stone comes from Africa. It is black but exudes three fluids: one that is black in color from its root; a blood-colored one from its center; and an ochre-colored one from the top.

📖 Pliny 37, 183; Isidore of Sevilla 16, 11, 7.

Triglitis: A bezoar that takes its name from a fish, the mullet.

📖 Pliny 37, 187; Damigeron 65; Meliteniotes v. 1184.

Trisite: This gem is the result of a flawed spelling of the name of the *chrysite*. It is red, white, and green. Anyone who wears it on their finger will never be possessed by harmful rage.

Because of all the defective spellings, a wealth of confusion prevails here and the name may well refer to the *iris*.

✦ MFr. *trisuces, trisutes, crifuces.*

📖 Alphabetical Lapidary 78.

Turcois: Turquoise, a natural hydrated aluminum phosphate, comes in two colors: green and blue. The blues ones, the variety Dimishiqî calls *Besh'âqi,* are the best. They are good for horses because, when placed in their mangers, the animals will not suffer from heat or cold. Any person touching this stone cannot be poisoned, and it changes color when poison is present. It is said to make eyesight clear and to strengthen it, that it is good against dropsy and diarrhea, it enlivens the soul, and it facilitates birth. Anyone who wears a turquoise ring runs no risk of being murdered or drowning. But its virtues are only acquired if its bearer leads an honest life. It gives patience and resignation to those who wear it in a ring or other object; it gives one a venerable and serious air and a good character. There is a tradition about this stone derived from the prophet's words "Carnelian is for us and onyx is for our foes," because the latter stone inspires wild, difficult moods, causes stubbornness, and arouses sorrow and anxiety.

Turquoise is used to make the Saturn talisman, which has the property of making its owner drink copiously and live until a ripe old age!

If a turquoise bears the image of a kneeling man looking upward and holding a piece of cloth, this stone is useful for sales and purchases, but its bearer must behave virtuously. "If an Aquarius is engraved upon a green turquoise, its owner will profit on all sales and purchases—so much so that his buyers will stay hot on his trail."

Turquoise is considered to be the stone for horsemen because if a horse falls upon its rider, he will not be crushed if he is wearing this gem. It also protects the steed from many ills.

✦ *turchion, turchogis, turchesia, turgei;* MFr. *turcheise, turkoys, turcas, turquemaux, turquemaf, turqueniaf, turquemac, turcaman, torquemant, truquamans, cucremas, curquema(n)s, curquemaf, curtemaf, surquemac, purquemaf, turmak, crismaf, curc(re)maf, crasnuez, gurgum;* MSp. *turquesa;* MHG *turkoyse, turgei, turcke;* MItal. *turchiman;* Ar. *firôsag, feyrizech, erfebronug, ahtat, farasquin.*

📖 2nd Lapidary in prose 36; *Sidrac* 24; Arnoldus Saxo 76; Bartholomaeus Anglicus XVI, 97; *De la vertu des tailles* 34 (*turcheise verte* [green turquoise]); *De l'entaille des gemmes* 43; Dimishqî II, 5, 1; Luka ben Serapion 11; *De lapidibus preciosis* 11; Wolfram von Eschenbach 741, 6; 791, 24; Closener 1516 (given for *gurgus*); Albertus Magnus 2, 18, 2; *Picatrix* II, 10, 41; Volmar v. 558–63; Pseudo-Mandeville 60; Mandeville I (Amiens ms.) 7; Closener tu 39; Leonardi II, 7, 262; *Libro di Sidrach* chap. 477; *Phisice* 98.

U–V

Unio: This is another name for pearl, which medieval authors justified with the assertion that there was only one pearl per oyster. The pearl heals gout, leprosy, and stomachaches; it is good against the bites of rabid animals. A person who habitually eats pearls will never die suddenly or from poisoning.

When the *Romance of Alexander* describes the palace of the Indian king Porus, it mentions a grapevine that hangs between its columns. Its leaves and branches are made of gold and some of its grapes are crystals and pearls, as "big as a man's thumb," or onyx, depending on the text. When he was crossing through the Land of Darkness, Alexander and his soldiers found stones, which they gathered up. On their return to daylight, they discovered these stones were pearls and gold. See *margarita*.

✦ MFr. *uniun, oignon;* MHG *unjô*.

📖 Alexander Neckham v. 317ff.; Pseudo-Hugues de Saint-Victor II, 35; Wolfram von Eschenbach 791, 5; *Sidrac* 13; Leonardi II, 7, 276; Closener un 26.

Varach: A red stone that is also called "dragon's blood" (*sanguis draconis*). It has hemostatic properties.

 📖 Arnoldus Saxo 77; Albertus Magnus 2,19, 1; Leonardi II, 7, 270.

Vatrachius, Vatrachites: Another name for *batrachites* and *ranius*.

 📖 *Kyranides* 1, 21; *Secrez* 19; Leonardi II, 7, 275.

Veientana: A stone found in Veii, Italy. It is black but bordered by a white line.

 ✦ *vegenterna, vejentana.*

 📖 Pliny 37, 184; Solin 2, 44; Isidore of Sevilla 16, 11, 5; Lambert de Saint-Omer 55, 62; Leonardi II, 7, 272.

Veneris Crines: The "hair of Venus" is an extremely shiny black gem with something that looks like red hair inside.

 📖 Pliny 37, 184; Solin 37, 20; Isidore of Sevilla 16, 11, 6; Meliteniotes v. 1136.

Vermidor: This is a stone found in the mountains of India. It shines at night like a candle. It is good for all the illnesses of the heart and body.

 ✦ *vermidoyr, vermidour, vermindor, verinidor, vermidoine, vermudor, veroudor, verendor, verondor, berondor, derondor, termidor;* MItal. *vermidori.*

 📖 *Sidrac* 21; Mandeville I (Amiens ms.) 4; *Libro di Sidrach* chap. 474.

Vernix: Another name for the pale stone also known as the "Armenian stone" (*lapis armenicus*). It is good against the harmful effects of black bile, spleen and liver disorders, and also heart attacks. See *armenius*.

 📖 Arnoldus Saxo 78; Albertus Magnus 2, 19, 2; Konrad von Megenberg VI, 80; Leonardi II, 7, 271.

Vertillus: This clear, radiant stone calms the libido of its bearer; it is also good for eye problems, liver problems, and heart trouble.

📖 Konrad von Megenberg VI, 79.

Victory Stone: A victory stone appears in the thirteenth-century Arthurian romance *Diu Crône* (The Crown; v. 28060–63) by Heinrich von dem Türlîn. In this story, it was originally set in a belt made by a fairy. For Icelandic references to a victory stone (*sigrsteinn*), see the entry for *náttúrusteinar*. See also *alectorias, corvia, gagatromeus, pyrophilus, memnonius*.

Virites: A stone identical to pyrite that is brilliant in color and will burn the hand of anyone who touches it. See *pyrite*.

📖 Leonardi II, 7, 274; *Liber secretorum* II, 1, 34; *De virtutis lapidum* II, 20.

Vitrum: *Vitrum* is glass, about which Avicenna said, "Glass is to stones what the idiot is to humans." It is a hot, dry stone that is useful for the teeth and eyes. Drunk with wine, it is good for the bladder and kidneys. Glass is astringent and purifies scurf patches when the mouth is rinsed out with it.

Glass had a magical aura during the Middle Ages. *Diu Crône* (The Crown), the Arthurian romance written by Heinrich von dem Türlîn around 1230, tells how Gauwain came to a glass castle that spun like a windmill, built by the magician Gaugoter (v. 12940–66). This same romance mentions a smooth, pointed glass mountain that stands in the land of the giant Assiles (v. 6782–86).

Glass castles are not foreign to folk tales—six of the Brothers Grimm stories mention them—and there are even coffins made from the same substance. There is the one in the tale of Snow White, as well as the one that appears in the fairy tale *The Glass Coffin*.

📖 *Summarium Heinrici* VI, 6, 11; Luka ben Serapion 43 (*zezeg*); Avicenna II, 2, 731.

Vulcanis: See *hephaestitis*.

Vulture Stone: See *quanidros*.

Vulturis Lapis: The "vulture stone" comes from the skull of this bird. It gives health to its bearer and milk to women's breasts. It permits the realization of one's requests. See also *quanidros*.

 Leonardi II, 7, 273.

W

Water Stone: This is a white stone that, if bound to the navel of a dropsy sufferer at night and left there until morning, will secrete drops of water when exposed to the sun. This procedure is repeated several times and the patient is healed.

📖 Dimishqî II, 6, 13.

Werewolf Stone: In the anonymous thirteenth-century lay *Melion*, the eponymous hero wears a ring with two stones that possess wonderful properties.

> "On my hand I have a ring," he says to his wife, "there it is on my finger. Its setting holds two peerless stones, one is white and one is vermilion. Learn now of their marvelous virtues. Touch me with the white stone and set it on my head: when stripped of my clothes I will be completely naked and become a large wolf with a powerful body . . . If I am not touched by the other stone, it's all over—I will never turn back into a man." (v. 155–72)

📖 *Les lais anonymes des XIIe et XIIIe siècles,* ed. Prudence Mary O'Hara Tobin (Geneva: Droz, 1979); Claude Lecouteux, *Elle courait le garou: lycanthropes, hommes-ours, hommes-tigres, une anthologie* (Paris: J. Corti, 2008).

Wishing Stone: Called *önkesteinn* in Iceland, this stone has the power to grant all one's wishes. It is found in the sea at low tide, when the moon is nineteen days old and the sun is at its zenith in the south. See also the entry for *náttúrusteinar.*

📖 Jón Árnason, *Íslenzkar Þióðsögur og Æventýri* (Leipzig: J. C. Hinrich, 1862–1864).

X–Y–Z

Xanthus, Xuthos: The name given to a variety of hematite whose yellow color verges on white. In Greek, *xuthos* means "blond." It is more likely a chrysolith.

📖 Theophrastus 37; Pliny 37, 169.

Xiphios: This is a blue stone of Cappadocia. Some regard it as another name for sapphire. A sparrowhawk is carved on it with the *xiphios* fish by its claws; some gladiola root is then enclosed beneath the stone. This ring helps a person's undertakings; placed upon an animal or any statue sacred to the gods, the oracle will respond to your question. In Assyria, it was reduced into a powder that was used as a perfume to burn in the sacrifice of four-legged animals.

✦ *xiphinos*.

📖 *Kyranides* 1, 14; *Secrez* 4, 12; Leonardi II, 7, 277.

Xuthon: The name for a variety of chrysolith, which is the stone of the commoners. Its name is a variant of *uthos, xanthos*.

📖 Pliny 37, 128.

Ydrinus: See *enhydros*.

 Leonardi II, 7, 279.

Yetios: This is a hard, dull stone the color of blood. It is used to separate the *paragonius* from metals. It is utilized in the crafting of an amulet. An eagle rending an eel should be carved upon it, then beneath it some root of the *hypericum* or *dyonisa estiva* and a small piece of eagle's wing should be placed, with the whole set into a ring of gold or silver. This ring is good for all afflictions of the uterus and all afflictions spawned by this organ.

✦ *hyetites, yecticos, genos.*

 Kyranides 1, 20; *Secrez* 4, 18; Leonardi II, 7, 278.

Yquisis: A stone found in the nest of the hoopoe. If it is placed on the head of a sleeper, he will recount all he has done without lying. *Yquisis* is a distortion of the word *quirin*. See *quirin*.

 Lapidary of King Philip, Paris, National Library of France, French ms. 2043, folio 147 v°– 148 r°.

Ysoberillus: See *chrysoberulli*.

 Leonardi II, 7, 280.

Zalata: A stone resembling a thunderbolt; nothing more is known about it.

 Closener za 27.

Zandarakes: Another name for realgar.

 Pliny 32, 39f.; Pseudo-Dioscorides 122; Lombard Dioscorides 131; Vincent de Beauvais VII, 102.

Zanus: A stone found in the Green Sea. Whosoever uses it as a seal shall see cares and woes vanish by the wayside.

 📖 Qazwînî (Ruska 87).

Zarite, Zirite: *Zarite* has the color of glass. If worn around the neck, it is said to arrest hemorrhages and to cure alienation.

 📖 Leonardi II, 7, 282.

Zathene: This gem is native to Media, and has the color of amber. Crushed with palm wine and saffron, it softens like wax and releases a pleasant odor.

 📖 Pliny 37, 187.

Zemech: See *lapis lazuli*.

Ziazaa: This white-and-black stone, which contains other shades of color, causes horrible dreams. A person wearing it will be drawn into litigations.

 📖 Leonardi II, 7, 283.

Zignites: This stone has the color of glass and is also called *evax*. Worn around the neck, it stops bleeding, extinguishes ardor, and represses desire.

 ✦ zingnites, zigrites, zignies, eugenites, evas, lychnites; MFr. *zinguite*.

 📖 Arnoldus Saxo 81; Bartholomaeus Anglicus 104; Vincent de Beauvais VII, 31 (*chalcitis*); VIII, 108; Albertus Magnus 2, 20, 2; Konrad von Megenberg VI, 82.

Zimech, Zimiech: This stone appears to be a kind of lapis lazuli. *Zimech* is blue with golden specks. It is effective against quartan fever and the fainting fits caused by the vapors of the black bile.

 📖 Arnoldus Saxo 80; Bartholomaeus Anglicus XVI, 103; Albertus Magnus 2, 20, 1.

Zimur: This stone is found on Mount Zimurc in the land of Prester John; it is so burning hot by nature that it can only be picked up by iron tongs. It is used to make "vessels" in which food is cooked without fire.

 ✦ *zimurt, zirmich, zimmt, zimirth.*

 📖 Prester John E §38 (Zarncke); §96.38 (Wagner, 458).

Zmaragdachates: A kind of agate. See *achates*.

 📖 Pliny 37, 139.

Zmilaces: See *zamilampis*.

 📖 Isidore of Sevilla 16, 15, 14; Leonardi II, 7, 284.

Zamilampis: A stone found in the Euphrates River that resembles Proconnesian marble. Its center is sea-green in color. It is said to have been beloved by Dionysios. If worn by the person who gives sacrifices to this god, it causes the grapevines to prosper. When attached to the rootstocks, it makes them fertile.

 ✦ *zmilanthis.*

 📖 Pliny 37, 185; Solin 37, 7; Orpheus v. 260–66; *Kerygma* 5; Pseudo-Hippocrates 31; Meliteniotes v. 1151.

Zoraniscaea: This stone is found in the Indus River. It is said to be the stone of the Magi.

✦ *zoronysios.*

📖 Pliny 37, 185; Leonardi II, 7, 285.

Zumemellazuri: This name is formed by combining two of the names for lapis lazuli, the Arabic *zemech* and the Latin *lazurus.* See *lapis lazuli.*

📖 Leonardi II, 7, 281.

Zunich: See *lapis lazuli.*

Notes

Introduction

1. Cf. Claude Lecouteux, "La face cachée des pierres," in *La pierre dans le Monde medieval,* ed. C. Thomasset and D. James-Raoul (Paris: PUPS, 2010), 133–61.
2. Max Wellmann, "Die Stein- und Gemmenbücher der Antike," *Quellen und Studien zur Geschichte der Naturwissenschaften und der Medizin* IV (1936): 427–89.
3. *Collectanea rerum memorabilium*, ed. Theodor Mommsen (Dublin and Zürich: Weidmann, 1979).
4. Isidore of Sevilla "Isidori Hispalensis Episcopi," *Etymologiarvm sive Originvm Libri XX,* ed. Wallace Martin Lindsay, vol 1 (Oxford: Oxford University Press, 1911).
5. *Marbode of Rennes (1035–1123) De lapidibus,* ed. John M. Riddle (Wiesbaden: Franz Steiner Verlag, 1977).
6. *Textes latins et vieux français relatifs aux Cyranides,* ed. L. Delatte (Liège, Paris: Bibliothèque de philosophie et lettres de l'Université de Liège, 1942), XCIII.
7. L. Pannier, *Les lapidaires du Moyen Age des XIIe, XIIIe et XIVe siècles* (Paris: Vieweg, 1882; reprinted Geneva: Slatkine, 1973), v.
8. Part I, Act III, Scene I, ll. 1317–18.
9. See also: *lapis lapidem terit; altera manu fert lapidem, altera panem ostendit.*

10. C. Thomasset, ed., *Placides et Timéo ou Li secrés as philosophes* (Paris and Geneva: Droz, 1980), 186; also 55ff.
11. D. Gottschall and G. Steer, eds., *Der deutsche Lucidarius* I, TTG 35 (Tübingen: Niemeyer, 1994), 43.
12. M. Letts, ed., *Mandeville's Travel*, vol. 2 (London: Hakluyt Society, 1953), 318ff.
13. Cf. J. Wittichius, *Bericht von den wunderbaren Bezoardischen Steinen* (Leipzig: Steinmann, 1589).
14. Cf. F. de Mély, *Les lapidaires de l'Antiquité au Moyen Age*, vol. 3 (Paris: E. Leroux 1902), LXIV.
15. Cf. C. Lecouteux, *Les monstres dans la littérature allemande du Moyen Age*, vol. 2 (Göppingen: Kümmerle, 1982), 190.
16. *David de Sassoun*, trans. F. Feydit (Paris: Gallimard, 1964), 124ff.
17. *De proprietatibus rerum* XVI, 84. The same opinion on the *quandros* can be found in Albertus Magnus.
18. Cf., for example, *Ruodlieb* v. 99ff.
19. Isidore of Sevilla, *Etymologiae* XVI, 15, 25.
20. Alfonso X, Rey de Castilla, *Lapidario*, Odres Nuevos Maria Brey Mariño, ed. (Madrid: Castalia, 1970); *Alfonso X lapidario, segun el manuscrito escurialense H.1.15*, ed. Rodriguez M. Montalvo (Madrid: Gredos, 1981).
21. Albert le Grand, *De mineralibus* II, 2, 1.
22. *Mandeville's Travels*, 319.
23. Here are some variants found in manuscripts: *turrobole(i)n, chirobolos, cerobolim, piropolis, pirobolis*.
24. Bartholomaeus Anglicus, *De proprietatibus rerum* XVI, 102, 112 (Frankfurt: N.p., 1650).
25. Information provided by Professor Chiwaki Shinoda (Hiroshima University).
26. Cf. J. E. Merceron, "De la grotte-refuge au château-prison: itinéraire mythologique de quelques vierges," *Mythologie française* 208 (2002): 14–16.
27. *Kérygmes lapidaires d'Orphée* 16, in R. Halleux, J. Schamp, *Les lapidaires grecs* (Paris: Les Belles Lettres, 1985), 157.
28. Ibid., 101ff., *Lapidaire orphique* v. 366ff.
29. Jacob [. . .] *tulit lapidum quem supposuerat capiti suo et erexit in titulum,*

fundens oleum Desuper . . . Genesis 28:11–19. For an amazing parallel with Cú Chulainn, see Philippe Walter, *Merlin,* 106.
30. Ca. 54, Mansi XIX, 69ff.
31. *Veluti ibi quoddam numen sit;* Concile d'Agde c. 5, anno 506. This notion can also be found in Réginon de Prüm, Burchard of Worms, and Yves de Chartres, cf. D. Harmening, *Superstitio* (Berlin: Erich Schmidt Verlag, 1979), 63.
32. *Kristni saga,* ed. G. Jónsson, in *Islendinga sögur* I (Reykjavik: Islendinga-sagnautgafan, 1954), 243–80; *At Giljá stóð steinn sá, er þeir frændr höfðu blótat, ok kölluðu þar búa í ármann sin.* For more on this kind of spirit, see C. Lecouteux, *Démons et génies du terroir au Moyen Age* (Paris: Imago, 1995).
33. *Þórvalds þáttr ens víðförla,* ed. G. Jónsson, in *Islendinga sögur* VII (Reykjavik: Islendinga-sagnautgafan, 1947), 437–63. The text says: *Hvár byggir spámaðr þinn? Har býr hann skammt frá bæ mínum í einum miklum stein ok vegligum* (Thorvald asks, "Where lives your seer?" And Kodran answers: "He dwells next to my farm, in a large stone").
34. Cf. M. Eliade, *Traité d'histoire des religions* (Paris: Payot, 1949), 188–207.
35. Philippe Walter, *Merlin ou le savoir du monde* (Paris: Imago, 2000), 98.
36. Ulrich Engelen. *Die Edelsteine in der deutschen Dichtung des 12. und 13. Jhs.,* MMS 2 (Munich: Wilhelm Fink Verlag, 1978).
37. M. Zink. ed., *Le roman d'Apollonius de Tyr* (Paris, UGE, 1982), 92; *Eracle,* ed. G. Raynaud de Lage, CFMA 102 (Paris, 1981). I have used *Eraclius,* the German text by Otte.
38. Hedda Ragotzky, Horst Wenzel, *Höfische Repräsentation. Das Zeremoniell und die Zeichen* (Tübingen: Niemeyer, 1990).
39. Cf. *Samsons saga fagra* (Saga of Fair Samson), ed. J. Wilson (Copenhagen: SUGNL, 1953), *Samfund til udgivelse af Gammel Nordisk Litteratur, LXV,* chap. 8.
40. *Heinrich von dem Türlîn: Die Krone,* ed. Fritz Peter Knapp and Manuela Niesner (Tübingen: Niemeyer, 2000–2005), v. 15664ff.
41. Bettina Wagner, *Die Epistola presbiteri Johannis lateinisch und deutsch. Überlieferung, Textgeschichte, Rezeption und Übertragungen im Mittelalter mit bisher unedierten Texten,* Münchener Texte und Untersuchungen, 115 (Tübingen: Niemeyer, 2000).

42. Cf. Christel Meier, *Gemma spiritualis. Methode und Gebrauch der Edelsteinallegorese vom frühen Christentum bis ins 18. Jh.* MTS 34/1 (Munich: Wilhelm Fink Verlag, 1977); for a superb example of deciphering their meaning: Chr. Gerhardt, "Zu den Edelsteinstrophen in Heinrichs von Mügeln 'Tum,'" *Beiträge zur Geschichte der deutschen Sprache und Literatur* 105 (1983): 80–116.
43. *Lapidaire apocalyptique,* trans. V. Gontéro, *Sagesses minérales* (Paris: Garnier, 2010), 233.
44. Long text I, §65 (ed. Wagner, *op. cit. supra,* 354). The second long text (§ 66, 363) explains: *Virtus quidem lapidis huius est, quod non permittit aliquem inebriari.*
45. Long text II, §63 (ed. Wagner, *op. cit. supra,* 36). Hildesheim's version (§ 63, 424, offers the lesson: *Lectus vero noster est eburneus, intus ornatus saphiro ad custodiam castitatis.*
46. Cf. C. Lecouteux, "Les pierres magiques et le merveilleux," in S. Hartmann and C. Lecouteux, ed. *Deutsch-französische Germanistik: Mélanges pour G.E. Zink,* G.A.G. 364 (Göppingen: Kümmerle, 1984), 53–67; C. Lecouteux, *Au-delà du Merveilleux,* Culture et Civilisation médiévales XIII (Paris: P.U.P.S., 1998), 24–26.
47. *De civitate Dei* X, 11 *(eo quod lapidibus et herbis adhibitis et adligent quosdam...)*
48. Thomas de Cantimpré, *De natura rerum* XIV, 51 and 29, in which there is question of " legitimo carmine sacrata."
49. Ibid., XIV, 56.
50. Chap. 70, 118, and 120; *Saga de Théodoric de Vérone,* trans. C. Lecouteux (Paris: Champion, 2001).
51. "*Si posueris eum (i.e., lapidem) in alio lapide et tecum portaveris, non est possibile, quod aliquis exercitus possit durare contre te vel tibi resistere, sed fugiet coram te*" (chap. 59); cf. R. Steele, ed., *Secretum secretorum... Fratris Rogeri* (Oxford: Oxford Press, 1920); Roger Bacon, *De mirabilibus lapidis* II, 2.
52. He that beareth it on his left arm, shall overcome all his enemies; M. R. Best and F. H. Brightman, ed., *The Book of Secrets of Albertus Magnus* (Oxford: Oxford Press, 1973), 45.
53. Cf. Caesarius von Heisterbach, *Dialogus miraculorum* IV, 10: Segerus received from Bernard a gem of varied colors, "*et dixisset si illam attulisse de Septia (= Ceuta), et tantae esse virtutes, ut victoriosos efficeret, qui ea uterentur.*"

54. Cf. *Les Lapidaire grecs: lapidaire orphique, Kérygmes lapidaires d'Orphée, Socrate et Denys, lapidaire nautique, Damigéron-Evax,* trans. Robert Halleux and Jacques Schamp (Paris: Les Belles Lettres, 1985); Evax, 231–90.
55. *Anglo-Norman Lapidaries,* 130.
56. For more on this latter see C. Lecouteux, "Der Menschenmagnet: eine orientalische Sage in Apollonius von Tyrland," *Fabula* 24 (1983): 195–214.
57. Cf. Dimishqî, *Manuel de la cosmographie du Moyen Age,* trans. A. F. Mehren (Copenhagen: Imprimerie Bianco Luno, 1874), 88ff.
58. Ibid., 83.
59. "Les pierres talismaniques au Moyen Age," *Nouvelle Plume, Revue d'études mythologiques et symboliques* 1 (2000): 2–19; C. Leonardi, *Les pierres talismaniques* (liber lapidum III), trans. C. Lecouteux and A. Monfort (Paris: PUPS, 2002).
60. Cf. N. Weill-Parot, *Les images astrologiques au Moyen Age et à la Renaissance. Spéculation intellectuelles et pratiques magiques* (Paris: Champion, 2002).
61. *Anglo-Norman Lapidaries,* 293; concerning *aphroselenite.*
62. A good introduction to the subject is: H. Fühner, *Lithotherapie. Historische Studien über die medizinische Verwendung der Edelsteine* (Ulm: Haug Verlag, 1956).
63. Ed. Migne, *Pat. lat.* 197, col. 1247–66.
64. Thomas de Cantimpré, *De natura rerum* XIV, 71, ed. Boese (Berlin: DeGruyter, 1973), 373ff.
65. Ed. H. Rückert, Quedlinburg and Leipzig, 1858173. Cf. also, inter alia, *Biterolf und Dietleib* v. 7050–55, ed. O. Jänicke (Berlin and Zurich: Weidmann, 1963).
66. Ed. K. A. Hahn (Frankfurt, 1845); reprint Berlin: De Gruyter, 1965.
67. Wirnt von Grafenberg, *Wigalois, le chevalier à la roue d'or,* trans. with text and notes by C. Lecouteux and V. Lévy (Grenoble: Ellug, 2001); *Viegoleis à la roue d'or,* trans. A.-H. Delavigne and C. Lecouteux (Paris: PUPS, 2000).
68. R. Munz, ed., *Ulrich Füetrer: Persibein, aus dem Buch der Abenteuer,* ATB 62 (Tübingen: Ulrich Müller, 1967).
69. F. Weber, *Poytislier aus dem Buch der Abenteuer von Ulrich Füetrer,* ATB 52 (Tübingen: Ulrich Müller, 1960).
70. In her book on the trials of prowess and chastity, Christine Kasper does not

mention *Poytislier* and *Persibein*. Cf. *Von miesen Rittern und sündhaften Frauen und solchen, die besser waren: Tugend- und Keuschheitsproben in der mittelalterlichen Literatur,* GAG 547 (Göppingen: Kümmerle, 1995), 256–67.

71. F. H. von der Hagen and G. Büsching, eds., in *Deutsche Gedichte des Mittelalters,* vol. 1 (Berlin: N.p., 1808), 12ff.
72. Ferlampin-Acher, *Fées,* 346.
73. J. Grimm, *Deutsche Rechtsalterthümer,* vol. 2 (Hildesheim/New York: Georg Olms, 1998), 425.
74. J. Goossens, ed., *Reynaert Historie, Reynke de Vos,* Texte zur Forschung, 42 (Darmstadt: Wissenschaftliche Buchgesellschaft, 1983), 206: [Nobel] *ghinc staen up ene hoghe stage van stene.*
75. F. Liebrecht, *Zur Volkskunde* (Heilbronn: Henninger, 1879), 425.
76. Philippe Walter, *Canicule. Essai de mythologie sur Yvain de Chrétien de Troyes* (Paris: SEDES, 1988), 124.
77. Titus-Livy, *The History of Rome* I, 24, 7ff.; Cf. also Aulus Gellius, *Noctae atticae* I, 21, 4; Cicero, *Epistulae* VII, 2, 2; Festus 115, ed. O. Müller.
78. *Hænsa Þoris saga* chap. 12, ed. S. Nordal and G. Jónsson, in *Borgfirðinga sögur* (Reykjavik: Islendinga-sagnautgafan, 1938) Islenzk: Fornrit, 3.
79. *Lebor Gabála Erenn,* ed. R. A. S. MacAlister, IV, 110–12; cited in *Ogam* XVII, 185.
80. *Third Lay of Gudrun,* str. 9, in *The Poetic Edda,* trans. Carolyn Larrington (Oxford: Oxford University Press, 1996), 204.
81. *Decretum XIX, 5: Bibisti chrisma ad subvertendum Dei iudicium vel aliquid . . . in lapide . . . aut in ore tuo tenuisti aut in vestimentis tuis insutum vel circa te ligatum habuisti . . . ut crederes divinum iudicium subvertere posse?* Ed. of Cologne, 1548.
82. H. J. Schmitz, ed., *Die Bußbücher,* vol. 1 (Düsseldorf: 1898); reprint (Graz: 1958), 437–65.
83. Cf. also Mark 9:42 and Luke 17:1–2.
84. *Hrafnkels saga Freysgoða,* chap. 6.
85. F. Liebrecht, *op. cit. supra,* 513.
86. *Si mulier mulierem percusserit [. . .] portabit lapides catenatos.*
87. Olaus Magnus, *Historia de gentis septentrionalibus* VI, 12 (Rome: N.p., 1555).
88. Cited by Liebrecht, *op. cit. supra,* 513. See also the account by Olaus

Magnus, *Historia de gentibus septentrionalibus* XIV,6: *Si poenam pecuniariam dare nequierit adulter, tunc duo saxa mulieri homo tenus imponi debent: et ipsa, virilibus adulteri funiculo ligatis, ipsum per plateas civitatis aspicientibus cunctis pertrahere, ac demum abjurare civitatem, deinceps non ingrediendam, cogetur.*

89. Saxo Grammaticus, *Gesta Danorum*, bk. VIII, 16. Translation from Saxo Grammaticus, *The History of the Danes Books I–IX*, trans. Hilda Ellis Davidson (Cambridge: Brewer, 1996), 272.
90. Snorri Sturluson, *Edda*, trans. Anthony Faulkes (London: Dent, 1987), 62.
91. Cf. F. Liebrecht, *Zur Volkskunde* (Heilbronn: Henninger 1879), 298.
92. Cited from P. Walter, *Canicule*, 124.
93. Snorri Sturluson, *La Saga d'Olaf Tryggvason*, chap. 63, trans. R. Boyer (Paris: Imprimerie nationale, 1992), 124ff.
94. *Edda Snorra, Skáldskaparmál*, chap. 5, ed. Á. Björnsson (Reykjavik: Islendinga-sagnautgafan, 1975), 104ff.
95. *Historia naturalis* IV, 12, 89.
96. *Chorographia* III, 5, 37.
97. Translation slightly amended from *Gautrek's Saga and Other Medieval Tales*, trans. Hermann Pálsson and Paul Edwards (London: University of London Press, 1968), 27–28. In his translation of *Gautrek's Saga*, R. Boyer interprets *Ætternisstapi* as "Family Precipice" but *stapi* means "steep rock" or "boulder" so my preference is "Family Rock." Cf. Régis Boyer, *Deux sagas islandaises légendaires* (Paris: Les Belles Lettres, 1996).
98. Ed. G. Jónsson, in *Fornaldar sögur Norðurlanda* IV (Reykjavik: Islendinga-sagnautgafan, 1959), 5.
99. Cf. C. Lecouteux, "Les pierres magiques et le merveilleux" in *Deutsch-französische Mediävistik. Mélanges pour G. E. Zink*, GAG 364 (Göppingen: Kümmerle, 1984), 53–67.
100. Max Wellmann, "Die Stein- und Gemmenbücher der Antike," *Quellen und Studien z. Geschichte d. Naturwissenschaften und der Medizin* 4 (1935): 426–89; M. Steinschneider, "Arabische Lapidarien," *Zeitschrift der deutschen morgenländischen Gesellschaft* 49 (1895): 244–78.
101. H. Lüschen, *Die Namen der Steine. Das Mineralreich im Spiegel der Sprache* (Thun, Munich: 1968). On the other hand the *Lexikon der Zaubersteine* by C. Rätsch and A. Guhr (Graz, 1989) is quite disappointing.

102. Ed. I. del Sotto, *Le lapidaire du XIVe siècle* (Vienne: 1862); L. Mourin, "Les lapidaires attribués à Jean de Mandeville et à Jean à la Barbe," *Romanica Gandensia* IV: 159–91.
103. In *The Book of Sidrach*, we find a similar list: *soryge, crassimulf, veromidor, reflambine, cottrice, turquemas;* cf. L. Pannier, *Les lapidaries*, 214.
104. In addition to the languages of the medieval West, it is necessary to master Hebrew and Arabic.

Bibliography

Aetios of Aminda. *Aetii Amideni libri medicinales.* Vols. I–IV edited by Alessandro Olivieri in *Corpus Medicorum graecorum,* Leipzig: Teubner, 1935. Vols. V–VIII, Berlin: Akademie Verlag, 1950.

Agricola, Georgius. *De re metallica libri XII.* Basel: N.p. 1556; Brussells facsimile, 1967.

Albertus Magnus. *Opera Omnia,* vol. 5. Edited by Auguste Borgnet. Paris: Vives, 1890.

Alexander Neckham. *Alexandri Neckam De laudibus divinae sapientiae.* Edited by Thomas Wright. London: Longman, Green, 1863.

Alfonso X. *Lapidario, segun el manuscrito escurialense H.1.15.* Edited by Rodriguez M. Montalvo. Madrid: Gredos, 1981.

———. *Rey de Castilla, Lapidario.* Edited by Maria Brey Mariño. Madrid: La Iberia, 1970.

Alphabetical Lapidary (ascribed to Philippe de Thaon). In *Anglo-Norman Lapidaries,* edited by Paul Studer and Joan Evans. Paris: Champion, 1924.

Aristotle. *Liber Aristoteles de lapidibus* (Montpellier codex 277, XVth century, fol. 127 ff.). In *Das Steinbuch des Aristoteles,* edited by Julius Ruska. Heidelberg: C. Winter, 1911.

Arnaldi Saxonis. *Liber de coloribis gemmarum.* Transcription and commentary by Claude Lecouteux. www.sites.univ-rennes2.fr/celam/cetm/lapidaire/arnaldus.htm.

Avicenna. *Avicenna Liber Canonis.* Venice: Pagininis, 1507.

Baccius, Andreas. *De gemmis et lapidibus preciosis eorumque viribus et usu.* Frankfurt: N.p., 1603.

Baggio, Serenella. *Il lapidario attribuo a Zucchero Benciveni*. Padova: Presso l'autore, 1996.

Bakhouche, Béatrice, Frederic Fauquier, and Brigitte Perez-Jean. *Picatrix, un traité de magie médiévale*. Turnhout: Brepols, 2003.

Barb, A. A. "Birds and Medical Magic: 1. the Eagle Stone; 2. the Vulture Epistle," *Journal of the Warburg and Courtauld Institute* 13 (1950): 316–22.

———. "Gemme gnostiche." *Enciclopedia dell'arte antica*, vol. III, 1960, col. 971–79.

Bartholomäus Anglicus. *De rerum proprietatibus*. Frankfurt: Wolfgang Richter, 1601.

Bartholomeus Engelsman. *Van den proprieteyten der dinghen*. Haarlem: J. Bellaert, 1485.

Bartina, Sebastian. "Pietre preziose." *Enciclopedia della Biblia*, vol. 5, col. 1560–65. Turin: N.p., 1971.

Beauvais, Pierre de. *Le Bestiaire*. Edited by Guy R. Mermier. Paris: Nizet, 1977.

Beauvais, Vincent de. *Speculum natural*. Douai: Baltazar Belierus, 1624.

Bede, the Venerable. *Cives caelestis patriae*. In Jacques-Paul Migne, *Patrologia latina* 171, col. 1771, ff. (mistakenly attributed to Marbode).

Belleau, Rémy. *Les amours et nouveaux eschanges des pierres precieuses*. Edited by Maurice Verdier. Geneva, Paris: Droz, 1973.

Bianco, Ludmilla. *Le pietre mirabili. Magia e scienza nei lapidari greci*. Palermo: Sellerio, 1992.

Bingen, Hildegard von. *Hildegard von Bingen, Physica*. In Jacques-Paul Migne, *Patrologia latina*, 197, col. 1247–66.

———. *Physica*. Translated by Priscilla Throop. Rochester, Vt.: Inner Traditions, 1998.

Bodl. Digby 13 (manuscript). Oxford: Bodleian Library.

Breydenbach, Jacob (Jean de Cuba). *Hortus sanitatis*. Mainz: N.p. 1491.

Brodführer, Eduard. "Der Wernigeroder Lapidarius." *Zeitschrift f. deutsche Philologie* 46 (1915): 255–68.

Byrne, Eugene H. "Some Medieval Gem Stones and Relative Values." *Speculum* X (1935), 177–87.

"Cambridge lapidary." In *Anglo-Norman Lapidaries*, edited by Paul Studer and Joan Evans. Paris: Champion, 1924.

Cantimpré, Thomas de. *Thomas Cantimpratensis Liber de natura rerum*, Teil I: Text. Edited by Helmut Boese. Berlin/New York: De Gruyter, 1973.

Catalani, Jordan. *Mirabilia descripta*. In *Une Image de l'Orient au XIVe siècle*, edited and translated by Christine Gadrat. Paris: Écoles des Chartes, 2005.

Chael. *Trinum Magicum sive Secretorum Magicorum*. In Camillo Leonardi, *Speculum lapidum*, III, edited by Cesare Longinus, 94–103. Frankfurt: N.p., 1673.

Connochie-Bourgne, Chantal. "Le cas de l'Image du monde: une encyclopédie du XIIIe siècle, ses sources antiques, l'apport médiéval." *La transmission des connaissances techniques, Cahier d'histoire des techniques* 3, 88–98. Aix-en-Provence, 1995.

Costa, ben Luca. "De physicis ligaturis." *Constantini Africani Opera*. Basel: N.p., 1536.

Damigeron. *Les Lapidaire grecs: lapidaire orphique, Kérygmes lapidaires d'Orphée, Socrate et Denys, lapidaire nautique, Damigéron-Evax*. Text established and translated by Robert Halleux and Jacques Schamp. Paris: Les Belles Lettres, 1985.

De Boodt, Anselme Boèce. *Le parfait Joaillier, ou Histoire des pierreries*. Lyon: J.-A. Huguetan, 1644.

De figura. Ms. Sloane 1784, fol. 158ff. London: British Museum.

"De lapidibus preciosis." *Das Steinbuch des Aristoteles*. Edited by Julius Ruska. Heidelberg: C. Winter, 1911.

Delatte, Armand, and Philippe Derchain. *Les intailles magiques gréco-égyptiennes de la Bibliothèque nationale*. Paris: N.p., 1964.

Delatte, Louis, ed. *Textes latins et vieux français relatifs aux Cyranides*. Liège, Paris: Bibliothèque de philosophie et lettres de l'Université de Liège, 1942.

"De la vertu des tailles." In *Anglo-Norman Lapidaries*, edited by Paul Stuber and Joan Evans. Paris: Champion, 1924.

"De l'entaille des gemmes." In *Anglo-Norman Lapidaries*, edited by Paul Studer and Joan Evans. Paris: Champion, 1924.

De mirabilibus auscultationibus: Aristotelis quae feruntur De plantis, De mirabilibus Auscultationibus. Edited by Otto Apelt. Leipzig: B. G. Teubner, 1888.

Der Glîchezâre, Heinrich. *Das mittelhochdeutsche Gedicht vom Fuchs Reinhart*. Edited by G. Baesecke. ATB 7. Halle a. d. Saale, 1952.

Deutsche, Notker der. *Werke*. Edited by J. C. King. *Martianus Capella De nuptiis Philologiae et Mercurii*, vol. 4. ATB 87. Tübingen: Niemeyer, 1979.

De Virtutibus Lapidem or the Virtues of Stones. Translated by Patricia Tahil. Seattle: Ars Obscura Press, 1989, 2005.

Devoto, Guido, and Albert Molayem. *Archeogemmologia. Pietre antiche, glittica, magia e litoterapia*. Rome: La Meridiana, 1990.

Dimishqî. *Manuel de la cosmographie du Moyen Âge*. Translated by M. A. F. Mehren. Copenhagen: Imprimerie Bianco Luno, 1874.

Dioscorides. *Pedanii Dioscurides Anazarbei De materia mediaca libri quinque*, 3 vols. Berlin: Weidmann, 1958.

Di Venosa, Elena. *Die deutschen Steinbücher des Mittelalters. Magische und medizinische Einblicke in die Welt der Steine*. GAG 714. Göppingen: Kummerle, 2005.

———. "Diffuzione e ricezione die trattati mineralogici in area tedesca: considerazioni socioletterarie." *Labirinti* 76 (2004): 351–65.

Draelants, Isabelle. "Une mise au point sur les œuvres d'Arnoldus Saxo." *Bulletin de Philosophie médiévale* 34 (1992): 163–80; 35 (1993): 130–49.

Duaci, Balthazar Belleri, and Jacques de Vitry. *Historia Orientalis*. 1597; *De lapidibus preciosis*, 194–98.

Eis, Gerhard. "Nachricht von einem besonderen Krötenstein." *Medizinische Monatsschrift* 4 (1950): 861–62.

Engelen, Ulrich. *Die Edelsteine in der deutschen Dichtung des 12. und 13. Jahrhunderts*. Münstersche Mittelalterschriften, 27. Munich: Fink, 1978.

Engle, David G. "Edelstein." *Enzyklopädie des Märchens*, vol. 3, col. 1003–9. Berlin: Sternberg Press, 1981.

Evans, Joan. *Magical Jewels of the Middle Ages and the Renaissance, Particularly in England*. Oxford: Oxford University Press, 1922.

Evans, Joan, and Mary Serjeantson, eds. *English Medieval Lapidaries*. Oxford: Oxford University Press, 1933.

Faugère, Annie. *Les origines orientales du Graal chez Wolfram von Eschenbach. Etat des Recherches*. GAG 264. Göppingen: Kümmerle, 1979.

Ferrara, Filippo da. *Liber de introductione loquendi*. Edited by S. Vecchio in I castelli di Yale III (1998): 131–65.

Fery-Hue, Françoise. "La description de la 'pierre précieuse' au Moyen Âge: encyclopédies, lapidaires et textes littéraires." *Bien dire et bien aprandre* 11 (1993): 147–76.

———. "La tradition manuscrite du Lapidaire du Roi Philippe." *Scriptorium* 54 (2000): 91–192.

———. "Présences animales et végétales dans les lapidaires en moyen-français." *le Moyen Français* 55–56 (2004–2005): 107–28.

———. "Sidrac et les pierres précieuses." *Revue d'Histoire des Textes* 28 (1998): 93–181; 30 (2000): 315–21.

———. "Une version réécrite du chapitre minéralogique de *Sidrac*." *Scriptorium* 60 (2006): 124–46.

Flamand, Elie-Charles. *Les pierres magiques. Le règne minéral dans ses rapports avec l'alchimie, le symbolisme, l'astrologie, la musique, la médecine, etc. Le lapidaire fantastique.* Paris: Courrier du Livre, 1981.

Fleischacker, Robert von. "Ein altenglischer Lapidar." *Zeitschrift f. deutsches Altertum* 34 (1890): 229–35.

Foote, Peter. "Steinbøker." *Kultuhistorisk leksikon for nordisk Middelalder* vol. 17, col. 115–18. Oslo: Gyldendal Norsk Forlag, 1972.

Franckenberg, A. von. *Gemma magica oder magisches Edelgestein*. Amsterdam: Im Jahr Christi, 1688.

Führner, Hermann. *Lithotherapie. Historische Studien über die medizinische Verwendung der Edelsteine.* Ulm: Haug Verlag, Nachdruck, 1956.

Galland, Antoine, trans. *Mille et une Nuits*. 3 vols. Paris: Garnier-Flammarion, 1965.

Garrett, R. M. *Precious Stones in Old English Literature*. Leipzig: Hurzel, 1909.

Gart der Gesundheit. Edited by Jean de Cuba and Bernhard of Breydenbach. Augsbourg: N.p., 1488.

Gerhardt, Christoph. "Zu den Edelsteinstrophen in Heinrichs von Mügeln 'Tum.'" *Beiträge z. Geschichte der deutschen Sprache und Literatur* 105 (1983): 80–116.

Gesner, Conrad. *De omni rerum fossilium genere etc.* Zurich: N.p., 1565.

Gontero, Valérie. "La clarté de l'escarboucle dans les romans antiques." *PRIS-MA* 17 (2001): 57–71.

———. "L'anel faé. Analyse d'un motif merveilleux dans la littérature arthurienne en vers des XIIe et XIIIe siècles." *Les Lettres romanes* 57 (2003): 3–18.

———. "Les gemmes dans l'œuvre de Chrétien de Troyes." *Cahiers de Civilisation médiévale* 45 (2002): 237–54.

———. "Les gemmes marines: au carrefour du lapidaire et du bestiaire, d'après *Phisice*, une version du Lapidaire de Jean de Mandeville." *Mondes marins du Moyen Âge.* Edited by Chantal Connochie-Bourgne. Senefiance Aix-en-Provence: 2006.

———. "Un syncrétisme pagano-chrétien: la glose du Pectoral d'Aaron dans le lapidaire chrétien." *Revue d'Histoire des Religions* 223 (2006): 417–37.

Gontero-Lauze, Valérie. *Sagesses minérales. Médecine et magie des pierres précieuses au Moyen Âge.* Éditions Classiques Garnier. Paris: Garnier, 2010.

———. *Lapidaire alphabétique de Philippe de Thaon.* Paris: Éditions Classiques Garnier, 2010.

———. *Lapidaire apocalyptique de Philippe de Thaon.* Paris: Éditions Classiques Garnier, 2010.

———. *Lapidaire de Jean de Mandeville.* Paris: Éditions Classiques Garnier, 2010.

———. *Lapidaire de Marbode de Rennes, première traduction romane.* Paris: Éditions Classiques Garnier, 2010.

Gossouin de Metz. *Image du Monde.* In *L'Image du monde, une encyclopédie du XIIIe siècle,* edited by Chantal Connochie-Bourgne. Edition critique et commentaire de la première version. Thesis. Paris: IV-Sorbonne, 2000; lapidary, 1010–25.

Halleux, Robert. "Fécondité des mines et sexualité des pierres dans l'antiquité gréco-romaine." *Revue belge de Philologie et d'Histoire* 48 (1970): 16–25.

Halleux, Robert, and Jacques Schamp. "Damigéron, Evax et Marbode. L'héritage alexandrin dans les lapidaires médiévaux." *Studi Medievali* XV (1974): 327–47.

———. *Les lapidaires grec.* Paris: Les Belles Lettres, 1985.

Heinrich von dem Türlîn. *Die Krone.* 2 vols. Edited by Alfred Ebenbauer and Fl. Kragle. ATB 112 and 118. Tübingen: Niemeyer, 2000–2005.

Hermes. *Trinum magicum.* Edited by Cesare Longinus. Frankfurt: Conrad Eifridi, 1673.

———. In Leonardi, *Speculum lapidum* III, 122–24.

———. In *The Kyranides,* 241–88.

Hertzka, Gottfried, and Wighard Strehlow. *Die Edelsteinmedizin der heiligen Hildegard von Bingen.* Freibourg-im-Breisgau: Bauer, 1985.

Hiebner, Israël. *Mysterium sigillorum, herbarum et lapidum.* Erfurt: In Verlegung Johann Birckners Buchhändlers, 1651.

Holmes, Urban T. "Medieval gem stones." *Speculum* 9 (1934): 195–204.

Hüe, Denis. "*Le Jardin de Santé* de Jehan de Cuba: une encyclopédie tardive et sa Réception." *Discours et savoirs: l'encyclopédisme medieval* 173–200. Paris: Cahiers Diderot, n° 10, 1998.

———. "*Le Jardin de Santé* de Jean de Cuba: dans la traduction faite pour

A. Vérard autour de 1500. Note sur le lapidaire." In *le Moyen Français* 55–56 (2004–2005): 187–203.

Il Libro di Sidrach. Edited by Adolfo Bartoli. Bologne: Collezione di Opera inedite o rare, 1868.

Isidore of Sevilla. "Isidori Hispalensis Episcopi." *Etymologiarvm sive Originvm Libri XX,* vol. II. Edited by Wallace Martin Lindsay. Oxford: Oxford University Press, 1911.

Jüttner, Guido. "Lapidarien." In *Lexikon des Mittelalters*, t. 5, col. 1714ff. Munich and Zurich: N.p., N.d.

Kaimakis, Dimitris, ed. *Die Kyraniden*. Meisenheim on Glan: Anton Hain, 1976.

King, C. W. *The Natural History Ancient and Modern of Precious Stones and Gems, and of Precious Metals*. London: Bell and Daldy, 1865. Available online: www.farlang.com/gemstones/king-natural-history/page_001.

Kitson, Peter. "Lapidary Traditions in Anglo-Saxon England I; the Background: the Old English Lapidary." *Anglo-Saxon England* 12 (1983): 9–60.

———. "Lapidary Traditions in Anglo-Saxon England II; Bede's *Explanatio Apocalypsis* and related works." *Anglo-Saxon England* 12 (1983): 73–123.

Klein-Franke, Felix. "The Knowledge of Aristotle's Lapidary during the Latin Middle Ages." *Ambix* XVII (1970): 137–42.

Konrad von Megenberg. *Das Buch der Natur*. In *Kritischer Text nach den Handschriften,* vol. 2, edited by Robert Luff and Georg Steer. Tübingen: Max Niemeyer Verlag, 2003.

Kozminsky, Isadore. *The Magic and Science of Jewels and Stones*. New York: G. P. Putnam's Sons, 1922.

Kunz, George Frederick. *The Curious Lore of Precious Stones*. Philadelphia: Lippincott Company, 1913.

Laet, Johannes de. *De gemmis et lapidibus*. Leyden: Luguduni Batavorum, 1647.

Lapidaires astrologiques (Rhagael, Chael, Hermès, and Solomon). Transcription with commentary by Claude Lecouteux. www.sites.univ-rennes2.fr/celam/cetm/lapidaire/lapidairesastrologiques.html.

Lapidaire chrétien. Transcription of manuscrit 164 (Res. Ms. 12) Méjanes Municiple Library of Aix-en-Province by Valérie Gontero, www.uhb.fr/alc/medieval/lapidaire/Lapidairechretien.htm#_Ci_commence_le#_Ci_commence_le.

Lapidaire du Roi Philippe. Paris: Bibliothèque nationale, manuscrit français 2043, fol. 121r°–159 v°.

Latini, Brunetto. *Le livre dou tresor*. Edited and critiqued by Francis J. Carmody. Berkeley, Los Angeles: University of California Press, 1948.

Le Clerc, Guillaume. *Das Thierbuch des normannischen Dichters Guillaume Le Clerc*. Edited by Robert Reinsch. Altfranzösische Bibliothek 14. Wiesbaden: Sandig, 1967.

Lecouteux, Claude. "Arnoldus Saxo: Unveröffentlichte Texte, transkribiert und Kommentiert." *Euphorion* 76 (1982): 389–400.

———. "Les pierres talismaniques au Moyen Âge." *Nouvelle Plume, Revue d'études mythologiques et symboliques* 1 (Nagoya, 2000): 2–19.

———. "La face cachée des pierres." *Les pierres au Moyen Âge*. Edited by Claude Thomasset and Danièle James-Raoul. Paris: PUPS, 2010.

———. "Les pierres magiques et le merveilleux." *Deutsch-französische Mediävistik. Mélanges pour G.E. Zink*. GAG 364 Göppingen: Kümmerle, 1984.

———. "La Montagne d'aimant." *La montagne dans le texte médiéval: entre mythe et réalité*. Edited by Claude Thomasset and Danièle James-Raoul. Paris: PUPS, 2000.

———. "Der Menschenmagnet: eine orientalische Sage in Apollonius von Tyrland." *Fabula* 24 (1983): 195–214.

Le Livre du Graal. Edited and translated by Phillipe Walter. 2 vols. Paris: Gallimard, 2001–2003.

Lentini, Anselmo. "Il ritmo *Cives caelestis patriae* e il *Duodecim lapidibus* di Amato." *Benedictinia* XII (1938): 15–26.

Leonardi, Camillo. *Les pierres talismaniques (Speculum lapidum II)*. Edited, translated, and commentary by Claude Lecouteux and A. Monfort. Paris: PUPS, 2003.

———. Transcription and commentary by Claude Lecouteux. *De lapidibus liber secundus*. www.sites.univrennes2.fr/celam/cetm/lapidaire/leonardi%20de%20lapidibus%202.html.

———. *De lapidibus liber tertius*. Transcription and commentary by Claude Lecouteux. www.sites.univ-rennes2.fr/celam/cetm/lapidaire/leonardi_de_lapidibus.htm.

Les Lapidaire grecs: lapidaire orphique, Kérygmes lapidaires d'Orphée, Socrate et Denys, lapidaire nautique, Damigéron-Evax. Text established and translated by Robert Halleux and Jacques Schamp. Paris: Les Belles Lettres, 1985.

Lesser, Friedrich. *Lithotheologie, das ist natürliche Historie und geistliche Betrachtung der Steine.* Hamburg: Brandt, 1735.

Lettre du Prêtre Jean. Les versions en anciens français et en ancien occitan, textes et commentaires. Edited by Martin Gosman. Groningue: Bouma's Boekhuis, 1982.

Liber lapidarii. Ms. Sloane 1784. London, British Museum.

Liber ordinis rerum (Esse-Essencia-Glossar). Edited by Peter Schmitt. 2 vols. Texte and Textgeschichte, 5. Tübingen: Niemeyer, 1983.

Liber secretum. The Book of Secrets of Albertus Magnus of the Virtues of Herbs, Stones and certain Beasts, also a Book of the Marvels of the World. Edited by Michael R. Best and Frank H. Brightman. Oxford: Oxford University Press, 1973.

Liber sigillorum Ethel. Ms. Digby 79, fol. 178ff. Oxford, Bodleian Library,

———. In Leonardi. *Speculum lapidum II (Thetel).*

———. In Thomas de Cantimpré. *De natura rerum (Thetel).*

———. In Konrad von Megenberg. *Das Buch der Natur (Techef).*

Littmann, Enno. *Die Erzählungen aus den Tausendundein Nächten*, 12 vols. Wiesbaden: Sändig, 1981.

Lüschen, Hans. *Die Namen der Steine. Das Mineralreich im Spiegel der Sprache.* Thun: Ott Verlag, 1979.

Magni, Alberti. "De virtutibus herbarum, lapidum and animalium." *De secretis mvliervm.* Lyon: N.p., 1591 (non-paginated).

Major, Johann. *Epistola de cancris et serpentibus petrefactis.* Jena: Sumptibus Esaiae Fellgiebelii, typis Johannis Nisii, 1664.

Mandeville II. *Le lapidaire du XIVe siècle. Description des pierres précieuses et de leurs vertus magiques d'après le traité du chevalier Jean de Mandeville.* Edited by I. Del Sotto. Geneva: Slatkine, 1974.

Mandeville, John. *Voyages: The Travels of Sir John Mandeville.* London: Pynsons, 1496.

———. *Reisen.* Translated by Otto de Diemeringen. Basel: Berhard Richel, 1480–1481.

———. *Reisen.* Translated by Michel Velser. Augsbourg: Anton Sorg, 1480.

Månsson, Peter. *Stenbok.* In *Peder Månssons skrifter på svenska*, edited by Robert Geete. Stockholm: Svenska fornskrift-sällskapet, 1913–1915.

Marbode. *Lapidaire de Marbode de Rennes, 1ère traduction romane.* In

Anglo-Norman Lapidaries, edited by Paul Studer and Joan Evans. Paris: Champion, 1924.

———. *Marbode of Rennes (1035–1123) De lapidibus*. Edited by John M. Riddle. Sudhoffs Archiv, Beiheft 20. Wiesbaden: Franz Steiner Verlag, 1977.

———. *Poème des pierres précieuses*. Translated from the Latin, presented and annotated by Pierre Monat, followed by "Une lecture symbolique des lapidaires médiévaux" by Paul Louis-Combet. Collection ATOPIA. Grenoble: Jérôme Million, 1996.

Mas'udi, Ibrahim ibn Wasif Shah. *L'Abrégé des merveilles*. Translated from the Arab and annotated by Carra de Vaux. Paris: Sindbad, 1984.

Meier-Staubach, Christel. *Gemma spiritualis. Methode und Gebrauch der Edelsteinallegorese vom frühen Christentum bis ins 18. Jahrhundert*. Munich: Wilhelm Fink Verlag, 1977.

———. "Text und Kontext: Steine und Farben bei Bartholomäus Anglicus in ihren Werk- und Diskurszusammenhägen." *Bartholomaeus Anglicus, De Proprietatibus rerum, Texte latin et réception vernaculaire. Lateinischer Text und volkssprachige Rezeption.* Edited by Baudouin Van den Abeele and Heinz Meyer. Turnhout: Brepols, 2005.

Meineke, Eckhard. *Bernstein im Althochdeutschen*. Studien zum Althochddeutschen 6. Göttingen: Vandenhoeck and Ruprecht, 1984.

Mély, Fernand de. *Le Traité des fleuves de Plutarque*. Paris: Klincksieck, 1892.

Mély, Fernand D., and Charles-Emil Ruelle. *Les lapidaires de l'Antiquité et du Moyen Âge*, vol. 2. Paris: E. Leroux, 1896.

Mozzani, Eloïse. *Le livre des superstitions. Mythes, croyances et legends*. Paris: Robert Laffont, 2004.

Nunemaker, Horace J. "The Chaldean Stones in the Lapidary of Alfonso X." *Publications of the Modern Language Association* XLV (1930): 444–53.

———. "In Pursuit of the Sources of the Alfonsine Lapidary." *Speculum* XIV (1939): 483–89.

Pagel, Walter. "Paracelsus and Techellus the Jew." *Bulletin of the History of Medicine* 34 (1960): 274–77.

Pannier, Léopold. *Les lapidaires français du Moyen Âge des XIIe, XIIIe et XIVe siècles*. Paris: Vieweg, 1882. Reprinted Geneva: Slatkine, 1973.

Pazzini, Adalberto. *Le pietre precioze nella storia della medicina e nella legenda*. Rome: Mediterranea, 1939.

Perini, Gabriella. *Gemme, pietre dure e precioze*. Milan: A. Mondadori, 1994.

Phisice. Transcription of manuscript 1254 (XVth century) by Valérie Gontero. Méjanes Municipal Library of Aix-en-Provence. http://gsite.univ-provence .fr/gsite/Local/cuerma/dir/user-1086/Gontero-lapidaireFV.pdf.

Pingree David, ed. *Picatrix. The Latin Version of the Ghayat al-Hakîm*. London: Warburg Institute, 1986.

Pliny, Plinius Secundus. *Historiae naturalis*. Edited by Ludwig Jan. 6 vols. Leipzig: Teubner, 1865–1878.

Pliny the Elder. *Histoire naturelle livre XXXVII*. Text established and translated with commentary by E. de Saint-Denis. Paris: Collection des Universités de France, 2003.

Polo, Marco. *La description du monde*. Translated by Louis Hambis. Paris: Librairie Klincksieck, 1955.

Poridat. *Poridat de las poridades*. Edited by Lloyd A. Kasten. Madrid: HSMS, 1957.

Prester John. *Epistola presbiteri Johannis*. Edited by Bettina Wagner. Tübingen: Niemeyer, 2000.

———. *Priester Johannes*. Edited by Friedrich Zarncke. New York: Hildesheim, 1980.

———. *The letter of Prester John to the emperor Manuel of Constantinople: the anglo-norman rhymed version*. Edited by V. R. Anthony. Silver Spring: University of Maryland, 1975.

Psellos, Michel. *De lapidibus*. Edited by Jacques-Paul Migne. *Patrologia graeca* 122 (1889): col. 887–900.

Pseudo-Hugues de Saint-Victor. *De bestiis*. Edited by Jacques-Paul Migne. *Patrologia latina* 176, col. 16 ff. This edition mistakenly attributes the text to Hugues de Fouilloy.

Ragiel. *Trinum magicum; sive, Secretorum magicorum opus. Continens I. De magia naturali, artificiosa and superstitiosa diquisitiones axiomaticas. II. Theatrum naturae praeter curam magneticam, and veterum sophorum sigilla et imagines magicas . . . III. Oracula Zorastris, and mysteria mysticae philosophiae, Hebraeorum, Chaldaeorum, Aegyptiorum, Persarum, Orphicorum, and Pythagoricorum. Acessere nonnulla secretorum and mirabilia mundi et Tractatus de proprii cujusque nati daemonis inquisition*. In Camillo Leonardi, *Speculum lapidum* II, edited by Cesare Longinus. N.p. N.d.

Rantasalo, Aukusti Vilho. *Einige Zauberstein und Zauberpflantzen im*

Volksaberglauben der Finnen. Folklore Fellows Communications 176. Helsinki: Suomalainen Tiedeakatemia, 1959.

Rätsch, Christian, and Andreas Guhr. *Lexikon der Zaubersteine*. Graz: Akademische Druk und Velagstalt, 1989.

Reinach, Salomon. *Les pierres gravées*. Paris: Librairie de Firmin-Didot, 1895.

Reynke de Vos. Lübeck: Mohnkopf, 1498.

Riddle, John M. "Lithotherapy in the Middle Ages. Lapidaries Considered as Medical Texts." *Pharmacy and History* 12 (1970): 39–50.

Riethe, Peter. *Hildegard von Bingen, Das Buch von den Steinen*. Salzbourg: Otto Müller 1986.

Rosarius. *Le bestiaire et le lapidaire du Rosarius*. Edited by Sven Sandqvist. Lund: Lund University Press, 1996.

Rose, Valentin. "Aristoteles und Arnoldus Saxo." *Zeitschrift für deutsches Altertum* 19 (1875).

Rothe, Johannes. *Liber defota anima*. Manuscript of Copenhagen University Library (Arnamagnæanske Institut). AM 785 4°, fol. 100 v°–231 v°.

Ruodlieb. Edited by B. K. Vollmann. Wiesbaden: Reichert, 1985.

Saint Florian. *Il lapidario di Sankt Florian*. Edited by Elena Di Venosa. Edizione sinottica dei codici Sankt Florian XI 37 e Berlino Germ. Fol. 944, Milan: CUEM, 2001.

Saint-Omer, Lambert de. *Liber floridus*. Manuscrit autographe de Gand, Bibliothèque centrale, Cod. 9, fol. 66 v°ff.

Saintyves, Pierre. *Pierres magiques : béthyles, haches-amulettes et pierres de foudre, traditions savantes et traditions populaires*. Paris: Emile Nourry, 1936.

Salzer, Anselm. *Die Sinnbilder und Beiworte Mariens in der deutschen Literatur und lateinischen Hymnenpoesie des Mittelalters. Mit Berücksichtigung der patristischen Literatur. Eine literarhistorische Studie*. Nachdruck aus den Gymnasialprogrammen Seitenstetten 1886–1894. Darmstadt: Wissenschafliche Buchgesellschaft, 1967.

Schmidt, P. *Edelsteine. Ihr Wesen und Wert bei den Kulturvölkern*. Bonn: Nenzel Verlag, 1948.

Schwarzbaum, Haim. "Jewish, Christian, Moslem and Falasha Legends of the Death of Aaron, the High Priest." *Fabula* 5 (1962): 185–227.

Serapion, Joannes. *De simplicibus medicinis opus praeclarum et ingens*. Edited in *Joannes Serapion Breviarium*. Lyon: N.p., 1525.

———. *Breviarium medicinae*. Edited by Reynaldus de Novimagio, 1479.

Serapion, Luka ben. *Aristoteles de lapidibus* (codex de Leyde, XVe siècle). In *Das Steinbuch des Aristoteles,* edited by Julius Ruska. Heidelberg: C. Winter, 1911.

Solin, Caius Iulius Solinus. *Collectanea rerum memorabilium.* Edited by Theodor Mommsen. Dublin/Zürich: Weidmann, 1979.

Solomon. *Trinum magicum.* In Camillo Leonardi, *Speculum lapidum* III, edited by Cesare Longinus. Venice: N.p., 1502.

Stadler, Hermann, ed. "Dioscoridus Longobardus (Cod. Monac. 337)." *Romanische Forschungen* 13 (1902): 161–243.

Steinschneider, Moritz. *Die arabischen Überstezungen aus dem Arabischen bis Mitte des 17. Jahrhunderts.* 2 vols. Graz: Akademische Druck und Verlagsanstalt, 1956–1960.

———. *Zur pseudoepigraphischen Literatur insbesondere der geheimen Wissenschaften des Mittelalters; aus hebräischen und arabischen Quellen.* Berlin: N.p., 1862; Amsterdam: Philo Press: 1965.

Strunz, Franz. "Zaubersteine." *Sudhoffs Archiv* 33 (1941): 233–48.

Studer, Paul, and Joan Evans, eds. *Anglo-Norman Lapidaries.* Paris: Champion, 1924.

Theophrastus. *De lapidibus.* Edited by David E. Eichholz. Oxford: Oxford University Press, 1965.

Thorndike, Lynn. *A history of magic and experimental science.* 8 vols. London: Macmillan and Co., 1923–1958.

———. "De lapidibus." *Ambix* 8 (1960): 6–23.

———. "The Latin Pseudo-Aristotle and Médieval Occult Science." *Journal of English and Germanic Philology* XXI (1922): 229–58.

———. "Traditional medieval Tracts concerning engraved astronomical Images." *Mélanges Auguste Pelzer,* 217–74. Louvain, 1947.

Ullmann, Manfred. "Die arabische Überlieferung der Kyranis des Hermes Trismegistos." *Proceedings of the VIth Congress of Arabic and Islamic Studies.* Uppsala Symposium, 1975.

Van Maerlant, Jacob. *Der naturen bloeme.* Edited by Eelco Verwijs. Groningen: Bibliotheek van middelnederlands Letterkunde, 1872.

Vocabularius ex quo. Edited by Berhard Schnell, Klaus Grubmüller, Hans-Jürgen Stahl, Eltraud Auer, and Reinhard Pawis. 6 vols. TTG, 22–27. Tübingen: Niemeyer, 1988–1989.

Wirbelauer, Karl-Willy. *Antike Lapidarien*. Wurzbourg: K. Triltsch, 1937.

Wolfram von Eschenbach. *Parzival*. Edited by Karl Lachman. 2 vols. Revised by Eberhard Nellmann. Frankfurt: Bibliothek des Mittelalters, 1994.

Wyckoff, Dorothy. *Albertus Magnus, Book of Minerals*. Oxford: Oxford University Press, 1967.

Zazoff, Peter. *Die antiken Gemmen*. Handbuch der Archäologie. Munich: C. H. Beck'sche Verlagabuchhandlung, 1983.

Zettersten, Arne, ed. *A Middle English Lapidary*. Lund: Gleerups, 1968.

Zwickel, Wolfgang. "Die Edelsteine im Brustschild des Hohenpriesters und beim Himmlischen Jerusalem." *Edelsteine in der Bibel*. Mainz: Verlag Phippip von Zabern, 2002.

Books of Related Interest

The Secret History of Poltergeists and Haunted Houses
From Pagan Folklore to Modern Manifestations
by Claude Lecouteux

The Tradition of Household Spirits
Ancestral Lore and Practices
by Claude Lecouteux

Stones of the Seven Rays
The Science of the Seven Facets of the Soul
by Michel Coquet

The Metaphysical Book of Gems and Crystals
by Florence Mégemont

Power Crystals
Spiritual and Magical Practices, Crystal Skulls, and Alien Technology
by John DeSalvo, Ph.D.

Himalayan Salt Crystal Lamps
For Healing, Harmony, and Purification
by Clémence Lefèvre

Vibrational Medicine
The #1 Handbook of Subtle-Energy Therapies
by Richard Gerber, M.D.

The Elixir of Immortality
A Modern-Day Alchemist's Discovery of the Philosopher's Stone
by Robert E. Cox

INNER TRADITIONS • BEAR & COMPANY
P.O. Box 388
Rochester, VT 05767
1-800-246-8648
www.InnerTraditions.com

Or contact your local bookseller